Women in U.S. History

D1366970

DISCARD

Women in U.S. History

A Resource Guide

Lyda Mary Hardy

2000
LIBRARIES UNLIMITED, INC.
Englewood, Colorado

To My Mother
Eunicemary Bicknell Hardy

What does one mean by "the unity of the mind," . . . for clearly
the mind has so great a power of concentrating at any point at
any moment that it seems to have no single state of being. . . . It
can think back through its fathers or through its mothers, as I
have said that a woman writing thinks back through her mothers.

Virginia Woolf

Cover photo: Lyda Doherty Bicknell looks over the shoulder of Governor Sleeper as he
signs the proclamation granting suffrage to Michigan women in 1918. (Courtesy State
Archives of Michigan)

Excerpts from *A Room of One's Own* by Virginia Woolf, copyright 1929 by Harcourt, Inc.
and renewed 1957 by Leonard Woolf, reprinted by permission of the publisher.

Libraries Unlimited, Inc.
P.O. Box 6633
Englewood, CO 80155-6633
1-800-237-6124
www.lu.com

Library of Congress Cataloging-in-Publication Data

Hardy, Lyda Mary.
    Women in U.S. history : a resource guide / Lyda Mary Hardy.
        p. cm.
    Includes index.
    ISBN 1-56308-769-3 (softbound)
        1. Women--United States--History--Bibliography. 2. Women--United
States--Historiography. I. Title: Women in US history. II. Title.

Z7964.U49 H364 2000
[HQ1410]
016.973'082--dc21

                                                                            00-055849

Contents

1—Women in United States History: An Overview (*continued*)

3—The Province of Women (*continued*)

4—Historiography of Women in the United States 251

5—Women's History Theory and Methodology 279

Acknowledgments

Every book is a huge undertaking, and there are many who help it come to fruition in large and small ways. This book is no exception. I would like to thank, first, my family. My husband, Steve Schechter, did more than his share of cooking, cleaning, and child care for over a year. My family, including my sons, Dale "Fred" Schechter and Nathan Hardy, visited libraries, museums, and conferences with me. I thank my boys for being my book carriers and copy-makers. My mother, Eunicemary Hardy, helped with research, suggestions, and support, and would have done much more had she not lost her vision over the course of the project. My father-in-law, Dale Schechter, read the most difficult chapters and gave suggestions. Aunt Dorothy Morris, provided materials and read chapters, and my uncle, Frank Bicknell, who passed away before the book was finished, was genuinely interested in the project and very generous in providing materials.

I thank my colleagues in the library profession. Joan Pinamont, Susan Richards, and Jean Parry provided bibliographic resources. John Campbell of the Pathfinder Regional Library System, as well as the staff and friends of the system, especially Jeff Bobicki, Don Wilkerson, and Connie Zortman, provided both technical and interlibrary loan assistance. My friends and colleagues at both the Gunnison Public Library and Savage Library at Western State College were most generous with time and assistance. I specifically want to acknowledge Laurel Bain, Patrick Muckleroy, and Nancy Gauss from those institutions. I thank all the Colorado libraries who sent materials, and all the publishers and producers who provided review copies. My biggest thanks go to special friend and librarian Fran Carricato, who gave advice on books, listened to me always, and helped to proofread the manuscript.

Valuable assistance was given to me by numerous colleagues at Gunnison High School. My principal, Steve Coleman, followed the project, lending support and answering questions. The history department, Gloria Waggoner, John Francis Xavier McCarthy, Bob Howard, and Tommy Percival, provided books and information whenever I needed them. The foreign language department, Carol Pearson and JoDee Costello, answered many questions and helped with review materials. The language arts department, Lisa

Danos, Missy Kizer, Joann Arai-Brown, and Jan Borah, were very supportive. Huge special thanks go to Lisa and Jan, who helped with research, read and re-read the manuscript, and listened to all whining. Vicki Wattier answered health and sports questions as well as looked at materials, Kim Cooper and Jane Somero provided assistance, and many others were there to listen and lend support.

Finally, many friends must also be credited. Sharon Colson and Helen Johnson called books to my attention. Anne Ryter helped with material on women in the sciences. Very special friends Marsha Rose (a former Lucy Stoner) and Kathy Spear (a former English teacher) volunteered to proofread and performed hours of work. Their help was invaluable. In the last few minutes of writing this manuscript, I fear I have forgotten someone, and, if that is true, I hope that person will forgive me and know that I am grateful to all for the help and support over the seventeen-month duration of this project.

Introduction

As a child, growing up in Cleveland and Chicago during the 1950s and 1960s, women's history passed me by. I never learned about women's part in history in my school classes or saw women represented in the school and public libraries I frequented, except for an old series of blue-covered biographies of which I read Dolley Madison and probably Abigail Adams. I can think of no historic women role models who inspired me, not Mamie Eisenhower nor Jacqueline Kennedy, who were just show plates. Eleanor Roosevelt and Margaret Sanger died, and I had never heard of them. My mother told me that my grandmother was the first woman to vote in Clare County, Michigan, so I guess I held an unconscious notion that there was something in history for me as a woman, but I did not know what it was.

I went to college in Michigan in the 1970s, where I earned a bachelor's degree in English with a minor in the social sciences, and a master's degree in library science. I went to good schools where the women in history were missing. Women were not the subjects of any of my papers or research projects even though the second wave of the women's movement had begun. As a college senior, I took one seminar on the topic of women, but there was no history in it. Even in library school, a profession dominated by women, women's history was missing. Shirley Chisholm was a candidate for president, and Marion Wright Edelman founded the Children's Defense Fund. Because my mother had told me how my great-grandmother had started the library in her rural county, that subconscious notion held that there was something in history for me.

I became a librarian. For more than twenty years I worked in public school libraries where the women in history were missing. I worked hard to ensure that the library materials supported the school curriculum, but the curriculum did not include women. So whatever books on women the library owned (and I am sorry to say they were few and I did not add to them) were passed over by students, who made their book selections based on the insidious unwritten curriculum: If it's not taught, it's not important. The students, both male and female, knew this rule was true. Karen Silkwood died, and they made a movie about her; Geraldine Ferraro was a vice-presidential candidate, but she retired from politics. Students graduated having no idea of women's part in history. Still, my mother had told me how my great-great-great-grandmother walked across New York state in 1814 carrying her baby for thirty-four days. There had to be something in history for me.

Finally, as a teaching veteran of twenty years, I went to a summer workshop, "A Woman's Place Is . . . in the Curriculum," given by the National Women's History Project in California, where I finally found history's missing women. What a difference to see women as a part of history, and what a difference this knowledge would make for my female students. No wonder our standardized test scores in social studies were so low; there was no connection for the girls to male-dominated political history. Incredibly, that same summer, my mother was reading the *Detroit Free Press*, and, in an advertisement for a special supplement of the newspaper to celebrate Michigan woman suffrage, she saw her mother. Grandmother was looking over the governor's shoulder as he signed the proclamation giving women the right to vote (see the photo on the cover of this book). Finally, we knew we had found our place in history.

Until the latter half of the twentieth century, women's history has been ignored completely or determined professionally by male interpretation and explanation. Now, with expanding interest and attention and new methods of research that have broken the field wide open, the opportunity exists to fill in the missing half of the past, giving voice to the majority sex through women's own observations and according to their values. Since the early 1970s, there has been tremendous interest in women's history as evidenced by the hundreds of books published, thousands of articles written, and numerous products developed that have turned women's history into a small industry of publications, resources, and services. This growth could not have happened unless certain societal changes had taken place. The revitalization of the women's movement correlated directly to the growth in women's history. Feminist research and writing have highlighted important issues, helping women's history to flourish as well as making significant contributions to the improvement of women's condition. Studies of gender differences, gender biases, and educational equity have brought to the forefront the nature and extent of America's patriarchal society and how it has shaped what is known about history and how children are educated. New research and knowledge help to create a climate in which educational reform towards a more inclusive view of the past and equal instructional opportunity can be achieved.

Recent scholarship, coupled with the substantial amount of publishing in the 1990s on the topic of women in history, brought about the need for this book. Women's history, as the inclusion of women's experience into recorded history, does not fit itself neatly into chronological divisions based upon American political events, and because the experience of women encompasses all cultural groups engaged in all fields of endeavor, one straight chronological arrangement is not possible. The resource section of the book is divided into three main chapters. Chapter 1, Women in U.S. History: An Overview, includes materials that portray women in the history of the United States following a chronological arrangement, subdivided into events important to women from Colonial times to the present.

Wherever possible, materials are placed within this chapter, and an attempt is made to keep items on the same woman together even when they might fit into several categories. Chapter 2, The Female Experience, encompasses materials that represent the unique apperception of women of many backgrounds whose contributions have added to the history of the United States, including African American women, Asian American women, European American women, Jewish American women, Latinas, Native American women, and women of various regions of the country. In Chapter 2, materials generally are not matched to a historical period and are not by or about famous women. They include memoirs, contemporary accounts, writings with a broad historical focus, histories of groups, or collected biographies. The Province of Women, Chapter 3, covers the history of women in the broadly defined fields of endeavor and interest in the arts; literature; politics; religion; science and technology; sexuality, reproduction and identity; sports and recreation; and work. Each of the resource-reviewing chapters is organized with general and reference resources listed first, followed by books of nonfiction and biography, with a section of audiovisual materials and Internet resources listed last.

Because of the vast amount of material currently available in women's history, it is not possible for this guide to include it all, but the guide will give readers an ample overview of what is available. Although the book deals only with the history of women in the United States, it includes a variety of types of material, including primary source books, wherever available, as well as recent books and audiovisual materials, primarily published or produced since 1990. Items included are in print and available at the time this book goes to press. All resources included are recommended, and each entry is marked with the codes M, H, C, A, denoting appropriateness for middle school, high school, college, or adult levels.

It is important to point out what this resource guide does not cover. It does not review books and materials on modern feminism (also known as second-wave feminism, which began in the late 1960s), except where feminism influences or is integral to historical events. Feminism is defined here as theory and organized activity advanced to improve women's political, economic, and social equality. This book does not cover problems and concerns about women's studies, or courses and curricula designed to raise awareness of issues affecting women. In general, this book will not discuss motherhood and family, leaving those subjects for the fields of sociology and psychology. The focus here is on history, although the book should not be considered comprehensive. Not every important historical figure is included, and unfortunately, the chapters are uneven, with some including more materials than others. Although a balanced approach was attempted, it was not achieved.

The final chapters of the book focus on historiography, theory and methodology, and education in order to fix women's history within these contexts. It is important to know how the current interest in women's history came about, and how it fits into the field of history as a whole as well as the field of education as a tool to empower the next generation.

Chapter 4 looks at historiography in the field of women's history where there has always been a written record of women in American history, even from Colonial times. This record was created by men and women who saw a need to document a period or a particular topic, or by women intimately involved in some historical event who wanted to leave a record. As professionalism grew, it was constructed by those interested in the field and who wanted to complete the record of women's part in the history of the United States.

Chapter 5 discusses historical theories and the evolution of women's history theory and methodology. As it grew, women's history presented certain problems, and specific teaching methods became associated with it. The ultimate goal of women's history is integration, but the goal itself presents some dilemmas for the field of history and for educational institutions. Because of gender research, it is known that changing historical curricula to include those who have been previously underrepresented, cannot, by itself, change education. A corresponding change in teaching methods and the nature of schools themselves is necessary. Educational reform must encompass changes in curriculum, pedagogy, and school climates.

Chapter 6 reviews recent research from a number of fields and provides an overview of the changes necessary in educational institutions for women's history to have full impact and for a new transcended education to evolve. Only when all these revisions are accomplished will a universal history for all people be achieved. Fortunately, great strides are being made. The large body of literature being written on women's history is filling out the record and making women visible in curricula that have excluded them until very recently. Reform efforts ensure that a wider range of teaching methods appeal to all types of learners. Educational institutions across the country are reconsidering the unconscious practices that for years have served girls and boys differently. Without all of these changes in educational institutions, women's history will be meaningless, for it will never be fully incorporated.

Chapter 1

Women in United States History:

An Overview

General and Reference Materials

Books

Bernikow, Louise, and the National Women's History Project. **The American Women's Almanac: An Inspiring and Irreverent Women's History**. New York: Berkley, 1997. 388p. $29.95; $16.95pa. ISBN 0-425-15686-9; 0-425-15616-8pa.

> Divided into nine sections—politics, the body, sports, the mind, writers and artists, entertainers, media, domestic life, and work—*The American Women's Almanac* covers personalities, events, and organizations in history. Each section begins with an overview and is arranged chronologically with short entries. The information within each entry is not detailed, but a plenitude of articles are included in each chapter; these allow the reader to follow the historical advances and framework of each topic. The book is well illustrated, with sidebars and special sections that offer interesting tidbits, time lines, and quotations, making for great browsing. Nearly impossible to put down, the book achieves its purpose of sparking interest in women's history, but those looking for serious or in-depth treatment should go elsewhere. A bibliography and an index are appended, although the index tends toward proper names and does not lead the reader to every subject; readers must often search within the topical chapters. *The American Women's Almanac* is a good public library choice, and readers will find it fascinating. HCA.

Conway, Jill Ker, ed. **Written by Herself, Autobiographies of American Women: An Anthology**. New York: Vintage, 1992. 672p. $16.00pa. ISBN 0-679-73633-6pa.

> As a historian of American women, Jill Conway is well equipped to edit this collection of twenty-five women's autobiographical writings from the nineteenth and twentieth centuries. The anthology has four sections, each headed with a brief essay: African American women, scientists, artists and writers, and pioneers and reformers. Each woman is introduced by a short biography and is presented chronologically within each section. The oldest woman presented is the slave chronicler Harriet Ann Jacobs, born in 1813; the youngest is writer Maxine Hong Kingston, born in 1940. The others range from the well-known: anthropologist Margaret Mead, photographer Margaret Bourke-White, reformer Jane Addams, and feminist Gloria Steinem, to the obscure: physician Dorothy Reed Mendenhall, reformer Vida Dutton Scudder, and physician Anne Walter Fearn. As Conway herself notes, the pieces vary in quality. Taken together, they speak to the growth of women's achievements over two centuries and provide personal glimpses into lives and careers. For readers seeking more than the cuttings provided, a list of the complete works is appended. HCA.

Cott, Nancy F., ed. **Young Oxford History of Women in the United States**.
New York: Oxford University Press, 1994. $111.45pa. ISBN 0-19-512398-0pa.

Noted historian Nancy Cott provides an introduction to each of the eleven volumes of the *Young Oxford History of Women in the United States*. The books in this series present an expansive view of political and social history and include various classes, races, ethnicities, and sexual identities. While adhering to these general specifications, the authors admirably cover periods ranging from less than 20 years to more than 160 years. Each title contains a chronology, suggestions for further reading, an index, and black-and-white illustrations showing familiar historical personalities as well as representative women engaged in typical activities of their times. The volumes include:

1. *The Tried and the True: Native American Women Confronting Colonization* by John Demos

2. *The Colonial Mosaic: American Women, 1600–1760* by Jane Kamensky

3. *The Limits of Independence: American Woman, 1760–1800* by Marylynn Salmon

4. *Breaking New Ground: American Women, 1800–1848* by Michael Goldberg

5. *An Unfinished Battle: American Woman, 1848–1865* by Harriet Sigerman

6. *Laborers for Liberty: American Women 1865–1890* by Harriet Sigerman

7. *New Paths to Power: American Woman, 1890–1920* by Karen Manners Smith

8. *From Ballots to Breadlines: American Women, 1920–1940* by Sarah Jane Deutsch

9. *Pushing the Limits: American Women, 1940–1961* by Elaine Tyler May

10. *The Road to Equality: American Women Since 1962* by William H. Chafe

11. *Biographical Supplement and Index* by Harriet Sigerman

Each volume of about 150 pages is based on primary source material, including interviews, so the *Young Oxford* series can be used in a number of ways: as supplementary material in history classes, for recreational reading, and for research. With their strength in the broad overview rather than in great detail, the volumes should find homes in many schools and libraries. MHA.

Cott, Nancy F., Jeanne Boydston, Ann Braude, Lori D. Ginzberg, and Molly Ladd-Taylor, eds. **Root of Bitterness: Documents of the Social History of American Women**. 2d ed. Boston: Northeastern University Press, 1996. 440p. $16.95pa. ISBN 1-55553-256-Xpa.

> In a collection of over eighty documents by or addressed to women from 1637 to the 1930s, the editors have selected papers that reflect women's experiences concerning work, power and gender, physiology, collective efforts, diversity, and relations to political authority. The documents are arranged chronologically and thematically. Beginning with Anne Hutchison's trial for heresy, the book includes diaries, letters, legal documents, newspaper articles, and writing from unexplored multicultural voices. Each document contains a brief introduction about the writer and the historical context; but because the book lacks an index and the document titles are vague, it is less useful than it might be. The primary source material would be difficult to find outside this collection, however, and teachers will use the documents in a variety of assignments. HCA.

Cullen-DuPont, Kathryn. **The Encyclopedia of Women's History in America**. New York: Facts on File, 1996. 336p. $45.00. ISBN 0-8160-2625-4. New York: Da Capo Press, 1998. 340p. $22.50pa. ISBN 0-306-80868-4pa.

> An alphabetical listing of people, organizations, legislation, publications, events, and topics in American women's history makes up Kathryn Cullen-DuPont's encyclopedia. The concise but complete entries range from a paragraph to over a page, and each one contains from one to five references for further reading. Eighteen pages of full bibliographical citations are appended at the end of the book. The biographical entries follow the format of *Notable American Women* except that a subject's major contribution is not mentioned at the beginning; the reader must review the article to discover the person's significance. An appendix of primary sources includes thirty-four documents, from a 1647 request for suffrage to a 1992 sexual discrimination case presented before the Supreme Court. A section of black-and-white illustrations, mostly of the notable personalities, appears in the center of the book. Although not comprehensive or scholarly, the encyclopedia, with its exceptional index, can be used for research and browsing in school and public libraries. MHCA.

Evans, Sara M. **Born for Liberty: A History of Women in America**. New York: Free Press, 1997. 416p. $15.00pa. ISBN 0-684-83498-7pa.

> Still the best one-volume overview of women's history, Sara Evans writes a well-researched, heavily documented, readable volume that presents women's history within the larger context of American history. The book begins with a review of the role of Iroquois women within their society and how their lives changed after European contact. It concludes with an overview of the decade of the 1980s. With its chronological arrangement and substantial index, information is easy to find. The book includes three picture essays and covers domestic lives, the emergence of women in public

spaces, and sharing space, as well as suggestions for further reading. *Born for Liberty* is a book every library will want to own, and it can be used as a text in women's history classes. HCA.

Frost-Knappman, Elizabeth, and Kathryn Cullen-DuPont. **Women's Rights on Trial: 101 Historic Trials from Anne Hutchinson to the Virginia Military Institute Cadets**. Detroit: Gale, 1997. 478p. $66.00. ISBN 0-7876-0384-8.

Women's Rights on Trial is a windfall for history, government, and law classes everywhere. The highly recommended book is set up for ease of use with both chronological and alphabetical lists of the 101 legal cases included. The litigation is divided into six sections organized around the themes of crimes of conscience and nonconformity; crime and punishment; rights and responsibilities of citizenship; reproductive rights; marriage, parenting and divorce; and women at work. No popular-culture, Lizzie Borden–type cases appear among the precedent-setting and landmark trials. The book's short introduction, giving a historical overview, is followed by chapter headings on each theme. The clearly presented cases are introduced with a box outlining the people, dates, places, verdicts, sentences, and significance of each case, and footed with an extensive bibliography. Illustrations scattered throughout the book enhance the narrative, and appendices include a glossary of legal terms, citations for the legal sources, and a comprehensive index. MHCA.

Guernsey, JoAnn Bren. **Voices of Feminism: Past, Present, and Future**. Minneapolis: Lerner, 1996. 96p. (Frontline Series). $19.93. ISBN 0-8225-2626-3.

JoAnn Guernsey begins her short essay with a look at the reasons feminism is feared and follows with a review of 150 years of the movement; she then covers the backlash decade of the 1980s. The last half of the book outlines such new directions of feminism in the 1990s as third-wave and power feminism. She discusses feminists representing a variety of viewpoints, including Camille Paglia, Christina Hoff Sommers, Katie Roiphe, and Naomi Wolf; Guernsey uses events of the past two decades to illustrate these feminists' philosophies. The book is most notable for clearly outlining the current state of the feminist movement, although it should be noted that the research comes from printed sources, not from interviews. Color and black-and-white photos illustrate the book throughout. The footnotes, a list of feminist organizations, a bibliography, and an index will be useful for school research. MHA.

Heinemann, Sue. **Timelines of American Women's History**. New York: Perigee, 1996. 400p. $15.00pa. ISBN 0-399-51986-6pa.

Timelines of American Women's History is divided into fourteen chapters covering politics, work, social change, education, religion, health, science, the military, adventure, sports, journalism, literature, entertainment, and the arts. The author presents each section in a chronological arrangement of four centuries of events usually divided by decade, although she employs larger time divisions as well. Information comes in capsule form, and the many sidebars present quotations, special topics, illustrations, special time lines, and lists that augment the main presentation. Heinemann's solid work includes a selected bibliography and an excellent index; the book can be used for both research and browsing. MHCA.

Hymowitz, Carol, and Michaele Weissman. **A History of Women in America**. New York: Bantam, 1978. 400p. $7.99pa. ISBN 0-553-20762-8pa.

From colonization through the feminist movement of the 1970s, Carol Hymowitz and Michaele Weissman have written a comprehensive history of women in America. The authors, journalists who write in a breezy, readable style, include historical notation in the back of the book. The book covers the major women's history events and personalities and places them into the context of broader history. The text is useful auxiliary material to general history classes, and can serve as a text for women's history classes. A thirty-two-page section of illustrations in the center of the book contains photographs beyond the well-known images; however, the picture identified as Abigail Adams is that of her daughter, Abigail Adams Smith. The work includes notes and a well-defined index. MHCA.

James, Edward T., Janet Wilson James, and Paul S. Boyer, eds. **Notable American Women 1607-1950: A Biographical Dictionary**. Cambridge: Belknap Press of Harvard University Press, 1971. 3 vols. $50.00pa. ISBN 0-674-62734-2pa.

Sicherman, Barbara, and Carol Hurd Green, eds. **Notable American Women, the Modern Period: A Biographical Dictionary**. Cambridge: Belknap Press of Harvard University Press, 1980. 773p. $34.00pa. ISBN 0-674-62733-4pa.

The definitive work on women in American history, *Notable American Women*, is the work of numerous scholars over a fifteen-year period. The editors chose each woman (who died before 1950) for inclusion on the basis of national public significance. Each article, which is signed by the contributor and contains a list of source material, manuscripts, and archives, includes a full biography with genealogical background, father's and mother's occupations, birth order, geographic background, schooling, religious affiliation, date of marriage/s, husband's name and occupation, children's names and birth dates, cause and place of death, and place of burial. The introduction, written by Janet James, surveys American women's history, and the appendix presents a classified list of numerous occupations and interests. The update volume, *The Modern Period*, brings women's history into the twentieth century with the biographies of 442 women who died between 1951 and 1975. *The Modern Period* is more diverse ethnically, but retains the same formats and arrangements. Although it is not illustrated, *Notable American Women* provides one of the basic reference works of American women's history and should be owned by every library. MHCA.

Keenan, Sheila. **Scholastic Encyclopedia of Women in the United States**. New York: Scholastic, 1996. 206p. $17.95. ISBN 0-590-22792-0.

> The arrangement of this biographical encyclopedia makes it a great book for research and browsing. Divided into six chronological chapters and covering over 250 famous and lesser-known women, *Scholastic Encyclopedia of Women in the United States* is illustrated on every page and includes sidebars containing quotations and definitions, cameos, and social history; these enhance the presentation, expanding and smoothing it into more than a mere biographical presentation. Each chapter is introduced by a double-page spread about the history of the period. The encyclopedia, while containing most of the important personalities of women's history, encompasses a healthy selection of multicultural women; they are also listed in the topical index, which makes the book useful for multicultural courses. Ranging from a paragraph to almost two pages, the entries use boldface type to cross reference to additional articles. Note that the author has chosen over half her subjects from the 1930s and later, and that the work includes no bibliographical citations or suggestions for further reading. The index is complete, and many schools will use the book to incorporate women into the curriculum and for report material. MHA.

Keetley, Dawn, and John Pettegrew, eds. **Public Women, Public Words: A Documentary History of American Feminism**. Vol. 1, **Beginnings to 1900**. Madison, WI: Madison House, 1997. 377p. $37.95; $19.95pa. ISBN 0-945612-44-3; 0-945612-45-1pa.

> *Public Women, Public Words* is organized chronologically into four sections covering the Colonial, Revolutionary, ante-bellum, and post–Civil War periods. Within these periods, the authors look at 136 documents dealing with family, education, women's sphere, reform, women's rights, clubs, and labor; the documents concern and are mostly written by women from 1637 through 1898. Most of the important figures of the seventeenth and eighteenth centuries are included here: Anne Hutchinson, Mary Dyer, Judith Sargent Murray, Mercy Otis Warren, Emma Willard, Sarah Grimké, Catharine Beecher, Lucy Stone, Elizabeth Cady Stanton, Lydia Maria Child, Margaret Fuller, and Susan B. Anthony, as well as many other writers. The same is true of the documents, which range from the well-known, such as Sojourner Truth's "A'n't I a Woman?" speech and the 1848 "Declaration of Sentiments and Resolutions," to the unfamiliar, such as Fannie Barrier Williams's "Women's Influence in Politics." The collection covers literature, including the poems of Phillis Wheatley, and Anne Bradstreet, and pieces from *Godey's Lady's Book*. The source of each document is listed, each section of the book is introduced, and each chapter concludes with suggestions for further reading. An index is included in this well-rounded overview of documents tracing the roots of feminism. The second volume of the series includes the twentieth century. HCA.

Kerber, Linda K. **No Constitutional Right to Be Ladies: Women and the Obligations of Citizenship**. New York: Hill and Wang, 1998. 405p. $25.00. ISBN 0-8090-7383-8.

>Women's rights are often debated, but the obligations of citizens are seldom considered. Historian and scholar, Linda Kerber sought out legal cases that would demonstrate these issues, and she discovered five major themes that make for a singular look at history: the obligation to refrain from treason, the obligation to avoid vagrancy, the obligation to pay taxes, the obligation to serve on a jury, and the obligation to perform military service. Court cases have been mounted concerning each of these responsibilities based on the principle of coverture, laid out in the Blackstone Commentaries, English common law brought to the New Republic. The belief that a woman is one legal entity with her husband within marriage has continued in law and social practice, causing men and women to carry unequal weight in practicing the obligations of citizenship. Kerber's chapters lay out the cases, the personalities, and the reverberating implications. The book is for lay readers interested in historical and legal topics as well as for government and law classes. HCA.

Kerber, Linda K., Alice Kessler-Harris, and Kathryn Kish Sklar, eds. **U.S. History as Women's History: New Feminist Essays**. Chapel Hill: University of North Carolina Press, 1995. 477p. $17.95pa. ISBN 0-8078-4495-0pa.

>The essays in this book are written to honor Gerda Lerner, the pioneering women's historian who believes that a knowledge of women's history would bring about a change of consciousness and that women need to understand their past to fully engage in their future. Each contributor has been touched by and believes in Lerner's work. The authors are history professors from distinguished universities and have many books credited to them. For instance, Nancy F. Cott of Yale describes the institution of marriage in the 1800s, Linda Gordon from the University of Wisconsin writes on early twentieth century welfare for women, and Darlene Clark Hine of Michigan State University recounts how she created *Black Women in America: An Historical Encyclopedia*. The essays fall into three categories: state formation, power, and knowledge, areas not usually associated with women. Covering the nineteenth and twentieth centuries, the topics address labor, slavery, politics, and women's organizations. The book includes a few illustrations among the well-researched and well-written articles on subjects that are not readily found anywhere else. HCA.

Kerber, Linda K., and Jane Sherron De Hart, eds. **Women's America: Refocusing the Past**. 4th ed. New York: Oxford University Press, 1995. 656p. $27.95pa. ISBN 0-19-509147-7pa.

>To illustrate women's involvement in history and centering on the themes of biology, economics, ideology, and politics, Linda Kerber and Jane De Hart have collected documents and essays by distinguished historians such as Julia Cherry Spruill, Anne Firor Scott, Kathryn Kish Sklar, Carroll

Smith-Rosenberg, Alice Kessler-Harris, Blanche Wiesen Cook, and William H. Chafe. The material is divided into four sections covering traditional America from 1600 to 1820, early industrialization from 1820 to 1880, later industrialization from 1880 to 1920, and modern America from 1920 to the present. Each chapter is introduced and each piece is headed with explanatory notes. The topics range from Colonial obstetric practice and slave testimonies to the creation of women's colleges and contemporary changes in household technology. De Hart writes a conclusion that draws all the themes together in relation to current advancements in women's history. A collection of "essential documents"—important legislation and papers pertaining especially to women; suggestions for further reading correlated to the chapters and themes; and an index are appended. The book can be used as textual and supplementary material in history classes. HCA.

Lerner, Gerda, ed. **The Female Experience: An American Documentary**. New York: Oxford University Press, 1992. 509p. $15.95pa. ISBN 0-19-507258-8pa.

First published in 1977, *The Female Experience* is Gerda Lerner's test of her theories concerning the documentation of women and of placing women in historical time lines. The book, which covers over 100 female writers from Anne Hutchinson in 1637 to the National Women's Agenda in 1975, proves Lerner's belief that there is evidence of women's participation in all of history. Lerner has been troubled throughout her career on how to fit women into the time line of a history dependent on such male turning points as wars and political elections. The historian demonstrates her idea of female periodization by dividing the book into three sections: the first part focuses on the female life cycle and includes text about childhood, marriage, housewifery, and death; the second part deals with male-defined society, discussing education, work, and politics; and the final section defines women by their individuality, body, communal work, and autonomy. The writings are from a variety of women including Dr. Mary Jacobi, Martha Coffin Wright, Mary A. Livermore, Catharine Beecher, Victoria Woodhull, and others. As the first women's history documentary, the book can be used in a variety of classes or for independent reading and research. It remains a worthy choice for all types of libraries. HCA.

Lunardini, Christine. **What Every American Should Know About Women's History: 200 Events That Shaped Our Destiny**. Holbrook, MA: Adams Media, 1997. 393p. $16.00; $11.95pa. ISBN 1-55850-417-6; 0-55850-687-Xpa.

Two hundred events in women's history, from the arrival of European women in Jamestown in 1607 to Maya Angelou's reading of her poem "On the Pulse of Morning" at President Bill Clinton's inauguration in 1993, are packed into an approximately six-inch-by-six-inch format. The events are arranged in chronological order, and some years may contain more than one event. For instance, 1852 is cited for Harriet Beecher Stowe and her writing *Uncle Tom's Cabin;* and for Emily Dickinson's publication of her first poem. The selected incidents cover subjects from literature to science, and from politics to family life; each selection is designated with one or more of these categories, allowing the reader to follow a particular topic through history. The events are given adequate coverage in three pages or less, including a short heading that allows the reader to preview the incident. Cross references are not included, and the index does not include all subtopics discussed within an entry, but a selected bibliography is included. The book has no illustrations. *What Every American Should Know About Women's History* is useful for quick reference, short reports, and browsing. MHCA.

Mankiller, Wilma, Gwendolyn Mink, Marysa Navarro, Barbara Smith, and Gloria Steinem, eds. **The Reader's Companion to U.S. Women's History**. New York: Houghton Mifflin, 1998. 696p. $45.00. ISBN 0-395-67173-6.

Providing an overview of women's issues and women's involvement in American history through a topical collection of essays is the intent of *The Reader's Companion to U.S. Women's History*. The most notable aspects of the book are adherence in every article to a multicultural presentation of the information, and the outstanding list of contributors. Major women's historians as well as additional experts have contributed to the publication, including Darlene Clark Hine, Judy Yung, Kathryn Kish Sklar, Angela Y. Davis, Bella Abzug, Rita Mae Brown, Andrea Dworkin, Joy Harjo, Patricia Ireland, Patsy T. Mink, Vicki L. Ruiz, Anne Firor Scott, and many others. Researchers seeking a straightforward, chronological history will not be satisfied, for the book chronicles women's connections to historical, religious, social, economic, political, cultural, and health topics, giving a focus not found anywhere else. Black-and-white photographs are scattered throughout, and the work contains an outstanding index. Libraries will consider the volume a unique offering and a fine scholastic contribution to the field, useful for all types of reference questions. HCA.

McElroy, Lorie Jenkins, ed. **Women's Voices: A Documentary History of Women in America**. 2 vols. Detroit: UXL, 1997. 350p. $63.00. ISBN 0-7876-0664-2.

Designed as a textbook, *Women's Voices* contains thirty-two documents tracing the evolution of women's rights and incorporates six topics: education, abolition, and suffrage in the first volume; and labor, women's rights, and reproduction in the second volume. Not all the documents are strictly American: Virginia Woolf, Simone de Beauvoir, and other non-Americans who affected thought and events in the United States are included. Each chapter has an introduction; and each document has a preface, a list of important points, a glossary, a closing that tells what happened next, a biographical sketch of the author, a list of interesting facts about the author, and suggestions for further reading. The book, which is aimed at school users, is well set up and easy to navigate. The selections are familiar documents, brought up-to-date with sidebars relating events such as Shannon Faulkner's attempt to enter the all-male Citadel and Operation Rescue's abortion protests. The text is scattered with black-and-white illustrations, mostly portraits. Each volume includes the same table of contents, a preface, a time line, and an index. *Women's Voices* will serve as the basis for women's history classes in middle schools and high schools. MH.

Mills, Kay. **From Pocahontas to Power Suits: Everything You Need to Know About Women's History in America**. New York: Plume, 1995. 325p. $10.95pa. ISBN 0-452-27152-5pa.

Kay Mills's book is a readable and entertaining overview of women's history. It is not comprehensive, as probably no single volume ever could be; however, the book is useful for beginning researchers and for research on the latest topics, including events in the 1990s. The book is arranged chronologically, with some topical coverage on education, work, and culture. A number of useful time lines are included on the right to vote, reproductive rights, sex discrimination, and religion. Each chapter begins with a list of questions, allowing for an easy overview. The questions are repeated as headings throughout the chapter for ease in finding information. The book contains information on subjects not readily found elsewhere, such as bra-burning. The lengthy index, which excludes titles, does not point to all the information in the text; Pocahontas is represented, but power suits are not, nor are all female Pulitzer Prize winners. *From Pocahontas to Power Suits* ends with sixteen pages of sources divided by topic. MHCA.

Sheafer, Silvia Anne. **Women in America's Wars**. Springfield, NJ: Enslow, 1996. 112p. (Collective Biographies). $19.95. ISBN 0-89490-553-8.

Sheafer profiles ten women who have served in a variety of capacities in all of America's wars since the American Revolution. The familiar figures are Molly Pitcher, a soldier from the Revolution; Mary Walker, a doctor in the Civil War; and Margaret Bourke-White, a photographer during World War II. Also included are a Civil War spy; nurses from World Wars I and II, and the Vietnam War; a Korean War correspondent; and a helicopter pilot and chaplain from the Gulf War. Each portrait is well drawn and includes two black-and-white illustrations. Designed to show the variety of women's involvement in American military actions, the book can be used for research and for independent reading. MH.

Weatherford, Doris. **Milestones: A Chronology of American Women's History**. New York: Facts on File, 1997. 394p. $45.00. ISBN 0-8160-3200-9.

Doris Weatherford breaks her chronological time line into eleven chapters. The chapter titles contribute a historical framework, but provide no other introductory information. Because the year headings are not set off in large type or boldface, they are easily overlooked on the page; and there is no attempt to categorize events into subtopics. Several pages are included for some years, and single events for others, and the entries themselves are uneven, running from one sentence to almost a page. The book has a scattering of black-and-white illustrations, a selected bibliography, and an index. Weatherford's *Milestones* appears flat and unappealing when compared to Heinemann's

Timelines, with its sidebars, comparative data, topical approach, and comprehensiveness; however, libraries will probably want to own both, as Weatherford's simple chronological arrangement has its place. MHCA.

Non-Book Material

American Memory: Historical Collections for the National Digital Library. 1999. Library of Congress, 101 Independence Avenue SE, Washington, DC 20540. 202-707-5000. E-mail: ndlpcoll@loc.gov. URL: http://lcweb2.loc.gov/amhome.html.

American Memory is the Library of Congress's digital project, which makes documents and illustrations available to a wider audience through the Internet. At least forty-four collections have been mounted on the World Wide Web, with more planned. Among those available are the National American Woman Suffrage Association's collection, portraits of the first ladies, and several multicultural collections. Each picture in this searchable site includes full archival detail. Another Library of Congress feature, exhibits, can be reached from this site or at http://lcweb.loc.gov/exhibits/. The exhibits, such as the one featuring women journalists in World War II, resemble a museum display and feature more background, explanation, and interconnectivity than the *American Memory* collections. Because the Library of Congress intends permanent display for the material posted, teachers can expect the same collections to be available from year to year. American history researchers and history teachers may want to bookmark this site. MHCA.

The Emerging Woman. Directed by Helena Solberg-Ladd. 40 min. Cinema Guild, 1974. Videocassette. Purchase $295.00; Rental $60.00.

Named by the Bicentennial Commission as the official film on the history of women, *The Emerging Woman* is filmed in black and white and shows the creators working on typewriters and reel-to-reel tape recorders. Although it is dated, this well-presented video documents a comprehensive overview of U.S. women's history, the only one available on video. Narrated by Leslie Cass, the film begins with the legal rights of women in the nineteenth century and covers the issues of slavery, the beginnings of the woman's rights movement, labor organization, the push to the Nineteenth Amendment, birth control, equal pay, work during World War II, and women's rights protests during the 1960s. It moves quickly, using engravings, photographs, and film to cover many of the women and events. The creative teacher of social studies and women's history classes will find ways to add to this presentation and bring it up-to-date. MHC.

The Feminist Revolution. Lake Mary, FL: Documentary Photo Aids, n.d. Posters. $45.00.

A series of twenty-seven black-and-white photographs and documents tracing the feminist movement from 1848 through the early 1970s is reproduced on glossy cardstock in an eleven-by-fourteen-inch size. The set presents a good historical view of the first and second waves of the feminist movement, including documents on women's liberation not readily found in other sources. The series begins with a photograph of Elizabeth Cady Stanton and Susan B. Anthony and moves on to an 1869 Currier and Ives cartoon lampooning woman out of her "sphere." The photographs include working women, protesting women, and advertisements and cartoons promoting women in their typical roles. Each illustration is captioned and many contain quotations from major feminists, from Mary Wollstonecraft and William Lloyd Garrison to Betty Friedan and Germaine Greer. The set is organized chronologically with only about five illustrations covering the suffrage movement. In the modern period, the material depicts protests against publications, beauty contests, advertising, single-sex organizations, and unequal wages. The accompanying guide gives background information, mostly linked to economic issues, from the Industrial Revolution to the 1970s. The discussion questions are somewhat dated and leading, and the bibliography needs to be augmented. Still, social studies and women's studies teachers will find the quotations and documentary material useful, especially in relation to women's liberation, where the full flavor of the controversy is evident. HCA.

General Federation of Women's Clubs. 1998. 1734 N Street NW, Washington, DC 20036-2990. 202-347-3168; fax 202-835-0246. E-mail: gfwc@gfwc.org. URL: http://www.gfwc.org/.

In 1984, the General Federation of Women's Clubs founded the Women's History and Resource Center as an archive and library to document women's volunteer activities. Documents from 1890 to the present are included in the GFWC archives; the GFWC's library includes over 1,000 volumes covering the women's club movement; and the organization has mounted a collection of photographs on its Web site. As the world's oldest and largest women's volunteer organization, the GFWC works to support local needs in the arts, natural resources, education, health, and civic causes. The GFWC is an important research site, providing links to the history of women's clubs, women's history research sites, and university collections. HCA.

Great American Women. Madison, WI: Knowledge Unlimited, 1998. Posters. $39.95.

This set of ten posters measures seventeen-by-twenty-two inches and is printed on heavy, coated stock. Designed to familiarize people with a wide range of women from many disciplines and periods, each poster includes a large artist's portrait of the subject, a headline of her name, and a short biography. The brightly colored prints depict women from the eighteenth century to the present; their many fields of endeavor include politics and government with Abigail Adams, Eleanor Roosevelt, and Sandra Day O'Connor; the reform movements with Susan B. Anthony and Jane Addams; and women who have overcome physical obstacles with Helen Keller and

Wilma Rudolph. Coming from the arts are Emily Dickinson and Georgia O'Keeffe, and Rachel Carson represents the field of science. The artwork on the posters is attractive enough for display in libraries and schools. A guide giving a historical overview, suggested activities, and a bibliography accompanies the set. MHCA.

Great Women Leaders. Madison, WI: Knowledge Unlimited, 1993. Posters. $34.95.

Framed in navy or maroon, these fifteen posters present women leaders from three centuries. Each poster, printed on heavy, coated stock, contains a six-inch-by-eight-inch black-and-white portrait of the subject, a caption giving name and dates, a quotation, and a short biography. The biographies are informative and include the notable achievements of each woman. Mary Wollstonecraft is the only non-American depicted among Lucretia Mott, Sojourner Truth, Elizabeth Cady Stanton, Susan B. Anthony, Jane Addams, Mary McLeod Bethune, Jeannette Rankin, Frances Perkins, Margaret Sanger, Eleanor Roosevelt, Bella Abzug, Betty Friedan, Shirley Chisholm, and Gloria Steinem. Their accomplishments range from writing *A Vindication of the Rights of Woman* to publishing *Ms.* magazine; and from working for abolition, women's rights, and peace to promoting education and birth control. They have served in the United Nations and the United States Congress; they have run for president of the United States and won the Nobel Peace Prize. The posters can be displayed in schools and libraries, but they should be hung where the captions can be easily read. MHCA.

A Guide to Uncovering Women's History in Archival Collections. 1999. The University of Texas San Antonio Libraries, Special Collections and Archives Department, 6900 N. Loop 1604 West, San Antonio, TX 78249-0671. 210-458-5505. E-mail: Jill Jackson, Archivist, jjackson@utsa.edu. URL: http://www.lib.utsa.edu/Archives/links.htm.

The University of Texas at San Antonio has brought together a useful listing of Web pages throughout the fifty states of archives, libraries, and other repositories owning primary source materials on women's history. The site also links to other finding resources and should be the first stop for any serious researcher. This site may gain importance as libraries continue to digitize collections, making them available via the Internet. HCA.

The History Channel. 1999. 235 E. Forty-Fifth Street, New York, NY 10017. URL: http://www.historychannel.com/index.html.

During March, *The History Channel* Web site offers exhibits, interactive polls and quizzes, and information related to women's history. Women's profiles are made available from biography.com, a part of the A & E Network with The History Channel. Features on woman's suffrage are mounted and special television programming is broadcast as part of the celebration. The channel also provides highlights such as "This Day in History," historical speeches, classroom study guides, and various exhibits throughout the year. Teachers and students engaging in Women's History Month activities will want to be familiar with this site and its useful information. MHCA.

National Archives and Records Administration. 1999. Seventh Street and Pennsylvania Avenue NW, Washington, DC 20408. 301-712-6400. URL: http://www.nara.gov/.

> As an independent agency of the federal government, the National Archives and Records Administration is charged with managing government records and preserving American history. NARA oversees the Presidential libraries, the federal register, two archive facilities, and a fine electronic database that makes many primary source documents and photographs available via the Internet. The NARA Web site is divided into an online exhibit hall, a digital classroom, and a research room. The digital classroom, set up for educators and students, includes archival source material, activities, and professional development opportunities. The lessons available are developed by educational staff and are correlated to the national history standards. One of the units, woman suffrage and the Nineteenth Amendment, accesses ten documents, teaching activities, a dramatic script, and links to related Web sites. For beginning researchers, the digital classroom also contains a series of activities that demonstrate how to navigate and use the resources of NARA. Teachers who want to include primary source material, and those using National History Day activities, will find this location invaluable. MHCA.

National Museum of Women's History. n.d. E-mail: info@nmwh.org. URL: http://www.nmwh.org/.

> The *National Museum of Women's History* is a virtual museum, although the organization would like to open a site on the Mall in Washington, D.C. within the next five years. For now, NMWH is celebrating its success in spearheading the effort to have the woman suffrage statue, honoring Susan B. Anthony, Elizabeth Cady Stanton, and Lucretia Mott, restored to the rotunda from its years in exile in the basement of the Capitol. The NMWH Web site features an exhibit of images from the woman suffrage movement, a time line, a quiz, and a bibliography. This site should be watched for future developments. MHCA.

National Register of Historic Places. 1999. National Park Service, P.O. Box 37127, Washington, DC 20013. URL: http://www.cr.nps.gov/nr/.

> During March, Women's History Month, the *National Register of Historic Places* Web page offers a special feature highlighting such historic places connected to women's history as the Clara Barton House; the Adeline Hornbek homestead; the M'Clintock house in Seneca Falls; and the home of Eleanor Roosevelt, Val-Kill. Lesson plans are offered about these locations and include skills in reading, cartography, and visual literacy. Additionally, a women's history bibliography; links to other Web sites; and overviews of women in connection to historic preservation, equal rights, the Progressive era, the

arts, and the professions are included. Teachers should be aware of the possibilities of this ready-made, searchable Web site. MHCA.

The National Women's Hall of Fame. 1999. 76 Fall Street, P.O. Box 335, Seneca Falls, NY 13148. 315-568-8060; fax 315-568-2976. E-mail: womenshall@aol.com. URL: http://www.greatwomen.org/.

In Seneca Falls, New York, the National Women's Hall of Fame was established by local residents in 1969 to permanently honor America's great women in the location where the woman's rights movement began in 1848. The Hall itself contains exhibits, artifacts and a research library. The Web site offers short biographies of the more than 150 inductees, the opportunity to nominate new members, and a learning center containing exhibits, resources, games, exercises and contests about women's history. The site does not link to state halls of fame, a notable drawback; however, the national museum may be an inspiration to groups to create their own memorials. Educators will use this site for curriculum ideas. MHCA.

National Women's History Project. 1999. 7738 Bell Road, Windsor, CA 95492-8518. 707-838-6000; fax 707-838-0478. E-mail: nwhp@aol.com. URL: http://www.nwhp.org/.

The National Women's History Project, established in 1980, created the celebration of Women's History Month each March. The organization provides a variety of services such as outreach to anyone interested in women's history and operating as a clearinghouse for curriculum and program resources. The staff serve as consultants, lecturers, and trainers, and offer in-service programs for schools and organizations, including a yearly workshop in California. Through its catalog, the NWHP offers curriculum units, program planning guides, video programs, posters, and high-quality materials from other publishers and producers. NWHP operates the Women's History Network, which publishes an annual directory and quarterly newsletter to encourage networking among individuals and organizations involved in all aspects of women's history. Teachers and educational leaders will use NWHP for material selection, curriculum development, and consultation, but the Web site is exceptional for all types of users. As the official Web site of Women's History Month, it furnishes basic information and lists programs from all over the country. Students will appreciate the interactive quiz and outstanding selection of historical links arranged thematically. Educational leaders will consult the page for links to women's history organizations, for curriculum updates, and for such programming ideas as the list of costumed performers. Everything having to do with women's history can be found at the *National Women's History Project*. MHCA.

The Sophia Smith Collection. 1999. Smith College, Northampton, MA 01063. 413-585-2970; fax 413-585-2886. E-mail: ssc-wmhist@smith.edu. URL: http://www.smith.edu/libraries/ssc/home.html.

The Sophia Smith Collection at Smith College is recognized as one of the largest women's history archives in the country. Founded in 1942 and named after the college's founder, the manuscript, print, and audio-visual collection portrays American women at home and abroad from Colonial times to the present. The collection is particularly strong in the areas of birth control, women's rights, suffrage, the women's movement, women working abroad, the arts, the professions, and family life. Included are the papers of Margaret Sanger; Ellen Gates Starr; Mary van Kleeck; Gloria Steinem; Sorosis, the first national club for professional women; the YWCA; and *Ms.* magazine. The Web site offers information about events, exhibits, the collection and its access, as well as subject guides and further Web links. Part of the collection has been digitized and is available online in a searchable format. The friendly site is an example of what archival access should and can be. MHCA.

Susan B. Anthony Slept Here. Directed by Alvin Cooperman. 56 min. Films for the Humanities and Sciences, 1995. Videocassette. Purchase $129.00; Rental $75.00.

Based on a book of the same name (now out of print) by Lynn Sherr and Jurate Kazickas, *Susan B. Anthony Slept Here* uses the roadside attraction motif to journey across America visiting locations important to women's history, narrated by ABC News correspondent Lynn Sherr, who travels in a red sports car. Even though maps are used as transitions, the film loses some of its geographical character when it organizes itself around themes, and introduces co-anchors to illustrate those themes. Olympic gold medal holder Donna de Varona helps to profile athletes and adventurers Babe Didrikson Zaharias, founder of the Ladies Professional Golf Association, and Annie Oakley, the sharpshooter and performer. In the other sections of the film, actress Blair Brown presents artist Georgia O'Keeffe and singer Bessie Smith; astronaut Mae Jemison introduces the first Black woman inventor and millionaire, Madame C. J. Walker, and the first teacher in space, Christa McAuliffe; and first lady Hillary Rodham Clinton profiles suffragist Susan B. Anthony, reminding of the importance of the right to vote. Black-and-white photos and film clips, including interviews with the subjects themselves, or with their descendants or friends, add authenticity. Within each section, many additional women are briefly profiled, among them Amelia Earhart, Jacqueline Cochran, Willa Cather, Isadora Duncan, Sacajawea, Helen Keller, Maria Mitchell, Jeannette Rankin, and Eleanor Roosevelt. The film is entertaining and informative and may spark school projects using geographical or women's hall of fame themes to research local heroines. MHCA.

Women in American Life. 5 parts, 15 to 25 min. ea. National Women's History Project, 1988, 1990. Videocassettes. $325.00 set; $69.95 ea.

Depicting women in American life from 1861 through 1977, this series of videos, produced by the National Women's History Project, features outstanding research and an excellent overview of women's history divided into five parts. The able narration, by project director Molly Murphy MacGregor, is pronounced over hundreds of black-and-white photographs and documents chosen from archives around the country. In the series, the transitions between topics are smooth, the narration and illustrations correspond well, and the experiences of women of color are included throughout. A study guide containing the script and biographical information on the many women mentioned accompanies each video.

Part one, *1861–1880: Civil War, Recovery, and Westward Expansion*, begins with women's contributions to the war effort in many different endeavors: as spies, in hospitals, and in organizing Sanitary Commissions to supply the armies. Included are Harriet Tubman, Bell Boyd, Dr. Elizabeth Blackwell, Dorothea Dix, Dr. Mary Walker, Louisa May Alcott, and Clara Barton. The end of the war brought changes for Northern, Southern, Black, and immigrant women, and some women chose to move west. The program ends with a solid explanation of the 1869 split in the woman's suffrage movement.

Part two, *1880–1920: Immigration, New Work and New Roles* covers the rise of unions, including the 1909 New York garment strike and the 1911 Triangle Shirtwaist fire; Mexican immigration northward due to the 1911 revolution; and new work opportunities gained from the invention of the typewriter and telephone. The various aspects of the reform movement, settlement houses, the WCTU, women's clubs, and the antilynching campaign of Ida B. Wells-Barnett, as well as the unification of the suffrage groups and their new tactics, which finally brought passage of the Nineteenth Amendment, are solidly covered.

In part three, *1917–1942: Cultural Image and Economic Reality*, women broaden their employment horizons during World War I; the peace movement is headed by Jeannette Rankin and Jane Addams; and the post-suffrage generation, aided by media images, see themselves much differently than previous generations. Black culture flourishes in the Harlem Renaissance while government policies discriminate against Asian, Native American, and Mexican women. The antilynching campaign, supported by Black and white women, makes gains against the Ku Klux Klan. During the Great Depression, women such as Frances Perkins and Mary McLeod Bethune gain key government posts for the first time.

Covering *1942–1955: War Work, Housework, and Growing Discontent*, part four includes women (excluding Japanese American women who were held in internment camps) who were recruited to industrial work and military service in World War II. Although the vast majority of women wanted to keep those jobs, they were laid off within months of the end of the war, and a new media campaign promoting happy housewives was begun. Despite the message telling women to stay home, and the childrearing advise of Dr. Spock, more women entered the workplace; but the limited post-war roles available to women left many unhappy. In the South, Mexican women and Black women organized to fight racial discrimination.

In the final part, *1955–1977: New Attitudes Force Dramatic Change*, women continued to enter the job market during the 1960s, and the divorce rate climbed. Ada Deer challenged unfair Native American determination acts, women entered tribal government, Mexican women unionized, the Chicano movement began on college campuses, and many Black women became leaders in the Civil Rights movement. Vietnam war protests made women realize that they had their own issues to address, and they formed groups such as the National Organization for Women. Styles changed, government policy changed, and women entered government service. Although the Equal Rights Amendment failed to be ratified, women recognized the issues that affected them and took advantage of greater opportunities and expanded roles.

History teachers will like the five-part division of the series and can use the guide to further subdivide the material along chronological, thematic, or cultural lines. Libraries may wish to use the series during Women's History Month; rentals are available. MHCA.

Women's History Celebration: The President's Commission on the Celebration of Women in American History. n.d. U.S. General Services Administration, Room 6002, 1800 F Street NW, Washington, DC 20405. E-mail: beth.newburger@gsa.gov. URL: http://www.gsa.gov/staff/pa/whc.htm.

The General Services Administration has established this Web site on the President's Commission on the Celebration of Women in American History, established by executive order in 1998. The purpose of the commission is to consider how best to honor the achievements of women in American history, which might include a focal point in Washington, D.C. and a national celebration. The commission is also considering connecting historical sites, museums, and libraries through the use of technology. The Web site allows visitors to read the executive order, to access committee member biographies, to examine posted minutes and schedules, and to use links to other women's history sites. Because the work of this commission is ongoing, students and other interested parties may enjoy watching it evolve and interacting with it. MHCA.

Women's Studies Database. 1999. University of Maryland, Women's Studies Department and Program, 2101 Woods Hall, College Park, MD 20742. 301-405-6877; fax 301-314-9190. E-mail: ws-editor@umail.umd.edu. URL: http://www.inform.umd.edu/EdRes/Topic/WomensStudies/.

By following the Reference Room link to American Women's History, a research guide to all types of women's history materials, both traditional print and new digital Internet resources, is available. Materials include reference and biographical sources, subject indexes, state and regional sources, primary sources, digital collections, books, journals, and theses. Because it is searchable, this is a great place to start student researchers, and teachers will be glad to know about its special section on finding digital collections. HCA.

WWWomen! The Premier Search Directory for Women Online. 1998. URL: http://www.wwwomen.com/.

Maintained by a privately owned company in San Francisco, *WWWomen!* focuses on finding worthy women-related Web pages, to which links are created by using a two-tiered approach. First, the site uses its search engines to locate sites that are current and relevant to women, and, second, sites may nominate themselves for inclusion. All new sites are screened. *WWWomen!* is searchable and browsable through organized categories. The main subjects covered are business, computers, diversity, education, entertainment, feminism, government, health, history, leisure, lesbianism, publications, resources, science, shopping, and sports. The history section offers a wide variety of pages on all aspects of women in history, through all times and from all places. Alphabetical arrangement makes the search function easy to use. Other features of the site include message boards for questions, announcements, and news; surveys; chat rooms; and site awards, which point to truly outstanding work based on content, inspiration, exploration, and presentation. *WWWomen!* is a site worthy of bookmarking because of its ease of use, thematic content, number of historical links, and the currency of the material. MHCA.

New World to New Nation, Prehistory to 1820

General

Books

Crane, Elaine Forman. **Ebb Tide in New England: Women, Seaports, and Social Change, 1630–1800**. Boston: Northeastern University Press, 1998. $50.00; $17.95pa. ISBN 1-55553-337-X; 1-55553-336-1pa.

> Elaine Crane concentrates on the four New England seaport towns of Boston, Newport, Portsmouth, and Salem to prove that during urbanization women lost autonomy. Women became increasingly invisible over two centuries in religion, economics, and law as patriarchal systems became institutionalized, even though women outnumbered men in these towns. American women's experience compares to the freedoms of European women in family, religion, economics, and law; however, the European intellectual tradition influenced American society so that female opportunity diminished as institution-building flourished. The result was that the limiting and silencing of women helped create a class of poor women. The implications of the study, which can be used for research or personal reading, progress far beyond its limited geographical context. A bibliography and an index are appended. HCA.

Jensen, Joan M. **Loosening the Bonds: Mid-Atlantic Farm Women, 1750–1850**. New Haven, CT: Yale University Press, 1986. 271p. $19.00pa. ISBN 0-300-04265-5pa.

> In another regional study, Joan Jensen examines women living outside Philadelphia, in Pennsylvania and Delaware, and the complexities of their lives as they function in the home, in the marketplace, and in the public arena. The purpose of the book is to chronicle farm women, rather than urban women. Although most women in this area were Quakers, the book embraces

all groups, including Native American and Black women. Jensen concludes that rural women, while engaged in hard work, built networks of support within their communities; developed a cottage industry around the butter trade; and became active in religion, education, and reform. By engaging in these activities, the agrarian women "loosened their bonds," becoming more autonomous and egalitarian. The book is illustrated with several black-and-white photographs and prints, has a number of graphical appendices, and is indexed. In addition to women's history, *Loosening the Bonds* can be used in regional and agricultural studies. HCA.

The Colonial Period

Books

Andrews, William L., ed. **Journeys in New Worlds: Early American Women's Narratives**. Madison: University of Wisconsin Press, 1990. 232p. (Wisconsin Studies in American Autobiography). $13.95pa. ISBN 0-299-12584-Xpa.

The travels of four Colonial women depicted in this collection, while different in many ways, are brought together symbolically as journeys to an enhanced sense of self. Mary Rowlandson relates the story of her capture by Indians in 1676 and tells how she traveled with them for eleven weeks before being ransomed. Sarah Kemble Knight keeps a travel diary on her business trip to New Haven in 1704. Elizabeth Ashbridge records a religious journey to peace as a Quaker preacher from a history of indentured servitude and a marriage to an abusive husband. Elizabeth House Trist travels from Philadelphia to meet her husband on a new plantation at Natchez, in the Louisiana Province, and keeps a diary of her travels for Thomas Jefferson. Beyond the enlightenment of the journey, all the women, through their writing, show evidence of personal growth from their experiences. Five historians wrote the introductions, which will be popular with those studying Colonial America. The various types of illustrations are black-and-white photographs, sketches, maps, documents, landscapes, and portraits. HCA.

Berkin, Carol. **First Generations: Women in Colonial America**. New York: Hill and Wang, 1996. 234p. $23.00; $12.00pa. ISBN 0-8090-4561-3; 0-8090-1616-0pa.

Carol Berkin tells the stories of Colonial women up through the time of the American Revolution. She intends her history to be inclusive, giving chapters to Native American women and African American women. All social classes and ethnic backgrounds are included in other chapters, which cover women of the Chesapeake, New England, and the middle colonies. Berkin considers inheritance, power, household production, religious life, rites of passage, and activism in showing the roles that women played in the early history of the country. The book adds to the scholarship on the period and can be used for research and individual reading. HCA.

Berkin, Carol, and Leslie Horowitz, eds. **Women's Voices, Women's Lives: Documents in Early American History**. Boston: Northeastern University Press, 1998. 203p. $42.50; $15.95pa. ISBN 1-55553-351-5; 1-55553-350-7pa.

> *Women's Voices, Women's Lives* brings the story of Colonial women to life in six chapters covering sex and reproduction, marriage and family, work, religion, politics and law, and gender ideology. Each section is introduced and divided into prescriptive and descriptive parts. The prescriptive documents are often written by men, who define various areas of women's lives; because Colonial women were subject to their fathers, brothers, and husbands, many of the descriptive writings are also by men, although female voices are included wherever possible. Each document, whether prescriptive or descriptive, is prefaced; this structure brings the court records, wills, letters, diaries, literature, sermons, advice books, and newspaper articles into perspective. The fascinating items portray women from all classes, regions, and races, and open up new ways of thinking about early residents of the New World. Unfortunately, there is no index, but, even so, libraries and schools where Colonial history is studied will want to own the book. HCA.

Brown, Kathleen M. **Good Wives, Nasty Wenches, and Anxious Patriarchs: Gender, Race, and Power in Colonial Virginia**. Chapel Hill: University of North Carolina Press, 1996. 496p. $19.95pa. ISBN 0-8078-4623-6pa.

> Winner of the Berkshire Prize, *Good Wives, Nasty Wenches, and Anxious Patriarchs* is a sagacious study investigating the role of gender in the rise of the slave system in Colonial Virginia and the institutionalization of patriarchy within social, cultural, and legal systems. Kathleen Brown contemplates the meaning of gender in England and how this foundation changed in the new world, leaving English women as embodiments of goodness and virtue, and women of African descent with connotations of evil and sinfulness. Brown explores the confrontations between English invaders and the Powhatan Indians; Bacon's Rebellion of planters against the English governor, which burned Jamestown in 1676, and the subsequent growth of the gentry class to which all white women aspired; and how all these events led to stratification along racial lines such as had never existed in England. Brown recognizes the overlap of race, class, and gender in the development of the earliest history of the United States. Her book, including black-and-white illustrations, maps, tables, notes, and an index, will be of particular interest in multicultural and Colonial studies. HCA.

Mossiker, Frances. **Pocahontas: The Life and the Legend**. New York: Da Capo, 1976. 383p. $15.95pa. ISBN 0-306-80699-1pa.

> Pocahontas looms larger in legend than her short life of twenty-two years would seem to allow. As the favorite daughter of Chief Powhatan, she had contact with the English settlers at Jamestown as she moved among them to carry food and messages; but Pocahontas was often at the center of misunderstandings between two cultures. When Captain John Smith was captured and held by her father, Pocahontas intervened to save his life. When

her father was ready to attack the Jamestown settlement, Pocahontas warned the colony, but, later, she was captured by the colonists and held in one of their ships. She married John Rolfe, was baptized, and sailed with him to England, where she was received at court; but she died in the foreign land, leaving an infant son. Mossiker calls upon both historical and anthropological data to recreate the story of the Native American girl. In an afterword, the author gathers the legends and literature that use Pocahontas as a central figure; however, because of its 1976 copyright date, the Disney myth is not a part of this discussion. The book's center section has fourteen black-and-white illustrations showing various artistic treatments of Pocahontas; four documents concerning Smith and Rolfe are appended; and a bibliography and an index are included. The well-researched, well-written biography will serve readers in schools and libraries. HCA.

Norton, Mary Beth. **Founding Mothers and Fathers: Gendered Power and the Forming of American Society**. New York: Knopf, 1996. 496p. $35.00. ISBN 0-679-42965-4.

Historian Mary Beth Norton investigated the period from 1620 to 1670 to determine the roots of gendered society. Although the Pilgrims founded their colony on a socialistic (and gendered) system, this was given up as a failure. The roots of family, community, and state power in the colonies were based on the philosophies of Sir Robert Filmer, which equated the power of the head of the family to the head of state; however, given that women, as mothers, wielded family power, because women could become widowed and thus heads of families, and women of status outranked lower-class men, power for women was a possibility. The Filmerian system produced Anne Hutchinson, a religious leader who created much dissension in the Massachusetts Bay colony; Margaret Brent, a financier who saved Maryland from dissolving; and Thomas/Thomasine Hall, for whom the courts created a dual sexual status. In the Chesapeake colonies, it was not possible to establish normal family structures because of the imbalance in sex ratios. This abnormality allowed for the advent of the Enlightened Lockean philosophy, which confined women's authority to the home by defining public and private spheres. Norton's scholarly study is based on the analysis of seventeenth-century civil and criminal court records, some of the few primary sources remaining from the period. With an appendix explaining the data collection and methodology, notes, and an index, this study enhances our knowledge of the Colonial period. CA.

Pinckney, Eliza Lucas. **The Letterbook of Eliza Lucas Pinckney, 1739-1762**. Edited by Elise Pinckney and Marvin R. Zahniser. Columbia: University of South Carolina Press, 1972. 195p. $16.95pa. ISBN 1-57003-186-Xpa.

The letterbook of Eliza Pinckney, recognized as the largest written record of a Colonial woman, provides a view of a privileged southern lady in the years before the Revolution. Eliza was born on the island of Antigua, where her father, a British army officer, served. After moving the family to a South Carolina plantation in 1738, when Eliza was fifteen years old, Colonel

George Lucas returned to Antigua to fulfill his military obligation. From this time, Eliza managed the extensive plantation affairs for the family, keeping a letterbook in which she recorded her correspondence. By nursing plants and seeds over a five-year period until they became profitable, Eliza was instrumental in establishing indigo as a cash crop for South Carolina. The money earned from the dye helped to sustain the Pinckney family through the Revolution. Because Eliza was widowed early from Charles Pinckney, to whom she was devoted, she managed plantation activity for most of her life. She raised three children, and both her sons served in the Revolutionary War. This edition of her journal includes color and black-and-white illustrations of the Pinckney belongings; maps; portraits; introductory material; a biographical sketch; and an index. With its singular portrayal of plantation life and Eliza's many interests, including the education of her slaves, the book should become the nucleus of any Colonial collection. HCA.

Treckel, Paula A. **To Comfort the Heart: Women in Seventeenth-Century America**. New York: Twayne, 1996. 267p. (American Women, 1600-1900). $33.00. ISBN 0-8057-9917-6.

Challenging the view of early twentieth-century historians that Colonial America was a golden age for women, Paula Treckel calls on more recent research to show that the period from 1588 to 1748 was a time of continuity and change. In extremely readable short sections, Treckel takes a broad view of the period, looking at family and legal roots in Europe, North America, and Africa to help explain women's experiences and roles during the settlement of the New World. The focus of the book is on resettlement, family life, law, and religion among immigrants, Native American women, slaves, and indentured servants from different regions over several generations. Containing fifteen black-and-white illustrations, notes, and an index, the easy-to-use book should be first choice in covering Colonial women. MHCA.

Winslow, Anna Green. **Diary of Anna Green Winslow: A Boston School Girl of 1771**. Bedford, MA: Applewood, 1996. 121p. $9.95pa. ISBN 1-55709-447-0pa.

When she was ten years old, Anna Green Winslow traveled to Boston from Nova Scotia in 1770 to live with an aunt and to be finished by attending school and social events. She kept her diary to practice her penmanship and to provide her parents with a picture of her life. Two themes, her vanity and her piety, ran through her narrative, which provides a picture of domesticity. When she was twelve, Winslow "came out," and she recorded this as well as other typical celebrations of the time. Winslow's diary covered only two years, but she did not live long after she stopped writing it. It is believed that she died in Marshfield, her mother's hometown, in 1779, although this fact is unrecorded. Providing a first-hand look at Boston in the years leading up to the Revolution, the diary is illustrated with seven black-and-white period illustrations. Early Colonial historian Alice Morse Earle introduces the diary, establishes the family's genealogy, and provides notes on the text, which make the material approachable, even for middle school students. MHCA.

Non-Book Material

Lacey, Bill. **The Trial of Anne Hutchinson**. El Cajon, CA: Interact, 1992. Simulation. $39.00.

The student can gain a clear understanding of the Puritans' religious beliefs by using this simulation, which re-creates the 1637 trial that convicted Anne Hutchinson of heresy and banished her from Boston. After following John Cotton, whom she revered, from England, Hutchinson held Tuesday meetings in her parlor to discuss the previous week's sermon. Hutchinson disagreed with the Puritan clergy on certain doctrines and was not afraid to explain her beliefs. Simmering religious differences and unfolding political events combined over three years to bring about Hutchinson's demise. The kit includes background and preparation materials for the teacher as well as student guides that clearly present the history and personalities of the time. Thirteen roles are available, but every class member is responsible for documenting the trial. Follow-up discussion questions and activities are suggested. The activity is well organized and offers a hands-on approach to studying Colonial America through a classroom event that can be used in social studies, religion, or drama classes. H.

Pocahontas: Ambassador of the World. Produced and directed by Monte Markham and Adam Friedman. 50 min. A & E, 1995. (A & E Biography). Videocassette. $19.95.

Commentary from five narrators, art, and live-action sequences help to tell the story of Pocahontas. Surprisingly, quite a lot is known about the seventeenth-century daughter of Chief Powhatan. As her father's advisor, Pocahontas was sent to observe the Jamestown settlers and was surprised to find that John Smith could speak her language. She believed in peaceful coexistence, helped the settlers with food gifts, and acted as intermediary to her father. Multiple interpretations are presented for the capture of Smith and his rescue by Pocahontas. In one account, the film explains that the tribe was a matrilineal society in which women had the power to pardon prisoners. Smith's own written account of his capture must be measured against what is known about the tribe's culture and what Powhatan may have been planning. Relations did not improve. When Smith later tried to carry out orders from King James to Powhatan, distrust reigned; Pocahontas had to warn Smith of her father's intent to harm the colony. Pocahontas was kidnapped by the English and kept prisoner aboard a ship. Here she met John Rolfe, whom she would eventually marry and with whom she would bear a son. Rolfe's intent was to Christianize her, and Rebecca was the name Pocahontas took at her baptism. With their newborn son, the Rolfes sailed to England, where they were received at the court of Queen Ann. When she was about twenty-two years old, Pocahontas became ill and died before she could return home. The film makes good use of primary source accounts, including the words of Pocahontas. With little illustration to draw on, some of the visual images become repetitive; still, the film is solid and will be popular with history classes. MHCA.

Salem Witchcraft

Books

Hall, David D., ed. **Witch-Hunting in Seventeenth-Century New England: A Documentary History, 1658–1692**. Boston: Northeastern University Press, 1991. 332p. $15.95pa. ISBN 1-55553-085-0pa.

> Not only does David Hall collect the major documents relating to witchcraft in the seventeenth century, he transposes them into standard English for ease in reading. He then presents a social history of New England by allowing the documents to speak for themselves. Although the book seems complete, it offers only a selection of documents including, with few exceptions, every case resulting in execution and every case for which extensive documentation exists. *Witch-Hunting* is arranged chronologically from 1638 through the Salem trials. Hall's introduction is concise, recounting historical context, witchcraft lore, and witch-hunting in relation to the social system, gender, religion, and law. He introduces each case before presenting the documents related to it. Some cases are short, half a page with two one-line diary entries marking an execution. Other cases take up entire chapters. Readers who want to know about witches will find sick children, quarreling neighbors, psychological disturbances, and all manner of shape-shifting, magic, and counter-magic. An appendix lists the New England statutes relating to witchcraft; the work also includes a selected bibliography and an index. Hall's delightful presentation on an absorbing subject is highly recommended. MHCA.

Hill, Frances. **A Delusion of Satan: The Full Story of the Salem Witch Trials**. New York: Da Capo, 1995. 270p. $14.95pa. ISBN 0-306-80797-1pa.

> Like many, Frances Hill was fascinated by the Salem witchcraft trials, and, even though she was a British subject, she wanted to write a comprehensive history. Hill believed that a satisfactory account did not exist, that all the answers had not yet surfaced, and that the 300-hundred-year-old story held implications for society today. Beyond the Salem trials, the McCarthy hearings of the 1950s and the persecution of people for undocumented satanic crimes prove that witch-hunts still occur in society. After detailing the Salem story, Hill concludes that disinheritance was a major theme in the Salem tragedy. Many of those involved had been denied their freedom, inheritance, wealth, or family, and both Salem and Massachusetts were in decline. The answer, no doubt, lies in many factors, and readers will draw their own conclusions. A picture section displays portraits of key figures, documents, and landmarks. The book also includes the Putnam family tree, a list of key people, a chronology, a list of the dead, and an index. Observant

research and writing make *A Delusion of Satan* an admirable choice for all libraries. MHCA.

Karlsen, Carol F. **The Devil in the Shape of a Woman: Witchcraft in Colonial New England**. New York: W. W. Norton, 1998. 370p. $13.95pa. ISBN 0-393-31759-5pa.

Witchcraft is the story of women. This is the point of view Carol Karlsen takes in her heavily documented study of witchcraft in Colonial New England. After contextualizing the beliefs about witchcraft during the period, Karlsen makes a careful analysis of the characteristics and patterns among those accused of witchcraft, both male and female. Using court records and other primary sources, she catalogs prosecutions, convictions, and executions, using over twenty tables to present gender statistics. Karlsen believes that women's relationship to witchcraft is tied to religion, social structures, and women's own struggle to define themselves. *The Devil in the Shape of a Woman* is a focused treatment, a gender study of the period rather than a history or chronology. An appendix lists most of the accused witches, and an index is included. HCA.

Non-Book Material

Salem Witchcraft Hysteria. 1997. National Geographic Society, 1145 Seventeenth Street NW, Washington, DC 20036-4688. 800-647-5463. URL: http://www.nationalgeographic.com/features/97/salem/splash.html.

This interactive site allows students to experience the 1692 Salem witchcraft trials by advancing in a carefully paced tutorial and deciding if they will plead guilty or innocent to the charge of witchcraft. Lettering of various colors on a black background gives the pages an eerie appeal. Plenty of background information is available in pop-up screens that tell about each person involved in the trials. One area of the site allows visitors to ask questions of a historian; another is designated for discussion. A bibliography and travel information are available, boosting the research value of the Web site. History teachers and students alike will love the game-like appeal of this Web site. MHCA.

The Witches of Salem: The Horror and the Hope. Produced and directed by Dennis Azzarella. 35 min. Phoenix Learning Group, 1972. Videocassette. Purchase $79.00; Rental $35.00.

The words and events dramatized in this live-action film about the Salem witchcraft trials are all taken from court records. The film does not parallel *The Crucible*, but rather takes a broader, more political view of the events, painting the Puritans as intolerant in a new land that was rapidly gaining an identity based on equal justice. In 1692, the royal charter to the Massachusetts Bay colony was revoked, and a new governor was to be appointed by the king. Beyond the political unrest, several events could have influenced the local girls to behave as though they were bewitched. Several of the adolescent girls of Salem read a book about a witchcraft incident that had happened four years earlier in Boston, and they heard enchanting stories from the slave, Tituba. When these girls made their accusations, the deputy governor insisted on accepting only "scientific proof" of witchcraft; thus, throughout the trials, questions were raised about the legal assumptions and evidence accepted. After nineteen hangings, and with over 100 accused still in jail awaiting trial, the new governor, Sir William Phips, ended the debacle, and the power of the Puritans went into decline. Throughout the film, the bewitched girls act quite out of control, even though their individual characters are not defined. Students will enjoy doing further research on this unique incident in American history, and teachers may choose to connect this film to the study of Anne Hutchinson's trial. The film offers good background material, and can be used wherever *The Crucible* is taught as well as in American history classes. MHCA.

American Revolution

Books

DePauw, Linda Grant. **Founding Mothers: Women in America in the Revolutionary Era**. New York: Sandpiper, 1975. 228p. $5.95pa. ISBN 0-395-70109-0pa.

> Linda DePauw offers a well-researched and readable overview of American women during the time of the Revolution. Covering women's work inside and outside the home, women's societal role, the legal rights of females, women's part in the war, and how the war affected the rights of women, the book contains very clear explanations aimed at the middle school and high school reader or researcher. The book includes coverage of Black women, Native American women, loyalist women, and patriot women during the second half of the eighteenth century. All the major female figures of the period are reviewed: Abigail Adams, Margaret Corbin, Deborah Sampson, Sally Hemings, Sybil Ludington, Betsy Ross, and Mercy Otis Warren, along with many other women. Although the book does not have footnotes, it contains numerous quotations from newspapers, letters, diaries, and other writings. Suggestions for further reading and an excellent index are appended. MH.

Gundersen, Joan R. **To Be Useful to the World: Women in Revolutionary America, 1740–1790**. New York: Twayne, 1996. 273p. (American Women, 1600–1900). $33.00. ISBN 0-8057-9916-8.

> To portray women of the Revolutionary period, Joan Gundersen follows three families through three generations in her heavily researched study. The grandmothers are adults before the Revolution, the mothers come of age during the conflict, and the daughters are women of the New Republic. Chosen to represent a variety of situations, but tied to the conflict in some way, the first generation women include Elizabeth Porter, from a small Virginia

plantation owning several slaves; Deborah Franklin, wife of Benjamin Franklin of Philadelphia; and Margaret Brant, an Iroquois who sided with the British during the war. Gunderson ably demonstrates the diversity and the commonality of women's experience throughout her characters' lives while including the perspectives of several cultures and classes. The author concludes that expanded or restricted opportunity is dependent on many factors, including immigration, marriage, social class, education, religion, cultural group, and changing social structures. The book includes ten black-and-white illustrations and an index. The comparisons of the three families make for interesting reading while bringing the Revolution and changes for women into focus. HCA.

Kerber, Linda K. **Women of the Republic: Intellect and Ideology in Revolutionary America**. Chapel Hill: University of North Carolina Press, 1980. 318p. $12.95pa. ISBN 0-8078-4065-3pa.

Linda Kerber considers the roles of women in the Revolution and how the period affected them. Through letters, diaries, court records, legal documents, pamphlets, and books, she proves women of the period were multifaceted: They participated with the Revolutionary army as cooks, washers, and nurses, or maintained homes, farms, and businesses during the absence of their spouses. After the Revolution, a number of changes occurred. The laws of coverture, or common law, which gave husbands legal control over the property of their wives, were not altered; and because women were under the jurisdiction of their husbands, their political persuasions were considered to be the same as those of their husbands. After the war, however, divorce became easier because many states passed laws the British had not permitted. Education was seen as more important, but women rejected reading political theory in favor of fiction. Although the female had gained a place in politics within the home, Kerber describes her as the "republican mother," a limited participant lacking power. *Women of the Republic* contains period illustrations and documents in black and white as well as a note on sources, and an index. This work will be a useful addition to Colonial studies collections in schools and libraries. HCA.

Norton, Mary Beth. **Liberty's Daughters: The Revolutionary Experience of American Women, 1750–1800**. Ithaca, NY: Cornell University Press, 1980. 384p. $16.95pa. ISBN 0-8014-8347-6pa.

Liberty's Daughters, admired as one of the first studies of the female experience, is based on the written records of approximately 450 families of the Revolutionary period. In organizing the book, the author is guided by the voices of the women as she perceives them through their writing. The topics important to them were household obligation, marriage, child-raising, self-perception, and independence. These subjects make up the first section of the book, which deals with the unchanging nature of women's lives. A second section examines changes wrought by the Revolution when activism, the course of the war, changing self-image, and female education became important to women. Mary Beth Norton concludes that in the second half of the eighteenth century, women's lives were affected by changing personal aspirations and by the breakdown of the barriers keeping women from participating in the public sector. Illustrated with black-and-white paintings, engravings, sketches, copies of documents, and graphs, the book, which was the winner of the 1981 Berkshire Conference Prize, includes notes, an appendix of major families studied, an essay on sources, and an index. HCA.

Warren, Mercy Otis. **History of the Rise, Progress and Termination of the American Revolution: Interspersed with Biographical, Political and Moral Observations**. 2 vols. Edited by Lester H. Cohen. Indianapolis: Liberty Fund, 1994. 762p. $25.00; $15.00pa. ISBN 0-86597-066-1; 0-86597-069-6pa.

This comprehensive history of the Revolutionary period was originally published in 1805. Although not specifically focusing on women, the history is interesting for the female perspective on the times and for Warren's assessments of the people she knew. Warren was considered an educated woman, having studied at home along with her brothers. Her classical education shows in her writing, which includes footnotes and quotations. Because Warren seldom worked with sources in front of her, her quotations came from memory. Historical methods have changed considerably in 200 years. The volumes are illustrated with a black-and-white portrait of Warren and the cover of the original edition. Indexing includes Warren's original index and a modern, more expanded version. Schools and libraries may want to have this early, although not definitive, record available. HCA.

Zeinert, Karen. **Those Remarkable Women of the American Revolution**. Brookfield, CT: Millbrook, 1996. 96p. $27.40. ISBN 1-56294-657-9.

Karen Zeinert makes Revolutionary women accessible to younger readers. Organized around the themes of army service, spies, politics, ladies associations, and the home front, Zeinert presents all the ways in which women contributed to the war effort. Covering women of different cultures and regions of the country, the author uses anecdotes and quotations to bring the stories alive. The book contains sidebars on such personalities as Martha Washington, Betsy Ross, Mary Jemison, and Phillis Wheatley. Also included are a time line, a bibliography, suggestions for further reading, and an index. Students will find *Those Remarkable Women* interesting reading and useful for reports. MH.

Non-Book Material

Deborah Sampson: A Woman in the Revolution. Directed by Dennis Joseph Passaggio. 17 min. Phoenix Learning Group, 1976. Videocassette. Purchase $195.00; Rental $46.00.

Because Deborah Sampson was discouraged by women's contributions to war work, she enlisted in the Revolutionary Army under the assumed name of Robert Shurtlieff. Serving under Colonel Jackson in the final years of the war, Sampson fought at Tarrytown and Yorktown and was wounded twice. She doctored herself to avoid being discovered. A malignant fever proved her undoing near the end of the war, and when her sex was discovered, she begged to keep her uniform and her rank until peace was declared, only three weeks later. Jackson awarded her a pension and a piece of land, where Sampson settled, married, and raised a family. Linda Atkinson plays Sampson in this short reenactment transferred to video from film. The credits are slightly off-screen, but that is the only fault with a production that brings women's roles as soldiers in the Revolution into focus. Discussion questions are included in the package with the video, which can be used in social studies classes. MHCA.

Women in the American Revolution. Compiled by Carol Berkin. 15 pieces with guide. Jackdaw Publications, 1975. Document portfolio. $35.00.

The documents in *Women in the American Revolution* were carefully selected to illustrate the range of activities women engaged in during the fight for America's independence. Mercy Otis Warren and Phillis Wheatley used their writing skills as propagandists. Women went to work in the factories, as well as in the home, creatively finding ways to compensate for the lack of goods. Raising money for supplies and following the army to serve in support positions as well as in combat were other ways women contributed. Both rebel and loyalist women opened their homes, lives, and fortunes to the war effort; however, loyalist women faced discrimination and displacement after the war. Even with a full range of participation during the war, women did not gain any rights after the war. Although Abigail Adams raised the issue during the forming of the Constitution, it would be years before the idea of basic rights for women would be seriously discussed. The kit contains five essays on various topics concerning women's participation in the Revolution as well as ten documents that are accompanied by plain text transcriptions, an aide in deciphering the handwritten scripts. Social studies teachers will appreciate this collection of primary sources, especially as their loose-leaf format allows for a variety of applications. MHCA.

Period of the New Republic

Books

Bober, Natalie S. **Abigail Adams: Witness to a Revolution**. New York: Aladdin, 1995. 248p. $8.99pa. ISBN 0-689-81916-1pa.

Over 2,000 letters written by Abigail Adams survived, helping to bring her personality and character to life. Even though her wish was that her correspondence be destroyed after her death, her family saved the letters from which Natalie Bober quotes generously in this biography. Abigail was the wife of the second American president, John Adams, and the mother for the fifth president, John Quincy Adams. She witnessed the Battle of Bunker

Hill from an elevation near her Massachusetts home, and she admonished her husband to "remember the ladies" when he served as a delegate to the Continental Congress. During the Revolutionary War, when John Adams spent a great deal of time abroad as a diplomat, Abigail used all of her resources to keep family and home together. As the first presidential wife to live in the White House, she set precedents for those who followed. Bober includes many period illustrations depicting a time that does not encompass a large visual record. A chronology, family trees, maps, notes, a bibliography, and an index complete the well-written book. MHCA.

Cott, Nancy F. **The Bonds of Womanhood: "Woman's Sphere" in New England, 1780–1835**. 2d ed. New Haven, CT: Yale University Press, 1977. 225p. $15.00pa. ISBN 0-300-07298-8pa.

Written more than twenty years ago, Nancy Cott's *The Bonds of Womanhood* established the cult of domesticity, the paradigm of nineteenth century women. In her research, the author reviewed the letters and diaries of more than 100 New England women from 1780 to 1835, a time of social change in the New Republic. From these documents, female voices outline women's sphere as work, home, education, religion, and mutual support. Cott's study still stands as a defining work in women's history, elucidating the lives of women from one region during one era. An index is included. HCA.

Gelles, Edith B. **Portia: The World of Abigail Adams**. Bloomington: Indiana University Press, 1992. 227p. $25.95; $12.95pa. ISBN 0-253-32553-6; 0-253-21023-2pa.

Abigail Adams, a prolific letter writer, left a full record of her life. Married to John Adams for over fifty years, she often lived away from him, thus the need to correspond. Adams, whose correspondence shapes the core of *Portia,* knew and wrote to many of the prominent figures of the day, including Thomas Jefferson, and she remained close to her two sisters and her five children. Edith Gelles places Adams as the central figure in this biography, using a topical arrangement to present her life story. Gelles discovered seven different personalities in the letters of Portia, Adams's pen name, but the book is not specifically organized around these themes of piety, romance, flirtatiousness, feminism, politics, self-analysis, and termagantism. Gelles encompasses some of these topics, constructing the book around courtship, marriage, gossip, friendship, war, sisterhood, and motherhood. Many biography readers may be surprised by this arrangement, although an intimate portrait of Adams does emerge. A black-and-white portrait section, a time line, notes, a bibliography, and a short index are included. HCA.

Pflueger, Lynda. **Dolley Madison: Courageous First Lady**. Springfield, NJ: Enslow, 1999. 128p. (Historical American Biographies). $19.95. ISBN 0-7660-1092-9.

Dolley Madison, only the second president's wife to live in the White House, had to save the artifacts and abandon the building to the British. This short, well-written biography details Madison's life as a Quaker girl, wife of President James Madison, and hostess in the White House. The first lady set many precedents that remain in place today. The book contains black-and-white illustrations, portraits, maps, and sidebars supplying interesting historical tidbits. A chronology, a glossary, suggestions for further reading, and an index are included in a book that will be used for research and reading. MH.

Skemp, Sheila L. **Judith Sargent Murray: A Brief Biography with Documents**. Boston: Bedford, 1998. 210p. (Bedford Series in History and Culture). $35.00. ISBN 0-312-17770-4.

Born to a wealthy merchant family in Gloucester, Massachusetts, Judith Sargent Murray showed such keen intellect that she was educated beside her brother, who was preparing for Harvard. From her twenties on, she engaged in writing poetry, essays, and plays on a wide range of topics. The Sargent family helped to found the Universalist church in America, and Murray wrote the catechism for the new church. When her first husband died, she married the pastor, John Murray. After the Revolution, when the ban on dramatic presentations was lifted in Boston, Murray mounted three of her plays at the Federal Street Theater. Sheila Skemp's book is divided into two parts, the first covering the writer's life and the second presenting samples of her work. Both sections are organized around Murray's major topics: religion, politics, women's rights, marriage, motherhood, education, and literature. Fifteen pieces of Murray's writing are included, and appendices provide a chronology, a selected bibliography, and an index. Murray's writing can be used to supplement discussions of the Revolution and the development of the new nation. HCA.

Ulrich, Laurel Thatcher. **A Midwife's Tale: The Life of Martha Ballard, Based on Her Diary, 1785–1812**. New York: Random House, 1990. 444p. $13.00pa. ISBN 0-679-73376-0pa.

The existence of the Martha Ballard diary, which is housed in the Maine State Library, has always been known because several authors have referenced it and quoted from it in their works; however, it took the work of historian Laurel Thatcher Ulrich to uncover the stories that the diary contains hidden beneath its mundane listing of accounts, weather conditions, and household chores. The diary entries are not long, seldom more than a paragraph, but within them a phrase can tell a complete story. Ballard, the mother of nine children, moved to Hallowell, Maine, in the fall of 1777, where she became a midwife, attending 816 births over twenty-seven years. Ulrich chose ten stories from the diary to illustrate health issues, home industries, social mores, family life, and politics at the turn of the nineteenth century. The incidents, which Ulrich explains in essays following a section of the diary, include a scarlet fever epidemic, a rape, the marriages of Ballard's children, and the imprisonment of her husband. The reader will find that half the joy of reading *A Midwife's Tale* lies in becoming acquainted with this indistinct period through a woman's eyes; the other half is admiration for the historian whose work brought the stories to life. The author won the Pulitzer Prize as well as prizes from the American Historical Association and the Berkshire Conference of Women Historians. It is illustrated with documents, maps, and charts, and an appendix lists the medical ingredients Ballard used. Full bibliographic citations and an index are included. There are plans to make the entire diary, with teaching activities, available via the Internet; such availability will greatly expand possibilities for learning about this period in American history. HCA.

Non-Book Material

A Midwife's Tale. Produced by Laurie Kahn-Leavitt. 88 min. PBS Video, 1997. (The American Experience). Videocassette. Public performance rights $79.95; Home use $19.95.

Based on the book by historian Laurel Thatcher Ulrich, *A Midwife's Tale* portrays events drawn from the diary of Martha Ballard written between 1785 and 1812. The film contains interviews with the author discussing how she approached her study of the diary and how she arrived at certain interpretations. The diary is important for what it adds to the body of knowledge about women in the post-Revolutionary era. As Ulrich says, "Without documents there is no history." On the surface, the diary appears to be filled with trivia, a record of work rather than of Ballard's feelings. As the historian interprets it, she uncovers far more than the surface discloses. The first story Ulrich examines is Ballard's work as a midwife and healer. Through this story, the author follows the course of a disease epidemic and discovers how Ballard lost three daughters in an earlier outbreak. Another plot involves the working dynamic of the Ballard family. When the father, Ephram, a tax collector, is thrown into debtors' prison for failing to collect the taxes, son Jonathan, a drunkard, exerts control over his mother. It is only when Ephram returns home that a measure of respect is restored to Ballard, who at the age of seventy is still engaged in daily hard physical labor as well as her midwifery. The video cuts back and forth between Ulrich and reenactments of the Ballard family, carefully reconstructing the clothes, manners, tools, and songs common during the period of the New Republic. The film is useful to illustrate this period in history, to demonstrate the construction of social history, and to depict the work of historians. *A Midwife's Tale* makes an excellent addition to school and library collections. HCA.

Victorians to Voters, 1820 to 1920

General

Books

Bryant, Jennifer Fisher. **Lucretia Mott: A Guiding Light**. Grand Rapids, MI:
William B. Eerdmans, 1996. 182p. (Women of Spirit). $15.00; $8.00pa.
ISBN 0-8028-5115-0; 0-8028-5098-7pa.

> Lucretia Mott was one of the most renowned women of the nineteenth cen-
> tury, influential in the fields of religion, abolition, and woman's rights.
> Born Lucretia Coffin, she married James Mott, whom she met at school, in
> 1811. As a Quaker, Mott was permitted to preach in her church, a privilege
> other churches and custom of the time denied women. It was through her
> church that Mott learned about the evils of slavery, and she became active
> in the abolition movement, traveling to speak on the subject, until Emanci-
> pation. As a delegate to the World's Anti-Slavery Convention in London in
> 1840, she was denied participation because of her sex. Because of this
> slight, Mott and Elizabeth Cady Stanton, who had also attended the con-
> vention, were moved to organize the first convention on the subject of
> woman's rights, which was held at Seneca Falls, New York, in July 1848.
> Mott lived an eventful life until her death in 1880 at the age of eighty-
> seven. Her biography contains a section of black-and-white illustrations,
> suggestions for further reading, and an index. The book uses several
> twentieth-century terms and fails to put Mott in the context of her times;
> still, it is a serviceable account of an inspiring woman, suitable for school
> use. MHA.

Clinton, Catherine. **The Other Civil War: American Women in the Nineteenth Century**. Rev. ed. New York: Hill and Wang, 1999. 320p. $13.00pa.
ISBN 0-8090-1622-2pa.

> Catherine Clinton creates a one-volume history chronicling women in the
> nineteenth century, with some topical consideration. Beginning with an over-
> view of the generations who lived before the nineteenth century, Clinton
> proceeds to cover industrialization, domesticity, the initial movements
> towards political organization, the Civil War, westward migration, feminist
> crusades, sexuality, reform, and integration into broader national move-
> ments. The book is a brief but comprehensive history, including a biblio-
> graphic essay and an index, suitable for research at all levels. MHCA.

Gabriel, Mary. **Notorious Victoria: The Life of Victoria Woodhull, Uncensored**. Chapel Hill, NC: Algonquin Books of Chapel Hill, 1998. 372p. $24.95. ISBN 1-56512-132-5.

> Proving that the Victorians could live up to their reputation for naughty behavior, Victoria Woodhull lived a fast life. Her father, often on the wrong side of the law, married Woodhull off at the age of fifteen to a drunkard. Woodhull and her sister, Tennessee Claflin, traveled as spiritualists until Woodhull's second husband brought them to New York. There they met Cornelius Vanderbilt, who helped them make a killing on Wall Street. The sisters opened their own brokerage house, the first run by women, and founded a newspaper, which they used to express their views on socialism, feminism, politics, and free love. Woodhull openly professed the ideals of the free love movement. As a feminist, she founded the Equal Rights Party and was nominated as the organization's presidential candidate in 1872; however, election day found Woodhull in jail, a ruined woman. She was brought down trying to demonstrate the hypocrisy of the double standard that existed for women. By the time she was thirty-four, her career was over; like many shooting stars, she had burned out quickly. Woodhull exiled herself to Great Britain and spent the rest of her life denying her past and reinventing herself. Illustrated with black-and-white photographs, Mary Gabriel's biography is very readable, but, as a journalist, Gabriel tends to lean on the newspaper record, quoting from it extensively. The book contains Woodhull's party platform, a bibliography, and an index. As a major participant in the woman's rights movement and the first woman to testify before Congress, Woodhull deserves to have her name a household word. HCA.

Ginzberg, Lori D. **Women and the Work of Benevolence: Morality, Politics, and Class in the Nineteenth-Century United States**. New Haven, CT: Yale University Press, 1990. 230p. (Yale Historical Publications). $27.00; $12.00pa. ISBN 0-300-04704-5; 0-300-05254-5pa.

> Lori Ginzberg's study of women in their reform role covers the period encompassing the Civil War, from 1820 to 1885. In the early years, women believed in the moral superiority of their sex; however, in carrying out acts of charity, women took on roles opposed to their higher nature as they became involved in business and political operations. In creating organizations and working for legislative changes in the ante-bellum period, the work of benevolence changed in style and in tradition. Because these changes occurred before the war, women emerged from the war with many independent experiences and looked at charitable work more as a business than a feminine pursuit. Ginzberg's complicated study is carefully researched and filled with primary source quotations. It is appropriate for advanced research and large collections. *Women and the Work of Benevolence* includes an index. CA.

Hedges, Elaine, Julie Silber, and Pat Ferrero. **Hearts and Hands: Women, Quilts, and American Society**. Nashville: Rutledge Hill, 1987. 107p. $19.95pa. ISBN 1-55853-434-2pa.

A companion volume to the video of the same name listed below, this book focuses mostly on women's relationships to the textile arts throughout the nineteenth century. While following the same topics and arrangement as the video, the book offers an amazing collection of black-and-white period photographs and color illustrations of quilts from the 1800s. Most of the photos tie to quilts and sewing in some way: Pioneers are shown in front of their sod house with their sewing machine; hospitalized Civil War soldiers are photographed in the ward, quilts covering their cots; African American women stand in front of a cabin while one irons a quilt; and a Lakota family is pictured with quilts hanging in the background. Most of the women featured in the video are pictured and quoted in the book; however, cultural groups are more of a presence in the book than they are in the video. An excellent reference list and an index will aid researchers. Although companion pieces, the book and video each stands on its own, and, because each serves a different purpose, libraries should not feel that they are duplicating by owning both. HCA.

Kelly, Catherine E. **In the New England Fashion: Reshaping Women's Lives in the Nineteenth Century**. Ithaca, NY: Cornell University Press, 1999. 258p. $39.95. ISBN 0-8014-3076-3.

Using diaries, letters, and other writings, Catherine Kelly illustrates how the lives of women changed during the first half of the nineteenth century in New England. The model of the self-supporting rural household was giving way to a rising consumer culture, thus creating a larger middle class. Through their writings to family and friends, middle-class, rural women of Massachusetts, New Hampshire, and Vermont explain the changes and continuities in their lives at home and at school as they balance traditional domestic values and the new values of the emerging culture. By exploring views on courtship, marriage, sentimentality, sociability, fashion, consumption, and class, the author illustrates how gender relations changed during this period and affected middle-class formation. At the same time, faith in rural values created the myth of the New England small town. Black-and-white illustrations and an index are included. CA.

Kitch, Sally. **This Strange Society of Women: Reading the Letters and Lives of the Woman's Commonwealth**. Columbus: Ohio State University Press, 1993. 391p. $45.00. ISBN 0-8142-0579-8.

Using a large cache of letters, Sally Kitch reconstructs the Woman's Commonwealth, a utopian community of celibate women operating in Belton, Texas. Although the Sanctificationist community existed between 1866 and 1983, the letters cover the years 1896 to 1904, the period covered in the book. Formed through religious conviction, the influence of other utopian movements at the time, and the cultural upheaval in women's position, the community of around twenty women sustained itself economically by owning and operating boarding houses. Not only does Kitch tell about the community and its personalities and interactions but she also analyzes the letters according to historical and feminist theories. The book provides insight into an obscure but engaging group and sheds light on the larger societal issues of the late nineteenth century. The book is sparsely illustrated with one group photo and a copy of a letter from Susan B. Anthony. Charts of the members and their real estate, a bibliography, and an index are appended. HCA.

Lipsett, Linda Otto. **To Love and to Cherish: Brides Remembered**. Lincolnwood, IL: Quilt Digest, 1997. 133p. $26.95pa. ISBN 0-8442-2651-3pa.

Examining brides of the nineteenth and early twentieth centuries, Linda Lipsett traces courtship, weddings, and marriage. The book includes a stunning collection of black-and-white and color photographs of weddings, wedding clothes, and friendship quilts made for weddings. Some interesting history has surfaced in diaries, scrapbooks, and magazines, and is documented with footnotes. Although Lipsett covers no well-known women, she creates a history of wedding traditions, including multicultural aspects. The book is a long narrative that would benefit from headings or chapter designations; nevertheless, *To Love and to Cherish* is useful for researching social topics and clothing, and browsers will love it. Sidebars explain many wedding customs, and an index and instructions and patterns for three quilts are included. HCA.

O'Brien, Michael, ed. **An Evening When Alone: Four Journals of Single Women in the South, 1827–67**. Charlottesville: University Press of Virginia, 1993. 460p. (Publications of the Southern Texts Society). $45.00; $15.00pa. ISBN 0-8139-1440-X; 0-8139-1732-8pa.

In an effort to make more source documents available to scholars and the general public, Michael O'Brien has edited four ante-bellum journals of single Southern women. Although diverse in time, place, background, and circumstance, the journals also reflect commonalties of the female condition. Elizabeth Ruffin was a twenty-year-old living on her family's Virginia plantation in 1827. Her life was complicated by an older step-brother, whom she begged to care for her financial affairs; but all the while she dreamed of independence. The Selma Plantation Diarist was believed to be Margaret Wilson, a governess from Pennsylvania who lived at the Mississippi plantation between 1835 and 1837. She was in her thirties and educated, but, as her diary shows, lonely for home. Jane Caroline North was the consummate South Carolina belle who kept her diary during the heyday of her early twenties in 1851 and 1852. Finally, Ann Lewis Hardeman, although single, was raising her deceased sister's six children on the Mississippi plantation belonging to her widowed brother-in-law during the 1850s and 1860s. Although the journal is a female art form, particularly popular during the nineteenth century, each writer engaged in the process for her own reasons. The diaries' similar themes center around the family, marriage, religion, and the desire for independence. O'Brien does a superb job of editing, making the text, which includes a handful of illustrations of the subjects and their locations, very readable. Genealogical charts of the families, notes, and an index are included. The book is useful for regional, sociological, and period studies. HCA.

Plummer, Nellie Arnold. **Out of the Depths or the Triumph of the Cross**. New York: G. K. Hall, 1997. 412p. (African-American Women Writers, 1910-1940). $30.00. ISBN 0-7838-1425-9.

> Nellie Arnold Plummer's memoir of her family's history in slavery and as the first emancipated generation reads like a scrapbook, but it also contains elements of the oral tradition, telling family stories handed down through several generations. The first part of the book is a generational chronicle of the grandparents and parents and their lives as Maryland slaves, their separations from each other, and their abuses. Immediately after the war, the family makes a concerted effort to gather itself together. A small piece of land is purchased; here they build a house and start a church. In the second part of the book, Plummer chronicles the history of the church, with her brother as pastor, and her forty-five-year teaching career in Washington, D.C. schools. Although the book is a narrative, it is also a compendium of organizational records, obituaries, pictures, letters, poetry, and documents collected throughout a lifetime. As such, it remains part slave narrative, part eclectic archive of a family of diaspora. MHCA.

Sterling, Dorothy, ed. **We Are Your Sisters: Black Women in the Nineteenth Century**. New York: W. W. Norton, 1984. 539p. $15.95pa. ISBN 0-393-31629-7pa.

> *We Are Your Sisters* is a collection of documents, letters, diaries, court records, newspapers articles, and interviews telling the story of African American women from 1800 to 1880. While concentrating on private, not published, writings, the book is more than a mere collection: Dorothy Sterling narrates the account and takes care to include a variety of her subjects' experiences during this time of upheaval. Sterling has organized the work into sections on slavery, ante-bellum free women, the war years, freedwomen, and the postwar North; she gleaned archives to assemble an edifying account that exists nowhere else. The book, illustrated throughout with black-and-white photographs, paintings, and engravings, concludes with sections from the diaries of four young women: Frances Anne Rollin, a teacher seeking justice from the Freedman's Bureau; Mary Virginia Montgomery, the daughter of a privileged Southern planting family; Laura Hamilton, a pregnant Virginia housekeeper; and Ida B. Wells-Barnett, a hard-working teacher who became a muckraking journalist for African American causes. A selected bibliography, notes, and an index are included in this highly recommended book. HCA.

Underhill, Lois Beachy. **The Woman Who Ran for President: The Many Lives of Victoria Woodhull**. New York: Penguin, 1995. 347p. $13.95pa. ISBN 0-14-025638-5pa.

> Victoria Woodhull was written out of history. Frederick Douglass, her running mate on the 1872 Equal Rights Party presidential ticket, did not acknowledge the event in his autobiography. Susan B. Anthony failed to mention her in *The History of Woman Suffrage in America*, even though Woodhull was the first woman to address Congress on the suffrage question. And Woodhull who

denied her past, spent the later years of her life abroad. No wonder it has taken so long for her to be treated biographically. Lois Underhill, with full bibliography and notes, speaks with authority on Woodhull in an excellent biography that concentrates on Woodhull's years in New York as a Wall Street broker, newspaper editor, feminist, lecturer, and arbiter of moral values. The book is introduced by Gloria Steinem, and includes a section of illustrations and an index. Every library should include Woodhull in its biography section. HCA.

Weatherford, Doris. **Foreign and Female: Immigrant Women in America, 1840–1930**. Rev. ed. New York: Facts on File, 1995. 432p. $35.00; $16.95pa. ISBN 0-8160-3100-2; 0-8160-3446-Xpa.

Using primary sources, Doris Weatherford elucidates the immigrant experience of European women in the period of heaviest migration, 1840 through 1930. Weatherford collects the information around rather wide and ambivalent topics, but the book covers many experiences from childbirth, death, illicit sex, cleaning methods, and appearance to religious faith, changing roles, and disillusionment with the New World. The book covers all variations of the immigrant experience: women working in factories, as domestics, and on family farms. Weatherford recognizes the need to bring together information on immigrant women that is not covered in other sources. She admits that the book is not comprehensive, ignoring Mexican and Asian migration and the topics of education, politics, and language; however, the book covers so many other points that these oversights can be forgiven. Illustrated throughout with period photographs, the book includes notes, a selected bibliography, and an index. *Foreign and Female* fills a gap in scholarship, and it should be a high priority purchase in every school and library where immigration is studied. MHCA.

Non-Book Material

America's Victoria: Remembering Victoria Woodhull. Produced and directed by Victoria Weston. 82 min. Women Make Movies, 1995. Videocassette. Purchase $250.00; Rental $60.00.

Few people could name the first female presidential candidate. Indeed, her life was so scandal-ridden that she was deposited into the dustbin of history. Several new biographies and this movie help to reconstruct Victoria Woodhull. Born to a poor and violent childhood in Ohio, Victoria Claflin was married young to help support her family. She moved often and engaged in a variety of professions, including acting and spiritualism. A feminist and free thinker who hated hypocrisy, Woodhull made a fortune on Wall Street using tips from Cornelius Vanderbilt, and she was the first woman to testify on the suffrage issue before a congressional committee. The major scandal of her life involved her uncovering and disclosing in her newspaper an affair between preacher Henry Ward Beecher and Elizabeth Tilton, which took place at approximately the same time as Woodhull's presidential bid. When the newspaper hit the streets, Woodhull was arrested under the Comstock law for distributing pornography. She spent election day 1872 in jail before being acquitted. The scandal wore on for years, but Woodhull was already ruined personally and financially. She moved to England where she lived quietly until her death at eighty-nine. The film is presented through black-and-white photographs and documents, and color interviews with various writers and historians, including Ellen DuBois and Gloria Steinem who, impressed with the life of Woodhull, are amazed by how thoroughly her story was expunged from history. With its exploration of double standards and reform efforts, the video will add to the study of the Victorian age. It is also a reminder that much in women's history remains to be uncovered. HCA.

Hearts and Hands: The Influence of Women and Quilts on American Society. Produced by Pat Ferrero. 63 min. New Day Films, 1988. Videocassette. $99.00.

> *Hearts and Hands* uses quilts, sewing, and related arts and industries as the vehicles to deliver American history from 1820 to 1917. A geographical pattern emerges as the locations travel from New England to the deep South, the Midwest, and the West. Much of the narration is in the form of diaries and letters of women; Lucy Larcom, Angelina Grimké, Elizabeth Keckley, Harriet Powers, Harriet Tubman, Abigail Scott Dunniway, and Frances Willard are the main figures represented. The power of the video lies in its focus on quilts, imparting a totally female-centered view of history. The Civil War becomes the story of how many uniforms, blankets, and socks were needed to clothe the armies; women of both the North and South had to find ways to manufacture these items when the Northern textile mills closed. Southern women gave up their silk dresses to make an observation balloon that was subsequently captured by the Yankees. A juxtaposition of period photographs, from soldiers in battle to Civil War-era quilts showing the designs of the period, brings women into the forefront of this event. Women are, likewise, the focus in the topics of industrialization, abolition, westward expansion, temperance, and suffrage. Although the film uses art, photographs, quilts, and music, it is not comprehensive, and teachers should be prepared to fill in dates, events, and personalities that are not covered. Creative teachers may choose to show the film in segments rather than as a whole. MHCA.

Hawaii's Last Queen. Produced by Vivian Ducat. 56 min. PBS Video, 1997. (The American Experience). Videocassette. Public performance rights $59.95; Home use $19.98.

> *Hawaii's Last Queen* moves step-by-step through the surrender of Queen Lili'uokalani to the forces of the United States government on January 16, 1893, and her later abdication of the throne of the independent nation of Hawaii. The film covers the plight of the native Hawaiians from first foreign

contact in 1778, the arrival of New England Congregational missionaries in 1818, the loss of native land to American sugarcane growers, the migration to city jobs, and the replacement by Asian immigrant agricultural workers. Lili'uokalani, educated at missionary school, was a traditionalist and nationalist. A poet and composer schooled in the ways of Victorian manners as well as in her native culture, she could foresee the future of her people. She took steps to protect the dwindling native population from harm as the doctrine of Manifest Destiny directed the grandchildren of the missionaries, who built a stable economy based on sugar production, as they placed themselves in positions of political power and moved to protect their economic interests by aligning themselves with the United States. Besides laying out the positions of the two sides, the film carefully presents the political intricacies leading to the overthrow of the nation of Hawaii and its "presentation" to the United States. The film includes black-and-white photographs and film as well as interviews with historians and curators. The historical detail is meticulous, the telling straightforward. Beyond regional interest, the video can be used in social studies units on expansionism and multiculturalism. HCA.

A Historical Investigation into the Past: The Lizzie Borden/Fall River Case Study. 1996. University of Massachusetts History Department, 612 Herter Hall, Amherst, MA 01003. 413-545-1330; fax 413-545-6137. URL: http://ccbit.cs.umass.edu/lizzie/intro/home.html.

Primary source materials related to the Lizzie Borden ax-murder trial are mounted here, although their accessibility is limited by their being posted within the course outlines for various history classes at the University of Massachusetts. The Lizzie Borden/Fall River Case Study project was created to teach students to practice history as historians practice it, that is, by looking at the documentary evidence. The case, still a mystery in many ways, is very appealing to students and lends itself to debate activities. In 1892, Borden, a thirty-two-year-old spinster, allegedly killed her stepmother and father in the home they all occupied in Fall River, Massachusetts. Borden was acquitted of the crime because of conflicting evidence. Having the case documents available opens opportunities for high-interest activities with students in government and social studies classes. MHCA.

She Even Chewed Tobacco: Passing Women in Nineteenth Century America. Produced by Liz Stevens and Estelle Freedman. 40 min. Women Make Movies, 1983. Videocassette. Purchase $275.00; Rental $75.00.

Based on the research of Alan Berube, this video was converted from a slide presentation made by the San Francisco Lesbian and Gay History Project. The still, black-and-white presentation works because most pictures from the nineteenth century are in this format anyway. Berube's research uncovered a myriad of women (mostly from California) who "passed" as men, including Cora Anderson, Marie Hall, Charlotte Arnold, Charley Parkhurst, Jeanne Bonnet, and Babe Bean. There were many reasons women wanted or needed to impersonate men during California's gold rush years. Some wanted to engage in careers that were closed to them as women, some faced economic necessity, some wanted to escape bad marriages, some wanted to exercise political rights forbidden to them, some wished to travel freely, and some desired to marry women they loved. After profiling a number of passing women, the film closes by outlining lesbian history through the 1940s. Many other women disguised themselves as men throughout history; they engaged in many occupations throughout the United States. This film can broaden perspectives regarding women soldiers in various wars, or open discussions on gender roles. HCA.

U.S. Women's History Workshop. n.d. Assumption College, Worcester, MA 01609. 888-882-7786. E-mail: John McClymer, Professor of History, jmcclyme@assumption.edu. URL: http://www.assumption.edu/whw/.

Created by Massachusetts middle school through college teachers, and sponsored by Assumption College, the American Antiquarian Society, the Alliance for Education, and the Worcester Women's History Project (WWHP), the *U.S. Women's History Workshop* mounts several activities for student use based on primary source material and an interactive format. Students can analyze the readings, pictures, and other material, and form answers to the questions poised. The topics include gender, nineteenth-century women, popular music, fashion and dress reform, and spiritualism. A plethora of documents are available here because the site also links to the material of the Worcester Women's History Project (http://www.assumption.edu/html /academic/history/WWHP/), which is making available, via the Internet, documents relating to the 1850 Worcester, Massachusetts, woman's rights convention, and women in the nineteenth century in general. The WWHP commemorates the first national woman's rights convention and continues the national discussion of women's rights. Information about the recreation of the 1850 convention and teaching suggestions on using the archival material are available. Although the *U.S. Women's History Workshop* could offer a better outline of its site, social studies and language arts teachers will find its primary source offerings very helpful. MHCA.

Writing on the Lakes: 1848. Produced by Jocelyn Riley. 28 min. Her Own Words, 1998. Videocassette. $95.00.

Based on the first-person travel accounts of Margaret Fuller, Lucy Bird, Eliza Steele, and others, *Writing on the Lakes: 1848* follows the fictional character Eliza Burton from her Seneca Falls, New York, home to the home of her sister in Wisconsin. She travels over the Erie Canal, stops at Niagara Falls, and crosses the Great Lakes. Her journey is narrated in the first person over still, color slides of travel documents, artifacts, handiwork, and land-scapes. The narration of the joys and problems of travel is interspersed with songs of the period. The film brings the period to life through a woman's eyes, and audiences of all types will enjoy it. Because it has special regional interest, it is especially useful where Great Lake's history is studied. A useful 114-page resource guide is available for $45.00. MHCA.

Industrial Revolution and the Labor Movement

Books

Dash, Joan. **We Shall Not Be Moved: The Women's Factory Strike of 1909**. New York: Scholastic, 1996. 165p. $15.95; $5.99pa. ISBN 0-590-48409-5; 0-590-48410-9pa.

> Poor working conditions and low wages united women garment workers in New York to strike for better conditions in 1909. The rising of the 20,000 pushed some women, such as Clara Lemlich, Leonora O'Reilly, and Rose Schneiderman, into positions of leadership. The strike was aided by educated and wealthy women who took up the cause and provided resources. While attaining reasonable goals, the strike taught the leaders how to organize, raised the membership in the women's garment workers unions, and directed women workers away from the American Federation of Labor, which was not fully committed to their goals. Unfortunately, inferior working conditions caused the Triangle Shirtwaist Factory disaster in 1911 in which 146 workers died. Joan Dash's digestible history of this two-year period concentrates on personalities and includes many quotations. Illustrated with two sections of black-and-white photographs, the book includes a bibliography and an index. MHCA.

Dublin, Thomas. **Transforming Women's Work: New England Lives in the Industrial Revolution**. Ithaca, NY: Cornell University Press, 1994. 324p. $16.95pa. ISBN 0-8014-8090-6pa.

> Beginning with rural women bringing "outwork," weaving and hat manufacture, into their homes, Thomas Dublin traces the growth of women into a paid workforce in the century of industrialization. The author uses corporate records as his primary sources in tracing the Lowell mill hands, the Lynn shoemakers, Boston servants and garment workers, and New Hampshire teachers to synthesize a collage of the lives of New England working women. To this picture, Dublin adds census data, deeds, wills, diaries, and letters to construct a social history in addition to an economic history. The workforce was created in a two-step process that first infiltrated farming homes and later capitalized on urban migration and immigration to firmly place women into the economic cycle. Over twenty-five illustrations and over forty graphs help to interpret the story. Dublin's research is impeccable, appending seven explanations of his methods, a selected bibliography, and an index. CA.

Dublin, Thomas. **Women at Work: The Transformation of Work and Community in Lowell, Massachusetts, 1826–1860**. 2d ed. New York: Columbia University Press, 1993. 312p. $20.00pa. ISBN 0-231-04167-5pa.

> *Women at Work* uses the corporate records of the Hamilton Company to create the social and economic history of the first industrial women workers. Focused on the Lowell community, the study covers life in the boardinghouses,

the careers of women workers, early strikes, the ten-hour movement, and the rise of the immigrant worker. Using writings from the workers, Dublin constructs a detailed picture of mill work and mill life, and includes the jobs of carding, spinning, weaving, and dressing. The book includes a handful of black-and-white illustrations, many graphs, and several appendices, which help to explain the study. Notes, a selected bibliography, and an index are included. CA.

Eisler, Benita, ed. **The Lowell Offering: Writings by New England Mill Women, 1840–1845**. New York: W. W. Norton, 1977. 223p. $12.95pa. ISBN 0-393-31685-8pa.

Benita Eisler offers commentary to set the writings of the mill girls, published in the *Lowell Offering*, into perspective. The *Offering* was the most consistent of several publications that grew up in the mill towns, the outgrowth of literary clubs sponsored by local churches and other organizations. Reverend Able C. Thomas was the first publisher of the *Offering*, which was later edited by Harriet F. Farley and Harriott Curtis; several of the worker contributors, who are traced in an epilogue, later produced published works. The subject matter of the *Offering* includes everything that would cross a mill girl's mind: mill life; new cultural experiences; reminisces on home, childhood, and family; and the discordant feelings of new independence and the choices associated with it. Editorials covered the social and political issues of mutual relief, the ten-hour movement, and suicides. Although monocultural, covering the period when the workers were overwhelmingly Protestant, New England girls, the *Offering* permits a closer look into a mutable period. The book contains black-and-white illustrations, notes, and a selected bibliography. MHCA.

Flynn, Elizabeth Gurley. **The Rebel Girl: An Autobiography, My First Life, 1906–1926**. New York: International, 1955. 351p. $9.95pa. ISBN 0-7178-0368-6pa.

This is the first half of the autobiography of Elizabeth Gurley Flynn, who died in Moscow in 1964. Although she lived the second half of her life as a communist, the first half details her childhood and involvement in the labor movement, beginning at the age of sixteen. In 1906, Flynn became a Socialist, speaking at rallies in New York City. As an agitator and strike leader for the International Workers of the World (IWW), she knew the important personalities of the day: James Connolly, Mother Jones, Big Bill Haywood, and Eugene Debs. During World War I, Flynn worked to defend civil liberties, and during the 1920s, she labored to free Sacco and Vanzetti. The autobiography presents labor history from the inside, focusing on planning the strategies, carrying out the actions, and dealing with the consequences such as jail time, which Flynn served on several occasions. The book, narrated in the first person, includes a smattering of black-and-white photographs, documents of the time, and an index. The title comes from Joe Hill, who dedicated his song "The Rebel Girl" to Flynn, the music to which is included in the book. HCA.

Gourley, Catherine. **Good Girl Work: Factories, Sweatshops, and How Women Changed Their Role in the American Workforce**. Brookfield, CT: Millbrook, 1999. 96p. $23.40. ISBN 0-7613-0951-9.

> *Good Girl Work* takes a broad look at women in labor, beginning with the apprenticeship system and moving to the textile factories and beyond. Catherine Gourley uses quotations set off in boxes to explain the working conditions and lives of laboring girls. Social reform, labor investigations, class issues, and the rise of female labor leaders are covered in this account, which ends in the aftermath of the Triangle Shirtwaist Factory fire. Although brief, the exposé provides a thorough introduction for younger readers, and is studded with pictures and documents. Notes and an index are appended. MH.

Kraft, Betsy Harvey. **Mother Jones: One Woman's Fight for Labor**. New York: Clarion, 1995. 116p. $16.95. ISBN 0-395-67163-9.

> Mary Harris Jones lived to be 100 years old, and she spent most of those years fighting for the rights of workers. A white-haired Irish immigrant, Jones was feistier than her meek demeanor suggested. She lost her husband and children to yellow fever in Memphis, and her business to the great Chicago fire; then, throughout the end of the nineteenth century, she lost many labor strikes and saw death and destruction, but she kept on fighting for an eight-hour day, child labor laws, and better working conditions. Mother Jones had just the personality to defy authority and stir up the workers, and she did not mind spending a night in jail. She organized miners in West Virginia and Colorado and various other workers in between. Betsy Kraft's book is exceedingly well-written and detailed, formatted with full-page black-and-white illustrations, many of child workers photographed by Lewis Hine. Notes, further reading, and an index are appended. MHA.

Leavitt, Judith Walzer. **Typhoid Mary: Captive to the Public's Health**. Boston: Beacon, 1996. 331p. $25.00; $15.00pa. ISBN 0-8070-2102-4; 0-8070-2103-2pa.

> Mary Mallon immigrated into the United States from Ireland in 1883 at the age of fourteen. She was a popular cook with New York's upper class; however, twice she was arrested and incarcerated as a public health nuisance for spreading typhoid to almost fifty people, three of whom died. As a result, she spent twenty-six years of her life in isolated captivity. The public knew her as Typhoid Mary, and the name is still a part of the vernacular. Judith Leavitt tells of Mallon's life through her own viewpoint as well as from various perspectives: those of the medical community, public policy makers, lawyers, the media, the social expectations of the time, and as continuing myth. In this way, a full portrayal of the events and their significance emerges, foreshadowing the events' continuing impact on current health epidemics. Black-and-white photographs and artwork illustrate the book, and a time line of Mallon's life, notes, and an index are appended. Not just a history, the book is useful in relation to health topics both historical and contemporary. HCA.

Stanley, Jerry. **Big Annie of Calumet: A True Story of the Industrial Revolution**. New York: Crown, 1996. 102p. $19.00. ISBN 0-517-70097-2.

> The 1913 copper miner's strike in the upper peninsula of Michigan is the setting for the story of "Big" Annie Clemenc, who became a strike leader. Clemenc was lost in history until the 1970s, and the details of her life are sketchy. Born in Calumet, Michigan, in 1888 of Croatian immigrant parents, Clemenc grew up in poverty and lived amidst various ethnic factions who did not always get along. Clemenc organized the miners' wives to provide social functions for the community and to work to improve mining conditions. In protest to a harsh working environment, the local miners went on strike in the summer of 1913. Every day from the third day of the strike until it was over, Big Annie put a huge American flag on her shoulder and led the strike parade. During December, Clemenc held a Christmas party for the strikers' children upstairs at Italian Hall. At the height of the party, someone unknown yelled "fire," causing a stampede down the stairs to the doors, which opened inward. Seventy-four people were crushed to death in the stairwell as they ran to escape, sixty-three of them children. It took another four months and intense public pressure to settle the strike. *Big Annie*, told in a straightforward, simple way, suitable for younger readers, explains the strike within the larger framework of the Industrial Revolution and the rise of the labor movement. The book is illustrated throughout and includes bibliographic notes and an index. Schools teaching integrated curriculums can use Arlo Guthrie's song "The 1913 Massacre," which is based on the Christmas Eve events. *Big Annie* will be of interest in regional history collections and where labor history is covered in-depth. MH.

Non-Book Material

The Emma Goldman Papers. 1998. 2372 Ellsworth Street, Berkeley, CA 94720-6030. 510-643-8518. E-mail: emma@uclink.berkeley.edu. URL: http://sunsite.berkeley.edu/Goldman/.

> An advocate of free speech, birth control, and organized labor, Emma Goldman was an anarchist and feminist in the early part of the twentieth century. Born in the Balkan states, Goldman immigrated to New York, where she spoke out and engaged in radical activities until she was deported in 1919. She spent the rest of her life organizing causes abroad. *The Emma Goldman Papers* Web site collects and makes available documents by and about Goldman. The Web site is organized into two parts: publications of the project, including a biographical and source guide, a traveling exhibit, and a curriculum for middle school and above; and primary source materials, including writings, documents, images, and moving pictures. The site's curriculum guide is well planned, linking to the themes of immigration, freedom of speech, women's rights, antimilitarism, and social change. Teachers will be impressed with *The Emma Goldman Papers*, and so will researchers. MHCA.

The Triangle Shirtwaist Factory Fire. 1999. Cornell University School of Industrial and Labor Relations, Kheel Center for Labor-Management Documentation and Archives, Ives Hall, Ithaca, NY 14853-3901. 607-255-3183; fax 607-255-9641. E-mail: Kheel_center@cornell.edu. URL: http://www.ilr.cornell.edu/trianglefire/.

> *The Triangle Shirtwaist Factory Fire* Web site, hosted by Cornell University, is a model historical Web site with its collection of all types of documents: cartoons, photographs, oral histories, newspaper and magazine articles, investigative reports, and letters, all relating to the tragic fire that killed 146 workers on March 25, 1911. The fire broke out near closing time in the ten-story building housing the Triangle Shirtwaist Factory in New York. The doors to the shop, which was not unionized, were locked. The mostly female workers could not escape, and many died when they jumped to the street below. Some of the survivors' interviews are available in audio format on the Web site. A short history, selected bibliography, links to other sites, and advice to student researchers round out the exceedingly well-put-together and easy-to-navigate site. Students and teachers will wish for many more sites of this caliber, that offer the broad range of primary and secondary source material related to such an important event as labor history. MHCA.

Victorian Domesticity

Books

Douglas, Ann. **The Feminization of American Culture**. New York: Noonday, 1998. 403p. $15.00pa. ISBN 0-374-52558-7pa.

> The United States was still a new nation during the nineteenth century, and its popular culture was just developing. During this time, industrialization removed women from the household industries in which they had been involved; they were excluded from male-dominated activities in politics and economics; and religion had lost its influence on society. Lacking power, women attempted to create a place for themselves through sentimental literature, thus creating a simpering female culture of timidity that has affected popular culture to this day. Ann Douglas traces the rise of this female culture through the literature and religious writings of women and ministers of the nineteenth century. Although many of the writings were extremely popular during the Victorian age, that they did not endure called into question the nature of the budding mass culture. The book is intellectual in scope, and it has far-reaching implications, especially in literature studies. Notes and an index are included. HCA.

Sklar, Kathryn Kish. **Catharine Beecher: A Study in American Domesticity**.
New York: W. W. Norton, 1976. 356p. $12.95pa. ISBN 0-393-00812-6pa.

> As part of the large and influential Beecher family, Catharine Beecher
> became renowned in the nineteenth century for her advice to Victorian
> women, at times outshining her preacher father and brothers and her
> novel-writing sister. Beecher was a teacher; a promoter of women's educa-
> tion; and a writer on moral, religious, educational, and domestic topics. Her
> best-known work, *A Treatise on Domestic Economy*, was published in 1841
> and reprinted many times, and, although she was not responsible for the
> cult of domesticity, her writing did much to encourage and perpetuate it.
> Cool to the abolitionist movement, which her family supported (her sister,
> Harriet Beecher Stowe, wrote *Uncle Tom's Cabin*), neither could Beecher
> support suffrage because it took women out of their most important role in
> the home. She believed her status as a woman was most important in her
> life, causing her many contradictions, even mental breakdown, in blending
> her domestic and public spheres. Kathryn Sklar's book, the winner of the
> Berkshire Conference annual prize, remains the scholarly study more than
> the popular biographical treatment. A small section of black-and-white
> illustrations, notes, a bibliography, and an index are included. HCA.

Smith-Rosenberg, Carroll. **Disorderly Conduct: Visions of Gender in
Victorian America**. New York: Oxford University Press, 1985. 357p.
$13.95pa. ISBN 0-19-504039-2pa.

> A collection of eleven essays written by Carroll Smith-Rosenberg, *Disorderly
> Conduct* is divided into three sections covering the nineteenth century,
> although the first essay expounds on the growth of women's history in the
> 1970s and the final article explores androgonist women from 1870 to 1936.
> Smith-Rosenberg's other themes include love and ritual, militant women,
> the Victorian life cycle of femininity, sex role conflict, and the abortion
> movement in the mid-nineteenth century. The essays, written over the
> twelve-year-period prior to 1985, are presented without dates and context,
> which some readers may want to know. A section of black-and-white illus-
> trations is included, but the pictures could belong to one or a number of the
> articles, for identifying information is not specific. Despite the format draw-
> backs, Smith-Rosenberg is an original and careful researcher, and her insights
> add substantially to knowledge of women during Victorian times. Notes
> and an index are appended. HCA.

Stephens, Autumn. **Wild Women: Crusaders, Curmudgeons and Completely
Corsetless Ladies in the Otherwise Virtuous Victorian Era**. Berkeley:
Conari, 1992. 248p. $12.95pa. ISBN 0-943233-36-4pa.

> Written in the overblown, flowery language of the Victorians, Autumn
> Stephens's delightful little book presents 150 women who did not fit the
> mold of their times. In two-page spreads, often accompanied by a black-
> and-white illustration or sidebar, the outrageous aspects of each personality
> are presented. Prostitutes, cross-dressers, murderers, and spies, including

women of all races, line up for inspection. Even the venerated ladies of the period disclose some hidden attributes. Not a serious study, but certainly fun for library browsers, *Wild Women* presents a liberal look at nineteenth-century women. A bibliography and an index are included. MHCA.

Non-Book Material

Godey's Lady's Book Online. 1995. University of Rochester Department of History, 364 Rush Rhees Library, Rochester, NY 14627. 716-275-2052; fax 716-756-4425. E-mail: rahz@dbv.cc.rochester.edu. URL: http://www .history.rochester.edu/godeys/intro.htm.

> *Godey's Lady's Book* was an immensely popular magazine for women during the nineteenth century, edited for many years by Sarah Josepha Hale, whose Victorian moral sensibilities shaped the content. This site includes the full text of five issues from 1850. The fashion plates, poems, stories, and advice are all included, making it an excellent source for ante-bellum studies. A few other links are available, but no teaching suggestions. Still, educators will be happy to give students access to this type of historical material. MHCA.

Westward Migration

Books

Armitage, Susan, and Elizabeth Jameson, eds. **The Women's West**. Norman: University of Oklahoma Press, 1987. 323p. $17.95pa. ISBN 0-8061-2067-3pa.

> The twenty-one articles collected in *The Women's West* were presented at the 1983 Women's West Conference. Their intent is to dissolve the myths of the West while building a broader, multicultural history. The papers cover a wide variety of topics, from the Ingalls family and the Harvey girls to childrearing and prostitution; places, from Canada to California; and times, from the Colonial fur trade to the twentieth-century sun belt. The scholars again confront the questions of how liberating the West was as an environment for women and how much of the attitude of domesticity women brought with them in migration, while at the same time raising many new questions for future research. The book does much to provide a more diffuse view of women's experience. Black-and-white illustrations, contributors' biographies, and an index are included. HCA.

Backus, Harriet Fish. **Tomboy Bride**. Boulder, CO: Pruett, 1969. 273p. $14.95pa. ISBN 0-87108-512-7pa.

> *Tomboy Bride* is Harriet Backus's memoir of married life spent in the mining camps of Colorado and Idaho. After the 1906 San Francisco earthquake, Harriet traveled alone by train to Denver to marry George Backus; the author proceeds with him to their new home in Telluride at the Tomboy

mine. Later, they live and work in British Columbia and Elk City, Idaho. They end up in Leadville, Colorado, where George Backus finds new ways to process molybdenum in the huge Climax mine. Backus's story is full of love and adventure along with historical and geographical details. The book, which includes black-and-white photographs, will be a joy for many readers. MHCA.

Brown, Dee. **The Gentle Tamers: Women of the Old Wild West**. Lincoln: University of Nebraska Press, 1958. 317p. $10.00pa. ISBN 0-8032-5025-8pa.

> Although Dee Brown acknowledges that fewer women came west than men, he believes they had a major role in its development, and he chronicles all the various reasons why they emigrated, as well as their occupations and experiences. Brown, the author of *Bury My Heart at Wounded Knee*, is an established Western scholar. He uses a thematic arrangement to tell many entertaining stories of the teachers, army followers, adventurers, suffragists, authors, performers, and reformers, quoting often from primary source material. Both the famous and the infamous are discovered in *The Gentle Tamers*: Ute Indian captive Josephine Meeker, Donner Party survivor Virginia Reed, missionaries Eliza Hart Spalding and Narcissa Whitman, actress Lotta Crabtree, and Justice of the Peace Esther McQuigg Morris, who helped win the vote for Wyoming's women. Wives followed their husbands west for various reasons: Elizabeth Custer promoted George Armstrong Custer; and Ann Eliza Young, the nineteenth wife of Brigham Young, denounced polygamy. With a picture section and a useful index, *The Gentle Tamers* will be read for enjoyment as well as for research, but it should be noted that these are mainly the experiences of white women moving west; other ethnic groups do not play a large role here. MHCA.

Butruille, Susan G. **Women's Voices from the Mother Lode: Tales from the California Gold Rush**. Boise: Tamarack, 1998. 272p. $16.95pa. ISBN 1-886609-14-4pa.

> Using sketches, historical photographs, pictures of present-day monuments, and many quotations, Susan Butruille traces the women of the California gold rush, including Native, migrating, and immigrant women. The narrative follows chronological and thematic lines, always incorporating the words, songs, poetry, and recipes of women. The book is written with expression and many audiences will enjoy it; students will find it useful for research. Notes, a bibliography, and an index are added. MHCA.

Butruille, Susan G. **Women's Voices from the Oregon Trail: The Times That Tried Women's Souls, and A Guide to Women's History Along the Oregon Trail**. Boise: Tamarack, 1993. 251p. $14.95pa. ISBN 0-9634839-8-6pa.

> This two-part book reveals both the stories of women and the locations of women's history along the Oregon Trail. Incorporating many quotations, songs, and recipes, the book traces the history of the trail, the backgrounds of the women who migrated, their reasons for moving, their preparations, their experiences on the trail, and their creation of new homes on the West

Coast. Susan Butruille is a colorful writer who brings the narrative alive. In the second part of the book, Butruille retraces the Oregon Trail through six states, from Missouri to Oregon, identifying and explaining the locations important to women's history. Besides the set-off quotations, the book is well illustrated with sketches, photographs, and maps. The volume serves both as a history and a guidebook and will have research and regional interest. MHCA.

Butruille, Susan G. **Women's Voices from the Western Frontier**. Boise: Tamarack, 1995. 322p. $16.95pa. ISBN 1-886609-00-4pa.

Following the pattern of her other books, using photographs and sketches, Susan Butruille illustrates a variety of western women. Women of all nationalities are included, as well as the famous women of the West. The book covers all classes of women, from saloon girls to society women. This is Butruille's most historical effort, gaining its strength from the myriad of quotations it incorporates into the narrative. The book is useful for research in libraries and classrooms. Notes, a bibliography, and an index are appended. MHCA.

Chapman, Helen. **The News from Brownsville: Helen Chapman's Letters from the Texas Military Frontier, 1848–1852**. Edited by Caleb Coker. Austin: Texas State Historical Association, 1992. 410p. $29.95. ISBN 0-87611-115-0.

Helen Ellsworth Blair Chapman was a prolific letter writer. In the collection published here, edited by her great-great-grandson, she chronicles the building of Brownsville in the early days of Texas statehood through correspondence sent to her mother in New England. Chapman sailed from New York to meet her husband, William, in Mexico, on the Rio Grande, where he served as first quartermaster in the Army. She describes the Army's move across the river to Fort Brown, and comments on such political and social events of the day as Zachary Taylor's suitability for the presidency and the difficulties of locating a copy of *Uncle Tom's Cabin* to read in the deep South. A product of the mid-century, Chapman believed in abolition and temperance, but she also spoke out against racial prejudice towards the Mexican people. Chapman's descendent, Caleb Coker, wrote the introduction, the letter headings, and the epilogue; and the work is illustrated with black-and-white photographs of the family and maps. Along with a bibliography and an index, the appendices list military personnel described in the letters and newspaper articles about the Chapman family. Because the book provides both social and military history, it should have a wide audience. HCA.

Clappe, Louise Amelia Knapp Smith. **The Shirley Letters: From the California Mines, 1851–1852**. Berkeley: Heyday, 1998. 195p. $12.95pa. ISBN 1-890771-00-7pa.

Containing twenty-three letters composed in the gold mining region along the Feather River in California, *The Shirley Letters* imparts one woman's perspective of mine camp life. Signed by Dame Shirley, the letters were composed by Louise Clappe, the wife of the doctor, who followed her husband to California by sailing from the East Coast to San Francisco. Written to her sister at home, Dame Shirley's letters give a first-hand account of the beautiful setting and a memorable Fourth of July celebration, but also of racial prejudice, drinking, gambling, and mob violence. In 1854, the letters were published in *The Pioneer*, a San Francisco literary magazine. Although the original letters have been lost, it is known that Clappe returned to San Francisco, divorced, and worked as a school teacher for the rest of her life. The book, containing black-and-white artwork, an introduction, notes, a glossary of place names, and an index, presents a woman's perspective on the California gold rush; it is ideal for use in schools and for independent readers. MHCA.

Ellis, Anne. **The Life of an Ordinary Woman**. Boston: Houghton Mifflin, 1990. 301p. $12.95pa. ISBN 0-395-54412-2pa.

> *The Life of an Ordinary Woman* is an uncommon book. Anne Ellis started to write her memories in 1924 at the age of forty-nine, although she had no education beyond the fifth grade. Having held all kinds of jobs in her life, she did not shy away from this one. Throughout her life, she faced extraordinary hardships, losing two husbands and a daughter; yet she made friends easily, and she remembered everything about the West. Born in Missouri, Ellis traveled west with her family, where she was raised in the boom-and-bust mining towns of Colorado. The family moved frequently in search of a better life, but Ellis remained poor all her life. Ellis provides a child's view of school, of immigrant men, and of holidays; and a young woman's view of fixing meals, caring for children, and making a living anyway you can. The events Ellis recounts are often surprising. She remembers a miner telling her about hearing Susan B. Anthony lecture at a suffrage rally in Lake City; she knew Captain Ellen Jack, the mountain woman and author of her own memoirs, *Fate of a Fairy*; and she was familiar with the long-lived Salida madam Laura Evans. This personal view of the Old West contains a few illustrations of the author and the places she lived; but with no index, it will be used mostly by those seeking an extraordinary story. MHCA.

Flynn, Jean. **Annie Oakley: Legendary Sharpshooter**. Springfield, NJ: Enslow, 1998. 128p. (Historical American Biographies). $19.95. ISBN 0-7660-1012-0.

> A fine biography of western legend Annie Oakley is recorded by Jean Flynn. Oakley's childhood was destitute. She learned to hunt to provide for her mother and siblings, and, as her rifle skill grew, she was entered into shooting contests; these opened the door for her career as an entertainer in the Wild West shows, pioneered by Buffalo Bill Cody. Although Oakley gained fame and traveled the world as a prototype western woman, she still tried to maintain an identity as a wife and a lady. After her death in 1926, her legend continued to grow. Flynn's complete book, illustrated with black-and-white photographs, contains sidebars, a chronology, a glossary, notes, suggestions for further reading, and an index. For younger readers, *Annie Oakley* is suitable for independent reading and research. MH.

Jeffrey, Julie Roy. **Converting the West: A Biography of Narcissa Whitman**.
Norman: University of Oklahoma Press, 1991. 238p. (Oklahoma Western
Biographies). $12.95pa. ISBN 0-8061-2623-Xpa.

> As one of the earliest women to travel west, Narcissa Whitman emigrated to
> Oregon in 1836, encountering Native Americans who had never before seen
> a white woman. Whitman settled at the Waiilatpu mission, near Walla
> Walla, to minister to the Cayuse Indians. Unfortunately, the work was not
> as ideal as she had imagined, and, in her eleven years there, she failed to
> convert any tribal members. Whitman, who lost a daughter in Oregon, adopted
> several other children and spent her time teaching. In 1847, the Whitmans
> were murdered by the Cayuse in response to cultural misunderstandings
> between the missionaries and the tribe; immigration pressures also played
> a part in the murders. Julie Jeffrey's biography sets Whitman into the per-
> spective of her religion, which was most important to her, from her child-
> hood in New York, when her only wish was to become a missionary, to her
> marriage to Marcus Whitman, which made her life's work possible. Black-
> and-white photographs and maps, sources, and an index are included. HCA.

Jeffrey, Julie Roy. **Frontier Women: "Civilizing" the West? 1840–1880**. Rev.
ed. New York: Hill and Wang, 1998. 278p. $12.00pa. ISBN 0-8090-1601-Xpa.

> In the revised edition to *Frontier Women*, Julie Jeffrey adds women of color
> to expand her original 1979 study, which focused on the experiences of
> white women. Her definition of the frontier expands to include immigra-
> tions from directions other than the East, as well as internal emigrations. In
> the nineteenth century, the women's sphere was so culturally pervasive
> that it moved with white women into the West, where they centered their
> new lives around the same social definitions. Using such documents as
> women's journals; letters; interviews; and legal, educational, and church
> records, the book is arranged in a topical manner, covering reports on the
> West, the overland journey, establishing new homes, founding communities
> and organizations, mining camps, Mormon culture, and growing political
> action. The book contains no illustrations, but does include a bibliography
> and an index. A good introduction to western women, Jeffrey's history is suit-
> able for reading and research. HCA.

Katz, William Loren. **Black Women of the Old West**. New York: Atheneum
Books for Young Readers, 1995. 84p. $18.00. ISBN 0-689-31944-4.

> William Katz creates a brief, but thorough, history of Black women in the
> West filled with amazing photographs on every page. The history begins in
> Revolutionary times, when slaves ran away to join Native American tribes,
> and continues through the immigration waves into the frontier states and
> the West. Women moved west as mail-order brides to found African American
> communities and to participate in such expanded opportunities as serving
> with the Buffalo soldiers, driving stagecoaches, and striking it rich in the
> gold fields. The author supplies brief biographies of pioneers to almost every
> state west of the Mississippi River; these sketches include the recognized,

such as Clara Brown, Mammy Pleasant, and Biddy Mason, and the unexplored, such as Harriet Scott and Susan McKinney Stewart. With its wealth of information and photographs, *Black Women of the Old West* will find many uses in school libraries. A bibliography and an index are included. MH.

Murphy, Claire Rudolf, and Jane G. Haigh. **Gold Rush Women**. Anchorage: Alaska Northwest, 1997. 126p. $16.95pa. ISBN 0-88240-484-9pa.

Covering the years from 1849 to 1914, *Gold Rush Women* describes both Native and immigrating females who played a part in the various Alaskan and Canadian mining fevers. With black-and-white photographs on every page, twenty-three women are profiled, ranging from Kate Carmack, a Tagish native who discovered Klondike gold but failed to profit from it, to Kate Rockwell, the dance hall girl who was never too ashamed to talk about her past. The book is notable for showing the women actually smiling in the photographs, a rarity in nineteenth-century photography, and for recounting how each woman physically arrived in the gold rush areas. Their reasons for immigrating were many: for adventure and opportunity, as brides, and as businesswomen. The Native women, while adapting to the invasion, generally tried to maintain traditional values. The book is divided into five chronologically arranged chapters that correspond to the geographical areas in which gold was discovered. An introduction and map head each chapter, and the book contains a time line, notes, suggestions for further reading, and an index. This exciting history will be used for browsing and research, as well as in regional studies. MHCA.

Riley, Glenda. **The Female Frontier: A Comparative View of Women on the Prairie and the Plains**. Lawrence: University Press of Kansas, 1988. 299p. $14.95pa. ISBN 0-7006-0424-3pa.

In a comparative study of frontierswomen, Glenda Riley measures the lives of women from the prairies and the plains. The prairie states of the Midwest were settled first: Minnesota, Iowa, Illinois, Indiana, and Missouri. The plains states are defined as the tier including Montana, North Dakota, Wyoming, South Dakota, Nebraska, Kansas, and Oklahoma. Riley shows that while men may have lived variegated lives, women's lives were characterized by sameness. The domestic and social chores they labored at in the East followed them to their new frontier homes, regardless of where they settled. The book compares the two groups of women in the home, at work, and in the community, noting that their efforts were necessary in building the West. Although Riley does not use many quotations in her broad coverage, her book is heavily footnoted, and it makes a fine contribution to the study of women in the expanding United States. Black-and-white photographs, graphs, notes, and an index are included. MHCA.

Riley, Glenda. **The Life and Legacy of Annie Oakley**. Norman: University of Oklahoma Press, 1994. 252p. (Oklahoma Western Biographies). $24.95. ISBN 0-8061-2656-6.

> Glenda Riley presents an interpretive biography of western legend Annie Oakley. Oakley's life is hard to piece together because she did not save correspondence or memorabilia; she chose instead to give away such mementos as her shooting medals, which she had melted to aid World War I causes. After treating Oakley's early life through her marriage at the age of sixteen, the chapters concentrate on Oakley as a professional entertainer, supreme sport shooter, Victorian lady, romanticized Western woman, and her continuing legend. Oakley lived in accordance with her Quaker background and failed to recognize her fame. Black-and-white photographs add to the interesting text, which is suitable for independent reading and research; the work provides source notes and an index. HCA.

Savage, Candace. **Cowgirls**. Berkeley: Ten Speed, 1996. 134p. $22.95pa. ISBN 0-89815-830-3pa.

> Candace Savage portrays cowgirls in three manifestations: real ranching women, legends, and as portrayed in the media. The first section covers women in western history, on trail drives, as homesteaders, and on ranches. Rodeo, Wild West show, movie, and television performers are later versions of the cowgirl. Savage's book is filled with black-and-white and color photographs and artwork, some of which are full-page illustrations. Notes, references, and an index are included in a great book for browsers and researchers looking for material on the old West and media history. MHCA.

Schlissel, Lillian. **Women's Diaries of the Westward Journey**. New York: Schocken, 1992. 278p. (Studies in the Life of Women). $14.00pa. ISBN 0-8052-1004-0pa.

> In creating this book, Lillian Schlissel used the diaries of over 100 women who emigrated to Oregon or California between 1840 and 1870. Although the overland journey was a family affair, few women willingly engaged in the journey, which they found fraught with danger from Indians, stampeding animals, snakes, disease, and accidents. Additionally, one-fifth of the women were pregnant during the journey and feared for their own lives. In the first half of her book, Schlissel gives an overview of migration periods from 1841 to 1850, 1851 to 1855, and 1856 to 1867. Many black-and-white photographs, some full-page, and extensive quotations from diaries are included. The last half of the book presents selections from six diaries dating from 1849 to 1867 and written by Catherine Haun, Lydia Allen Rudd, Amelia Stewart Knight, Jane Gould Tourtillott, Rebecca Hildreth Nutting Woodson, and Barsina Rogers French, along with photographs of the women or of their diaries. A map of the western trails, a table of information about the women diarists, a bibliography of primary sources, and an index are included. Carl N. Degler wrote the preface, and Gerda Lerner is the supervising editor to the series. *Women's Diaries* is superior as an overview of women's experience

on the westward journey and for providing a sampling of primary source material. MHCA.

Seagraves, Anne. **High-Spirited Women of the West**. Hayden, ID: Wesanne, 1992. 174p. $11.95pa. ISBN 0-9619088-3-1pa.

> Biographies of ten women who did not fit into the Victorian mold are presented in *High-Spirited Women of the West*. The subjects include Jessie Benton Fremont, Abigail Scott Dunniway, Sarah Winnemucca, Belle Starr, and others not as well known. As suffragists, public speakers, bandits, historians, miners, and artists, the women broke with traditional roles from Oregon to Texas. Anne Seagraves uses many sources in putting together her sketches, which can be used for independent reading and research. Black-and-white illustrations and a bibliography are included in this entertaining account. MHCA.

Seagraves, Anne. **Soiled Doves: Prostitution in the Early West**. Hayden, ID: Wesanne, 1994. 173p. $11.95pa. ISBN 0-9619088-4-Xpa.

> Anne Seagraves writes a comprehensive history of western prostitution, including accounts of many of the well-known madams: Mattie Silks of Colorado, Lottie Johl of California, "Chicago Joe" Hensley of Montana, and Maggie Hall, or "Molly b' Dam," of Idaho. Along with the sketches, Seagraves documents the variety of working conditions under which the girls labored, from street, to crib, to parlor house, and discusses the occupational hazards. A notable chapter covers Chinese women kept in slavery. Told in a straightforward manner, the book is not lewd or suggestive and can be used for research, even in schools. Sidebars present additional details, and the black-and-white photographs are exceptional. A glossary of terms and a bibliography are appended. HCA.

Stefoff, Rebecca. **Women Pioneers**. New York: Facts on File, 1995. 126p. (American Profiles). $19.95. ISBN 0-8160-3134-7.

> Nine women worthy of inclusion in discussions of the West are profiled in Rebecca Stefoff's *Women Pioneers*. Each chapter is more than ten pages long and includes black-and-white illustrations, a chronology, and suggestions for further reading. Although several of these women wrote memoirs or are the subjects of other writing, most are not well known. Among the multicultural cast are Rebecca Burlend of Illinois, Virginia Reed of the Donner Party, Tabitha Brown of Oregon, Louise Clappe of the California gold fields, Pamelia Fergus of Montana, Clara Brown of Colorado, Martha Gay Masterson of the Pacific Northwest, Elinore Pruitt Stewart of Wyoming, and Polly Bemis of Idaho. The book includes a brief introduction to western history, a map showing the locations discussed, and an index. *Women Pioneers* makes a useful addition to school libraries looking for additional report material. MHA.

Stewart, Elinore Pruitt. **Letters of a Woman Homesteader**. Lincoln: University of Nebraska Press, 1961. 282p. $7.95pa. ISBN 0-8032-5193-9pa.

> Elinore Rupert, as she signs her letters to her former employer, Mrs. Coney of Denver, wants to homestead. She puts an advertisement in the Sunday paper to find employment as a housekeeper for a rancher. When she is employed by Mr. Stewart, Elinore and her young daughter relocate to the high plains of Burnt Fork, Wyoming, where Elinore files a claim for land adjoining Stewart's homestead. She is determined to "prove up" on her claim even though she knows this will take several years of hard work. Between 1909 and 1913 she continues to correspond with Mrs. Coney, writing letters with a great deal of humor and filled with news of the neighbors she meets and of her ranching experiences. Elinore eventually marries Stewart and becomes the owner of her own land. Her hard work toward this accomplishment makes her very proud. The film *Heartland* is based on this delightful book, a picture of late-day homesteading. HCA.

Stratton, Joanna L. **Pioneer Women: Voices from the Kansas Frontier**. New York: Simon and Schuster, 1981. 319p. $12.95pa. ISBN 0-671-44748-3pa.

> With a book in mind, Joanna Stratton's great-grandmother, Lilla Day Monroe, began collecting reminiscences of Kansas pioneer women in the 1920s. After Monroe's death, her daughter took up the project and cataloged and annotated the manuscripts. The memoirs had been filed in an attic when Stratton found them. Eight hundred personal stories form the basis of *Pioneer Women*, which Stratton organizes around the topics of immigration, settlement, daily life, the wild environment, fighting the elements, Indians, education, religion, growing communities, the Civil War, and women's reform efforts for temperance and suffrage. Stratton incorporates many quotations into her own smooth narrative, but the writing must be taken for what it is: memory. The women recruited to share their thoughts were generally white homesteaders, and they did not write about topics they were not comfortable sharing. Missing from the book are the voices of women of color and other women outside the centrist sphere. Still, the book gives an eye-opening examination of how women dealt with such ordinary problems as maintaining homes in primitive conditions, as well as the unexpected: fires, blizzards, and illness. The introduction is written by Arthur M. Schlesinger, Jr., and an appendix chronicles the women in the Lilla Day Monroe Collection. Two black-and-white illustration sections, a bibliography, and an index are included. The book will have great appeal beyond its regional interest. MHCA.

Non-Book Material

As the Wind Rocks the Wagon. Directed by Michael Haney. 52 min. Great Plains Network, 1990. Videocassette. $149.00.

> Using extensive research from libraries and archives in California, Colorado, Idaho, Oregon, and Washington, Amy Warner characterizes five women who traveled the Oregon Trail. These five women, to each of which

Warner imparts a distinctive personality, are composite characters based on twenty-five of the over 2,000 overland trail diaries in existence. Kit Belshaw appears to be of Irish descent. She loses a baby girl before leaving Iowa for Oregon in 1848 with her husband, George, and son, Jamie. She has already moved once, from Ohio, with her new husband, and she remains optimistic throughout the journey, even in the face of hardship. Kit opens the video as a young woman in Ohio and closes it in her new home in Oregon, where she is not unhappy. Lucy Haun is a southern lady with a great sense of humor. Because she has more money at her disposal, her journey is comfortable while emigrating from Missouri to Sacramento, California in 1849. Phoebe is a child who finds everything about the trip exciting, and who tells some of the most fascinating stories. Mary Walker is pregnant and homesick, which makes the trip a greater burden for her. She feels as though she does not even know her husband, and, in the end, she loses her baby. The final character is based on a real person, Sarah Winnemucca of the Paiute tribe. Although the pioneers obsess about the Indians, Winnemucca provides the counterpoint by describing the Indians' view of the "white brother." There are many topics of concern on the trail: death, sickness, weather, wild animals, food, wagons, and livestock all compete as worries. Warner does an admirable job of acting the five parts, changing only her accessories to change identities. The set is minimal, but the focus is on the words of the pioneer women. The production will interest students in social studies classes covering the study of the West, and public libraries may find the video a popular acquisition. MHCA.

Nobody's Girls: Five Women of the West. Produced and directed by Mirra Bank. 90 min. New Video Group, distributed by Marjorie Poore Productions, 1995. Videocassette. $29.95.

Nobody's Girls introduces multicultural women who came into the West from different directions and for different reasons. Each woman came alone and made her way on her own terms. The segments include black-and-white photos, historical documents, and reenactments of the historical characters by outstanding actresses interpreting the actual words of the subjects. Narration of the carefully researched and developed histories is given by Blair Brown.

The first segment is about Paiute Indian and activist Sarah Winnemucca, played by Tantoo Cardinal. Winnemucca was educated in San Jose, California, became a Methodist, and married a white man. She served as a scout for the U.S. Army, which she trusted. It was the U.S. government she did not trust, and she spoke across the country against government policies that were unfair to the Paiutes. Although Winnemucca was the first Native American woman to visit Washington, D.C., where she met President Hayes, she never found justice for her people.

The second segment describes Clara Brown, played by Esther Rolle. Brown was born a slave and freed in her master's will. She headed west, joining a wagon train bound for the gold fields of Colorado, where she worked as a laundress, and invested her money. After the Civil War, Brown returned to Kentucky to find her family, but discovered that postwar conditions made this impossible. Instead, she chose to use her money to bring sixteen former slaves back to Colorado. Shortly before her death, Brown was reunited with her daughter through the help of a friend. She was honored as a member of the Society of Colorado Pioneers, who changed their rules to admit "Aunt Clara."

The subject of the third segment is Teresa Urrea, played by Angela Alvarado. Urrea was a Mexican national who was adored as a healer and a saint. Soldiers carried her picture into battle, but she was accused of fomenting rebellion against the government of Porfirio Diaz. For this she was deported to Arizona, where she continued to heal and support the poor until she died at a young age of tuberculosis.

In the fourth part, Bai Ling depicts "China" Mary Bong. Bong earned enough money by the time she was thirteen for passage to the "Golden Mountain." She may have come under an indentured contract as a prostitute, although she refused to remember the exact details of her immigration. Because of the Chinese Exclusion Act, she arrived in Canada and moved to Alaska. She worked at every type of job and gained many skills. The first Chinese woman in Sitka, Alaska, Bong made that city her home and remained there for the rest of her life.

The final episode is the story of Laura Evans, a Colorado prostitute. Evans is performed by Cloris Leachman, who has a wonderful sense of the voice and mannerisms of the hard-living woman. Evans, apparently, ran away from a marriage and ended up in Leadville during the silver boom. She used her body to support herself until a strike in 1893 closed the mines. She moved on to Salida, a railhead, where she started a house catering to the rail workers. She died there in 1953, "the last of the Red Light Queens." *Nobody's Girls* gives a completely different view of the West from that of the traditional wagon trains. A unique element of the programs is that multiple pictures of each woman are included; these show them at different life stages, both young and old. The video is recommended for use in social studies and women's studies classes, as well as for general public library circulation. HCA.

Petticoat Pioneers. Produced and directed by Wendel Craighead. 52 min. Kaw Valley Films, 1998. Videocassette. $49.95.

Rather than the purely biographical treatment of nineteenth-century women, *Petticoat Pioneers* includes institutions, organizations, and places important to the social progress of this period. The petticoat, layers of cloth hidden from view, serves as an analogy for the numerous unacknowledged women who worked to improve societal conditions during westward expansion. Beyond Sacajawea, most viewers will not be familiar with the women who surface here: Mary Easton Sibley, Amanda Young Brown, Christiana Pope McCoy, Susan Shelby Magoffin, and others. These are not the names commonly associated with the opening of the West, and the writers have done a good job in researching and presenting women from a variety of cultures. Perhaps more important than the women are the places and institutions. The Santa Fe and Oregon Trails are traced through the use of quotations from a variety of women who traveled over them. The histories of Oberlin College, the Harvey Girls, and the Daughters of the American Revolution impacted the times. The video is narrated by Richard Fatherly over artwork, photographs, landscapes, and reenactments, and is divided into two parts, covering the first and second halves of the century, though the Civil War is not discussed. The framing device of brief lists of the notable, well-known women of the century will give viewers a touch point. Where women's history is well established, this film will be appreciated for presenting new material in the study of the westward movement. HCA.

Pioneer Women's Diaries. Produced by Jocelyn Riley. 15 min. Her Own Words, 1998. Videocassette. $95.00.

Cuttings from the diaries of five pioneer women of Wisconsin narrated over a slide show of homestead artifacts and landscapes is the basis of this artful video. The segments, which describe the women's hopes, fears, and interests, are given in a chronological order from early marriage to childbearing years to later married life. The selections of the diaries do not give many hints as to the time frame or the locations, a weakness in the film. *Pioneer Women's Diaries* is most suitable for older, general audiences who have lived through several life stages and will recognize the historical artifacts in the photographs. The film's Midwestern regional interest can lead to more local, primary-source research. A resource guide, over 100 pages, is available for $45.00. HCA.

Prairie Cabin: A Norwegian Pioneer Woman's Story. Produced by Jocelyn Riley. 17 min. Her Own Words, 1991. Videocassette. $95.00.

Prairie Cabin expresses the universals of the immigrant experience, the longing for the homeland, the importance of traditions, and the concern for children growing up in a different culture. The narrator in this film, never identified, muses over the few small heirlooms that would fit into the trunks brought from Norway, describes her skill in making necessities for the new home, and shares her fear of fires and snakes on the prairie. She is glad to have written down the words to many songs, and several Norwegian songs are sung in the film in a fine a cappella soprano voice. Still photographs of settings in Wisconsin and Norway, as well as Norwegian artifacts, crafts, foods, and artwork, form the background to the narration. A special section on Christmas traditions is included. In all, the film gives a respectable overview of immigrant concerns and can be used in social studies classes as well as in regional study. For $45.00, a resource guide containing many primary source materials is available. MHCA.

Sacajawea. Produced and directed by Tom Robertson. 24 min. Films for the Humanities and Sciences, 1974. Videocassette. $79.00.

Sacajawea journeyed with Lewis and Clark between April and November of 1805, accompanying her husband, Charbonneau, a French trapper and guide. This dramatization of the trip mentions that Sacajawea was captured from her Shoshone tribe as a child and was sold to her trapper husband. She gave birth to a son several months before the trip began, and the baby boy traveled with the party. The words of Sacajawea are narrated in English over the native language recitation, which makes some of the audio slightly confusing. Incidents recounted in the film include Sacajawea's jumping into the river to save the sextant, encountering grizzly bears, discovering the Great Falls, and meeting Sacajawea's brother, who helps the party obtain horses for their portage over the mountains into the Columbia River basin. Last seen walking on the Pacific Ocean shore, it is obvious that Sacajawea played a role in the success of the expedition and that her part was appreciated by the leaders. The film, based on primary source documents, will be enjoyed by all audiences, who may wish to expand their study beyond this focused view. MHCA.

The Spirit of Pioneer Women. Produced by William J. Burling. Directed by William J. Burling and Francie Rottmann. (Wolff). 27 min. Denlinger's Publishers, 1993. Videocassette. $35.00.

The Spirit of Pioneer Women is a well-researched and well-assembled production, which includes pictures and writings from women who migrated west of the Mississippi. The majority of Western states are represented in the all-encompassing tale of the journey and the hardships of settling in the new environment. Generally, the women felt unprepared for the hard work, health issues, natural disasters, and poverty they faced. They wrote of homesickness and fear. Women who could not stand up to the rigors of this life became mentally impaired. Featuring both live-action color landscape shots and black-and-white still photographs, the film presents familiar and unknown images of the West. The journal writers, too, are well known, for instance, Elinore Pruitt Stewart, and obscure. There is a meager attempt at including women of different cultures with a still photograph of Black pioneer Clara Brown. A section on Paiute Indian Sarah Winnemucca offers a nice counterpoint to the production as she describes the great fear her tribe felt towards the white settlers and how her mother tried to hide her by burying her on the prairie. Rich in primary sources, the film offers an overview of the women of courage who relocated into unknown territory during the expansionist period of U.S. history. It is useful in school social studies classes, and it may serve as a discussion starter for book groups studying the West or women's journals. MHCA.

Women of the West Museum. n.d. 4001 Discovery Drive, Boulder, CO 80303. 303-541-1000; fax 303-541-1042. E-mail: staff@wowmuseum.org. URL: http://www.wowmuseum.org/.

Incorporated in 1991, the Women of the West Museum currently exists in a virtual environment and in western communities, where its educational programs, exhibits, and activities about western women of the past and present, and their continuing roles in shaping the West, are presented. The museum has a design and a location for a permanent structure in Boulder,

Colorado, where it has not yet broken ground. For now, the WOW Web site showcases the ongoing programs of the museum. These programs include a partnership with Women Writing the West to review books and profile an author each month. The site also facilitates local book groups, and readers surfing the Internet will be interested to see what books these groups are selecting to read. Each week, the WOW site features a new woman and a new quotation. Exhibits and features are not permanent on the site, but they do offer pictures and documents focusing on primary source material. One feature explores on the sod house; another, the story quilt, rotates memoirs of western women. Activities, lesson plans, recreational reading, articles, links, and expert advice from the museum historian enhance the educational intent of the WOW Web site. Teachers will appreciate the work being done here on their behalf. For a new institution, the Women of the West Museum has a solid footing, and it bears watching for future developments. MHCA.

Abolition and Civil War

Books

Chang, Ina. **A Separate Battle: Women and the Civil War**. New York: Penguin, 1991. 103p. (Young Readers' History of the Civil War). $17.99; $6.99pa. ISBN 0-525-67365-2; 0-14-038106-6pa.

Ina Chang's treatment of women in the Civil War is filled with special boxed topics and lots of black-and-white pictures. Incorporating a variety of primary source material into the account, Chang discusses women who spoke for freedom, women who worked to supply the armies, women who became soldiers and spies, women on the home front, and women and the war's aftermath. Beyond these topics, many individual personalities are woven into this story, both the well-known, such as Harriet Beecher Stowe, Harriet Tubman, and Clara Barton; and the obscure, such as Mary Livermore, Charlotte Forten, and Frances Clalin. Even adults who have never studied this Civil War history, will enjoy *A Separate Battle*. The work includes a bibliography and an index. MHA.

Clinton, Catherine. **The Plantation Mistress: Woman's World in the Old South**. New York: Random, 1982. 331p. $13.00pa. ISBN 0-394-72253-1pa.

The first to concentrate on the woman in the plantation house, Catherine Clinton uncovers the archival records of 750 females in the planter class. The households under consideration own more than twenty slaves and were located in the eastern seaboard states; the women discussed were born between 1765 and 1815. While recognizing that the women remained under male control and that the Southern experience was not the same as that of women in New England, Clinton shows that the mistress played an important role in the cotton economy. Quoting directly from the women, she demonstrates that they were educated and that they acted as the "conscience" of the plantation. Besides this pious model, Clinton also looks at sexual mores, addicts, and invalids in an examination of women who lived outside the traditional boundaries. As a result, Southern women emerge as active family members rather than shadowy figures. Appendices compare the Southern sampling to 100 Dutch farmers of New York's Hudson Valley. Notes, bibliography, and an index are attached. HCA.

DeCredico, Mary A. **Mary Boykin Chesnut: A Confederate Woman's Life**. Madison, WI: Madison House, 1996. 176p. (American Profiles). $29.95; $14.95pa. ISBN 0-945612-46-X; 0-945612-47-8pa.

A well-known socialite and woman of privilege, Mary Boykin Chesnut was the wife of James Chesnut Jr., who served in the Confederate army and on the staff of President Jefferson Davis. Chesnut's journals ran to ten volumes and gave a complete insider's view of the Civil War. Although the journals are not reproduced here, they are quoted from extensively to illustrate the biographical portrait of this intriguing woman. Born to wealth, Chesnut was educated at boarding school, and married, at the age of seventeen, into another planter family. Although she knew most of the prominent figures of the Confederacy and lived comfortably throughout the war, Chesnut's life was not untouched by the events. She was removed from several homes, all of which were ruined in the fighting. The family fortune, invested in Confederate notes and bonds, was lost. The Chesnuts never recovered, and Mary worked a small egg-and-dairy business until her death. Several black-and-white illustrations and maps are included, as well as reading suggestions and an index. HCA.

Forten, Charlotte. **The Journal of Charlotte Forten: A Free Negro in the Slave Era**. Edited by Ray Allen Billington. New York: W. W. Norton, 1953. 286p. $9.95pa. ISBN 0-393-00046-Xpa.

Charlotte Forten was a third-generation free Black woman raised in Philadelphia. Her journal, written between 1854 and 1864, covers the years of her education, teaching, and involvement in the great social experiment of the Civil War, the education of the freed slaves at Port Royal, South Carolina. Forten traveled to Salem, Massachusetts, to receive her education. Her preoccupation with her race motivated her to learn all she could. After a short teaching career, events of the Civil War led her to the South, where the Union army had invaded Port Royal to create a base for naval operations. As white residents fled the area, over 10,000 slaves, who had had little contact with civilized society, were left in need of education and skills; Forten was one of many who traveled to the sea islands to help with this effort. Although her journal ends at this point, Forten returned to her home in Philadelphia satisfied that the Black race was capable of the same achievements as the white race. She published several reports on the Sea Island experiment before marrying the Reverend Francis J. Grimké, nephew of the abolitionist sisters Angelina and Sarah Grimké. Two maps, notes, and an index round out this book that presents the perspective of an educated, northern free Black woman. HCA.

Fox-Genovese, Elizabeth. **Within the Plantation Household: Black and White Women of the Old South**. Chapel Hill: University of North Carolina Press, 1988. 544p. (Gender and American Culture). $45.00; $17.95pa. ISBN 0-8078-1808-9; 0-8078-4232-Xpa.

Framed by examinations of slaveholder Sarah Ann Haynsworth Gayle and escaped slave Harriet Jacobs, *Within the Plantation Household* investigates women in the ante-bellum slaveholding states. Elizabeth Fox-Genovese points to the rural nature of the South as a major form of identity. She sees gender as a dominant factor shaping the lives of white women, and the institution of slavery the overriding consideration to Black women. Although both groups shared a culture dominated by a white master, there were no shared bonds of womanhood in their world of "mutual antagonism" and "emotional intimacy." The author studied the writings of slaveholding women, those who opposed slavery, and the slaves themselves. She did not find evidence of the beginnings of feminism and abolitionism among the slaveholding women; rather she found them to be racist and class-conscious. The author discovers that, because slave women were victims of forced illiteracy, written records concerning their lives are few; the records that do exist are usually tainted with the bias of white interviewers. It was almost impossible to attempt interpretation of slave women unless through the recollections of their children and the records of slave resistance. *Within the Plantation Household* explores the nature of the southern household in terms of the social sciences, the experiences of the women as portrayed in their own writings, the gender conventions of slaveholding women, and how those conventions were expressed in their imaginative writings. Fox-Genovese uses case studies to make her points. Rather than assimilate quotations from many women, she presents representative full biographical interpretations of such women as Mary Boykin Chesnut; she then supplements these stories with writings from additional subjects. Fox-Genovese's study differs from Catherine Clinton's *The Plantation Mistress* in both regional emphasis and time period. Centered in the deep South in the period directly before the Civil War, *Within the Plantation Household* suggests a broader picture. Tables, black-and-white illustrations, notes, bibliography, and an index complete the work, which will be useful for research. HCA.

Fritz, Jean. **Harriet Beecher Stowe and the Beecher Preachers**. New York: Putnam's, 1994. 144p. $15.99; $5.99pa. ISBN 0-399-22666-4; 0-698-11660-7pa.

Jean Fritz's mission is to bring Harriet Beecher Stowe and the Beecher family to life for young readers. Because the family, consisting of a domineering father and eleven children all bent on living up to his expectations and their own destinies, held considerable power in the nineteenth century,

Harriet is only part of the focus of the book. Although the most enduring Beecher, Harriet was by no means the most renowned during her day. Her sister Catharine was also a writer who wielded great influence on women with her belief that a woman could make her most lasting contribution from within the home. Harriet, who held to this belief, married a sensitive man and had seven children. She wrote *Uncle Tom's Cabin* partly to fulfill familial expectations and partly to satisfy herself; certainly she did not foresee its impact on ante-bellum society. Overcoming shyness, Harriet became a public speaker, and like the rest of her orating family, enjoyed it. Although all the Beechers are tied into the text, an afterword details their later careers. Black-and-white illustrations, family tree, notes, a bibliography, and an index are included. Fritz's enjoyable book is a good introduction to this complicated family, but students, engaged in independent reading and research, will want to know more. MH.

Gilbert, Olive. **Narrative of Sojourner Truth**. Mineola, NY: Dover, 1997. 74p. (Dover Thrift Editions). $1.00pa. ISBN 0-486-29899-Xpa.

Olive Gilbert was the Connecticut abolitionist woman who wrote down the life story of Sojourner Truth, who remained illiterate throughout her life. *Narrative* covers Truth's time in slavery until she escaped as a young woman, her religious conversion and association with a cult group, and her travels and preaching. The book, first published in 1850, was intended as a propaganda piece for northern audiences, and Truth used sales of the book to support herself. *Narrative* does not mention many of the later famous incidents in Truth's life. Although it contains errors and omissions, it is the account closest to the source, and, with its low price, no library can afford to be without it. MHCA.

House, Ellen Renshaw. **A Very Violent Rebel: The Civil War Diary of Ellen Renshaw House**. Edited by Daniel E. Sutherland. Knoxville: University of Tennessee Press, 1996. 285p. (Voices of the Civil War). $34.00. ISBN 0-87049-944-0.

The House family moved to Knoxville, Tennessee, from Georgia just before the start of the Civil War. Eastern Tennessee was a place of divided loyalties, but the Houses were hard-core Confederates. Ellen House's favorite brother, Johnnie, rushed to enlist, and Ellen began a journal in September 1863 to record the local events for him. As a "very violent rebel," Ellen made no apologies for her politics, criticizing Federal rule and anyone sympathetic to the North, especially her neighbor Parson Brownlow. She was eventually deported from Knoxville, alleged to be a spy, although her journal does not bear this out. Johnnie, who was taken prisoner at Missionary Ridge, spent almost two years in prison. Shortly after his reunion with the family, he was murdered by a highwayman, an event detailed in the diary, which concludes shortly afterward in December 1865. The book, which portrays the extent of Rebel loyalty, includes a section of black-and-white illustrations, maps, notes, bibliography, and an index. MHCA.

Jacobs, Harriet. **Incidents in the Life of a Slave Girl**. New York: Oxford University Press, 1988. 306p. (Schomburg Library of Nineteenth-Century Black Women Writers). $13.95pa. ISBN 0-19-506670-7pa.

> First published in 1861, with an introduction by the abolitionist Lydia Maria Child, *Incidents in the Life of a Slave Girl* was written under the pseudonym Linda Brent. The author, who felt the need to protect her identity during the Civil War, was Harriet Jacobs. Influenced by the extremely popular nineteenth-century sentimental novel, Jacobs used that structure in her writing to serve two purposes: It allowed an audience of Northern female readers to identify with her through a familiar literary vehicle, and it allowed her a way in which to carefully express her sexual exploitation, a story which had not been told before and for which there were no models or conventions. The story itself is a chronological narrative beginning with Jacobs's childhood, and with some detours, following her escape, flight, and relocation. As Jacobs's master presses her to have a sexual relationship with him, she evades him by choosing a white lover with whom she has two children. Eventually, Jacobs goes into hiding to escape her master. Her children are purchased out of slavery by her lover and sent North where, after seven years in hiding, Jacobs escapes and joins them; however, the Fugitive Slave Law continues to haunt her as she settles in New York. Jacobs's document is one of a limited number of slave narratives written by women and expressing their unique experiences. It will be used as a primary source in social studies classes as well as for independent reading. HCA.

Johnston, Norma. **Harriet: The Life and World of Harriet Beecher Stowe**. New York: Beech Tree, 1994. 242p. $4.95pa. ISBN 0-688-14586-8pa.

> As part of a famous, high-achieving family, Harriet Beecher Stowe could not escape certain tragedies and scandals. Norma Johnston does not try to avoid these in telling the complete story of Stowe, author of *Uncle Tom's Cabin*. A Calvinistic background and a determined father, who sent all his boys to college and ignored his girls, were important to Stowe's outlook and drive to live up to considerable expectations. With that drive, Stowe became a writer and orator while still fulfilling her Victorian domestic destiny by caring for her hypochondriac husband and seven children. Her income was often needed to support the large family, especially when her husband did not work, two of her children died, and a son, Frederick, a veteran of Gettysburg, became addicted to alcohol. Despite personal problems, Stowe was a product of the Beecher family upbringing and of her times, and Johnston's study situates her within this destiny. The book, written in short chapters using many quotations, reads like the best twentieth-century divulgence, and readers will see the past century's connections to this day. Included are a few black-and-white illustrations, a bibliography, and an index. HCA.

Karcher, Carolyn L. **The First Woman in the Republic: A Cultural Biography of Lydia Maria Child**. Durham, NC: Duke University Press, 1994. 804p. $37.95; $22.95pa. ISBN 0-8223-1485-1; 0-8223-2163-7pa.

Lydia Maria Child was a major literary presence in the nineteenth century, publishing forty-seven books of fiction and nonfiction as well as journalistic accounts, and encompassing personal correspondence of some 2,600 letters. Child pioneered new ground in the historical novel, short stories, children's literature, domestic advice books, women's history, antislavery fiction, and journalistic sketches, yet names other than Child's have become associated with the founding of these genres. Although immensely popular at times, Child lost public favor when she exposed her abolitionist views; and she never achieved monetary success, living a life of poverty while supporting her ne'er-do-well husband. Still, Child's moralist stands made her "the first woman in the republic," as William Lloyd Garrison called her. Although chiefly an abolitionist, Child also supported Native American rights, the rights of the poor, and, to a lesser degree, woman's rights. Karcher's monumental study of Child, her times, and her literature, restores this nineteenth-century woman to her rightful place in history. Black-and-white illustrations, a chronology, a list of Child's works, notes, and an index are included. Because of the scholarly nature of this book, the door remains open for a biography with general readers in mind. CA.

Keckley, Elizabeth. **Behind the Scenes: or, Thirty Years a Slave, and Four Years in the White House**. New York: Oxford University Press, 1988. 371p. $29.95; $13.95pa. ISBN 0-19-505259-5; 0-19-506084-9pa.

Elizabeth Keckley was a slave until she managed to buy her freedom, and that of her son, through the subscriptions of people who knew and loved her. Using her skills as a seamstress, Keckley paid back her subscribers and moved on to Washington, D.C., where she became dressmaker to Varina Davis, wife of Jefferson Davis, and Mary Todd Lincoln. Only the first three chapters of the book cover Keckley's thirty years as a slave, while the more substantial part details her four years with the Lincolns, including the death of son Willie, the second inauguration, the assassination, and the sale of Mrs. Lincoln's personal belongings to raise money for her support. The book has elements of slave narrative, sentimental novel, and political tattle-tale as it becomes less about Keckley and more about Mary Todd Lincoln; however, that does not make it any less interesting. A black-and-white portrait of Keckley is included as well as an appendix of correspondence between the two women. The book will have multiple uses in studies of the Civil War era. MHCA.

Lerner, Gerda. **The Grimké Sisters from South Carolina: Pioneers for Woman's Rights and Abolition**. New York: Oxford University Press, 1998. 416p. $17.95pa. ISBN 0-19-510603-2pa.

The Grimké Sisters is Gerda Lerner's thesis for Columbia University, published in 1967 at a time when virtually nothing was being written about women in American history. The book is the chronological story of Sarah and Angelina Grimké, the daughters of a slaveholding family from Charleston, South Carolina. The sisters abhorred slavery, but each in her own way, because the girls were born thirteen years apart. They moved separately to Philadelphia, where they joined the abolitionist movement and became two of the first American women to speak publicly to "mixed" audiences, men and women together. The sisters later added their voices to the cause of woman's rights, which they saw as a corollary to the rights of the Black race. Lerner's book incorporates extensive quotations and involves the context of the times. It concludes with the sisters accepting the off-spring of their brother and his female slave into the family. The story of the Grimké sisters is remarkable; they lived to see their wish for abolition fulfilled, but not their hope for woman's rights. Worthy of its place in opening the floodgates of publishing in women's history, the book, which includes notes, a bibliography, and an index, deserves a wide audience. HCA.

Livermore, Mary A. **My Story of the War: A Woman's Narrative of Four Years Personal Experience As Nurse in the Union Army, and in Relief Work at Home, in Hospitals, Camps, and at the Front, During the War of the Rebellion**. New York: Da Capo, 1995. 700p. $19.95pa. ISBN 0-306-80658-4pa.

Published in 1887, Mary Livermore's stories of the Civil War are a remarkable document. Livermore was a Chicago newspaper co-editor whose reports and letters, sent home during her wartime travels on behalf of the U.S. Sanitary Commission, were collected by her husband. When the war commenced, Livermore volunteered her services, and, at the end of 1862, she and her associate, Jane C. Hoge, were put in charge of the Chicago office of the Sanitary Commission. In this position, Livermore visited battlefields, hospitals, and camps; worked as a nurse and a cook; raised money; delivered supplies; organized the great Sanitary Fair of 1863; and even journeyed to Washington to meet Lincoln. All this work is detailed in her book within a narrative about the course of the war. The book contains several topical sections, including soldiers' letters from the battlefield and a sketch of the career of Mother Bickerdyke; this extraordinary nurse, who served tirelessly at the battlefront and helped to improve hospital conditions, was not afraid to face down a general by telling him *her* authority came "from God." Several chapters outline Livermore's reminiscences of Lincoln and how she covered the Republican convention that nominated him in 1860; she was the first woman to cover a political convention, and she caused quite a stir on the convention floor. Livermore, who devoted herself to woman suffrage after the war, includes in her book a wealth of information on women's contributions to the war effort at home, in battle, as nurses, and in volunteer work. The publisher added illustrations and the history of many of the battle flags of the war as well as black-and-white engravings of Livermore, several nursing colleagues, and scenes described in the book. Although the book is not indexed, the content descriptions of the chapters are complete and will lead readers to many topics. The broad-based yet personal account, with stories both gruesome and touching, will complement many Civil War collections that focus on battles, strategies, and generals. MHCA.

Mabee, Carleton, and Susan Mabee Newhouse. **Sojourner Truth: Slave, Prophet, Legend**. New York: New York University Press, 1995. 293p. $16.95pa. ISBN 0-8147-5525-9pa.

Carleton Mabee's well-researched biography of Sojourner Truth sheds new light on the historic figure. Because Truth lived in slavery for her first thirty years, many problems arise in documenting her life. Truth, probably born in 1797, operated in the oral tradition through preaching and speaking, but unfortunately she lived before the days of the tape recorder. Mabee's goal was to uncover the best sources on Truth and to stick closely to them. Although this biography is an academic work, Mabee's chronological account of Truth's life is also for general audiences. Straight biography would not have done the subject justice because so many aspects of Truth's life are open to interpretation; therefore Mabee pauses during each chapter to discuss the issues and tell the reader how he arrived at his conclusions. For instance, the author does not believe the words attributed to Truth by Frances Dana Gage's account of the 1851 Akron woman's convention speech in which Truth supposedly thundered "Ain't I a Woman," because that account was not written until twelve years later. Because Mabee keeps the reader so closely informed, his portrait is all the more believable, and his work as a historian is to be valued. The book contains a section of black-and-white illustrations, a time line, notes, and an index, and is the most readable portrait to date of Truth's life. HCA.

McDonald, Cornelia Peake. **A Woman's Civil War: A Diary, with Reminiscences of the War, from March 1862**. Edited by Minrose C. Gwin. Madison: University of Wisconsin Press, 1992. 303p. $15.95pa. ISBN 0-299-13264-1pa.

The mother of nine children, Cornelia Peake McDonald waited out the war at home when her husband, Angus W. McDonald III, marched off with Stonewall Jackson's troops in March 1862. The home in Winchester, Virginia was in an area that saw constant troop movement, and the family sometimes watched battles from their windows or from nearby hills. McDonald defended the house, its contents, and their food supply, although soldiers managed to steal her Christmas cakes from the oven. On one occasion, McDonald found a human foot in her garden. Within months of her husband's departure, McDonald lost her youngest baby girl, and, within a year, the family was forced to evacuate to Lexington, Virginia, where they lived as refugees. When Angus McDonald fell ill in Richmond, McDonald rushed to his side, but he died before she could reach him; she was shown her husband's corpse before anyone told her of his death. McDonald began her diary to record daily events for her husband; however, she finished it for her children as a legacy to them for all they had endured. Because part of the log was lost during the family's exile, in 1875 McDonald added her reminiscences to what remained of the diary. Containing a few black-and-white photographs, an appendix of Angus McDonald's eighteen children by two wives (Cornelia was the second), notes, and an index, the narrative stands as a testament to one woman's courage in keeping her children safe in time of war. MHCA.

McKissack, Patricia C., and Fredrick McKissack. **Sojourner Truth: Ain't I a Woman?** New York: Scholastic, 1992. 186p. $13.95; $3.99pa. ISBN 0-590-44690-8; 0-590-44691-6pa.

> This biography, complete and well written, is aimed at younger audiences. The McKissacks do an admirable job of writing escaped slave and speaker Sojourner Truth's story within the context of the changing laws regarding slavery and the many abolitionists Truth came to know. The nineteenth century was a complicated time, and Truth was associated both with abolition and woman's rights. The book is studded with black-and-white illustrations—helpful to young readers—and an appendix profiles the major figures of the day. A bibliography and an index are included. MH.

McLaurin, Melton A. **Celia: A Slave**. New York: Avon, 1991. 148p. $12.00pa. ISBN 0-380-71935-5pa.

> *Celia: A Slave* has the look and feel of a novel, but readers will admire how historian Melton McLaurin has recreated the 1850s story of an anonymous slave from Missouri about whom few documents exist. Celia, fourteen years old, was purchased by John Newsom in 1850 and brought to his farm in Callaway County, where she lived in a cabin close to Newsom's house. From the first, Newsom sexually abused the girl; he continued the abuse over the next five years, and Celia bore him two children. When Celia entered into a romantic relationship with a male slave on the farm, she was pressured to end her relationship with Newsom. Caught in a web with no satisfactory resolution possible, Celia murdered Newsom. She was easily discovered and even energetically defended at her trial in 1855; but she was found guilty and hanged. McLaurin explores the moral quandaries of slavery, the political debate about Missouri as a slave state, and the legal maneuverings that attempted to justify the peculiar institution. He also pieces together the life of a slave woman, using court documents, county and state records, and the best knowledge of other historians of slavery. Where details are not available, he admits it; where emotions can only be theorized, he suggests a variety of possible responses. He makes evident the task of the historian in recreating events, and that process, revealed through notes, a bibliography, and an index, is as interesting as the story itself. History teachers may find multiple uses for the book, which will also be useful in ante-bellum studies. HCA.

Morton, Patricia, ed. **Discovering the Women in Slavery: Emancipating Perspectives on the American Past**. Athens: University of Georgia Press, 1996. 320p. $40.00; $20.00pa. ISBN 0-8203-1756-X; 0-8203-1757-8pa.

> Patricia Morton has assembled a collection of fourteen essays showing the breadth and depth of women's experiences with slavery. Grouped as case studies and group studies, the subjects range from Rachel Knight, Mary Bell, and Lydia Maria Child to Black Methodist women, clothing and adornment, and breast feeding. The book covers a variety of races and classes from a woman-centered view, which, as editor Morton describes it, sees slavery through a microscope rather than through a telescope. Although

only one essay is illustrated, a selected bibliography and notes on the contributors are included. HCA.

Painter, Nell Irvin. **Sojourner Truth: A Life, A Symbol**. New York: W. W. Norton, 1996. 370p. $20.00; $14.95pa. ISBN 0-393-02739-2; 0-393-31708-0pa.

In her biography, Nell Painter treats Sojourner Truth as a symbol, a process that began even during Truth's own time. Both Frances Dana Gage, in her account of the 1851 "Ain't I a Woman" speech, and Harriet Beecher Stowe, in her article "The Libyan Sibyl," for various reasons portrayed Truth in ways that were not strictly factual, but fulfilled the public's need to believe in the former slave as a larger-than-life figure. Painter's heavily documented study is presented in three parts: Truth's life in slavery, her early work as a feminist and abolitionist, and the myth-making surrounding her later work. The book has black-and-white illustrations throughout, and includes notes and an index. Painter's is the largest account of Truth and adds much to the understanding of this important woman. HCA.

Petry, Ann. **Harriet Tubman: Conductor on the Underground Railroad**. New York: HarperTrophy, 1996. $4.95pa. ISBN 0-06-446181-5pa.

Ann Petry's is a very readable, long-in-print biography of Harriet Tubman, who brought between 60 and 300 people out of slavery, including most of her own family. Born in the Tidewater area of Maryland, Tubman ran away before she was thirty years old. She worked at different jobs to gain enough money to return, again and again, into Maryland to lead other slaves to freedom. Although illiterate, Tubman had "street sense" and was never discovered. During the Civil War, Tubman worked as a scout, spy, and nurse, and claimed a pension when the war was over. Petry's straightforward account includes an index. MHCA.

Ropes, Hannah. **Civil War Nurse: The Diary and Letters of Hannah Ropes**. Edited by John R. Brumgardt. Knoxville: University of Tennessee Press, 1980. 149p. $11.95pa. ISBN 0-870-49790-2pa.

With a Yankee background, service with the freesoilers in Kansas, and experience as a novel-writer, Hannah Ropes enlisted as a nurse during the Civil War, serving in the Union Hotel Hospital in Washington, D.C. Louisa May Alcott served under Ropes, and mentions her in *Hospital Sketches*. Because nursing was not yet a professional field, training and methods were still developing. Ropes had an independent, take-charge attitude which, while beneficial to the patients, caused friction with the military doctors. As a person who had been politically involved, she knew senators and generals, whom she comments on in her diary, and who are identified in a glossary at the end of the book. The introduction to the book, written by John R. Brumgardt, is notable for portraying the development of nursing, and the personalities associated with it, during the Civil War. The letters and diary of Hannah Ropes are arranged by date from June 1862 to January 1863; the book shows one photograph of Ropes, and has a bibliography and an index. HCA.

Sandburg, Carl. **Mary Lincoln: Wife and Widow**. Bedford, MA: Applewood, 1995. 164p. $12.95pa. ISBN 1-55709-248-6pa.

> Stunning prose characterizes Carl Sandburg's portrait of Mary Todd Lincoln. Sandburg, poet and Abraham Lincoln's biographer, covers Mary Lincoln's childhood, her courtship, her marriage to Abraham Lincoln, their devotion to each other, her villainization by the press, and her institutionalization by her son Robert for insanity. Sandburg is kind to his subject while agreeing that she was mentally unstable. Mary Lincoln saw more than her share of grief when she lost three of her four sons, and was splattered with blood during the assassination of her husband. She was vain, extravagant, and temperamental, but, had she had lived today, the cause of her mental instability would probably be known and treated. Quotations from those who knew Mary Lincoln add interesting contemporary views to this biography. The book is illustrated with black-and-white photographs and documents, and has an index. Although brief, the profile is complete, well written, and judiciously documented. It will serve all types of readers. MHCA.

Seabury, Caroline. **The Diary of Caroline Seabury, 1854–1863**. Edited by Suzanne L. Bunkers. Madison: University of Wisconsin Press, 1991. 148p. $12.95pa. ISBN 0-299-12874-1pa.

> In 1854, Caroline Seabury left New York to become a teacher in a private school for young ladies in Columbus, Mississippi. She determined at that time to keep a diary. Her account portrayed her impressions of the "peculiar institution" of slavery, the thoughts a Northern woman was supposed to keep to herself. Because Seabury was dependent on her work to support herself, her diary is the only place she could record her reflections. When she was forced out of her job in 1862 because the school decided to retain only Southern teachers, she found several other situations; she was able to escape North when Union forces penetrated Confederate lines in the summer of 1863. Thus she ended her diary and closed that chapter in her life. A complete story of the years preceding and during the Civil War, the document portrays an outsider's view of the South. Several black-and-white illustrations, notes, bibliography, and index complete the book. MHCA.

Sterling, Dorothy. **Ahead of Her Time: Abby Kelley and the Politics of Antislavery**. New York: W. W. Norton, 1991. 436p. $14.95pa. ISBN 0-393-31131-7pa.

> It is surprising that Abby Kelley, and all the antislavery people who knew her and worked with her, disappeared from history. Kelley was a simple and modest woman of Quaker background who chose to remain single until she was in her forties. Instead of pursuing married life, Kelley left her teaching job to travel and lecture against slavery at a time when women were forbidden by church doctrine and social custom from speaking in public. As a woman lecturer, Kelley was preceded only by the Grimké sisters of South Carolina. For almost ten years before recruiting other women—Lucy Stone and Susan B. Anthony among them—to join her on the lecture circuit,

Kelley worked at convincing people throughout New England and the Midwest that they must take personal responsibility for ending the institution of slavery. Kelley, as a radical from the William Lloyd Garrison faction of the abolitionists, faced personal disparagement and violence throughout her life, but she lived to see what she stood for enacted during the Civil War and Reconstruction. Dorothy Sterling's book, with its notes, bibliography, and index, resurrects the antislavery movement in an important piece of research that includes long-buried pictures of the notable participants. The name Abby Kelley should be recognized by every American. HCA.

Sullivan, Walter, ed. **The War the Women Lived: Female Voices from the Confederate South**. Nashville: J. S. Sanders, 1995. 319p. $24.95. ISBN 1-879941-30-9.

Walter Sullivan has collected the diaries and memoirs of twenty-three Southern women and organized them chronologically to reveal a female history of the Southern Civil War years. The pieces can be read individually, each being headed with background information giving date, location, and context. Many of the writers are unknowns who spent the war years raising food, mustering supplies, and nursing. Some of the women are familiar diarists, for instance, South Carolina socialite Mary Boykin Chesnut and spies Rose Greenhow and Belle Boyd. The lengthy journal sections allow the women to tell their own stories. A brief chronology of the war, notes on the writers, a bibliography, and an index are included. Sullivan's book will be useful primary source material wherever the Civil War is studied. MHCA.

Todras, Ellen H. **Angelina Grimké: Voice of Abolition**. North Haven, CT: Linnet, 1999. 178p. $25.00. ISBN 0-208-02485-9.

On the evening of May 16, 1838, Angelina Grimké addressed the unfriendly crowd at Pennsylvania Hall in Philadelphia on the subject of slavery. The next night, the brand new hall was burned to the ground. In the early days of abolition, feelings ran strong, but Grimké was not afraid to face a crowd for, as the daughter of a South Carolina slaveholding family, she knew the horrors of slavery. Grimké left the South, wrote for the cause, and became one of the first women to speak in public in a time when such conduct was unacceptable. After the Civil War, Grimké became acquainted with her nephews, her brother's sons by one of his slaves, whom she welcomed into the family. Ellen Todras's biography is an excellent study, incorporating many quotes. The use of black-and-white illustrations, special topical sections, appendices of Grimké's writings, a time line, a bibliography, and an index make the book useful for research and reading. MH.

Weisenburger, Steven. **Modern Medea: A Family Story of Slavery and Child-Murder from the Old South**. New York: Hill and Wang, 1998. 352p. $25.00. ISBN 0-8090-6953-9.

The story of Margaret Garner's near decapitation of her two-year-old daughter with a butcher knife made headlines in 1856, as it would today, and the media followed the event during the last years before the Civil War. The case was dramatic in Cincinnati, a border crossing between slave and free country, because Garner was a cornered fugitive slave who refused to see her child taken back into slavery. Steven Weisenburger re-created the events because Toni Morrison drew upon them in crafting her Pulitzer Prize–winning novel *Beloved*. In resurrecting the escape, capture, and trial of the Garner family, who fled from Kentucky across the frozen Ohio River, the author also explores the associated characters: the slave master, John Pollard Gaines; the abolitionist defense attorney, John Jolliffe; and numerous others. One of many fugitive-slave trials occurring across the country, the complicated case ends with the Garners being returned to slavery. The book presents an excellent picture of ante-bellum sensationalism that has long been forgotten, but which Weisenburger uncovers by quoting from newspapers and court reports. The book includes black-and-white illustrations, notes, a bibliography, and an index. HCA.

White, Deborah Gray. **Ar'n't I a Woman? Female Slaves in the Plantation South**. Rev. ed. New York: W. W. Norton, 1999. 244p. $11.00pa. ISBN 0-393-31481-2pa.

A new edition of Deborah White's 1985 study of female slaves revises her sense of the differences between males and females in bondage. One of the first to explore slave women, White acknowledges that, in enduring the triple threat of racism, sexism, and powerlessness, slave women assumed different roles within society. Black women were stereotyped as either Jezebels or Mammies, but they created networks of cohesion to help each other. Life cycles, families, and reconstruction are other topics covered in this worthwhile study, which includes notes, a bibliography, and an index. HCA.

Whitelaw, Nancy. **Clara Barton: Civil War Nurse**. Springfield, NJ: Enslow, 1997. 128p. (Historical American Biographies). $19.95. ISBN 0-89490-778-6.

Although Clara Barton is venerated as the founder of the Red Cross and one who helped professionalize nursing, her life was not without its difficulties; she suffered from depression, and was sometimes criticized for her actions. During the Civil War, Barton gained permission to work on the front lines, where she brought food and supplies and aided soldiers under terrible conditions. At war's end, so many men were dead and missing that she asked President Lincoln to allow her to assist families in their searches for missing relatives. This project, which became the basis of the Red Cross, involved enormous correspondence, and all the writing was done by hand. Throughout her life, Barton was a woman who needed to be active, and she probably had the ability to accomplish even more than she did. The book is illustrated with black-and-white photographs, drawings, and maps, and boxed text contains topics for special consideration. Notes, a glossary, a bibliography, and an index are included. MH.

Zeinert, Karen. **Those Courageous Women of the Civil War**. Brookfield, CT: Millbrook, 1998. 96p. $27.40. ISBN 0-7613-0212-3.

> In a straightforward history, Karen Zeinert outlines women's involvement in the Civil War, covering soldiers, spies, nurses, first ladies, writers, and home-front workers. Her coverage is not as comprehensive as Chang's (listed above), and it has fewer illustrations; although color illustrations are included in Zeinert's book. The book has boxed treatments of topics such as Mary Chesnut's journal and Julia Gardiner Tyler, former first lady and Confederate sympathizer. A time line gives the major events of the war years, and notes, further reading, and an index are included in a book suitable for beginning research. MH.

Non-Book Material

Harriet Tubman and the Underground Railroad. Directed by Lloyd Richards. Produced by Vern Diamond. 22 min. Phoenix Learning Group, 1971. (You Are There). Videocassette. Purchase $285.00; Rental $72.00.

> Walter Cronkite anchors this *You Are There* production, which uses multiple reporters and an interview format to present a dramatic incident: Harriet Tubman helping four slaves to escape to the North. Today's students are probably not familiar with this CBS format, but they will find the production enjoyable. Through interviews with Tubman; her father, Ben Ross; a Quaker couple whose home is an underground railroad stop; a slave owner, William Hughlett; an abolitionist, William Lloyd Garrison; and the future president of the Confederacy, Jefferson Davis, all sides of the slavery issue are presented. Born a slave on a Maryland plantation, Tubman was injured during her childhood when a field hand escaped. This changed her, and she escaped herself, then returned to the South numerous times to bring as many as 300 slaves, including her own family, to freedom. Her biggest threat was the Fugitive Slave Law, so she made Canada her destination; even the North was unsafe for the escaped slaves. The film's only fault is an overly jubilant celebration at the Quaker safe house when the slaves arrive. Otherwise, the piece imparts a good deal of history and can be used with classes studying the events leading up to the Civil War. Discussion questions are enclosed. MH.

Rebel Hearts: Sarah and Angelina Grimké and the Anti-Slavery Movement. Produced by Betsy Newman. 58 min. Women Make Movies, 1994. Videocassette. Purchase $250.00; Rental $75.00.

> The Grimké sisters were born into a wealthy, slave-owning family in South Carolina. Sarah rejected her future as a Southern belle and embraced the Quaker religion, which she was introduced to on a trip to Philadelphia. After joining her sister in the North and becoming acquainted with the abolitionist movement, Angelina returned home to reform her family. The sisters educated and freed their own slaves, moved permanently to the North, and became

active as writers and speakers in the American Anti-Slavery Society in the 1830s. Because of religious and societal restrictions on women's speaking in public, the sisters began by speaking to private parties of females. As the sisters became better known and the antislavery movement grew, men began to attend their meetings. When the clergy moved against the sisters for speaking before mixed groups, the sisters were forced to recognize the injustices placed upon women. The Grimkés brought woman's rights into the reform movement even though the subject was rejected by most men in the antislavery movement. The Grimkés led the way as antislavery and woman's rights activists, opposing the Civil War on the grounds that the slaves had not been freed, and serving as models to other women who wished to speak publicly on the issues of the day. After the war, the sisters welcomed into their family former slaves who were their brother's children. Historians Gerda Lerner and Margaret Hope Bacon scrupulously advance the story and the historical context, which they narrate over black-and-white illustrations, documents, and filmed reenactments of the sisters. A well-developed production, *Rebel Hearts* will add to history classes' discussions of events leading up to the Civil War and of the beginnings of the woman's rights movement. HCA.

Sojourner Truth: Ain't I a Woman? Produced by Loren Stephens. Directed by Judy Chakin. 26 min. Phoenix Learning Group, 1989. Videocassette. Purchase $250.00; Rental $75.00.

Valeria Parker portrays Sojourner Truth in this video featuring biographical reenactments. Julie Harris plays Olive Gilbert, the author of *Narrative of Sojourner Truth*, and serves as the narrator for the production. Truth was born in New York state around 1797 to a master who promised to set her free. When this did not happen, Isabella, as was her birth name, took her infant child and escaped. She was sheltered by Quakers, and she accepted their religion and changed her name to Sojourner Truth. At the age of forty-six, she traveled on foot preaching throughout New England. Although she never learned to read or write, she became a spokesperson for abolition and woman's rights by using her wit and gift of speech. Her most famous speech, "Ain't I a Woman," was given at a woman's rights convention in Akron, Ohio, in 1851. Truth met many of the important public figures of her day, including Frederick Douglass, Harriet Beecher Stowe, and Abraham Lincoln, events that are dramatized in the video. Acting is most important in the film; the sets are minimal, featuring only curtains, a lattice, and lighting. Period music is featured, and documents and photographs are shown in sepia tones. The film has one inaccuracy: In describing the 1848 Seneca Falls Woman's Rights Convention, both Truth and Lucy Stone are described as attending; neither was there, and this event was no doubt confused with the 1850 Worcester, Massachusetts, Woman's Rights Convention, which was organized by Stone and attended by Truth. Overall, students will enjoy this production as a vehicle to learning about a female escaped slave who made her way in the world on the strength of her character. A discussion guide is included with the video, which can be used in social studies or biography units. MHCA.

Suffrage and Feminism

Books

Banner, Lois W. **Elizabeth Cady Stanton: A Radical for Woman's Rights**.
New York: HarperCollins, 1980. 189p. $17.00pa. ISBN 0-673-39319-4pa.

> Lois Banner's biography serves as an introduction to Elizabeth Cady Stanton, the mother of the woman's rights movement, who led the call for the first convention on the topic in 1848 at Seneca Falls, New York. Working closely with Susan B. Anthony, she was at the forefront of the suffrage movement until her death. Cady Stanton was a radical in a number of ways: She championed more liberal divorce laws, unheard of in the nineteenth century, and she wrote *The Woman's Bible,* in which she addressed religious anti-feminism. Cady Stanton was a proud writer, but little of her written and spoken words are included here. Although Banner's book presents the facts of Cady Stanton's life, readers will not feel they know the great feminist as a person. The book contains only one early portrait of Cady Stanton, still in her twenties; source notes and an index are included. MHCA.

Cullen-DuPont, Kathryn. **Elizabeth Cady Stanton and Women's Liberty**.
New York: Facts on File, 1992. 133p. (Makers of America). $19.95. ISBN
0-8160-2413-8.

> Beginning with Elizabeth Cady's elopement with Henry Stanton and their wedding voyage to London to attend the 1840 World Anti-Slavery Convention, where the women delegates were refused seats, Kathryn Cullen-DuPont gives a rich sense of the great feminist and the forces that created her. Quoting from Cady Stanton and those who knew her, the book covers her childhood, education, and work for woman suffrage. Black-and-white illustrations, further reading suggestions, and an index are included in this complete biography suitable for reading and reference use among younger readers. MH.

DuBois, Ellen Carol, ed. **The Elizabeth Cady Stanton—Susan B. Anthony Reader: Correspondence, Writings, Speeches**. Rev. ed. Boston: Northeastern University Press, 1992. 306p. $15.95pa. ISBN 1-55553-143-1pa.

> With insightful headings, historian Ellen Carol DuBois introduces the speeches and writings of the two great suffrage leaders Elizabeth Cady Stanton and Susan B. Anthony. These are divided into early, middle, and late life periods. The topics range from Cady Stanton's address at the 1848 Seneca Falls Woman's Rights Convention and Anthony's early writing on temperance to later letters addressed to legislative bodies and speeches presented at various conventions and public gatherings. Included are part of Cady Stanton's commentary on Genesis from *The Woman's Bible* and several pieces by Anna Howard Shaw lauding Anthony. The revised edition includes a final section of correspondence between the friends written late in their lives

between 1895 and 1902, along with their 1853 phrenological reports. With a forward by Gerda Lerner, the book provides a nice collection of primary sources to be used in studying the suffrage movement or the nineteenth century. A black-and-white photograph of the bronze cast of the clasped hands of the two suffrage leaders is the only illustration; an index is included. HCA.

DuBois, Ellen Carol. **Feminism and Suffrage: The Emergence of an Independent Women's Movement in America, 1848–1869**. Ithaca, NY: Cornell University Press, 1978. 220p. $14.95pa. ISBN 0-8014-9182-7pa.

> Feminist historian Ellen Carol DuBois looks at the roots of the suffrage struggle for an understanding of its development as a larger social movement. She considers suffrage, along with Black liberation and the labor movement, to be among the three great reform efforts in American history. Before the Civil War, suffrage was linked to abolition, and, although women leaders gained skills and confidence, they were not focused on their own priorities. After the war, women realized their need for an independent political base. Elizabeth Cady Stanton and Susan B. Anthony took the lead in breaking with the abolitionists, seeking, but failing, to form alliances with Democrats, labor unions, and working women before forming a suffrage-centered organization. The study is more a history of the origins of the feminist movement, giving a broader perspective on its meaning in the twentieth century. The well-laid out book includes sketches and quotations from the suffrage mothers as well as a bibliography and index. HCA.

Flexner, Eleanor. **Century of Struggle: The Woman's Rights Movement in the United States**. Cambridge: Belknap Press of Harvard University Press, 1996. 384p. $16.95pa. ISBN 0-674-10653-9pa.

> Eleanor Flexner's *Century of Struggle* was the first full account written of the suffrage battle, and although it covers that aspect of history thoroughly, it tells much more. The book is an overview of women's history from 1608. The historical summary is excellent, drawing on a wealth of primary source material and quoting extensively. Flexner pays particular attention to the chronological development of the themes of education, organization, reform, and labor. The book is known to be the most thorough report of the last fourteen years of the suffrage struggle—almost a third of the book chronicles these years—before the ratification of the Nineteenth Amendment. As a basic text in women's history, for its incorporation of primary source material, and for its extensive coverage of the suffrage movement, the book deserves to be in every library. MHCA.

Friedl, Bettina, ed. **On to Victory: Propaganda Plays of the Woman Suffrage Movement**. Boston: Northeastern University Press, 1987. 378p. $16.95pa. ISBN 1-55553-073-7pa.

> Bettina Friedl has uncovered parlor plays, Victorian amateur entertainments, on the topic of woman suffrage, some of which are collected in this volume. The twenty plays, a few of them mere scenes, were published from

1856 onwards; however, most of them date from the 1910s. Charlotte Perkins Gilman and Catharine Waugh McCulloch were the most notable authors. The plays, which began as propaganda pieces for the suffrage movement, were performed as part of suffrage pageants. The works are accompanied by an introductory chapter, explaining their context and significance, and a chapter that critiques the plays. In many ways, the presentations show that human nature has not changed significantly. Adding to the social history of the suffrage movement, the volume will be used where women's rights are studied in depth and with drama studies at all levels. A section of black-and-white photographs, etchings, document reproductions, and illustrations, and a complete bibliography of similar materials are included. MHCA.

Frost, Elizabeth, and Kathryn Cullen-DuPont. **Woman's Suffrage in America: An Eyewitness History**. New York: Facts on File, 1992. 452p. (Eyewitness History). $45.00. ISBN 0-8160-2309-3.

Woman's Suffrage in America contains an excellent overview of the period from 1800 to 1920; the thirteen chronological chapters are introduced by a historical essay, and contain a time line of key events and a hearty selection of documents. The documents come from diaries, newspapers, sermons, speeches, letters, government reports, political resolutions, and meeting proceedings. The book is studded with black-and-white etchings, paintings, and photographs, and contains an appendix of full-length documents, from Angelina Grimké's "Appeal to the Christian Women of the South" to the Nineteenth Amendment to the Constitution. Another appendix briefly profiles 100 personalities of the suffrage movement, and notes, a bibliography, and an index are included. Although history teachers will love having all this material available in one source, the documents are presented without individual explanation. Given the complicated infighting surrounding suffrage and its many personalities, it is unrealistic to expect young readers to decipher it all without a teacher's support. MHCA.

Fuller, Margaret. **Woman in the Nineteenth Century: An Authoritative Text, Backgrounds, Criticism**. New York: W. W. Norton, 1998. 308p. (Norton Critical Edition). $12.50pa. ISBN 0-393-97157-0pa.

Not a history, *Woman in the Nineteenth Century* is Margaret Fuller's feminist treatise, blending her free spirituality to the search for perfection. The essay, published in 1845, directly influenced early feminists and the Seneca Falls Woman's Rights Convention. Fuller was considered the first American woman intellectual, a part of the Transcendental movement. A friend to all the best minds, she supported herself through a series of "conversations" among women of Boston's intellectual elite. Unfortunately, Fuller only lived to be forty, dying in a shipwreck off New York. In the Norton Critical Edition, many of Fuller's other writings, fiction, nonfiction, personal documents, and correspondence demonstrate how she came to her womanist philosophy. Reviews of *Woman in the Nineteenth Century*, written by Lydia Maria Child, Edgar Allan Poe, George Eliot, and others, illustrate how the work was received at midcentury; and recent essays, published in the last fifteen years, explain Fuller's influence today. A chronology and a selected bibliography are also included. HCA.

Gilman, Charlotte Perkins. **The Living of Charlotte Perkins Gilman: An Autobiography**. Madison: University of Wisconsin Press, 1990. 341p. (Wisconsin Studies in American Autobiography). $15.95pa. ISBN 0-299-12744-3pa.

Charlotte Perkins Gilman was an intellectual who influenced the woman's movement with her 1898 book *Women and Economics,* which argued for female economic independence and pointed out social discrimination against women. Gilman, a descendent of the Beecher family, became a lecturer and writer after an unhappy marriage and the birth of a daughter drove her into madness. She reflected on this episode in an autobiographical short story, "The Yellow Wallpaper." Always a champion of women, although not through the large suffrage organizations, Gilman wrote her memoirs late in life, adding a last chapter when she knew she was dying of breast cancer. She took her own life, as she had planned, when the pain became too much to endure. With an introduction by biographer Ann J. Lane, a forward by friend Zona Gale, and an index, the book can be used in autobiographical studies, literature courses, or women's studies. HCA.

Graham, Sara Hunter. **Woman Suffrage and the New Democracy**. New Haven, CT: Yale University Press, 1996. 234p. $32.00. ISBN 0-300-06346-6.

Sara Graham concentrates on the development of the National American Woman Suffrage Association as a single-issue pressure group from the 1890 reunification of the divided suffrage movement to the 1920 passage of the Nineteenth Amendment. The book is divided into two parts, the first part focusing on new image creation for the group from 1890 to 1915. Suffering from low membership, lack of funding, poor political strategy, and no public support, this was the period when Susan B. Anthony was elevated to sainthood. During this time, when no significant progress toward the vote was being made, the group redefined itself by using a variety of strategies to lobby politicians and by employing more professional publicity campaigns. The second section deals with the creation of the suffrage "machine" from 1915 to 1920, when the NAWSA was committed to carrying out Carrie Chapman Catt's "Winning Plan" by defining the cause as strictly suffrage and by removing themselves from the radical tactics of Alice Paul's National Woman's Party. Graham's study is unique in its political look at suffrage organizations, and it will bring insight to those interested in a more in-depth look at the march to the vote. HCA.

Gurko, Miriam. **The Ladies of Seneca Falls: The Birth of the Woman's Rights Movement**. New York: Schocken, 1974. 328p. $13.95pa. ISBN 0-8052-0545-4pa.

Miriam Gurko's history of woman's rights, aimed at younger readers, covers developments from the seventeenth century through the deaths of the first generation of suffrage leaders. All the major personalities get chapter coverage, including the Grimké sisters, Lucretia Mott, Elizabeth Cady Stanton, Margaret Fuller, Susan B. Anthony, Lucy Stone, and even the anti-suffragists, or "antis." The topical coverage advances in a chronological progression with two black-and-white sections of photographs and illustrations included. The book contains the text of the 1848 Seneca Falls "The Declaration of Sentiments and Resolutions," a chronology, a bibliography, and an index. Although the book is very serviceable for use in middle school, teachers need to be aware that it stops short of covering the eventual passage of suffrage. MHA.

Helmer, Diana Star. **Women Suffragists**. New York: Facts on File, 1998. 146p. (American Profiles). $19.95. ISBN 0-8160-3579-2.

Ten leaders of the suffrage movement, from its beginnings at the Seneca Falls convention organized by Elizabeth Cady Stanton to its conclusion with the passing of the Nineteenth Amendment, which was introduced to Congress by Jeannette Rankin, are sketched in Diana Helmer's useful book. Representatives of the first and second generations, as well as Black women leaders, are included in profiles that include a portrait, a chronology, and sources for further reading. The book can be used in parts for reports or as a whole for free reading. As a whole, the book gives an idea of the range of approaches to suffrage and some of the internal squabbles that divided the movement. An index is included. MH.

Kendall, Martha E. **Susan B. Anthony: Voice for Women's Voting Rights**. Springfield, NJ: Enslow, 1997. 128p. (Historical American Biographies). $19.95. ISBN 0-89490-780-8.

Opening with Susan B. Anthony's arrest and trial for voting in the 1872 presidential election, Martha Kendall presents a high-interest portrait of the suffrage leader. She covers Anthony's Quaker childhood, teaching career, travels, and work in the various woman's rights campaigns. Although Anthony did not live to see the vote, the author discusses the passing of the Nineteenth Amendment and Anthony's legacy. Black-and-white illustrations, etchings, and documents are included, and several maps detail Anthony's huge travel schedule and the state by state enfranchisement of women. A chronology, notes, a glossary, an index, and suggestions for further reading are included in this accessible portrait for young readers. MH.

Kerr, Andrea Moore. **Lucy Stone: Speaking Out for Equality**. New Brunswick, NJ: Rutgers University Press, 1992. 301p. $19.00pa. ISBN 0-8135-1860-1pa.

Lucy Stone stands beside Elizabeth Cady Stanton and Susan B. Anthony at the pinnacle of the leadership of the suffrage movement. Stone was the first Massachusetts woman to earn a college degree, working her way through Oberlin in Ohio. Mentored by Abby Kelley, Stone became an orator for the Massachusetts Anti-Slavery Society, traveling alone at a time when women could not speak in mixed gatherings. When she married late in life, she was the first woman to keep her maiden name. Stone signed the call for the first national woman's rights convention held in Worcester, Massachusetts in 1850, and it was the report of the speech she gave there that converted Anthony to the woman's rights cause. She was an untiring worker for woman's rights, and when her principles caused her to disagree with Cady Stanton and Anthony over the ratification of the Fourteenth and Fifteenth Amendments, she formed her own organization, the American Woman Suffrage Association. Shortly after the division of the suffrage movement, Stone began to edit the enduring suffrage newspaper, *Woman's Journal.* Author Kerr believes that Stone was left out of suffrage history because of her detachment from Cady Stanton and Anthony during the years they were writing *History of Woman Suffrage*; however, Kerr also believes that the *Woman's Journal* is as important as *History of Woman Suffrage* as a documentary source in the suffrage movement. Libraries will want to place *Lucy Stone* back in her rightful place in their history and biography sections. The work contains a section of black-and-white photographs, notes, a bibliography, and an index. HCA.

Kolmerten, Carol A. **The American Life of Ernestine L. Rose.** Syracuse: Syracuse University Press, 1999. 300p. (Writing American Women). $34.95. ISBN 0-8156-0528-5.

Although Ernestine Rose was born abroad and died abroad, Carol Kolmerten concentrates on her life as queen of the suffrage platform. Rose was a great intellect, a sarcastic wit, and a wonderful lecturer, but her background and politics made her an easy target for those who opposed the vote for women. As a Polish immigrant of Jewish descent, a freethinker, and an atheist, Rose was neglected by many within the reform movements, although Susan B. Anthony remained a constant friend. Supported by her husband, Rose traveled across the United States for the suffrage movement; but the work exhausted her, and she returned to Europe to live out her life. A section of black-and-white illustrations, a bibliography, and an index round out a fine contribution that restores an important personality in the woman's rights movement. HCA.

Kraditor, Aileen S. **The Ideas of the Woman Suffrage Movement, 1890–1920.** New York: W. W. Norton, 1981. 313p. $12.95pa. ISBN 0-393-00039-7pa.

In analyzing twenty-six women who held an office in the National American Woman Suffrage Association for three or more years between 1890 and 1918, Aileen Kraditor is able to make some generalizations about suffrage philosophy. The majority of these women, the principal first and second generation leaders, including Susan B. Anthony, Elizabeth Cady Stanton, Lucy Stone, Carrie Chapman Catt, and Alice Paul, were college graduates, married, of Anglo-Saxon origin, Protestant, and employed on their own behalf for part of their lifetimes. From an examination of their papers, Kraditor presents their views on religion, home, immigration, and labor. Beyond this analysis, Kraditor examines the views of antisuffragists and southern suffragists. An appendix lists biographical information for the subjects, and a bibliography and an index are included. Kraditor's book, first published in 1965, was one of the first studies to use the papers of the suffrage leaders as the basis of investigation. HCA.

Lane, Ann J. **To *Herland* and Beyond: The Life and Work of Charlotte Perkins Gilman**. Charlottesville: University Press of Virginia, 1990. 413p. $17.50pa. ISBN 0-8139-1742-5pa.

Charlotte Perkins Gilman left an abundance of written material, which biographer Ann Lane accesses in creating this unusual portrait. Giving up the chronological approach, Lane shows Gilman's relationship to her father, mother, three intimate female friends, two husbands, doctor, work, and daughter. From a childhood of abandonment, and after suffering a postpartum mental breakdown, which was exacerbated by her medical care, Gilman lived in constant fear of attacks of depression. She suffered public abuse for sending her daughter to live with her divorced husband, who had married her good friend. As a feminist theorist and writer who dealt with the origins of patriarchal society, the struggle to achieve autonomy, and women's need for economic independence, Gilman was doomed to poverty. Lane's strength lies in her interwoven analysis of Gilman's writings. With black-and-white photographs, notes, a bibliography, and an index, the book will be used in women's studies, psychology, and literature. HCA.

Matthews, Jean V. **Women's Struggle for Equality: The First Phase, 1828–1876**. Chicago: Ivan R. Dee, 1997. 212p. (American Way). $24.95; $12.95pa. ISBN 1-56663-145-9; 1-56663-146-7pa.

In dating her study from the 1828 founding of the newspaper the *Free Enquirer*, published in New York by freethinkers Frances Wright and Robert Dale Owen, to the country's centennial in 1876, Jean Matthews centers on the origins of the women's movement as we know it today. The movement, then as now, wanted equal rights, opportunities, and respect with men, rather than the long-accepted patriarchal view, which was considered natural and divinely ordained. Although the movement would come to focus on suffrage, many other rights for women were more immediate during this early period, including education and legal rights in marriage. Matthews gives a forthright, detailed account of the period, containing such well-known and newly uncovered subjects as freedwoman Maria Stewart, who lectured in public even before trailblazer Angelina Grimké. Matthews clarifies how sex invaded and affected the suffrage question during the 1870s with the issues of divorce, free love, and birth control. Those interested in the history of the nineteenth century beyond the suffrage question will find the information in *Women's Struggle for Equality* useful. Source notes, the 1848 "Declaration of Sentiments," and an index are appended. HCA.

Monroe, Judy. **The Nineteenth Amendment: Women's Right to Vote**. Springfield, NJ: Enslow, 1998. 128p. (Constitution). $19.95. ISBN 0-89490-922-3.

Judy Monroe's book puts the suffrage struggle into the context of constitutional history. Covering the annals of suffrage from Seneca Falls to the passage of the amendment, the book provides a good introduction for those unfamiliar with the topic. Monroe outlines the history of the Constitution and how an amendment is passed, and, in a final section, the author shows how the new law affected women in the 1920s as well as its continuing influence. Besides black-and-white illustrations, supplementary sections include the text of the Constitution, a glossary, notes, charts, suggestions for further reading, and an index. The book will be most useful in government studies. MH.

Shaw, Anna Howard. **Anna Howard Shaw: The Story of a Pioneer**. Cleveland: Pilgrim Press, 1994. 338p. $13.95pa. ISBN 0-8298-1018-8pa.

In her autobiography, Anna Howard Shaw tells the story of how, starting at the age of twelve, she managed her family's homestead in Michigan, caring for a disabled mother while her father worked in Massachusetts and enlisted in the Civil War. Determined to make her own way and searching for a field where she could do the most good, Shaw became both an ordained minister and a doctor; but she was convinced that only through enfranchisement could women achieve social equality, so she took up the suffrage cause. She worked for both nationwide suffrage organizations before they were reunited in 1890 as the National American Woman Suffrage Association. In 1904, she assumed the presidency of this group and held that post for almost twelve years. *The Story of a Pioneer* was written near the end of Shaw's presidential term and enumerated many of the suffrage battles at the turn of the century. As a close friend to Susan B. Anthony, Shaw wrote several laudatory chapters on "Aunt Susan" as well as detailing Shaw's own service as a minister. Because few suffrage leaders left autobiographies, Shaw's is all the more important. It is the portrait of a woman pioneer in many fields. The book contains black-and-white photographs, but, alas, no index. MHCA.

Sherr, Lynn. **Failure Is Impossible: Susan B. Anthony in Her Own Words**. New York: Times Books, 1995. 384p. $15.00pa. ISBN 0-8129-2718-4pa.

Susan B. Anthony's life story is told through her own words, introduced and explained by Lynn Sherr, in *Failure Is Impossible*. Anthony kept copious diaries, scrapbooks, and memorabilia, which made this near-autobiography possible. Anthony's voice enables her powerful personality to emerge. She had a sense of humor, but it could be eclipsed by the important messages she felt the world must hear and understand. Sherr's book is illustrated with black-and-white photographs (some of Anthony's artifacts), illustrations, and documents. Boxed inserts contain such humorous and interesting facts as newspaper reporters' fondness for Anthony's omnipresent red shawl; they would not file their reports unless she was wearing it. Anthony's last public words were "failure is impossible," and Sherr's book imparts the full sense of Anthony as common woman and enduring legend. One color photograph depicts the stained glass window memorial to Anthony in the A.M.E.

Zion Church in Rochester, New York; notes, a bibliography, and an index are included. HCA.

Stanton, Elizabeth Cady. **Eighty Years and More: Reminiscences, 1815–1897**. Boston: Northeastern University Press, 1993. 490p. $15.95pa. ISBN 1-55553-137-7pa.

> The true nature of Elizabeth Cady Stanton comes through in her reminiscences. Cady Stanton hoped that these more personal sketches of herself as a wife, a reformer, a mother, and an "enthusiastic" housekeeper would amuse future generations. The text is taken from Cady Stanton's diary, with supplementary opinion and accounts added; Cady Stanton dedicated the book, first published in 1898, to Susan B. Anthony. The book is humorous in tone as it illuminates the many period personalities that Cady Stanton knew, worked with, and entertained, as well as the lives of her own seven children. With an introduction by Ellen Carol DuBois and an afterword by Ann D. Gordon, *Eighty Years and More* includes black-and-white photographs and a name index. The book will serve history collections as a primary source and add to biography collections. HCA.

Stevens, Doris. **Jailed for Freedom: American Women Win the Vote**. Edited by Carol O'Hare. Troutdale, OR: NewSage, 1995. 220p. $12.95pa. ISBN 0-939165-25-2pa.

> *Jailed for Freedom* is the original account of the militant tactics employed by the National Woman's Party to win the vote. The book was written in 1920 by party member Doris Stevens, who was herself incarcerated for the cause. It is edited for smoother reading by Carol O'Hare in this new edition, which keeps the drama of the incidents that began in 1913 with the first inauguration of Woodrow Wilson. Over a seven-year period, members of the NWP picketed the White House, which led to arrest and imprisonment; held hunger strikes; and endured forced feedings all to obtain the suffrage right they did not have. Although the account is one-sided and self-serving, it is important, for neither the National American Woman Suffrage Association nor the National Woman's Party acknowledged the accomplishments and contributions of the other in the final suffrage battle. Edith Mayo has written a complete introduction to the suffrage movement. Archival black-and-white photographs have been added to the text, as well as historical notes on the major personalities and important topics. Stevens includes a list of countries with woman suffrage in 1920 and a list of over 150 women who served sentences during the protest period (hundreds of others were arrested). *Jailed for Freedom* should be part of any serious suffrage collection. HCA.

Terborg-Penn, Rosalyn. **African American Women in the Struggle for the Vote, 1850–1920**. Bloomington: Indiana University Press, 1998. 192p. (Blacks in the Diaspora). $39.95; $16.95pa. ISBN 0-253-33378-4; 0-253-21176-Xpa.

> Scholar Rosalyn Terborg-Penn traces African American women in the suffrage movement from its beginnings in the 1850s, through the middle years

of the 1870s and 1880s, and to the ratification of the Nineteenth Amendment. Among the Black women who had worked to achieve suffrage were Mary Ann Shadd Cary, Ida B. Wells-Barnett, Angelina Weld Grimké, and Mary Church Terrell. Terborg-Penn documents many others, as well as African American women's organizations that contributed to the cause by developing their own strategies and ideas and responding to those who opposed Black woman suffrage. Tracing Black women as early voters and candidates, the author also illustrates the efforts in the southern states to disenfranchise Black women after 1920. Terborg-Penn's book includes black-and-white photographs, notes, a selected bibliography, and an index. HCA.

Van Voris, Jacqueline. **Carrie Chapman Catt: A Public Life**. New York: Feminist Press, 1987. 307p. $13.95pa. ISBN 1-55861-139-8pa.

Jacqueline Van Voris credits Carrie Chapman Catt with the organizational plan and leadership that finally achieved woman suffrage after a more than seventy-year effort. Catt was married twice and lost both husbands. Receiving nearly a million dollars, designated for the suffrage cause, from the estate of Mrs. Frank Leslie, Catt was a woman of means and a woman of ways with her centrist understanding of politics. Catt became president of the National American Woman Suffrage Association in 1915 when the movement was again dividing. A splinter group, the National Woman's Party, led by Alice Paul, favored much more radical tactics. Catt's devotion of suffrage, even through the years of World War I, her fairness, her hard work, and her inspiration won her much respect. In 1919, Catt called for the formation of the League of Women Voters, and, after the passage of the Nineteenth Amendment, she devoted her time to peace activity, a neglected part of her lifetime legacy that is fully disclosed here. Each of the five sections of Van Voris's book are headed with a black-and-white portrait of Catt from different stages of her life; notes, a bibliography, and an index are included. As a highly respected public figure, Catt deserves a place in biography collections. HCA.

Wheeler, Marjorie Spruill, ed. **One Woman, One Vote: Rediscovering the Woman Suffrage Movement**. Troutdale, OR: NewSage, 1995. 388p. $18.95pa. ISBN 0-939165-26-0pa.

Published to commemorate the seventy-fifth anniversary of the Nineteenth Amendment, *One Woman, One Vote* is a collection of nineteen essays by distinguished historians, including Linda K. Kerber, Alice S. Rossi, Ellen Carol DuBois, Rosalyn Terborg-Penn, and Nancy F. Cott, as well as some of the participants in the suffrage movement such as Jane Addams. Adding to scholarship on the topic, the research covers a wide range of topics: suffrage militance in the 1870s, western suffrage, the Woman's Christian Temperance Union, antisuffrage women, working women, and socialist women. Marjorie Wheeler offers a brief overview of the entire movement in a book that is scattered with black-and-white illustrations. Two notable appendices list state-by-state suffrage legislation and a time line of congressional actions.

Notes on the contributors, suggested readings, and an index finish the book, which is appropriate for expanding suffrage collections. HCA.

Wolff, Francie. **Give the Ballot to the Mothers: Songs of the Suffragists, A History in Song**. Springfield, MO: Denlinger's, 1998. 144p. $31.95pa. ISBN 0-87714-191-6pa.

A wonderful accompaniment to the video by the same name listed below, *Give the Ballot to the Mothers* contains the sheet music and lyrics to twenty-six songs, with source notes and explanations for each one. The book is spiral-bound for ease in playing the music and is divided into three sections: rally songs, songs of persuasion, and popular songs; each section is a treasure trove of suffrage illustrations, cartoons, and pictures. One song has been updated for contemporary use, and a bibliography is included. Neither the book nor the video contains a complete history of the suffrage movement, and they should not be expected to do so. The focus is on the music, which leads to a more humanistic, rather than political, view of the struggle to win the vote. Music students and historians will appreciate *Give the Ballot to the Mothers*, which will be popular in schools with integrated curriculums and where the suffrage movement is taught in depth. The items may also find uses in communities with active women's clubs. MHCA.

Non-Book Material

Amendment 19: Women's Right to Vote. Produced and directed by Rhonda Fabian and Jerry Baber. 7 min. Films for the Humanities and Sciences, 1998. (Amendments to the Constitution: Bill of Rights and Beyond). Videocassette. $49.95.

With its focus on constitutional law, this film is suitable for government classes because it places women's voting rights in relation to all constitutional history and all voting rights. Using color and black-and-white photographs and documents, the film gives a brief history of women's voting and the struggle for the Susan B. Anthony Amendment. Anthony and Elizabeth Cady Stanton are the only suffragists mentioned. After the passage of the Nineteenth Amendment, litigation centered around the state's rights issue in granting voting rights. Because the Equal Rights Amendment failed to pass, full equality for women is not guaranteed by the Constitution, but this has not prevented women from making advances in economic, social, and political equality. Its brief length structures the film as an introduction, and teachers will want to fill in historical details. HC.

Dekock, Paul. **Debate at Seneca Falls**. El Cajon, CA: Interact, 1992. Simulation. $34.00.

Debate at Seneca Falls is a classroom simulation to promote the understanding of the issues raised at the 1848 Woman's Rights Convention at Seneca Falls surrounding the social, legal, and religious customs of the nineteenth century.

The student guide lays out the background to the first convention on woman's rights and presents Elizabeth Cady Stanton's "Declaration of Sentiments" and the resolutions she presented to the assembly. In the simulation, the twelve resolutions are condensed to four motions, with eight students speaking, pro and con, about each motion, and using handouts, which are included. Each class member is responsible for tracking the arguments on each motion and for voting on each. Females in the class are given two votes to ensure passage of the resolutions, because many more women than men were present at Seneca Falls. Costumes and other special touches can add an authentic flavor to the debates, which end with debriefing questions to ensure students' understanding. The teacher's guide is well organized and includes all the elements necessary to carry out the activity, designed to last four days, in social studies classes. HC.

Dreams of Equality. Produced and directed by Allen Mondell and Cynthia Salzman Mondell. 28 min. Media Projects, 1994. Videocassette. Purchase $95.00; Rental $50.00.

Produced for the National Park Service in conjunction with the Women's Rights National Historic Park, *Dreams of Equality* portrays the woman's rights issues of the nineteenth century through the correspondence of Lucy Griswold, an attendee at the 1848 Seneca Falls Woman's Rights Convention, with her brother, Silas. In live-action dramatizations, acted in period costumes and accurate settings, Lucy prepares for the journey to Seneca Falls as her voice-over narration describes her excitement to her brother. In his responses, Silas emerges as a rather traditional man of the time. Although he is an abolitionist, he believes man offers woman the greatest protection, making education, career, and legal rights unnecessary. The dramatized sequences of the letters between Lucy and Silas are the most effective part of the film, which is marred by trying to do too much. It includes cuts of adolescent pairs of girls and boys discussing (in some cases arguing over) the status of women's rights today. The film narration between the dramatized sequences, which fills in historical facts in a straightforward accurate manner, is accompanied by black-and-white illustrations, documents, and newspapers. Unfortunately, the film contains too many cuts, such as the ones that interrupt Elizabeth Cady Stanton's reading of the Declaration of Sentiments. Although the purpose of the added scenes is to provide examples of the injustices of which Cady Stanton speaks, the result is confusing because the quickened pace tends to confound the message. Teachers can help to sort out how women did not have the right to vote, to attend college, to speak within their churches, to own property, or to pursue a vocation. In the concluding letter, Lucy provides the money for her granddaughter to attend medical school. The women of Seneca Falls would not live to see the right to vote procured by the Nineteenth Amendment, but the ending of the film shows a series of black-and-white still pictures of the protests that would bring about the right to vote as well as other women's firsts. These pictures are not narrated, but are generally recognizable historic events. Although better editing could have produced a stronger film, the major battles and problems for women in the 1800s are portrayed truthfully. Teachers of history and women's studies will want to be familiar with the film before using it so that they can smooth over the jumpy sequences. MHCA.

Elizabeth Cady Stanton and Susan B. Anthony. Produced by Marcus Keys. Directed by R. J. DeMaio. 24 min. Films for the Humanities and Sciences, 1983. (Against the Odds). Videocassette. $89.95.

> The film is almost misnamed because it spends as much time covering the British woman suffrage movement and the push for the Nineteenth Amendment, both of which occurred after the deaths of Elizabeth Cady Stanton and Susan B. Anthony, as it does covering their lives and careers. Although these two women were key players in the early suffrage movement, they are only briefly profiled here. Similarly, a few other women in the suffrage movement are mentioned, but receive no coverage. Bill Bixby begins the film's narration with an overview of woman's rights in the nineteenth century and the first woman's rights convention at Seneca Falls, New York. Cady Stanton and Anthony and the woman suffrage movement are accounted for before the video notably outlines the suffrage movement in England and of how the events there, spearheaded by Emmeline Pankhurst, led to similar styles of protest on this side of the Atlantic, which helped to achieve the vote. After relating the ratification of the Nineteenth Amendment, the narration turns to 1983 where, under the credits, unidentified women talk about their current conditions. The film includes black-and-white and color photographs and film clips. As an overview of the suffrage movement here and abroad, the video is a good starting point for more in-depth research, especially into the suffrage personalities. HCA.

Give the Ballot to the Mothers: Songs of the Suffragists. Produced and directed by Francie Wolff. 28 min. Delinger's, 1996. Videocassette. $35.00.

> A fun way to approach the suffrage movement is through its music, which comes together in this unique video, the work of Francie Wolff. Wolff narrates the video along with colleague Cynthia Green Libby, conveying not only the music of the seventy-two year suffrage movement, but the conscience of the time and the people. The video contains fourteen songs vocalized by men, women, and groups, with melodies that are both original and familiar. A remarkable job of finding suffrage documents, sheet-music covers, cartoons, photographs, and film, adds to the narration, which includes many quotations from men and women, known and unknown, who lived during the time. Imparting many little-known tidbits of the suffrage movement that are not included in other accounts, the video includes dress, symbols, banners, and stereotypes both of the suffragettes and of the "antis." The video concludes with some reenactments photographed during the seventy-fifth anniversary of suffrage. MHCA.

Laura Clay: Voice of Change. Directed by Heather Lyons. 56 min. Cinema Guild, 1992. Videocassette. Purchase $350.00; Rental $95.00.

Laura Clay is a controversial figure; although she played a major role in the suffrage movement, she is not well known. Clay's position in the movement was difficult because she was a Southern woman, an aristocratic daughter of Kentucky. Her mother ran the family estate and believed strongly in education for all her children. As the acting head of the household, Clay's mother came to believe in woman's rights and brought her daughters into the suffrage movement after the Civil War. Clay served as president of the Kentucky Woman Suffrage Association, formed the Kentucky Equal Rights Association, and worked within the National American Woman Suffrage Association, traveling to Oregon and Arizona to work in their state suffrage campaigns. When the Nineteenth Amendment was proposed, Clay worked against it, believing suffrage would be achieved through state measures, as was already happening in many states. As a believer in states' rights, she insisted this was the proper procedure, but the conviction alienated her from the movement. The film uses dramatic reenactments, interviews with historians, and the presentation of a wide variety of documents to portray Laura Clay, who emerges as a complex person. The locations and documentation are exceptional, including a film clip of Carrie Chapman Catt reading from the Seneca Falls "Declaration of Sentiments." Clay's story imparts a more comprehensive view of the suffrage movement, and the film can be used where the suffrage movement is studied in depth. HCA.

Lee, Myrra. **Elizabeth Cady Stanton**. El Cajon, CA: Interact, 1993. Simulation. (Great American Lives). $22.00.

Interact is a company specializing in participatory classroom activities. This simulation on the life of Elizabeth Cady Stanton will make the social conditions of the nineteenth century come alive. Cady Stanton, Susan B. Anthony's closest friend, was a visionary of the early woman's rights movement; she worked a lifetime for abolition, women's property rights, education, dress reform, and religious equality. The activity is based on the *This Is Your Life* television program of the 1950s. Cady Stanton is introduced as the honored guest, and important people in her life visit and are interviewed about their relationships to her. Some of the guests, for whom all scripts are included, are Cady Stanton's mother, father, and daughter, Amelia Bloomer, Susan B. Anthony, William Lloyd Garrison, Frederick Douglass, and Horace Greeley. There are parts for fourteen members of a classroom, but other class members participate by taking notes about the speakers on the "Studio Audience Form." Two student evaluations are included, a matching quiz, and an essay question. Extensive background material is provided for the teacher, as well as suggestions for timing the activity, preparation, and special flourishes. For teachers interested in creating more dynamic classrooms, the simulation is perfect for social studies or drama classes with advanced middle school students and above. MH.

Not for Ourselves Alone: The Story of Elizabeth Cady Stanton and Susan B. Anthony. Produced by Ken Burns and Paul Barnes. 2 parts, 90 min. ea. PBS Video, 1999. Videocassette. $29.98.

Ken Burns and Paul Barnes portray Elizabeth Cady Stanton and Susan B. Anthony side-by-side from their young womanhood through their more than fifty years of friendship and alliance in work for woman's rights. The film is framed by an introduction and an epilogue depicting women who participated in the final push for suffrage and voted for the first time in the 1920 election. They achieved the vote that Cady Stanton and Anthony spent their lives working for but never lived to see. The film uses color film of historical locations and interviews with a number of contemporary historians, black-and-white period film, and numerous black-and-white still photographs to tell the story of the two woman's rights pioneers. Innumerable quotations from the writings of Cady Stanton and Anthony, as well as others, are read throughout the video, but it is the narration written by Geoffrey C. Ward and read by Sally Kellerman that advances the story. Cady Stanton could never live up to the expectations of her father, who lost four sons, and she alienated him by marrying an abolitionist. She was the philosopher in her partnership with Anthony, but she was more radical, supporting divorce and challenging religious doctrine with her *Woman's Bible*. Anthony was always independently inclined, a strong organizer with leadership abilities who started out in the temperance and abolition movements. For over half a century her work for woman's rights and suffrage was single-minded as she traveled, wrote, spoke, and organized. The strength of *Not for Ourselves Alone* is in showing the relationship between the two women, a lasting bond that grew and changed but never broke. The video does a good job in presenting the lives of both women, portraying the political tactics they employed over the years, some of which were successful and many of which were not; however, the program stops short of discussing the most embarrassing episodes in the history of the suffrage movement, Anthony's endorsements of George Francis Train and Victoria Woodhull. How these may have set the suffrage movement back is never discussed. The video is suitable for general audiences and also can be used in classroom settings. MHCA.

One Woman, One Vote. Produced by Ruth Pollak. 106 min. PBS Video, 1995. (The American Experience). Videocassette. $79.95.

Narrated by Susan Sarandon, this film is the most comprehensive view of the seventy-two-year struggle for women's right to vote. Although its coverage of the final push to the vote is excellent, the film is a little light-handed with the early years of the suffrage movement. It profiles Elizabeth Cady Stanton, Susan B. Anthony, and Lucy Stone, but fails to mention the many other notable women involved in the early years or the obstacles they had to overcome to be heard. The film profiles the involvement of Carrie Chapman Catt, Alice Stone Blackwell, Mary Church Terrell, Harriet Stanton Blatch, Anna Howard Shaw, Alice Paul, Lucy Burns, and Maud Wood Park. The tactics of the woman suffrage movement in Great Britain that radicalized the movement in the United States are defined, and the treatment of the American suffragists arrested for protesting in front of the White House is shockingly revealed. The divisiveness over strategies between the National American Woman Suffrage Association and the National Woman's Party is continuously stressed. When the Nineteenth Amendment passed the House of Representatives, the Senate, and state ratification, in each case, it passed by only one vote. The film never theorizes as to why suffrage took so long; it seems that the complete story of suffrage is yet to be told. Until that happens, *One Woman, One Vote* gives the best coverage. The film is divided into fourteen sections for easier use in classroom settings. HCA.

Susan B. Anthony House. 1999. 17 Madison Street, Rochester, NY 14608. 716-235-6124. URL: http://www.susanbanthonyhouse.org/main.html.

A virtual tour of the historic home of Susan B. Anthony, where she was arrested for illegally voting in 1872, is the highlight of this site. Information and pictures are plentiful, as well as biographical information, a time line, and links to other sites. Teachers may use the site for a virtual field trip, and researchers will enjoy seeing the artifacts. MHCA.

The Trial of Susan B. Anthony. Directed by Burt Brinckerhoff. Produced by Vern Diamond. 22 min. Phoenix Learning Group, 1971. (You Are There). Videocassette. Purchase $225.00; Rental $72.00.

On June 18, 1873, Susan B. Anthony was tried for having voted in a national election during a period when women were not enfranchised. The nineteenth-century struggle for woman's rights and woman suffrage is uncovered through the *You Are There* format: With Walter Cronkite as anchor, multiple reporters interview subjects who reenact the incidents. The video gives scant background on Anthony, a teacher and Quaker turned reformer, who is arrested in the first scene. Anthony's friends Lucretia Mott and Elizabeth Cady Stanton do not appear in the film because they did not support her in her act of civil disobedience. The trial is moved from Rochester, New York, in an attempt to find an impartial jury; but the judge, Ward Hunt, who is firmly against suffrage, has already written a decision, and refuses to allow Anthony to speak in her own defense. Her lawyer, Henry Seldon, mounts a defense based on the Fourteenth and Fifteenth Amendments. District Attorney Crowley lets on that the jury will never be charged, and so it is. Judge Hunt throws out the arguments of the defense, finds Anthony guilty, and discharges the jury before they can deliberate. He fines Anthony $100 and court costs. When asked for a statement, Anthony finally has her say. Refusing to pay the fine, she declares that "resistance to tyranny is obedience to God." Colleen Dewhurst plays Susan B. Anthony in this production; beyond its historical utility, the film can be used alongside Henry David Thoreau's *Civil Disobedience* to illustrate the application of political protest. HCA.

Votes for Women: The Fight for Suffrage. 20 pieces with guide. Jackdaw Publications, 1992. Document portfolio. $35.00.

> Including documents from 1868 to 1917, *Votes for Women* covers the seventy-two-year history of the suffrage movement. The kit includes five historical essays that start from the beginnings of the suffrage movement, including the resolutions presented in 1848 at the Seneca Falls Woman's Rights Convention. The documents themselves include Susan B. Anthony's suffrage newspaper, *The Revolution*; publications and broadsides for and against suffrage; a resolution presented to Congress by suffragist Victoria C. Woodhull; sheet music supporting the cause; postcards sold to raise funds; a pledge-to-march card for a 1913 rally; and maps of the states where women could vote as a result of state legislation. The collection is remarkable for including the antisuffrage movement and the British suffrage movement. Many of the illustrations and artifacts come from the collection of the Museum of American Political Life, and the notes and guide include a bibliography and discussion questions. Teachers who concentrate on including primary source material in their instruction will appreciate this varied collection. MHCA.

Votes for Women?! The 1913 U.S. Senate Testimony. Produced by Jocelyn Riley. 17 min. Her Own Words, 1990. Videocassette. $95.00.

> *Votes for Women?!* introduces testimony given before the Senate committee charged with referring the Woman Suffrage Amendment to the full Senate in April 1913. The statements are narrated over color and black-and-white slides of suffrage artifacts and documents gleaned from collections in Wisconsin. Modern-day performers speak the parts of the reenacted committee introductions, which were made by Senator Charles S. Thomas of Colorado, who was the presiding officer. Speaking against the amendment was Kate Douglas Wiggin of New York, who was the author of *Rebecca of Sunnybrook Farm*. Belle Case La Follette of Wisconsin, the reformer and wife of "Fighting" Bob La Follette, spoke in favor of the amendment. Because the primary source material in the video makes it an excellent starting place for students who rarely hear historical congressional testimony, it can lead to classroom debates or other activities surrounding the study of suffrage. A resource guide, available for $45.00 and containing articles and cartoons published in 1913, as well as the script of the video, will prove extremely useful to teachers. HCA.

Reform

Books

Addams, Jane. **Twenty Years at Hull-House: With Autobiographical Notes**. New York: Penguin, 1998. 320p. (Penguin Twentieth Century Classics). $12.95pa. ISBN 0-14-118099-4pa.

> The founder of Hull House wrote her memoirs at the age of fifty after twenty years of involvement in Chicago politics and reform. Addams opens

the book by recalling her childhood in Illinois, where her father was a state senator and Lincoln devotee. After attending Rockford Female Seminary, Addams found herself unsuited to her desired career in medicine. She spent several years wandering through Europe before inventing a career in which she could "learn of life from life itself." With her friend Ellen Gates Starr, she purchased an aging mansion at Polk and Halstead streets and offered education, health, and social services to the Greeks, Italians, Russians, Germans, and Sicilians in the neighborhood. Addams admitted that she could hardly recall all the events that happened in a chronological order, so she offered topical consideration of how the settlement workers affected labor legislation in Illinois through their many social investigations. They learned to work with the city to better conditions in the Nineteenth Ward, all the while offering "clubs" that provided skills in cooking, sewing, child care, the arts, and any other trade that was needed. The book, which is indexed and illustrated with black-and-white sketches by a Hull House resident, does not go on to tell of Addams's long career in working for peace. It is, however, a first-hand account of the development of the field of sociology, and it belongs in every library. MHCA.

Cooper, Anna Julia. **The Voice of Anna Julia Cooper: Including *A Voice from the South* and Other Important Essays, Papers, and Letters**. Edited by Charles Lemert and Esme Bhan. Lanham, MD: Rowman and Littlefield, 1998. 357p. $61.00; $15.95pa. ISBN 0-8476-8407-5; 0-8476-8408-3pa.

The first Black woman to earn a doctorate degree, Anna Julia Cooper received her honor at the age of sixty-five after a lifetime of teaching and activism. Born in Raleigh, North Carolina before the Civil War, Cooper graduated from Oberlin College and taught across the United States. She was selected, as a representative from her gender and race, to speak at the Chicago World's Columbian Exposition in 1893. Her most important work, *A Voice from the South*, a collection of essays written between 1886 and 1892, supported equal education for men and women based on aptitude. As a high school principal in Washington, D.C., she was dismissed because of her high standards. Considered an early Black feminist, Cooper lectured on education, race, and manners, which she considered imperative to a civilized society. Her later interests included the history of slavery in colonies of France, the topic of her thesis from the Sorbonne, which she wrote in French. Introduced by Charles Lemert and including an index, Cooper's collected writings are revealing of an educated woman of the first generation out of slavery. HCA.

Daniels, Doris Groshen. **Always a Sister: The Feminism of Lillian D. Wald**. New York: Feminist Press, 1989. 207p. $12.95pa. ISBN 1-55861-113-4pa.

Doris Daniels's biography of Lillian D. Wald focuses on her life as a feminist, which influenced her life as an activist. As a major reformer of the Progressive era, Wald founded the Visiting Nurse Service and the Henry Street settlement house on the lower East Side of New York, where she witnessed first-hand the conditions of immigrant women living in the tenements. In the time before government subsidies for social work, Wald had to court wealthy patrons and government politicians so that she could fund her good works; to convert them to her causes, she emphasized straight facts. Daniels treats Wald's life topically, including her interests in nursing, education, working women, immigrants, and peace. With a career spanning seventy-three years, Wald deserves a place next to reformer Jane Addams. A section of black-and-white photographs, notes, bibliographical essays, and name and subjects indexes are appended. HCA.

Davis, Elizabeth Lindsay. **Lifting As They Climb**. New York: G. K. Hall, 1996. 424p. (African-American Women Writers, 1910–1940). $30.00. ISBN 0-7838-1419-4.

Illinois club woman Elizabeth Lindsay Davis wrote this history of the National Association of Colored Women in 1933, covering the development of the organization from its founding in 1895. The National Association of Colored Women was the largest organization of its kind, enrolling at its height up to 250,000 members from all over the nation. These women represented various regional interests in religion, business, politics, and literature, and membership included Mary Church Terrell, Mary McLeod Bethune, Madame C. J. Walker, Charlotte Hawkins Brown, and Anna Julia Cooper. The national organization was dedicated to "social embetterment" of Black women; but the work of the organization was carried out in the local branches, which awarded scholarships, provided services to orphans and wayward girls, and taught domestic improvement classes. The local achievements are chronicled in the history, which also sketches brief portraits of ninety-five Black women. Along with the narrative, the history contains a compendium of club documents and black-and-white photographs. The re-publication of *Lifting as They Climb* helps to restore the overlooked Black women's club movement to history. HCA.

Frankel, Noralee, and Nancy S. Dye, eds. **Gender, Class, Race, and Reform in the Progressive Era**. Lexington: University Press of Kentucky, 1991. 202p. $15.95pa. ISBN 0-8131-0841-1pa.

The Progressive era was characterized by industrial growth, corporate ascension, and urban expansion. Because of their domestic interests in clean food, family welfare, and education, women played a major role in reform, especially to end child labor and industrial piece work; however, not all women saw reforms in the same way. The twelve essays published here, from papers presented at the 1988 Conference on Women in the Progressive Era, show that issues of race, class, and ethnicity influenced how women perceived and participated in reform. Many of the scholars are well known: Nancy A. Hewitt, Alice Kessler-Harris, Molly Ladd-Taylor, Barbara Sicherman, Rosalyn Terborg-Penn, and Ellen Carol DuBois. Their topics cover African American women fighting segregation in Atlanta, working-class neighborhoods, Alice Hamilton, Hull House, and the antilynching crusade. While illustrating the variety of approaches to reform among different groups of women, they also show the complexity of the Progressive era. Notes on the contributors and an index are included. HCA.

Giele, Janet Zollinger. **Two Paths to Women's Equality: Temperance, Suffrage, and the Origins of Modern Feminism**. New York: Twayne, 1995. 295p. (Social Movements Past and Present). $29.95; $16.95pa. ISBN 0-8057-9700-9; 0-8057-4523-8pa.

> Over thirty years in the writing, Janet Giele's book traces the history of the temperance and the suffrage movements and compares their tactics, expressed in the publications of the groups, and the leadership of the organizations. Using new research on social movements, the author explains how the two groups laid the groundwork for the later feminist movement, and traces women's social movements from 1920 to the 1990s. Giele views the groups as equal because the feminism of the temperance group, centered on social issues such as alcoholism, poverty, and violence, as well as the politically focused ideology of the suffragists were needed to change women's traditional roles. The history of women's movements and the emergence of American feminism between 1830 and 1870 are also covered. Appendices detailing the author's analysis of the contents of the group's newspapers and comparison of biographical data on the leaders of the organizations as well as notes, references, and an index are included. HCA.

Keller, Helen. **The Story of My Life**. New York: Signet, 1988. $4.99pa. ISBN 0-451-52447-0pa.

> Helen Keller, born in 1880, was not blind, deaf, and mute at birth. Illness in her nineteenth month left her in darkness until the age of six, when Annie Sullivan became her teacher. Helen quickly learned the manual alphabet and how to write, and later she learned to speak with difficulty. *The Story of My Life* was written in Keller's sophomore year at Radcliffe College, where Sullivan accompanied her. The book is a testimonial to both women, to Sullivan for her teaching convictions, and to Keller for her courage and example. Because of Keller, those with physical challenges were able to seek equal educational opportunities and equal civil rights within society. MHCA.

McMurry, Linda O. **To Keep the Waters Troubled: The Life of Ida B. Wells**. New York: Oxford University Press, 1998. 400p. $30.00. ISBN 0-19-508812-3.

> Linda McMurry has written a complete biography of Ida B. Wells, attending to her childhood and the first half of her adult life, times that Wells did not treat fully in her own autobiography. Using Wells's writings and the accounts of others, McMurry traces her subject from her birth into slavery in Holly Springs, Mississippi through her long career as an activist for African American causes, especially against lynching. When Wells was orphaned at the age of sixteen, she taught school to support her siblings. At twenty, she sued a railroad company for removing her from a first-class coach.

Always one to speak out against injustice, her criticism of her employers in the school district, just as she was beginning her writing career in Memphis, caused her to be dismissed from her teaching job and forced her to write full time. Her watershed event was the lynching of friend Tom Moss in 1892; her outcry against this event as editor of the Memphis *Free Speech* caused a local backlash and closed the newspaper. From the 1890s until her death, Wells was involved in all significant African American events and reform movements, and she always placed race issues ahead of all others. Her gender and her singular focus alienated her from many, but also gained her respect for her unwavering view. With black-and-white illustrations and many quotations, *To Keep the Waters Troubled* includes notes, a bibliography, and an index. HCA.

Ovington, Mary White. **Black and White Sat Down Together: The Reminiscences of an NAACP Founder**. Edited by Ralph E. Luker. New York: Feminist Press, 1995. 167p. $19.95; $10.95pa. ISBN 1-55861-099-5; 1-55861-156-8pa.

First published in the *Baltimore Afro-American* in 1932 and 1933 in order to explain to the newspaper's Black audience why a white women would devote her life to this cause, Mary White Ovington's memoir details her history and her lifelong involvement with the National Association for the Advancement of Colored People (NAACP). A New Yorker by birth, Ovington did settlement-house work and investigated employment and housing problems for Black people in the city. Ovington was much maligned for attending biracial club dinner meetings, organized for the purpose of exchanging ideas, including Socialist ideas. Present during the organization of the NAACP in 1909, Ovington held continuous membership and served on the board of directors from 1919 until her retirement in 1947. The book is not a history of the organization, but does recount a variety of racial incidents that influenced one woman to find this organization important. MHCA.

Schneider, Dorothy, and Carl J. Schneider. **American Women in the Progressive Era, 1900–1920**. New York: Facts on File, 1993. 276p. $29.95. ISBN 0-8160-2513-4.

Drawing on letters, memoirs, and magazines, *American Women in the Progressive Era* covers the extensive range of activities in which women participated during the first twenty years of the twentieth century. In a well-documented text containing many pictures and quotations, the authors discuss women in the new labor-saving home, at work, in the labor movement, in the club movement, in settlement houses, in the suffrage movement, in the peace movement, and in the World War I effort at home and abroad. Changes for Black women and changes in sexual relations are also covered. With its bibliography and index, the book has tremendous research potential. MHCA.

Sklar, Kathryn Kish. **Florence Kelley and the Nation's Work: The Rise of Women's Political Culture, 1830–1900**. New Haven, CT: Yale University Press, 1995. 436p. $37.50. ISBN 0-300-05912-4.

> In the first of what is to be a two-volume work, Kathryn Kish Sklar uncovers Florence Kelley's background and life through her fortieth year. The strength of Sklar's book, which won the Berkshire Prize, lies in its weaving of the roots of reform history and political history into the biographical format. Kelley was born to a tariff-supporting senator father and a Quaker mother. She graduated from Cornell University and wanted to go on to law school, but was turned down because of her sex. When she finally earned her law degree twelve years later, she prosecuted labor abuse cases, which she uncovered as a resident of Hull House. Before she took up this work, Kelley toured Europe, was converted to Socialism, and married a Russian doctor. Returning with him to the United States, she participated in the Socialist Labor Party in New York City while raising her three children, but her marriage fell apart. Moving to Illinois, where the divorce laws were more lenient, Kelley joined Hull House as a labor investigator employed by the governor. Her work as general secretary for the National Consumers' League is the subject of the next volume. Notes, bibliography, and index complete this highly researched study appropriate for biography readers as well as researchers. HCA.

Stebner, Eleanor J. **The Women of Hull House: A Study in Spirituality, Vocation, and Friendship**. Albany: State University of New York Press, 1997. 246p. $19.95pa. ISBN 0-7914-3488-5pa.

> As an assistant professor of theology, Eleanor Stebner uses the themes of spirituality, vocation, and friendship to characterize the residents of Hull House. She presents her work in two parts: the context of Hull House as part of the settlement house movement and as part of Chicago at the end of the nineteenth century, and a group biography including nine women associated with Hull House, three portrayed in relation to each of three themes. Jane Addams, Ellen Gates Starr, and Mary Keyser, the housekeeper, illustrate spirituality or openness to the experiences of people and acknowledgment of the mystery of life. Alice Hamilton, Julia Lathrop, and Florence Kelley demonstrate the trait of vocation, a job as an expression of spirituality. Wealthy patrons Helen Culver, Louise deKoven Bowen, and Mary Rozet Smith portray friendship. A photograph of each woman and several other photographs are included. With notes, a bibliography, and an index, Stebner's study brings new meaning to the Hull House community. HCA.

Terrell, Mary Church. **A Colored Woman in a White World**. New York: G. K. Hall, 1996. 437p. (African-American Women Writers, 1910–1940). $30.00. ISBN 0-7838-1421-6.

> Although Mary Church Terrell grew up privileged, her main concern throughout her life was the advancement of the Black race. Terrell's parents, Memphis mulattos who both owned their own businesses, never spoke to her about slavery. They sent her north to be educated, and Terrell completed

the "gentlemen's course" at Oberlin, which was reserved for male students and required the study of Greek. Although her father opposed her working, Terrell felt an obligation to put her education to use and began teaching. After her marriage, when she could no longer pursue her career because only single women were allowed to teach, she joined community work, lecturing and writing on woman's rights, the advancement of Black women, Black history, and discrimination. She spoke before the National American Woman Suffrage Association and picketed the White House with the National Woman's Party. She traveled and lectured oversees several times, addressing the Women's International League for Peace and Freedom in 1919. She was a founding member of both the National Association of Colored Women and the National Association for the Advancement of Colored People (NAACP), and she believed these organizations were necessary and helpful to the race. Terrell enjoyed a social and economic position that allowed her to press for advances; however, she faced discrimination herself and sometimes chose to pass for white, which she was not proud of, to avoid segregated situations. Her autobiography, self-published in 1940, details her work in these various fields over a lifetime. MHCA.

Non-Book Material

Belle: The Life and Writings of Belle Case La Follette. Produced by Jocelyn Riley. 15 min. Her Own Words, 1987. Videocassette. $95.00.

The life of Belle Case La Follette is well depicted in this short film made up of black-and-white and color slides. Family photographs, documents, and artifacts are shown under narration from La Follette's writings. As the first woman to complete a law degree at the University of Wisconsin, La Follette did not enter the field of law, but enjoyed a noteworthy career as a teacher, mother, politician's wife, and magazine editor. She supported "Fighting" Bob La Follette of Wisconsin in his career as governor, senator, and presidential candidate. Together, they began *La Follette's Magazine*, which she continued to operate after her husband's death and which turned into *The Progressive*. Belle La Follette was outspoken on many of the issues of her day, believing in woman's suffrage, dress reform, exercise for health, and peace. This less well-known woman is certainly deserving of consideration in social studies classes and as part of regional studies. A resource guide to assist the educator is available for $45.00. MHCA.

Helen Keller: In Her Story. Produced by Nancy Hamilton. 56 min. Phoenix Learning Group, 1953. Videocassette. Purchase $295.00; Rental $50.00.

Although made in black-and-white in 1953, this film is an absolute gem, showing Helen Keller at seventy-three years of age with all her humor, good spirits, and love of life shining through. Keller was born in 1880, but at nineteen months, illness left her blind, deaf, and mute. She remained helpless in this condition until the end of her sixth year, when her mother read about the advances being made in teaching the blind and employed Annie Sullivan to instruct Helen. Sullivan was able to reach through the terrible darkness, and within months Helen was learning to write. She was a published author by the time she was ten years old. Together, Sullivan and Keller went to Radcliffe, where Helen graduated cum laude in 1919, the first person with her triple challenge to accomplish this task. The film shows Keller meeting Robert Smith, who was the only other college graduate at that time facing the same challenges. Keller worked as an inspiring speaker for the prevention of blindness. She regretted that her ability to speak was not stronger, but she did not let this stop her from traveling the world. The film is filled with newsreels of her extensive travels, and also follows her at her home in Akron Ridge, Connecticut, in her day-to-day activities. The video contains one fuzzy audio spot, which probably occurred when it was adapted from the film version. Narrated by Katharine Cornell, this inspirational video is an absolute must in any curriculum teaching Keller's *The Story of My Life*. The video includes the only footage of Annie Sullivan Macy talking, and seeing the teacher and student together will deeply affect all viewers. Teachers' training programs and public libraries will especially want to consider *Helen Keller* for purchase. MHCA.

Hull House: The House That Jane Built. Directed by Tim Ward. 58 min. Cinema Guild, 1990. Videocassette. Purchase, $350.00; Rental $95.00.

Hull House features a varied production of archival pictures and film; close-ups of narrator Ellen Burstyn; and characterizations of six remarkable women who lived in Chicago's Hull House presented by practiced actresses. Although background to each of these women is given, the film primarily portrays the history of the settlement house from its founding in 1889 over a twelve-year period through the turn of the twentieth century. Jane Addams, the founder of Hull House, was a college-educated woman of means who was disappointed with her meaningless life and determined to be useful. By buying a house in a poor, immigrant neighborhood in Chicago, Addams helped individuals and brought about changes for workers everywhere. She carefully selected the young women who lived in Hull House, and the settlement touched and improved the neighborhood because the women knew the conditions there. Ellen Gates Starr, an art lover and organizer for causes, co-founded Hull House. Others staff members included Julia Lathrop, a social researcher; Mary Kenney, a union organizer; Florence Kelley, an investigator and reformer whose work inspired state legislation to halt sweat shops; and Dr. Alice Hamilton, a medical researcher whose studies of toxic substances forced protective legislation. Hull House was remarkable for being the first institution of its kind, and the achievements of the women residents advanced beneficial social change. Addams founded the field of social work, and each of the other women enjoyed a more than successful career. This film about young women who started with a simple idea may inspire young people, who often feel that they cannot make a difference, and it will be useful for classes in history and sociology. MHCA.

Temperance and Prohibition. 1999. Ohio State University Department of History, 106 Dulles Hall, 230 W. Seventeenth Avenue, Columbus, OH 43210. 614-292-2674; fax 614-292-2282. E-mail: kerr.6@osu.edu. URL: http://www.history.ohio-state.edu/projects/prohibition/.

> Professor K. Austin Kerr of Ohio State University has mounted a nicely arranged, accessible collection of materials on the temperance movement and prohibition. Included are pictures, documents, and information of national and local (Ohio) interest. The Woman's Crusade of 1873 and Frances Willard, leader of the Woman's Christian Temperance Union, are covered, and a limited number of links to other sites, all dealing with prohibition, are available. Because the site's strength lies in its one topic focus, history students will enjoy using it for research. MHCA.

Women and Social Movements in the United States, 1830–1930. 1999. State University of New York at Binghamton History Department, Binghamton, NY 13902-6000. E-mail: Kathryn Kish Sklar, Professor, kksklar@binghamton.edu. URL: http://womhist.binghamton.edu/.

> Rich in primary source documents, *Women and Social Movements in the United States* posts the projects of students at the State University of New York at Binghamton in which students ask a question and collect fifteen to twenty documents that relate to that question. The documents come from the papers of the Women's Trade Union League, the National Association of Colored Women, the National Consumers' League, the Henry Street and Hull House settlements, the National Woman's Party, and the Women's International League for Peace and Freedom. The well-organized site is intended for use by high school and college students in American history and women's history classes. It is possible to search the site, and some additional links are available. The only caution for teachers is that the approximately sixteen projects posted here may not remain stable as newer ones are added and older ones removed. HCA.

World War I

Books

Gavin, Lettie. **American Women in World War I: They Also Served**. Niwot: University Press of Colorado, 1997. 295p. $29.95. ISBN 0-87081-432-X.

> Lettie Gavin divides her comprehensive study of women serving in World War I into nine sections describing organizations that sent women overseas: the Navy, the Marines, the Army Signal Corps, army nurses, army reconstruction aides, the YMCA, independent physicians, the Red Cross, and the Salvation Army. Although other countries recognized the necessity of using women in the war effort and sent them to the front, the United States was very slow to do this, causing branches of the armed services to borrow women from other countries. The Navy was the first to enlist women, over

11,000 yeomen who served in clerical jobs, and the Marines also recruited before the war was over. Many women in the armed services held no rank and received no benefits after the war, and some women had to find their own way to France, especially badly needed female doctors. Gavin uses interviews, diaries, and letters to personalize the experiences of those who led the way in professionalizing military careers. Her book includes black-and-white photographs for every chapter; a map; information on chemical warfare and shell shock; a list of women who were killed, wounded, or decorated during the war; and an index. It is suitable for collections on military history, World War I, and women's history. MHCA.

Greenwald, Maurine Weiner. **Women, War, and Work: The Impact of World War I on Women Workers in the United States**. Ithaca, NY: Cornell University Press, 1990. 309p. $15.95pa. ISBN 0-8014-9733-7pa.

Maurine Greenwald uses case studies to explore the impact of World War I on women workers. After showing how women were shifting from the service industries to business industries in the fifty years leading up to the war, Greenwald goes on to examine the railroad, streetcar, and telephone job sectors. Each area merits special consideration. The federal government ran the railroad between 1918 and 1920, and they also controlled telephone operations during the war when labor conflicts arose in that industry. Changes in the operations of streetcars precipitated class conflicts in several cities. The concept of working women was in flux during this time, even though women emerged from the war with a better concept of themselves as wage earners. Black-and-white photographs, illustrations, cartoons, sketches, graphs, notes, a bibliography, and an index are included. CA.

Non-Book Material

An American Nurse at War: The Story of World War I Red Cross Nurse Marion McCune Rice of Brattleboro, Vermont. Directed by Stephen Hooper. 36 min. An American Nurse at War, 1997. Videocassette. $39.95.

The material for this film came from 650 photographs and fifty letters produced by director Stephen Hooper's great-aunt during four years of Red Cross nursing service in France during World War I. Marion McCune Rice's original material is mixed with film footage and interviews to make an excellent documentary of both the course of World War I and the role of nurses. Rice was born in Brattleboro, Vermont, in 1882. With a degree in nursing and some tourist experience in Europe, she contacted the Red Cross in 1915 about volunteering overseas. Accompanied by three other nurses, she joined Dr. Ralph Fitch to form a team that would work together for the next four years in three different French hospitals. The major events of the war, the sinking of the Luisitania, trench warfare, mustard gas attacks, Wilson's declaration of war after the attacks on neutral ships, and the abdication of Wilhelm II are skillfully woven into the narrative of Rice's letters home describing hospital conditions. The nurses fought dirt, vermin, cold, and lack of supplies. At one point, rather than be recalled home, the nurses gave up their salaries and depended solely on donations to continue their work in creatively caring for both the physical and mental conditions of the men. Their inventiveness was carried into the operating theater, where new surgical methods were developed; and Rice's team was celebrated by the French government with some of its highest honors. The film footage of World War I is outstanding, and *An American Nurse at War* will supply collections where little on this period is available. The film will be an ace in courses that include *All Quiet on the Western Front.* MHCA.

New Milieu to New Millennium, 1920 to 2000

General

Books

Camp, Helen C. **Iron in Her Soul: Elizabeth Gurley Flynn and the American Left**. Pullman: Washington State University Press, 1995. 396p. $40.00; $28.00pa. ISBN 0-87422-105-6; 0-87422-106-4pa.

> As the "mortal enemy of capitalism," Elizabeth Gurley Flynn was the dominant radical of the twentieth century. A labor organizer by the time she was sixteen, Flynn took to the stump in New York City, stopping traffic on Broadway. Working for the Industrial Workers of the World (IWW or Wobblies), she organized all manner of labor strikes, and, supported by the American Civil Liberties Union, she defended Sacco and Vanzetti. After a ten-year retirement in the 1920s and 1930s for health reasons, Flynn officially joined the Communist Party in New York City, rising through the ranks to become the first female party chairman. She served a three-year prison sentence as an American political prisoner during the McCarthy era. When the communist movement declined, Flynn moved to the Soviet Union, where she died in 1964. In researching this keen biography, Helen Camp had access to Flynn's papers, FBI files, and people who had known her. The book, which will be used by biography readers and those researching the twentieth century, includes a section of black-and-white photographs, notes, bibliography, and an index. HCA.

Cook, Blanche Wiesen. **Eleanor Roosevelt: Volume One, 1884–1933**. New York: Penguin, 1992. 587p. $16.95pa. ISBN 0-14-009460-1pa.

Cook, Blanche Wiesen. **Eleanor Roosevelt: Volume Two, 1933–1938**. New York: Viking, 1999. 686p. $34.95. ISBN 0-670-84498-5.

Although Eleanor Roosevelt is commonly considered the first president's wife to expand the public role of the first lady, Blanche Cook's two-volume opus portrays Roosevelt as much more complex than universally imagined. Beginning with the privileged family background, volume one covers Eleanor's unhappy childhood, marriage to her cousin Franklin, family life as mother of six children, role as wife to a politician, and the upsetting scandal surrounding the uncovering of Franklin's affair with his secretary. Although the Roosevelts agreed to continue their marriage, they lived in separate domains, and Eleanor widened her circle of female friendships and returned to such fulfilling activities as teaching. The most surprising aspect of the book is Eleanor's more than close relationship with reporter Lorena Hickok, who often shared in family time. The first volume concludes after Franklin wins the presidential bid, and Eleanor prepares for life in the White House.

Volume two reveals the first six years of the presidential term during the Great Depression and the New Deal. Eleanor was active and influential in domestic concerns, including race, housing, and women's issues, often at odds with her husband. On the events occurring in Europe with the rise of Hitler, Eleanor had very little to say, which Cook explains within the social and political context of the 1930s. As a history professor and writer who met Eleanor on several occasions in her youth, Cook's research was made possible by the opening of the Hickok and Roosevelt archives. Considerably more than the first fifty-four years remains be told of Roosevelt's life, and, with her attention and technique, Cook will be the one to tell it. The detailed volumes contain sections of black-and-white photographs, notes, bibliographies, and indices. HCA.

Felder, Deborah G. **A Century of Women: The Most Influential Events in Twentieth-Century Women's History**. Secaucus, NJ: Birch Lane, 1999. 368p. $27.50. ISBN 1-55972-485-4.

"The influential events that have shaped the destiny of women" throughout the last 100 years are presented in this time line of articles covering the fields of psychology, fashion, labor, health, education, politics, the arts, journalism, and sociology. Author Deborah Felder chooses between four and fourteen events to represent each decade. The chronology presents some surprises: birth control preceded *The Feminine Mystique,* and women's studies preceded *Ms.* Each decade is headed with an illustration and a caption describing the look of that time, and each event is explained in a multiple-page article; almost every article includes at least one black-and-white photograph. An appendix lists women's firsts throughout the twentieth century, and a bibliography and index are included. The book is great for browsing, but will also be used in research. MHCA.

Freedman, Russell. **Eleanor Roosevelt: A Life of Discovery**. New York: Clarion, 1993. 198p. $17.95; $10.95pa. ISBN 0-89919-862-7; 0-395-84520-3pa.

Although she lived amid privilege and wealth, Eleanor Roosevelt's life was not an easy one. Both her parents died before she was ten, and one of her own children died in infancy. Although Eleanor Roosevelt was in love with her husband, his mother was critical; Franklin Roosevelt later betrayed his wife, an event the author deals with in a straightforward way. Education, friendships, and the confidence that comes through helping others changed Roosevelt. She reinvented the role of first lady by engaging in activities she believed were important and by traveling as the eyes and ears of her disabled husband. Her acts of charity were recognized when President Harry Truman appointed her a delegate to the newly organized United Nations, opening a new chapter in her life as a human rights activist. Russell Freedman's biography is well organized and well written, and includes many black-and-white photographs, quotations from Roosevelt, a bibliography, and an index. It is an excellent choice for all school libraries. MHA.

Kercheval, Jesse Lee. **Space: A Memoir**. Chapel Hill, NC: Algonquin Books of Chapel Hill, 1998. 325p. $18.95. ISBN 1-56512-146-5.

Jesse Lee Kercheval writes a golden memoir of her childhood as a happy-go-lucky ten-year-old enraptured with the space program. In 1966, her family moved from Washington, D.C., to Cocoa Beach, Florida, where her father, an army retiree, was happy to take on the business management of a community college, although her mother regretted giving up her Treasury Department job. In the new environment, the mother embraces substance abuse, and the father endures a series of heart attacks, leaving older sister Carol in charge. The pressures on the girls, who are coming of age in the sixties, along with the multiple health problems of the aging, unprepared parents, drive the family to the brink of many crises. Jesse makes unguided life choices; however, in the fashion of the times, she lets it all happen without placing value judgments on her own psyche. *Space* throws the controversy over the current female generation into a new light, and will be read by those interested in the era, the space program, and how young girls dealt with those times. MHCA.

Linden-Ward, Blanche, and Carol Hurd Green. **American Women in the 1960s: Changing the Future**. New York: Twayne, 1993. 585p. (American Women in the Twentieth Century). $19.95pa. ISBN 0-8057-9913-3pa.

Providing a comprehensive view of women's involvement in the turbulent decade of the 1960s is not an easy task. Blanche Linden-Ward and Carol Green have organized their book topically, covering women in politics, the Civil Rights movement, higher education, work and the professions, popular culture, youth culture, the arts, literature, and the women's movement. Dress and appearance are covered in a separate chapter, and the chapter on the body deals with the advent of the pill, abortion, childbirth, reproductive technologies, and various types of medicines, including thalidomide. The cultural institutions of marriage, family, children, divorce, sexuality, lesbianism, and mental health also receive chapter coverage. These and other establishments were confronted by women in students', peace, environmental, and religious movements. With its obviously expansive scope,

American Women in the 1960s should be placed among history books on the twentieth-century for its research value. Notes, a bibliography, and an index are included. HCA.

Milton, Joyce. **The First Partner: Hillary Rodham Clinton**. New York: Morrow, 1999. 435p. $27.00. ISBN 0-688-15501-4.

Because Hillary Rodham Clinton is an unfinished subject, this biography will not be the last on the first lady. Beginning with the controversies of the 1990s, Milton recounts Clinton's sequential history as a young school leader and activist, as a children's advocate, as a member of the legal staff for the Watergate investigation, as a corporate attorney, and as the first lady active in failed health care reform and connected with several political scandals. The author views Clinton's life as a series of contradictions in re-lation to feminism, family, power, and politics, but these opinions must be separated from facts that may not be known yet. With Clinton on the cusp of moving into her own future or fading from historical memory, the future will decide whether Milton's portrait has lasting value. No photographs, but notes and an index are included. MHCA.

Neuman, Nancy M., ed. **True to Ourselves: A Celebration of Women Making a Difference**. San Francisco: Jossey-Bass, 1998. 246p. $22.00. ISBN 0-7879-4175-1.

Assembled by the League of Women Voters, *True to Ourselves* is a collection of twenty-two essays by contemporary women from a variety of fields and ethnic backgrounds. Writing to inspire their readers, the authors include explorer Ann Bancroft, politician Bella Abzug, philanthropist Kathleen Kennedy Townsend, reformer Sarah Brady, political wife Tipper Gore, and others. Each chapter is headed by a portrait of the writer and biographical information. The use of captions within the essays makes for easy reading. *True to Ourselves* is a nice gift book; it could also be used for book discussion groups. MHCA.

Rogers, Mary Beth. **Barbara Jordan: American Hero**. New York: Bantam, 1998. 414p. $27.50. ISBN 0-553-10603-1.

Barbara Jordan may best be remembered for her stirring oratory, which galvanized all Americans around a common vision for the United States. Born in Houston, Jordan was elected to the Texas Senate in 1969, the sole woman and the sole African American. From there her political career grew. The first Black woman to represent the south, she gained national exposure when she went to the House of Representatives in 1972 and elo-quently defended the Constitution in the Watergate hearings. She spoke at the Democratic National Conventions in 1976 and 1992, but she retired after only six years in Congress and returned to teaching. Suffering from multiple health problems, Jordan insisted on fulfilling her obligations and a full work schedule until her death in 1996. A person of high integrity, Jordan's political career was too short for one who could have accomplished much more. Mary Beth Rogers, who knew Jordan personally, writes an inspiring biography of a woman who changed politics for the better. MHCA.

Rose, Kenneth D. **American Women and the Repeal of Prohibition**. New York: New York University Press, 1996. 215p. (American Social Experience). $47.50; $17.50pa. ISBN 0-8147-7464-4; 0-8147-7466-0pa.

In December 1933, by convening state constitutional conventions, the Twenty-First Amendment to the United States Constitution repealed the Eighteenth Amendment, which had begun prohibition in 1919. Kenneth Rose shows how women contributed to the repeal and what their tactics were. The Women's Organization for National Prohibition Reform (WONPR) was founded in 1929, its leadership drawn from elite society and membership from a broad spectrum of classes. WONPR centered their repeal argument on the threat to the home caused by prohibition, creating a criminal element in society, making drinking fashionable, and corrupting police and politicians. As the issue was couched in morality, it was divisive between this organization and the still-active WCTU, Woman's Christian Temperance Union. Rose profiles many women who took an active role in the debates, giving a more in-depth look at a singular occurrence in constitutional history. Black-and-white photographs, cartoons, and documents are included as well as the text of the amendments, notes, and an index. HCA.

Schott, Linda K. **Reconstructing Women's Thoughts: The Women's International League for Peace and Freedom before World War II**. Stanford: Stanford University Press, 1997. 211p. (Modern America). $39.50. ISBN 0-8047-2746-5.

The United States branch of the International League for Peace and Freedom was formed in 1919 from what remained of the Woman's Peace Party, an organization of American women formed in 1915 to protest World War I. Linda Schott identifies twenty-one women active in the national leadership of the U.S. section of the Women's International League for Peace and Freedom between the wars, examining their ideas and activities to determine the reasons they entered peace work, how they shaped policy, and their influence on intellectual history. Schott interprets the women's writings, organizational records, and personal correspondence in her research. The group members included many influential women of the period, including Jane Addams and Emily Greene Balch, both Nobel Peace Prize winners, along with Dorothy Detzer, Mary Church Terrell, and Jeannette Rankin. Accompanying Schott's scholarship are black-and-white photographs, a chart of biographical information on the subjects, notes, and an index. HCA.

Swerdlow, Amy. **Women Strike for Peace: Traditional Motherhood and Radical Politics in the 1960s**. Chicago: University of Chicago Press, 1993. 310p. (Women in Culture and Society). $17.95pa. ISBN 0-226-78636-6pa.

Descended from a tradition of women's peace organizations, Women Strike for Peace commenced on November 1, 1961, with a one-day national peace protest to end the arms race. The "middle-aged, middle-class white mothers" went on to protest strontium 90 (radiation found in milk), nuclear war, and the Vietnam War. Their tactics were unconventional and spontaneous, employing local autonomy and reliance on their appeal as housewives and mothers, and they forged international alliances with women in the Soviet Union and Vietnam. Amy Swerdlow, who became a historian, was a founding mother in Women Strike for Peace. Her intent with this book is to record the group's history, to uncover why housewives would be moved to such radical political actions, and to unearth the motives of female empowerment. With black-and-white photographs, cartoons, notes, a bibliography, and an index, *Women Strike for Peace* adds to the protest history of the 1960s. HCA.

Taylor, Ethel Barol. **We Made a Difference: My Personal Journey with Women Strike for Peace**. Philadelphia: Camino, 1998. 155p. $25.00. ISBN 0-940159-49-X.

Philadelphia resident Ethel Taylor recounts her association with Women Strike for Peace beginning in 1961. The first issue the women, who organized in Taylor's dining room, tackled was clean milk. Strontium 90 from radioactive fallout was contaminating cow's milk, and in working to protect their children, these ordinary housewives began to press for the Nuclear Test Ban Treaty. Other issues followed, specifically the Vietnam War. In her writing, Taylor has a knack for presenting issues very clearly and connecting them to current events. Black-and-white photographs and documents are included throughout the book which, unfortunately, does not contain an index. HCA.

Non-Book Material

A Century of Women. Produced by Kyra Thompson. 6 parts, 55 min. ea. Ambrose Video Publishing, 1994. Videocassettes. $495.00 set; $99.95 each.

A Century of Women is a fairly comprehensive history of American women in the twentieth century, narrated by Jane Fonda. The production is divided into six parts built around the themes of work, family, sexuality, social justice, image, and popular culture; these are held together with a framing device, the stories of five generations of women in a fictional family on a weekend retreat. These well-acted, interesting stories create the chronological and thematic transitions to the history and are of special interest to students who do not have a generational sense of history. Each part of the film follows a loosely chronological arrangement while striving to be inclusive within each topic. In-depth portraits on women, both notable and obscure, use archival and contemporary material. In the sexuality segment, Margaret Sanger's crusade for birth control is fully covered, from the antiobscenity Comstock law to a film clip of Morley Safer interviewing Sanger in 1957. This segment also discusses Dr. Celia Mosher, Edna St. Vincent Millay, Charlotte Perkins Gilman, Emma Goldman, Gloria Steinem, Katherine McCormick, and Erica Jong. There is a lengthy interview with Hillary Rodham Clinton in the family portion, and popular culture covers the careers of Bessie Smith, Willa Cather, Georgia O'Keeffe, and Martha Graham. Along with the archival film, photographs, and interviews, notable actresses, such as Marlo Thomas, Mary Steenburgen, Candace Bergen, and Sally Field, read from diaries, letters, and memoirs. The family tape seems to be a continuation into the postwar period of the tape on work, which covers the first half of the twentieth century. The framing dramatizations will work when the entire series is used, and they can lead to further discussion and, perhaps, interest in family documentation; these frames, however, will probably be confusing when series parts are used in isolation. In all, the ambitious *A Century of Women* will best be used in women's history and women's studies courses. The carefully prepared teacher who is familiar with the entire series could incorporate cuts from the series throughout the study of twentieth century history. MHCA.

Hillary Rodham Clinton: Changing the Rules. Produced by Andrea Blaugrund. 50 min. A & E, 1994. (A & E Biography). Videocassette. $19.95.

Hillary Rodham Clinton enjoyed a successful career before her tenure as first lady. Her life from birth through 1994, halfway through the first presidential term, is covered as part of the A & E Biography series. The film features many interviews, not only with Mrs. Clinton, but with her brother, Hugh, childhood and college friends, minister, media people, White House aides, and Arkansas friend Mary Steenburgen. Raised in Park Ridge, Illinois, Clinton's early experiences included hearing Martin Luther King, Jr., preach, and serving as a Goldwater Girl in the 1964 presidential election. The first lady went on to higher education at Wellesley where, as class president, she became the first student to speak at graduation. At Yale Law School, she introduced herself to Bill Clinton in the library. She worked with him on the McGovern presidential campaign in Texas in 1972, and, afterward, moved to Washington to work for Marian Wright Edelman and the Children's Defense Fund. Child advocacy remains a cause very dear to her. When Watergate began, Mrs. Clinton was one of the three women attorneys appointed to a team of forty-three lawyers. Later, she turned down an offer from a top law firm to follow Bill Clinton to Arkansas, where they were married; they raised their daughter, Chelsea, while Bill Clinton rose through the political ranks. Although the film factually remarks on events that have been troublesome for the Clintons—money made in the commodities market, the Whitewater real estate deal, and marital problems—it does not provide in-depth details, nor allude to the political debate surrounding each event. The overall image shows Mrs. Clinton as a brilliant woman who has held a string of leadership positions since her young adult years, beloved by people who know and work with her. Her own advice is that sometimes it is necessary to "transcend yourself." *Hillary Rodham Clinton* can be used in social studies classes, where the film will stand as an introduction: With Mrs. Clinton's potential, more chapters will certainly be written. MHCA.

Paving the Way. Produced and directed by Emma Jean Morris. 52 min. Filmakers Library, 1995. Videocassette. Purchase $350.00; Rental $75.00.

> *Paving the Way* presents four contemporary women in history who break into mostly male professions and covers their varied careers from the 1950s to the present. The narrator, Barbara Feldon, gives an overview of how women of the mid-twentieth century were expected to be housewives, even though one-third of women worked outside the home. She also discusses the 1960s women's movement, gender quotas, and Title IX legislation. These topics are illustrated with photographs, film clips, and interviews, which form the introduction to the stories of the film's four subjects. The first, Supreme Court Justice Ruth Bader Ginsburg, was one of nine women in Harvard's class of 1956. When she became pregnant while working at her first law job, she was demoted, and she lost that job when her baby was born. Ginsburg continued her legal career by prosecuting sex discrimination cases, work that led to her appointment to the Supreme Court. Next, Major General Jeanne Holm chose a career in the Air Force shortly after a 1948 law removed women from combat positions; within a few years, pregnant women were discharged from duty. After these setbacks, Holm witnessed and helped to bring about more equitable changes throughout her military career. Third, Reverend Addie Wyatt was afraid to tell her husband she was running for president of the meat packer's union. She managed to reform gender-based pay inequities for working women before switching to a religious vocation. Finally, Congresswoman Patsy Mink was the first woman admitted to the Hawaiian bar. Moving on to politics, where she served multiple terms in Congress, she promoted legislation for childcare and equal education. In the film, some of the most revealing comments come from the children who grew up with the four women exemplified as working mothers. The film offers a good overview of the changes for women during the turbulent middle decades of the twentieth century as well as interesting portraits of four successful women. MHCA.

She's Nobody's Baby: American Women in the Twentieth Century. Produced and directed by Ana Carrigan. 56 min. Phoenix Learning Group, 1981. Videocassette. $79.00.

> Narrated by Alan Alda and Marlo Thomas, the theme of *She's Nobody's Baby* centers on the different messages conveyed to women since the turn of the twentieth century from such sources as experts, the media, and the government, and how, on more than one occasion, these messages have reversed themselves. The film illustrates the theme using black-and-white and color film clips, photographs, documents, and a nice selection of period music. As a comprehensive history of American women in the twentieth century, the video begins with Alice Roosevelt and moves through labor strikes, World

War I, woman suffrage, the flapper, education, the Great Depression, World War II, stay-at-home mothers, rising divorce rates, the pill, the Civil Rights movement, and an increase in opportunities for women; it mentions many distinguished women in each period. The media's influence on women is illustrated with diverse examples, including Lillian Gish, Theda Bara, Zelda Fitzgerald, Josephine Baker, Mae West, Shirley Temple, Katherine Hepburn, Lucille Ball, Doris Day, Marilyn Monroe, Jean Stapleton, and Mary Tyler Moore. Before movies and television, the radio was an early medium to affect women; they listened to such experts as Sigmund Freud and Dr. Benjamin Spock. In the 1970s, after decades of competing and contradictory advise, women began to listen to other women. Although *She's Nobody's Baby* ends with the 1970s, it is a worthwhile film for use in social studies, women's studies, and media courses. It can also be used to promote discussion among adults, some of whom may remember much of what is related. MHCA.

The Women of Summer: The Bryn Mawr Summer School for Women Workers, 1921–1938. Produced and directed by Suzanne Bauman. 55 min. Filmakers Library, 1985. Videocassette. Purchase $425.00; Rental $85.00.

In the 1920s and 1930s, one of the Seven Sisters schools, Bryn Mawr, created a summer program to advance working women. The curriculum, which emphasized English and economics, was the brainchild of Hilda Worthington Smith, who directed the summer program. Funded by alumnae, friends, and union organizations from all over the country, the summer school program enabled women students who worked in factories for meager wages, having left formal education at early ages to help support struggling families. The documentary reports the story of what this opportunity meant to the women who attended. The film is a perfect example of the classic writing rule: show, don't tell. It is told from the perspective of a fiftieth class reunion and shows interviews with many alumnae and surviving faculty members. The film is narrated by Esther Peterson, a faculty member who became the highest ranking woman in U.S. government when President John F. Kennedy appointed her to the Department of Labor. Film clips, period photographs, documents, and student poetry are incorporated. A number of union and folk songs are sung by Holly Near and Suzanne Bauman; these are the perfect accompaniment to the message and help make the film more than a mere historical account. The summer school was avant-garde in its teaching methods, in admitting Black women in the 1920s, and in allowing the students to engage in political activities. The type of hands-on education offered to these nontraditional students was the school's downfall as the Great Depression deepened and the Red Scare commenced. Besides offering a good deal of labor history, the film is inspiring in it portrayal of students who went on to notable careers, many as union organizers. The women upheld the standards upon which the summer school was based and tried to pass them on as they resumed their careers. Although it depicts an obscure event, the movie packs a mighty message and should be shown right along with *Bound for Glory* in the study of the Great Depression. HCA.

The 1920s

Books

Andersen, Kristi. **After Suffrage: Women in Partisan and Electoral Politics Before the New Deal**. Chicago: University of Chicago Press, 1996. 191p. (American Politics and Political Economy). $38.00; $13.95pa. ISBN 0-226-01955-1; 0-226-01957-8pa.

> In their first decade with suffrage, Kristi Andersen thinks about women as voters, candidates, and officeholders and ponders their influence on citizenship, voting, party politics, and electoral politics. The experiences women gained from long years in the suffrage battle influenced their behavior in the political process. With a distrust for political parties, women were more independent, skeptical, and less likely to pledge their loyalty. Perceived as a distinct group with their own agenda, women were treated separately by politicians and the press. Women who entered politics used gender networks to extend reform agendas through a decade unfriendly to these causes. At the same time, as unseasoned voters, women built new networks and methods that changed the political process. Such organizations as the League of Women Voters, which held debates and surveyed candidates, transformed party-centered politics by utilizing advertising and interest groups, methods more familiar in the late twentieth century. Andersen uses cartoons and graphs to make her points, and a bibliography and an index are included. HCA.

Anthony, Carl Sferrazza. **Florence Harding: The First Lady, the Jazz Age, and the Death of America's Most Scandalous President**. New York: Morrow, 1998. 645p. $30.00. ISBN 0-688-07794-3.

> Reading like a best-seller, Florence Harding, first lady to the twenty-ninth president, is painted as even more outrageous than her adulterous husband. An unwed teenage mother, the daughter of an abusive father, Florence Harding lured Warren G. Harding into marriage and became his newspaper partner. She promoted him in politics from the Senate to the presidency, all the while ignoring his affairs. When the couple moved to Washington, the drug-addicted owner of the Hope Diamond, Evalyn McLean, became Harding's best friend. A few years into the term, the Hardings knew they could not escape the corruption of the administration and the Teapot Dome scandal, even with the help of the first lady's astrologers. After a trip to Alaska in 1923, the president died under the care of his wife's hand-picked homeopathic practitioner, amid rumors that she had poisoned him. In a little over a year, the first lady, who pioneered airplane travel, press conferences, White House entertainment, and feminism, was dead. Carl Anthony's research draws on the recent discovery of the first lady's diary and President Harding's letters. Photographs, sources, notes, and an index are included in a biography set in the Jazz Age. HCA.

Non-Book Material

The Flapper Story. Directed by Lauren Lazin. 29 min. Cinema Guild, 1985. Videocassette. Purchase $250.00; Rental $55.00.

> *The Flapper Story* is filled with well-reproduced newsreel footage, still photographs, advertisements, and numerous examples of music from the 1920s. Interspersed among these are interviews with women, now elderly, who were flappers, modern, rebellious post–World War I women. The film follows a loose chronological arrangement from the end of the war, covering the topics of suffrage, prohibition, jazz, the rise of Hollywood, and the coming of the Great Depression. The interviews are frank as the subjects discuss the expectations placed upon them by the suffragists, the look and dress of the 1920s, sexual mores, marriage, work, and life circumstances. What the women fail to discuss in any detail is education. The overall impression is that the 1920s was a fun time of greatly expanded possibilities for women who enjoyed much more freedom in hairstyle, dress, manners, and movement than in any previous time, and where they could choose, and many did, to work at a variety of available jobs. The film does not emphasize homemaking, instead focusing on the youth culture and zany activities of the Roaring Twenties. The strengths of the film are the newsreel clips and the interview subjects, who connect the present to the past. The film can be used in social studies classes and to open discussions of the changing roles of women. HCA.

The 1930s

Books

Faulkner, Howard J., and Virginia D. Pruitt, eds. **Dear Dr. Menninger: Women's Voices from the Thirties**. Columbia: University of Missouri Press, 1997. 258p. $24.95pa. ISBN 0-8262-1111-9pa.

> Dr. Karl A. Menninger was a psychiatrist who wrote an advice column for the *Ladies' Home Journal* for a short time during the 1930s to promote the idea of a healthy mind. Thousands of letters were sent to him, each of which he answered. Many of the letters survived, and the editors have collected the genuine voices of women from the era of the Great Depression. Many of their concerns had to do with sexual conflicts, frigidity, and extra-marital affairs. Problems with husbands, in-laws, parents, and children were also a common theme, and there were, of course, true mental problems related to depression, hostility, narcissism, and personality disorders. The letters are a treasure in recording the period concerns and the popular advice being dispensed to women. A portrait of Dr. Menninger is included in a publication that can be used in courses on psychology, women's studies, and history. HCA.

Sternsher, Bernard, and Judith Sealander, eds. **Women of Valor: The Struggle Against the Great Depression as Told in Their Own Life Stories**. Chicago: Ivan R. Dee, 1990. $26.95. ISBN 0-929587-34-0.

> Although women in the 1930s are often overlooked, the autobiographical writings of sixteen women who worked throughout the Great Depression show that social action and feminism did not die during this time. Although well-known women are represented—Lillian Wald, Eleanor Roosevelt, Margaret Bourke-White, and Frances Perkins—many are not household names. A degree of diversity is introduced with Ellen Tarry, a southern Black woman who worked for the Federal Writers' Project; Anzia Yezierska, a Russian Jewish immigrant who was also a writer; and Ella Reeve Bloor, Meridel Le Sueur, and Vera Buch Weisbord, labor organizers and members of the Communist Party. Generally, these women's jobs can be categorized into three areas: government work, labor organizing, and social work. In developing these fields, women laid the groundwork for later government welfare programs and the institution of organized labor. Their voices are rich and bring a broader perspective to the era than the often-portrayed housewife holding the family together. The editors provide introductions, and the illustrations are by artist Jorge Colombo, who depicts each woman. *Women of Valor* makes a fine contribution to collections of women's history and the Great Depression. HCA.

Ware, Susan. **Beyond Suffrage: Women in the New Deal**. Cambridge, MA: Harvard University Press, 1981. 204p. $14.50pa. ISBN 0-674-06922-6pa.

> Historian Susan Ware characterizes the 1930s as a period when more women were appointed to political positions, in the Democratic Party and in government New Deal agencies and programs, than at any previous time. She notes that this phenomenon has been largely overlooked in history, where the Depression years are seen as a time when married women were forced out of jobs. Women's participation in the New Deal is significant for its "network" developed from roots in suffrage and reform, which maximized influence through cooperation and association. Thus the New Deal brought to fruition many programs with origins in the various reform movements. Ware concentrates on twenty-eight women of national prominence in the New Deal period before 1945. Appendices outline her selection criteria and give comparative and individual biographical data. The women include first lady Eleanor Roosevelt, congressional members Mary T. Norton and Caroline O'Day, ambassadors Florence Jaffray Harriman and Ruth Bryan Owen, Labor Department appointees Grace Abbott and Francis Perkins, NRA appointees Emily Newell Blair and Rose Schneiderman, and others. Ware's worthy study, containing notes and an index, should be included in women's studies collections. HCA.

World War II

Books

Colman, Penny. **Rosie the Riveter: Women Working on the Home Front in World War II**. New York: Crown, 1995. 120p. $19.00; $10.99pa. ISBN 0-517-59790-X; 0-517-88567-0pa.

> Covering the entire war period, Penny Colman explains the government and business efforts that attracted women into the work force as the war started, and the campaigns that sent them home again when the war was over. Both the text and statistical appendices note the numbers and types of women who went to work, along with the kinds of jobs they held. A chapter details minority women in the work force. The author personalizes the text by interviewing Dot Chastney, who was a schoolgirl when the war began. Using quotations from magazines and government publications, Colman shows how the image of women was manipulated as well as the different forms of discrimination they faced while working to produce needed military supplies. Black-and-white photographs are used to augment the narrative, and a chronology, a bibliography, and an index help to make the book a useful research tool for younger readers. MH.

Gruhzit-Hoyt, Olga. **They Also Served: American Women in World War II**. New York: Birch Lane, 1995. 279p. $19.95. ISBN 1-55972-280-0.

> Olga Gruhzit-Hoyt solicited the war experiences of women veterans and was surprised by the overwhelming response she received. Many of those stories are used in this account of women in the service, which is divided by organization: Army Nurse Corps, Navy Nurse Corps, Women's Army Corps, U.S. Navy WAVES, Marine Corps Women's Reserve, Coast Guard SPARS, Women's Airforce Service Pilots, Office of War Information and Office of Strategic Services, and American Red Cross. After summarizing women's association with each group, the author recounts "war stories," because these women were serving on the front. The accounts, which range from one page to a chapter, tell of attack, capture, and death as well as of love and marriage. The author uses third-person narration in most of the text, with limited direct quotation; notwithstanding, at the end of each story, Gruhzit-Hoyt summarizes what happened to each woman after the war. Many women sent photographs of themselves in the war, which are interspersed throughout the text. *They Also Served*, with notes, a bibliography, and an index, will fit nicely into World War II collections. MHCA.

Holm, Jeanne M., ed. **In Defense of a Nation: Servicewomen in World War II**. Arlington: Vandamere, 1998. 192p. $29.95. ISBN 0-918339-43-X.

> Retired Major General Jeanne M. Holm, the first woman in the armed forces to hold two-star rank, and author of a history of women in the military, is well qualified to edit this collection of articles chronicling the war

record of women in each branch of the armed services. Included are the Army Nurse Corps, Navy Nurse Corps, Women's Army Corps, Navy Women's Reserve, Marine Corps Women's Reserve, Coast Guard Women Reserves, Women Airforce Service Pilots, army dietitians, physical therapists, and occupational therapists, and numerous civilian organizations. Experts from each organization write the chapters detailing the recruitment, training, theaters of operation, service record, and demobilization of women in World War II. A military history of women, *In Defense of a Nation* is filled with black-and-white photographs along with notes on the authors, a chronology highlighting military events and military women, notes, a bibliography, and an index. This important book belongs in every World War II collection. MHCA.

Houston, Jeanne Wakatsuki, and James D. Houston. **Farewell to Manzanar: A True Story of Japanese American Experience During and After the World War II Internment**. New York: Bantam, 1973. 145p. $5.50pa. ISBN 0-553-27258-6pa.

Only seven years old when her family was interred at Manzanar, Jeanne Wakatsuki Houston needed to tell the story of the camps when she became an adult. Although Houston writes *Farewell to Manzanar* from the distance of time and place, her memories are vivid. Written in 1973, before reparations were made to Japanese Americans, there is still a sense of bitterness to the story of how, after the attack on Pearl Harbor, the Wakatsuki family of Long Beach, California was sent first to a relocation center and then to Manzanar camp. Houston's father, taken to North Dakota for nine months, rejoined his family at Manzanar. Those members of the family who had not scattered to the military or other occupations lived there until 1945, when they returned to Long Beach to start over. While illuminating camp life, the book also represents the changes in family dynamics brought about by their humiliating experience. Moving enough to be read in one sitting, *Farewell to Manzanar* is for readers and report writers. MHCA.

Howe, Russell Warren. **The Hunt for "Tokyo Rose."** Lanham, MD: Madison, 1990. 254p. $14.95pa. ISBN 1-56833-013-8pa.

Suggesting that Iva Toguri, who was convicted of treason as the World War II radio personality Tokyo Rose, be given a congressional apology, Russell Howe determines to set the record straight on a midcentury miscarriage of justice. Toguri was sent to Japan before the war to nurse a sick aunt. Unable to leave and unhappy in the culture, she waited out the war, holding a variety of jobs. One job was as typist at Radio Tokyo, where she was recruited to broadcast for the English-speaking station. Throughout the war, she never renounced her American citizenship and was always loyal, but when reporters came looking for Tokyo Rose after the war, Toguri admitted to being that person. She was arrested and held in Japan until the Counter Intelligence Corps found no evidence against her and sent her home. Radio broadcaster Walter Winchell picked up her story and goaded the FBI into reopening the case. A victim of continuing anti-Japanese prejudice, Toguri was tried in the United States and convicted on one count, out of eight, of treason. She served six years in prison, although in 1977 she received a pardon from President Gerald Ford, the only one ever granted in a treason case. In a foreword, former Attorney General Ramsey Clark decries the incident and makes it clear there never was a Tokyo Rose; she was an invention. Howe's book is carefully researched and written, containing a section of black-and-white photographs. Great for research, the book can also be used in multicultural studies, sociology, and government classes. HCA.

Litoff, Judy Barrett, and David C. Smith. **American Women in a World at War: Contemporary Accounts from World War II**. Wilmington, DE: Scholarly Resources, 1997. 237p. (Worlds of Women). $45.00; $16.95pa. ISBN 0-8420-2570-7; 0-8420-2571-5pa.

Twenty-five pieces written by contemporary women concerning World War II are collected in *American Women in a World at War*. The writers, representing a broad spectrum of class and race, cover a range of material about war preparations, military service, overseas assignments, the home front, war jobs, and preparations for a postwar world. Included are pieces by communist Elizabeth Gurley Flynn, Navy nurse Page Cooper, photographer Margaret Bourke-White, army wife Barbara Klaw, the U.S. Department of Agriculture, Susan B. Anthony II, and Mary McLeod Bethune. The editors introduce each topic and essay; black-and-white photographs and suggested readings round out the volume. Teachers looking for primary source material about the war written by women should be interested in this material. MHCA.

Moore, Brenda L. **To Serve My Country, to Serve My Race: The Story of the Only African American Wacs** [sic] **Stationed Overseas During World War II**. New York: New York University Press, 1996. 272p. $40.00; $17.95pa. ISBN 0-8147-5522-4; 0-8147-5587-9pa.

A veteran of active duty in the Army, Brenda Moore interviews over fifty women of the 6888th Central Postal Directory Battalion, a unit of African Americans in the Women's Army Corps serving in England and France during World War II. Moore looks at why the women joined up and how the military changed its policy so that they could enlist. Exploring their experiences together, Moore notes the women confronted the double burden of racism and sexism as they served in the European theater. She uses extensive sections from her interviews throughout the book. Black-and-white photographs and graphs illustrate the study of the segregated armed forces. A list of the interview subjects as well as all the members of the 6888th, Moore's survey instrument, notes, a bibliography, and an index are appended. HCA.

Okubo, Miné. **Citizen 13660**. Seattle: University of Washington Press, 1983. 209p. $14.95pa. ISBN 0-295-95989-4pa.

Miné Okubo was an artist when, as a young woman, she was relocated with other Japanese Americans first to the Tanforan center and then to the Topaz camp in Utah, where she drew scenes of camp life for her loyal friends at home in Berkeley. In 1946, she published the nearly two hundred drawings, with descriptions written underneath, as *Citizen 13660*. The artwork adds immeasurably to the understanding of camp life by illustrating the crowded conditions; the lack of privacy; the housing, food, weather, and insects; and even the light moments. When Okubo left Topaz in April 1944, she moved to New York to work for *Fortune* magazine. She added a new foreword to the book in 1983 just before the Commission on Wartime Relocation and Internment was to issue its report on reparations. Students, as part of the visual generation, will love using this book for research, and it may find uses in art classes also. MHCA.

Weatherford, Doris. **American Women and World War II**. New York: Facts on File, 1990. 338p. (History of Women in America). $29.95. ISBN 0-8160-2038-8.

Although Doris Weatherford covers much the same material as other books on nursing, women in the military, and women in industry, her section on the home front sets her treatment apart. Rationing, managing the home around shortages, volunteer work, juggling home and job, the waiting and then being notified that a loved one will not be coming home, all give a much closer look at life under wartime conditions. On a brighter note, war weddings are one of the many interesting social aspects not found in other sources. Varied quotes are used throughout the book and four black-and-white photograph sections are included. Notes and an index complete a book that will be used for many types of research. MHCA.

Wise, Nancy Baker, and Christy Wise. **A Mouthful of Rivets: Women at Work in World War II**. San Francisco: Jossey-Bass, 1994. 283p. $25.00. ISBN 1-55542-703-0.

A mother-daughter team interviews over 100 women who went to work during World War II. The jobs they held ranged from movie house ushers to shipyard workers to WAC pilots. The interviews are arranged topically, starting with women relocating as the war began, and ending with the way women felt about leaving their jobs as the servicemen came home. In between, some of the topics include training, sexual harassment, mentoring, and self-confidence. In a final chapter, children and grandchildren of the war employees discuss their experiences while their mothers worked or what they remember hearing their relatives say about their jobs. Each chapter and interview is headed with comments by the authors, who also draft profiles of the interviewees. A black-and-white photograph section, a bibliography, and an index are included in a book that draws women into the history of World War II. MHCA.

Zeinert, Karen. **Those Incredible Women of World War II**. Brookfield, CT: Millbrook, 1994. 112p. $24.90. ISBN 1-56294-434-7.

Karen Zeinert gives a brief overview of the roles women played in World War II as pilots, in the armed forces, as nurses and doctors, with the press, and on the home front. These topics are framed by chapters telling about the beginning and ending of the war. Encompassing black-and-white photographs, *Those Incredible Women* also uses special boxed sections to treat biographical and other topics such as Eleanor Roosevelt, Dr. Emily Barringer, prisoners of war, and Japanese American women. The book uses quotations from women workers; a graph shows the numbers of women in the work force; a time line lists important dates; and notes, a bibliography, and an index are appended. MH.

Non-Book Material

The U.S.A. vs. "Tokyo Rose." Directed by Antonio A. Montanari, Jr. 48 min. Cinema Guild, 1995. Videocassette. Purchase $295.00; Rental $90.00.

Tokyo Rose, the World War II radio personality used by the Japanese to demoralize the U.S. troops, was not one woman, but several; and she had counterparts employed in the propaganda business in all the theaters of war. *The U.S.A. vs. "Tokyo Rose"* is a carefully researched production using documents from the FBI, court records, and archival film to tell the story of Iva Toguri, who was convicted of treason for acting as Tokyo Rose. Toguri, born a U.S. citizen, was sent to Japan to nurse a sick aunt before the bombing of Pearl Harbor. Toguri went instead of her immigrant mother because the 1924 Exclusion Act would not have allowed her mother to return to the United States. Toguri was caught in Japan when war was declared and could not return home. She went to work for Radio Tokyo, where she was recruited to broadcast. Toguri steadfastly refused to renounce her U.S. citizenship throughout the war, and her broadcasts were considered a joke by sailors who heard them around the Pacific theater. After the war, reporters convinced Toguri to admit to using the name Tokyo Rose, and she was filmed in a reenactment of her broadcasts. From this point on, Toguri was pursued by the U.S. Justice Department, tried for treason, convicted, and imprisoned for six years. The case of Tokyo Rose illustrates the anti-Japanese attitudes that prevailed in the United States before, during, and after the war. The film can be used in history and sociology courses to illustrate intolerance. Because of the details the film imparts, more than one viewing is necessary for research purposes. HCA.

The 1950s

Books

Breines, Wini. **Young, White, and Miserable: Growing up Female in the Fifties**. Boston: Beacon, 1992. 261p. $15.00pa. ISBN 0-8070-7503-5pa.

Wini Breines creates what she calls a "sociological memoir" to uncover the culture of white girls growing up in the 1950s and the defiance that would help create the feminist movement of the 1960s. Because the insulated

1950s embraced narrow gender roles and worship of the domestic sphere while consumerism, conformity, and commercialism expanded, sociologist Breines had to search hard to uncover the roots of rebellion. The 1950s was the decade of the mother; with nothing but the home to care for, women tended to be overly involved in their children's lives, while at the same time, girls were developing their own teen culture based on an abundance of new material goods. In another contradiction, the sexual double standard was confusing to girls, who witnessed the unapproachable alternative roles of the beat generation, movies stars, and rock and roll idols. Hints of forming resistance were found in interviews, fiction, sociological data, and the author's own memories where, hidden behind lipstick and push-up bras, a new consciousness was forming. Breines's study is interesting for those who grew up during the time and for those interested in girl culture today. Notes and an index are appended. HCA.

Eisenhower, Susan. **Mrs. Ike: Memories and Reflections on the Life of Mamie Eisenhower**. New York: Farrar, Straus & Giroux, 1996. 392p. $26.00. ISBN 0-374-21514-6.

Mamie Eisenhower symbolized the 1950s, when her husband reigned through two terms of the presidency, but her granddaughter shows that the first lady was more complicated than her prim image portrayed. Although the perfect White House hostess, who entertained Nikita Khrushchev, Mrs. Ike used a number of strategies to keep the press at bay, leaving her public image shadowy. In unpublished correspondence between the first lady and the president, used throughout the book, Mrs. Ike comes out from under her bangs, revealed as confident in herself and devoted to her husband. When Mamie Doud married the West Point graduate Dwight D. Eisenhower in 1916 and began to follow him around the world on assignments, she resigned herself to living with military discipline and life in the public sphere. The Eisenhowers faced hardships when they lost a three-year-old son, when they were separated during World War II, and when rumors spread about Ike's war-time secretary; but their happy marriage lasted over fifty years. Biography readers and history buffs will enjoy Susan Eisenhower's writing, which includes sections of photographs, notes, and an index. HCA.

Goodwin, Doris Kearns. **Wait Till Next Year: A Memoir**. New York: Simon and Schuster, 1997. 261p. $25.00; $13.00pa. ISBN 0-684-82489-2; 0-684-84795-7pa.

Growing up in Rockville Centre, on the South Shore of Long Island, New York, during the 1950s presented a problem. With three baseball teams, the choice of which one to support had to be made and defended with friends and neighbors. Doris Goodwin's father taught her to keep a score book and track the Brooklyn Dodgers when she was six years old. Interviewed as a woman fan by Ken Burns for his epic baseball documentary, Goodwin wanted to recreate the 1950s heyday of New York baseball when one of the three teams went to the World Series every year, but, in doing so, she had to re-create her girlhood in the neighborhood, at Morris Elementary

School and at St. Agnes Catholic Church, as well as childhood rituals and those of the game of baseball itself. The epoch, and Goodwin's youth, came to an end when the Dodgers moved to California, her mother died, the family relocated, and the neighborhood changed. Goodwin is the winner of the Pulitzer Prize in history for her book about the Roosevelts, *No Ordinary Time*. Her skills as a historian are put to use in interviewing former neighbors and reading the local newspaper as background to her memoir, which can be used as supplementary history on the period or just as a good read. MHCA.

Knight, Brenda. **Women of the Beat Generation: The Writers, Artists and Muses at the Heart of a Revolution**. Berkeley: Conari, 1996. 366p. $19.95; $14.95pa. ISBN 1-57324-061-3; 0-57324-138-5pa.

Everyone knows Jack Kerouac and Allen Ginsberg, but where are the women of the beat generation? Although they risked all as social outcasts, these supremely talented and intellectual women, like all women of their time, became submerged under the men who spoke for the generation. The beats of the 1950s were precursors to the 1960s hippies, nonconforming artists who lived on the margins. By breaking with social norms, the women paved the way for the next generation to exhibit more individuality, live on their own, and engage in the sexual relationships they chose. Many of the women collected in Brenda Knight's bio-bibliographical collection are now dead, but their works of poetry, fiction, and memoir remain to speak for them. The collection includes twenty-six women, including Carolyn Cassaday, Diane di Prima, Hetti Jones, ruth weiss, and Jan Kerouac, and sidebars treat another thirteen women associated with the beatniks. Black-and-white illustrations, lists of collected works, and an index are appended. HCA.

Meyerowitz, Joanne, ed. **Not June Cleaver: Women and Gender in Postwar America, 1945–1960**. Philadelphia: Temple University Press, 1994. 411p. $22.95pa. ISBN 1-56639-171-7pa.

In a collection of fifteen essays, editor Joanne Meyerowitz aims at reinterpreting the stereotyped view of the white suburban housewife of the 1950s. The book is divided into four topical sections dealing with labor, activism, womanhood, and rebels. Contributions by historians and sociologists such as Susan M. Hartmann, Rickie Solinger, and Wini Breines expand the period with subjects such as the immigration of Chinese women to New York after the repeal of the Chinese Exclusion Acts, married nurses' participation in the labor force, women peace activists of the McCarthy era, Mexican American social activism in California barrios, out-of-wedlock pregnancies among white and Black women, and the containment of female sexuality. Even with this range of topics, Meyerowitz believes there are still unexplored areas in postwar women's history, and she notes that not all the writers in this book agree in their interpretation of the era. Although a broader view of the period can be appreciated now, readers will welcome future writing on the 1950s. *Not June Cleaver* contains a few black-and-white illustrations, and brief biographical sketches on the contributors. HCA.

Civil Rights

Books

Bates, Daisy. **The Long Shadow of Little Rock: A Memoir**. Fayetteville: University of Arkansas Press, 1986. 234p. $16.00pa. ISBN 0-938626-75-2pa.

> Daisy Bates and her husband owned the *Arkansas State Press*, which they used to support the integration of Little Rock Central High School. As a result, Daisy Bates was at the center of the Civil Rights controversy, under constant threat; she appealed to President Dwight D. Eisenhower for protection, and eventually lost her newspaper. At the height of the struggle, on September 25, 1957, President Eisenhower ordered the 101st Airborne Division to help nine students exercise their right to free public education, against the wishes of Governor Orval E. Faubus. Bates's memoir, originally published in 1962, recounts the struggles that went on for years of the nine Black students and the community of Little Rock. The book is surprisingly emotionally charged for those unfamiliar with the era. Some of the highest moments occur when Bates, who grew up in a foster home after her mother was murdered by three white men for refusing their sexual advances, confronts the "drunken pig" who killed her mother. The foreword to the book is written by Eleanor Roosevelt; black-and-white photographs and an index are included. The book will be read as biography and used in Civil Rights-era research. HCA.

Crawford, Vicki L., Jacqueline Anne Rouse, and Barbara Woods, eds. **Women in the Civil Rights Movement: Trailblazers and Torchbearers, 1941–1965**. Bloomington: Indiana University Press, 1993. 290p. (Blacks in the Diaspora). $13.95pa. ISBN 0-253-20832-7pa.

> The seventeen essays presented in *Women in the Civil Rights Movement* were written for the conference of the same name given in October 1988 at the University of Georgia in response to the PBS series *Eyes on the Prize*. The goal of the conference was to bring forth and acknowledge the role women played in achieving equal rights. Many activist women were high-lighted in the papers, including Fannie Lou Hamer, Ella Baker, Septima P. Clark, Modjeska Simkins, Gloria Richardson, and Eleanor Roosevelt. In addition, papers were written about various places and events. The text is illustrated with black-and-white photographs; information on the contributors and an index are included. HCA.

Fleming, Cynthia Griggs. **Soon We Will Not Cry: The Liberation of Ruby Doris Smith Robinson**. Lanham, MD: Rowman and Littlefield, 1998. 224p. $24.95. ISBN 0-8476-8971-9.

> "Soon we will not cry" was a comment made in relation to the many deaths in the Civil Rights movement which, it was felt, were becoming beyond response capacity for many people. Ruby Doris Smith Robinson was one who died in the cause, not violently, just too young. A native of Atlanta whose father

was a minister, Robinson entered the cause at the age of seventeen when she joined a lunch counter sit-in. As a member of the Student Nonviolent Coordinating Committee (SNCC), she became a leader in the Atlanta office, riding the freedom buses throughout the South during the summer of 1964. Unhappily, in 1967 cancer cut her organizing career short. Never one to call attention to herself, her place in the movement was recognized by Julian Bond, Ralph Abernathy, and Martin Luther King, Jr., who were pallbearers at her funeral. Cynthia Fleming's book, including black-and-white photographs and an index, gives many details of Civil Rights organizing and women's roles in the struggle. HCA.

Mills, Kay. **This Little Light of Mine: The Life of Fannie Lou Hamer**. New York: Plume, 1993. 390p. $14.95pa. ISBN 0-452-27052-9pa.

Forty-four years old when the Civil Rights movement came to Sunflower County, Mississippi, Fannie Lou Hamer raised her hand to volunteer to register to vote. Although poor and lacking education, Hamer knew the Jim Crow system and for the next fifteen years, until her death in 1977, worked to change it. It took several attempts before Hamer was able to register; although victorious in citizenship, she was evicted from her home. Becoming more involved in Civil Rights, Hamer went to work for the Student Nonviolent Coordinating Committee, but, during the course of her work, she was arrested and later beaten in jail. These experiences made her an able spokesperson for the Mississippi Freedom Democratic Party as she challenged delegate rules during the 1964 and 1968 Democratic National Conventions. Hamer used the courts to challenge many unfair political practices, and worked to improve conditions for Black people in many fields. Mills's able and inspiring biography contains a map, a chronology, black-and-white photographs, a list of Civil Rights personalities mentioned in the text, notes, and an index. HCA.

Moody, Anne. **Coming of Age in Mississippi**. New York: Laurel, 1968. $6.99pa. ISBN 0-440-31488-7pa.

Anne Moody started out in a "rotten wood two-room shack" on a Mississippi plantation. Her narrative of her youth as a Black woman in the segregated South in the 1950s and 1960s is unrelenting in its harshness. Moody began cleaning houses at the age of nine to help her family eat. A bright and athletic child, she earned a scholarship to attend Natchez College. With a sense of righteousness, Moody joined the Civil Rights movement, registering voters and participating in sit-ins. At one point she found her own name on a Ku Klux Klan hit list. The book concludes in 1964, when Moody, at twenty-eight, sees no end to the Civil Rights struggle. *Coming of Age in Mississippi*, with its immediate first-hand experiences and angry voice, is a good choice to use alongside *Black Like Me*. HCA.

Murphy, Sara Alderman. **Breaking the Silence: Little Rock's Women's Emergency Committee to Open Our Schools, 1958–1963**. Edited by Patrick C. Murphy II. Fayetteville: University of Arkansas Press, 1997. 303p. $20.00pa. ISBN 1-55728-515-2pa.

The year after nine Black students integrated Little Rock Central High School, Governor Orval Faubus used a new state law to close the schools rather than continue with integration. Led by Adolphine Fletcher Terry, a prominent white woman from a respected family, a committee of women worked to keep the schools open. While trying to protect their identities so their husbands would not be fired, the women employed an effective, neutral-toned ad campaign, and eventually employed re-education efforts. Author Sara Murphy was a member of the WEC over the course of its existence. The book offers a counterpoint to Daisy Bates's memoir, listed above, and shows how both races had to work together to save education. *Breaking the Silence*, which expands information about the Civil Rights era, includes black-and-white photographs, notes, a bibliography, and an index. HCA.

Parks, Rosa, and Jim Haskins. **Rosa Parks: My Story**. New York: Dial, 1992. 192p. $17.00. ISBN 0-8037-0673-1.

By refusing to give up her seat as ordered by the bus driver, on December 1, 1955, Rosa Parks began a year-long court battle and a bus boycott that, in the end, desegregated bus transportation in Montgomery, Alabama. Parks's autobiography details her childhood and the influences that led to her courageous decision. As a child, she saw Ku Klux Klan members ride by her house. When she married, Parks was one of two female NAACP members in Montgomery and was active in the Civil Rights movement. After the bus incident and her arrest, Parks lost her job and relocated to Detroit. The book by this much-honored leader contains black-and-white photographs, a chronology, and an index. MHCA.

Robinson, Jo Ann Gibson. **The Montgomery Bus Boycott and the Women Who Started It**. Edited by David J. Garrow. Knoxville: University of Tennessee Press, 1987. 190p. $36.00; $15.95pa. ISBN 0-87049-524-0; 0-87049-527-5pa.

On the day after Rosa Parks was arrested for refusing to give up her seat on a segregated Montgomery, Alabama bus, a group of women headed by Jo Ann Robinson began to organize a boycott of city buses to begin the following Monday. The women had only the weekend to complete their plans and get the word out. The boycott lasted thirteen months, when a Supreme Court ruling served on the city forced the integration of the buses. For over a year, the Montgomery Improvement Association, headed by Dr. Martin Luther King, Jr., and including many women members, kept the bus boycott alive. Rides were organized, staging areas arranged, and station wagons purchased with money from northern contributions. Although Robinson, who was an English professor at Alabama State, takes little credit for herself in her memoir, her involvement and leadership are obvious. Included in the history are black-and-white photographs and documents, a glossary of individuals, a chronology, and an index. HCA.

Stanton, Mary. **From Selma to Sorrow: The Life and Death of Viola Liuzzo**. Athens: University of Georgia Press, 1998. 250p. $24.95. ISBN 0-8203-2045-5.

> The only white woman honored at the Civil Rights Memorial in Montgomery, Alabama, Viola Liuzzo was murdered by members of the Ku Klux Klan. Liuzzo, a Michigan housewife and mother of five children, was driving nineteen-year-old Leroy Moton, a Black man, to Montgomery on the night of March 25, 1965, after the historic march from Selma to Montgomery. After they were spotted at a stop light, their car was followed by an automobile holding three white Klansmen, who ran them down and shot Liuzzo in the head. Covered with blood, Moton played dead and escaped. In the publicity and trials the followed, Liuzzo was painted as a loose woman, a bad mother, and one who had no business in the South. Mary Stanton's purpose is to uncover the truth about Liuzzo and her involvement in the Civil Rights movement. She detected a cover-up, instigated by J. Edgar Hoover, to hide an FBI informant, a racist who was working undercover during the protest march and may have been the one who killed Liuzzo. A freelance writer, Stanton re-creates the crime, using interviews and all the documentation on the case she can find. The personal involvement that she brings to her investigation brings the decades-old story to life again while putting to rest many of the rumors. Black-and-white photographs, notes, a bibliography, and an index complete the book. HCA.

Tarry, Ellen. **The Third Door: The Autobiography of an American Negro Woman**. Tuscaloosa: University of Alabama Press, 1992. 319p. (Library of Alabama Classics). $19.95pa. ISBN 0-8173-0579-3pa.

> Ellen Tarry's autobiography will stand beside Richard Wright's *Black Boy* in documenting segregation in the early part of the twentieth century. Tarry, with no physically distinguishing African American characteristics, was born in Birmingham, Alabama. Planning a career as a writer, she moved to New York in 1929, just as the stock market crashed. Because of her parents' social position, Tarry had never faced the worst sorts of discrimination, but, as jobs dried up during the Depression, she took work at the lowest levels until she was hired by the Federal Writers Project in 1936. Tarry wrote, performed social work for the Catholic church, and directed a USO for Black soldiers in Alabama during the World War II. It was the treatment of her darker-skinned daughter, born in 1944, that moved Tarry to write *The Third Door,* in which she gave her vision of a world without racial discrimination, one in which a third door would not be marked for colored or white. An afterword written in 1965 outlined Tarry's experiences in the Civil Rights movement. At no time did Tarry ever deny her race, and at times she seemed surprised by cultural issues. The book can be used in conjunction with other books that portray systems of segregation. HCA.

Webb, Sheyann, Rachel West Nelson, and Frank Sikora. **Selma, Lord, Selma: Girlhood Memories of the Civil-Rights Days**. Tuscaloosa: University of Alabama Press, 1997 168p. $15.95pa. ISBN 0-8173-0898-9pa.

When Sheyann Webb and Rachel Nelson were eight and nine years old, respectively, they met Dr. Martin Luther King, Jr. and participated in some of the major protests of the Civil Rights battle in Selma, Alabama. Frank Sikora interviewed the girls when they were in their teens to record their memories of these events. Between January and March 1965, King was organizing citizens of Selma to register to vote and for a march to Montgomery. On March 7, Bloody Sunday, Webb began the march, which was turned back by state troopers at the Edmund Pettus Bridge in downtown Selma and resulted in a riot. Nelson had remained at a local church, where Andrew Young was making logistical arrangements. Within two weeks, a U.S. district judge allowed the march to continue. It was after this march that Civil Rights worker Viola Liuzzo was murdered by Ku Klux Klan members. The girls participated in part of the march to Montgomery and heard about the murder. Their reminiscences reveal the depth of their convictions, even at such a young age; students will relate to their story, which includes black-and-white photographs of Webb and Nelson and the events. There is no index, but Sikora heads each section with a historical overview. MHCA.

Non-Book Material

A Place of Rage. Produced and directed by Pratibha Parmar. 52 min. Women Make Movies, 1991. Videocassette. Purchase $225.00; Rental $90.00.

Two highly articulate women, June Jordan and Angela Davis, narrate the history of the Civil Rights struggle from their experiences with segregation as children, their involvement in the struggles, and their perspectives on the important issues today, including homosexual rights and women's rights. Between segments about the March on Washington, Rosa Parks, and Fannie Lou Hamer, Jordan reads stunningly from her own poetry ("a place of rage" is her phrase). Davis eloquently explains her involvement with the Black Panther Party, her arrest, and her commitment to the Communist Party. Black-and-white news footage, including Davis's 1970 prison interview, illustrate the historical sequences. Comments from writer Alice Walker and filmmaker Trinh T. Minh-ha add to the portraits. The film is backed with rock music from Prince, Janet Jackson, and others. It will find a variety of uses: in literature classes for the poetry, in history classes studying the Civil Rights movement, and in multicultural classes, where the narrators will certainly be admired. HCA.

Rosa Parks: The Path to Freedom. Produced by Patrick Moday. 20 min. Filmakers Library, 1996. Videocassette. Purchase $225.00; Rental $55.00.

Emery King serves as the narrator for this short film that tells of Rosa Parks's courageous act, which began the Civil Rights movement. Her arrest and conviction for failing to give her bus seat to a white passenger in Montgomery, Alabama, on December 1, 1955, was appealed all the way to the Supreme Court, which struck down segregation laws forever. The film details exactly how the segregation system on the buses operated, and it includes current interviews with Parks and people who knew her or were involved in the bus boycott. Film clips and photos are plentiful as Parks's entire life is outlined. As a child she witnessed Klan activity, and she was an NAACP (National Association for the Advancement of Colored People) member. At the time of her arrest, she was a seamstress working in a Montgomery department store. Although several other women were arrested for similar acts, Parks was chosen to be the catalyst that began the bus boycott. After the Supreme Court decision, Montgomery was racially divided, and Parks lost her job. She moved north and currently resides in Detroit, where she works in a variety of ways to improve the lives of students. The film delivers a full and clear presentation of the incident and its place in Civil Rights history; it is accessible to all ages, and will be especially useful in a social studies curriculum. MHCA.

Women's Movement

Books

DuPlessis, Rachel Blau, and Ann Snitow, eds. **The Feminist Memoir Project: Voices from Women's Liberation**. New York: Three Rivers, 1998. 531p. $20.00pa. ISBN 0-609-80384-0pa.

> Fearing that the beginnings of the second-wave feminist movement in the 1960s might be lost, editors Rachel DuPlessis and Ann Snitow called upon feminists to recall their roots in the movement. Around thirty essays are included here, from Vivian Gornick, Alix Kates Shulman, Dana Densmore, Naomi Weisstein, Michele Wallace, and others. In trying to put the movement in perspective, the editors then asked more than half a dozen writers, including Kate Millett, to comment upon the memoirs. Ample material is covered, including Black feminism and lesbian feminism. In their introduction, the editors give much credit to the Civil Rights movement as the spark fanning feminism, and they bear testimony to this in their chronology, which includes many Civil Rights-era events as well as more esoteric moments in history, noted in the memoirs themselves. Notes on the contributors are included. HCA.

Faludi, Susan. **Backlash: The Undeclared War Against American Women**. New York: Doubleday, 1991. 552p. $14.95pa. ISBN 0-385-42507-4pa.

> Feminist journalist Susan Faludi takes on the myths of the 1980s in a scintillating social history. Her premise asks why women were so unhappy in the 1980s if they won their battle for equality in the 1970s. The answer lies in a backlash against feminism. Faludi uses statistics to prove that biological

clocks and shortages of men never existed; she points out media, fashion, and beauty trends that demean women; she blames the New Right, the political climate, and many in positions of power and influence for acting against women; and she shows how these influences have affected popular psychology, working women, and reproductive rights. With sharp writing, Faludi produces massive evidence showing the 1980s were a misogynistic decade in which women never attained educational, wage, benefit, reproductive, or household parity. Sexism reigns while the dominant culture worries about what would happen if women really gained equality. Notes and an index are included. HCA.

Friedan, Betty. **The Feminine Mystique**. New York: Laurel, 1983. 452p. $6.99pa. ISBN 0-440-32497-1pa.

The Feminine Mystique was credited with starting the feminist movement after its publication in 1963. Betty Friedan defined the "feminine mystique" as the cultural images to which women were trying to conform. Women were unhappy, but, as they could not define their problem, it was referred to as "the problem that had no name." The postwar housewife was supposed to be happy at home raising her children, but, Friedan charged, this was a myth, and she believed that Freud, Margaret Mead, educational institutions, and the media helped to create it. Friedan encouraged women to strive to identify paths to self-fulfillment. The 1983, twentieth-anniversary edition of the book contains additional material from Friedan discussing the impact of her book, which she originally presented as an academic study, including notes and an index. HCA.

Horowitz, Daniel. **Betty Friedan and the Making of *The Feminine Mystique*: The American Left, the Cold War, and Modern Feminism**. Amherst: University of Massachusetts Press, 1998. 354p. (Culture, Politics, and the Cold War). $29.95. ISBN 1-55849-168-6.

Concerned that Betty Friedan was misrepresenting herself as a housewife who never had feminist leanings before she wrote *The Feminine Mystique*, Daniel Horowitz writes to set the record straight in an intellectual biography. Friedan attended Smith College and the University of California at Berkeley. She wrote for several union and industry publications in which she showed the roots of philosophies that Horowitz connects to her involvement in the Popular Front, a progressive, civil libertarian group active since the 1930s. Theorizing that Friedan hid this background for fear of McCarthyism, the author concludes that Friedan developed her feminism over a lifetime. Although Friedan has accused Horowitz of red-baiting, the author believes that Friedan and her work were seminal to an age, and that knowing her past makes her work more valuable. The book, even without its political agenda, is a credible biography; it includes notes and an index. HCA.

Ireland, Patricia. **What Women Want**. New York, Plume, 1996. 323p. $12.95pa. ISBN 0-452-27249-1pa.

To discover what women want, Patricia Ireland had to discover what it was she wanted. Ireland is a National Organization for Women activist who served as president through most of the 1990s. In her autobiography, she sees her life as a journey from stewardess school to law school to White House protest arrest. The story is not hers alone, but also the story of the women's movement with all the major personalities included. A black-and-white photograph section and an index are included. HCA.

Lazo, Caroline. **Gloria Steinem: Feminist Extraordinaire**. Minneapolis: Lerner, 1998. 128p. $25.26. ISBN 0-8225-4934-4.

Coming from a difficult childhood, Gloria Steinem realized that she should not marry. After attending Smith College and traveling in India, she began to forge a career as a writer. It was on a writing assignment that Steinem was introduced to the feminist movement; she became a leader of the movement and founded *Ms.* magazine and the National Women's Political Caucus. Caroline Lazo's biography for young readers incorporates many black-and-white and color photographs. The well-laid-out book includes the sources for all quotations, a bibliography, and an index. MH.

Mansbridge, Jane J. **Why We Lost the ERA**. Chicago: University of Chicago Press, 1986. 327p. $42.00; $15.95pa. ISBN 0-226-50357-7; 0-226-50358-5pa.

The social and political issues involved in the defeat of the Equal Rights Amendment are thoroughly analyzed in Jane Mansbridge's important reflection. Alice Paul proposed the Equal Rights Amendment immediately after the passage of the Nineteenth Amendment in 1920; however, the amendment was at odds with the special legislation agenda of such social reformers as Florence Kelley because it would end the protections they had proposed. Finally passed by Congress in 1972, the ERA died ten years later, lacking three states for ratification. During those ten years, a majority of people reported supporting the amendment, a belief that was not born out in the voting booth. Mansbridge portrays the ERA as an amendment of principle; it would not have evoked immediate or large changes in women's position. In a time when the public was not seeking gender role change, the ERA became political; and it was represented as legislation that would send women to war, mandate unisex restrooms, and allow homosexual marriage. While the movement from the principle to the effects of the amendment was damaging, part of the defeat had to do with the massing of volunteer effort. Large voluntary forces require simple causes, and the ERA became too complex. In addition, politics in the 1970s moved to the right with an added suspicion towards giving the Supreme Court more power. Mansbridge believes that the defeat of the amendment was detrimental to women's equality in the long term, because over the years it could have brought about beneficial legal interpretations and legislation. Her detailed study of this event will be helpful to any cause that bases its argument on the "common good." The book, which includes tables, figures, notes, and an index, will be useful in history and political science classes. MHC.

Stern, Sydney Ladensohn. **Gloria Steinem: Her Passions, Politics, and Mystique**. Secaucus, NJ: Birch Lane, 1997. 501p. $27.50. ISBN 1-55972-409-9.

Even while bemoaning the experience of writing the biography of a live person, Sydney Stern's respect and admiration for her subject are evident. Stern portrays Gloria Steinem, now over sixty years old, as one who has succeeded in her journalistic career, in political causes, and as a humanitarian. Even though a hard worker, Steinem always appears controlled, a trait she says was instilled in her as a child of the 1950s. Steinem's name is synonymous with feminism; however, she did not enter the movement until 1969. As the glamour girl of the movement, Steinem's series of male lovers and her public life hold great interest. Stern is confident that Steinem and her friends held nothing back in extensive interviews she held with them. The seriously researched, complete biography is accompanied by black-and-white photographs, notes, a selected bibliography, and an index. HCA.

Tobias, Sheila. **Faces of Feminism: An Activist's Reflections on the Women's Movement**. Boulder, CO: Westview, 1997. 332p. $27.00; $16.00pa. ISBN 0-8133-2842-X; 0-8133-2843-8pa.

> *Faces of Feminism* is Sheila Tobias's personalized history of the feminist movement from the perspective of her twenty-five years as an activist and academic. Tobias served on the NOW Legal Defense and Education Fund and is friends with many key feminists. Detailing "generations" of issues, Tobias arranges her material in a roughly chronological order, devoting more space to the topics that interest her the most. She starts with a historical overview, raising the issues important to the movement, then jumps to the post-suffrage era; she covers the turbulent years of the 1980s as well as other topics such as work, Betty Friedan, antifeminism, lesbianism, new theory, and disagreements. The most complete history of second-wave feminism on the market, the book includes several black-and-white photographs, a chronology, notes, and an index. HCA.

Non-Book Material

Some American Feminists. Produced by Luce Guilbeault, Nicole Brossard, and Margaret Wescott. 56 min. Women Make Movies, 1977. Videocassette. Purchase $225.00; Rental $90.00.

> The most illustrative film about the second wave of the feminist movement, *Some American Feminists* interviews six women who were heavily involved. The film was shot in New York City between 1975 and 1976 when the feminist movement was only about ten years old and already suffering growing pains on a number of issues. These problems are discussed by Rita Mae Brown, Margo Jefferson, Kate Millett, Lila Karp, Ti-Grace Atkinson, and Betty Friedan. Whether it is movement influences, economics, jobs, racism, homophobia, setbacks, or reactionary sways, the women agree that they are discovering and expressing themselves in exciting times and helping to construct a different future. Friedan and Millett have already published important books, *The Feminine Mystique* and *Sexual Politics*. Jefferson weighs in on the place of Black women in feminism. Brown and Millett support the gay liberation movement, but realize that this support is divisive among feminists. Karp and

Atkinson take an adamant stand, admitting that they have given up associating with men. Friedan notes the growth in the feminist movement and how legal changes and recognition have already created a better climate for women. Several protests of the early 1970s, the integration of the want ads at the *New York Times*, and the Stonewall gay rights protest are included in black-and-white and color news clips. The film will be useful in women's studies and social studies classes for teachers well versed in the issues. HCA.

Veteran Feminists of America. 1997. 220 Doucet Road, Lafayette, LA 70503. 318-984-3599. URL: http://www.fodreams.com/VFOA/.

A series of small reunions prompted the founding of the Veteran Feminists of America, a group dedicated to reunion, tribute, and conservation of the history of the second-wave feminists. The organization pursues continuing political, social, and outreach agendas and acts as a resource for young feminists. Any woman involved in the feminist movement between 1965 and 1975 is eligible to join. The *Veteran Feminists of America*, a searchable Web site, offers interactive opportunities, biographies, memories, writings, history, business, and events of the organization. Researchers will appreciate the way the site brings together information about the early years of the feminist movement and offers information not available other places. HCA.

Vietnam War and the Counterculture

Books

Bigler, Philip. **Hostile Fire: The Life and Death of First Lieutenant Sharon Lane**. Arlington: Vandamere, 1996. 192p. $21.95. ISBN 0-918339-37-5.

Among eight American military nurses who lost their lives in Vietnam, Sharon Lane was the only one killed as a result of enemy fire. While working at the 312th Evacuation Hospital in Chu Lai, Lane was killed on the job on June 8, 1969, when a rocket hit a building and exploded. A twelve-year-old Vietnamese girl was also killed. Lane, who was only twenty-four years old when she died, had been in Vietnam six weeks. From Canton, Ohio, she had attended the Aultman School of Nursing before enlisting in the Army. Philip Bigler had full access to Lane's ample correspondence, which her family had kept, and spent several years researching Lane's life for this biography; Lane's last missive from Vietnam is appended. Bigler includes black-and-white photographs and illustrations, appendices of military documents, a selected chronology, a bibliography, and an index. Students will read *Hostile Fire* as biography and use it for research. MHCA.

Brody, Leslie. **Red Star Sister**. St. Paul: Hungry Mind, 1998. 209p. $15.00pa. ISBN 1-886913-15-3pa.

By the time her memoir ends in 1972, Leslie Brody is nineteen years old and has visited the North Vietnamese embassy in France in a self-styled peace delegation of two. Brody wanted to, and did, become a writer, but she detoured through the 1960s on the way. Her youthful journals are included in her narrative, which begins in 1958 with her grammar school years in New York. Brody, already a rebel, was spanked by one of her teachers for a story she had written. Although she survives high school, Brody postpones college to drop out and join the prolific counterculture, traveling across the country from Woodstock to a White Panther commune to Ann Arbor, and then on to Europe. Weaving the historical background of the time with her own experiences and the things she reads, Brody recreates the spontaneity of her coming of age as a naive radical. Students, who are always looking for the authentic hippie experience, will love this very readable story. HCA.

Davis, Angela. **Angela Davis: An Autobiography**. New York: International, 1988. 400p. $12.95pa. ISBN 0-7178-0667-7pa.

Written at the age of twenty-eight, Angela Davis's intelligent and articulate autobiography is framed within the narrative of her arrest in New York as a fugitive from a California conspiracy charge. A gun owned by Davis had been used in a Marin County Courthouse hostage situation and murder. Although Davis was acquitted of all charges, it took several years, and she lost her job with the University of California. The charges against her in the Soledad brothers case were politically motivated by her race and politics: she was a Black member of the Communist Party. Born in Birmingham, Alabama, Davis learned righteous values from her family. Educated at private school in New York, Brandeis University, and abroad, Davis participated in the Civil Rights movement and politics from an early age. Although she thought it was presumptuous to write an autobiography, which dwells mostly on the Soledad incident, at such an early age, the book is a first-hand account of the unsettled politics of the 1960s and 1970s. Several black-and-white photographs of the author in her youth appear opposite the title page. HCA.

Mullen, Peg. **Unfriendly Fire: A Mother's Memoir**. Iowa City: University of Iowa Press, 1995. 156p. (Singular Lives). $12.95pa. ISBN 0-87745-507-4pa.

Peg Mullen's son was drafted into the Vietnam War in 1968. Within two years, Mullen was notified that her son had been killed by "friendly fire," a concept she could not comprehend. She started a one-woman campaign to protect other mothers' sons from the same fate. The incident, and Mullen's reactions, were documented in a book and television movie, *Friendly Fire*, but *Unfriendly Fire* is Mullen's own story, written from the distance of twenty-five years and after the death of her supportive husband. There is, after all, more of the story to report. Mullen was contacted by the American soldier who killed her son, as well as other people connected to the incident. Norman Schwarzkopf, her son's commanding officer, returned to military combat and his actions in the Gulf War prompted a reexamination of Mullen's son's letters home. (They are appended to the book.) Although Mullen's writing is cathartic, she represents one of thousands of women who faced similar situations during the war. The book includes black-and-white photographs. HCA.

Walker, Keith. **A Piece of My Heart: The Stories of 26 American Women Who Served in Vietnam**. Novato, CA: Presidio, 1985. 350p. $15.95pa. ISBN 0-89141-617-Xpa.

Artist and writer Keith Walker became interested in recording the stories of women who had served in Vietnam after meeting and talking to an army nurse. He was surprised to find that a number of veterans would not talk to him, canceled their interviews, or neglected to return their transcripts. Yes, feelings still ran high, even after several decades. Walker was also surprised to find that it was hard to determine how many military and civilian women had served in Vietnam, but he estimates about 15,000. In his appendix, he tries to list all the organizations and units in which women served, but he believes the list is not complete. Among the twenty-six women Walker did interview are nurses, WACs, Special Services operators, Red Cross workers, USO employees, entertainers, and others. Each interview is prefaced with a contemporary portrait of the subject and some background. Additional sections of black-and-white photographs would be better placed with the interview they accompany. Entertainer Martha Raye, who received two Purple Hearts for wounds received in Vietnam, writes the introduction. HCA.

Non-Book Material

The Other Angels. Produced and Directed by Patricia L. Walsh. 56 min. The Other Angels Productions, 1995. Videocassette. $39.00 for schools; $59.00 for libraries and colleges.

An excellent addition to Vietnam War studies is the moving video, *The Other Angels*. The film, made by Patricia L. Walsh, who served in Vietnam as a civilian nurse attached to the State Department's Public Health Service in the late 1960s, is recorded at a reunion of five nurses during the dedication of the Vietnam Women's Memorial on Veteran's Day 1993. The group is followed from their hotel meeting, through the parade and dedication ceremony, and to a private dinner. While the former nurses participate in the day's events, each one reveals her personality and recalls incidents from her time in Vietnam. The film would have succeeded with this alone, but the reminiscences are interspersed with newsreels, film clips, and stock and personal photographs in color and black-and-white. The juxtaposition of images and memories creates several layers and allows the film to convey volumes while remaining neutral on the controversial issues surrounding the war. The nurses maintain the qualities that most likely led them to this field in the first place: concern for humanity, a sense of humor, a willingness to serve, and adaptability. The production presents the history of the war balanced against its human side and its absurdity. The fond memories of encounters with the Vietnamese people and the speculation about how many parade spectators that day had lost someone in Vietnam help to weave the old and new together. Yes, the nurses gathered to heal themselves, and the film extends that healing power to all who see it. It is highly recommended for all audiences. HCA.

The Female Experience

General and Regional Materials

Books

Abbott, Shirley. **Womenfolks: Growing up down South**. Boston: Houghton Mifflin, 1998. 210p. $12.00pa. ISBN 0-395-90144-8pa.

> Shirley Abbott ran away from the South and her roots, but, when she returned to help her dying mother, she wondered why. *Womenfolks* is her effort to explore the culture of southern women. The book combines Abbott's own family history with the research of southern historians, diaries and journals, and the historical fiction of the South. When Abbott brings forth all the myths of the region for reexamination, we discover that the South creates myths about women like no other region of the country. In the end, women of the area are revealed as more important and more vital than the stereotyped southern belle. HCA.

Bernhard, Virginia, Betty Brandon, Elizabeth Fox-Genovese, and Theda Perdue, eds. **Southern Women: Histories and Identities**. Columbia: University of Missouri Press, 1992. 203p. $34.95. ISBN 0-8262-0868-1.

> The nine papers published in *Southern Women* were presented at the Southern Conference on Women's History, sponsored by the Southern Association for Women Historians at Converse College, Spartanburg, South Carolina in June 1988. The papers present a wide range of experiences, various periods, and different races and classes. Susan Westbury writes on women in Bacon's Rebellion; Kent Anderson Leslie presents a mulatto women, Amanda America Dickson; Cheryl Thurber develops the mammy image; Mary Martha Thomas and Elizabeth Hayes Turner both consider suffrage in the South; and Darlene Clark Hine reflects on Black women and rape. Notes on the contributors and an index are appended to the wide-ranging collection. HCA.

DuBois, Ellen Carol, and Vicki L. Ruiz, eds. **Unequal Sisters: A Multicultural Reader in U.S. Women's History**. 2d ed. New York: Routledge, 1994. 620p. $29.99pa. ISBN 0-415-90892-2pa.

> *Unequal Sisters* explains how, in the early stages of women's history in the United States, it was believed that there was one universal female experience, that of the white woman. Now a multicultural experience is assumed and research into all aspects of women's past is ongoing. The publication of *Unequal Sisters* presents the research of the finest historians: Nancy Hewitt on recent thought on women's history, Rayna Green on the portrayal of Native women in American culture, Kathryn Kish Sklar on Hull House, Linda Gordon on family violence, Meredith Tax on giving voice to immigrant women through fiction and nonfiction, Judy Yung on the feminization of Chinese-American women, and Elsa Barkley Brown on Maggie Lena Walker. The thirty essays cover cultural groups from many areas of the country,

and historical periods from settlement to the present. Taken together, the essays give a true feel for the vast experiences of women in U.S. history. The book would be useful in many courses of study where the essays could be assigned chronologically, by cultural group, or by topic. Selected bibliographies of Latinas, and women of African American, Asian American, and Native American descent are appended. HCA.

Farnham, Christie Anne, ed. **Women of the American South: A Multicultural Reader**. New York: New York University Press, 1997. 319p. $19.50pa. ISBN 0-8147-2655-0pa.

Christie Farnham's book is the *Unequal Sisters* of the South, including seventeen wide-ranging essays on the southern woman by a variety of contributors. As editor, Farnham places the material in chronological order and prefaces each selection with a note giving its historical context. The book begins with an essay by Anne Firor Scott, the historian who first researched the southern woman. Topics include Choctaw women, Cherokee women, Jewish women, Appalachian women, Mary McLeod Bethune, lesbian women, female slaves in planter wills, the Northern myth of the rebel girl, women in Reconstruction and the Depression, Garveyism, and second-wave feminism. No collection on southern women should be without the coverage of *Women in the American South*. Notes on the contributors and an index are included. HCA.

Hasselstrom, Linda, Gaydell Collier, and Nancy Curtis, eds. **Leaning Into the Wind: Women Write from the Heart of the West**. Boston: Houghton Mifflin, 1997. 388p. $25.00. ISBN 0-395-83738-3.

Although there are no well-known writers represented in *Leaning Into the Wind*, the amateur writing is as touching and poignant as any published work. The writers are ordinary women, from the high plains states of North Dakota, South Dakota, Nebraska, Montana, Wyoming, and Colorado, who took pen in hand at some point in their lives. The editors, three "ranch women" who lived several hundred miles apart, received so much material in response to their open solicitation that they had trouble winnowing it down. In the end, the writings of over 100 "tough and independent" women were selected for the collection, which is made up of poetry and memoir both humorous and heartfelt. This collection should not be read straight through, but rather savored over different stages of a lifetime. Although it speaks directly to women in the West, it will be enjoyed by women everywhere. Notes on the contributors are attached. HCA.

Niederman, Sharon. **A Quilt of Words: Women's Diaries, Letters and Original Accounts of Life in the Southwest, 1860–1960**. Boulder, CO: Johnson, 1988. 220p. $11.95pa. ISBN 1-55566-047-9pa.

Gleaned from historical societies and libraries in Colorado, Arizona, Utah, and New Mexico, the four corner states, Sharon Niederman introduces western women's journals as an art form. The women journal-keepers portrayed in

A Quilt of Words came to the West after the Civil War and throughout the beginning of the twentieth century for many reasons: as brides, as teachers, and to cure themselves. The writing of each of the fifteen subjects is prefaced by Niederman in chapters ranging from three to many more pages, some of which contain black-and-white photographs. An eighty-five-year-old described only as "Yavapai woman" was recorded in Arizona as part of an oral history program; Marietta Wetherill was adopted by the Navajo tribe and married Chaco Canyon excavator Richard Wetherill; Grace Mott Johnson was a sculptor visiting Taos in its early days as an art colony; and Isabella Greenway was a New Deal congresswoman for Arizona. The writings speak to the variety of adventures women enjoyed in the West and how they differed from the explorations of men. MHCA.

Rak, Mary Kidder. **A Cowman's Wife**. Austin: Texas State Historical Association, 1993. 301p. (DeGolyer Library, Cowboy and Ranch Life). $29.95pa. ISBN 0-87611-127-4pa.

In 1919, Mary Kidder Rak and her husband purchased the 22,000-acre Old Camp Rucker Ranch north of Douglas, Arizona. Although Rak had been a teacher and had no ranch experience, she learned to do everything required by her new life, including outdoor work and keeping house without the benefit of electricity. *A Cowman's Wife*, first published in 1934, details the joys of ranch life, all-night dances at the schoolhouse, the scenery, and rain in the desert; the dangers, such as strangers on the ranch, wolves, and flash floods are also discussed. Although the Raks sold their ranch in 1943, the book remains as a testimony from a woman who fully participated in agricultural life during the first half of the twentieth century. *A Cowman's Wife* will have regional interest, and is accessible for all who love the West. Introduced by western historian Sandra L. Myres, the book is illustrated with charcoal drawings and has an index. MHCA.

Rothschild, Mary Logan, and Pamela Claire Hronek. **Doing What the Day Brought: An Oral History of Arizona Women**. Tucson: University of Arizona Press, 1992. 174p. $17.95pa. ISBN 0-8165-1276-0pa.

For the Lives of Arizona Women Project, Mary Rothschild and Pamela Hronek interview over twenty women aged seventy and older, adding their stories to the rich history of the state. In choosing women to interview, the authors try to match the 1890 to 1930 census data in terms of ethnic makeup and geographical distribution while also representing the mining, agricultural, and business economies. The interviews are woven within a narrative created by the authors, covering immigration, childhood, daily life, community life, and work. The book presents varied cultural, religious, and class perspectives of the early years of the twentieth century as the subjects look back on their lives and their involvement in historical events. It is enjoyable reading for those interested in Arizona history, women's history, or pioneer life. A section of historical and current photographs of the interviewees is included, as well as notes, a bibliography, and an index. MHCA.

Scott, Anne Firor. **The Southern Lady: From Pedestal to Politics, 1830–1930**. Charlottesville: University Press of Virginia, 1995. 312p. $12.95pa. ISBN 0-8139-1644-5pa.

> Anne Firor Scott's book is acknowledged as a classic that initiated the field of women's history. When Scott noticed how many women were mentioned as playing significant roles in southern reform movements before suffrage, which was at odds with the standard view of the southern lady, she uncovered journals, diaries, and other writings that revealed a more active picture. Dividing her study, Scott looks at the image of southern women in the ante-bellum period, and she thoroughly documents the southern suffrage movement in the post–Civil War period. An afterword to the 1995, twenty-fifth anniversary edition discusses the book's impact and the author's opinion of it after a life's work in women's history. The book includes a section of black-and-white photographs, a bibliographic essay, and an index. HCA.

Varnell, Jeanne. **Women of Consequence: The Colorado Women's Hall of Fame**. Boulder, CO: Johnson, 1999. 384p. $32.50; $18.00pa. ISBN 1-55566-213-7; 1-55566-214-5pa.

> *Women of Consequence* is included in this bibliography as the type of publication that, it is to be hoped, exists in every state. It is a biographical collection of the women included in the Colorado Women's Hall of Fame. Although women's hall of fame organizations exist in many states, they vary in physical form from Web sites to museums to traveling exhibits, and their induction requirements are diverse. Colorado inducts, on an irregular schedule, both contemporary and historical women and now includes almost sixty women, who are profiled in short articles. Readers are encouraged to search for their own state or local women's hall of fame through the Yellow Pages or on the World Wide Web to find publications of regional interest. MHCA.

Non-Book Material

Documenting the American South. 1999. University of North Carolina at Chapel Hill, Walter Royal Davis Library, Chapel Hill, NC 27544-8890. 919-962-1301; fax 919-962-5537. E-mail: docsouth@listserv.unc.edu. URL: http://metalab.unc.edu/docsouth/index.html.

> Pulling material from its own collection, the University of North Carolina has mounted a large database of southern literature, first-person narratives, and slave narratives. Many women are represented within each of these sections. The collections are of full-text, primary source material covering southern history from colonization through the early twentieth century. An excellent source for research material, the searchable Web site will also be of regional interest. MHCA.

Teaching Tolerance. 1999. Southern Poverty Law Center, 400 Washington Avenue, Montgomery, AL 36104. fax 334-264-7310. URL: http://www.splcenter.org/teachingtolerance/tt-index.html.

A project of the Southern Poverty Law Center, *Teaching Tolerance* magazine was established in 1991 to help classroom educators promote equity, respect, and understanding. The periodical is published twice a year and mailed free to teachers. Resource kits on the Civil Rights movement and the history of intolerance in America, both of which include women's experiences, are also available at no cost to schools. The *Teaching Tolerance* Web site provides classroom resources, activities, and recommended reading suggestions. The site is searchable and links to the hate group research of the Southern Poverty Law Center, making it a useful spot for teachers. MH.

Women's Archives in the Special Collections Library at Duke University. 1997. Duke University, Perkins Library, Durham, NC 27708. 919-660-5880; fax 919-684-2855. E-mail: Elizabeth Dunn, Archivist, edunn@duke.edu. URL: http://scriptorium.lib.duke.edu/women/.

Duke University's Special Collections Library owns a rather extensive archival collection documenting women in the American South from the late eighteenth century to the present. Three parts of this collection have been chosen for online access. The Women's Liberation Movement section includes over forty transcribed texts and scanned images from documents that originated between 1969 and 1974. The African American Women zone contains scanned images and texts of the writings of four women, three of them slaves. The Civil War Women section contains a girl's diary and the papers of both a Confederate and a Union spy. The site is searchable and links to a few additional women's archives on the Web. The documents available are well selected, and teachers of the Civil War and of twentieth-century history will admire Duke's efforts in making these collections available online. MHCA.

African Americans

Books

Bolden, Tonya. **And Not Afraid to Dare: The Stories of Ten African-American Women**. New York: Scholastic, 1998. 216p. $16.95. ISBN 0-590-48080-4.

Chosen to represent the theme of courage across American history from the time of slavery to the present, the ten women included in *And Not Afraid to Dare* are arranged chronologically by their dates of birth. Their stories are exciting: Ellen Craft dressed as a man to escape slavery; Mary Fields was a stagecoach driver in Montana; Ida B. Wells-Barnett was threatened with death for speaking out against lynching; Clara Hale retired only to begin a new career nursing drug-addicted babies; and Mae Jemison traveled to space. The book also characterizes Charlotte Forten Grimké, Mary McLeod Bethune, Leontyne Price, Toni Morrison, and Jackie Joyner-Kersee, with each sketch including a portrait and quotations. Students can use this book, which appends a listing of additional daring women, a selected bibliography, and an index, for both independent reading and research. MH.

Cary, Lorene. **Black Ice**. New York: Vintage, 1991. 238p. $12.00pa. ISBN 0-679-73745-6pa.

Lorene Cary, a graduate of the University of Pennsylvania, has written for *Time* magazine. In *Black Ice,* she describes how, in her late adolescence, she is recruited to attend a private New Hampshire high school, formerly all-white and all-male, expanding the diversity of its student body for the first time in the 1970s. Cary chose to leave Philadelphia and attend St. Paul's, the sole Black woman enrolled. In this position, she pressured herself to achieve and questioned everything about her life. As a testament to St. Paul's impact on her, she later returned as a teacher and as a trustee who encouraged other Black students. Cary's story has impact, and students will understand her confusion and admire her determination. MHCA.

Chambers, Veronica. **Mama's Girl**. New York: Riverhead, 1996. 194p. $12.00pa. ISBN 1-57322-599-1pa.

A survivor of poverty and cruelty who grew up in Brooklyn in the 1970s, Veronica Chambers suffered abuse at the hands of her father, step-mother, and step-father. Because her mother, a secretary, was overwhelmed by the task of raising Chambers and her difficult younger brother, Chambers became the perfect child in order to help her. Growing up, but without being raised, Chambers started college at age sixteen and went on to a career in magazine writing and editing. The memoir of her youth is simply stated and emotional, one with which many teens will identify. HCA.

Delany, Sarah L., A. Elizabeth Delany, and Amy Hill Hearth. **Having Our Say: The Delany Sisters' First 100 Years**. New York: Dell, 1993. 299p. $6.99pa. ISBN 0-440-22042-4pa.

Both over 100 years old at the time they wrote the book, Sadie and Bessie Delany look back at a century of experiences. Raised on a college campus, Saint Augustine's in Raleigh, North Carolina, where their father was employed, the girls understood early the power of education. Although neither married, they both attended Columbia University; Bessie became a dentist and Sadie a teacher. Relocating in New York, the sisters lived in Harlem during its renaissance in the 1920s where they knew many of the important figures of the day. They outlived the Civil Rights period, they outlived the "Rebby" boys, and they lived to tell about it all in alternating and distinct voices. Their personal accounts of their 100 years provide students with a good sense of the advance of history. A section of black-and-white family photographs is included. HCA.

Dunham, Katherine. **A Touch of Innocence: Memoirs of Childhood**. Chicago: University of Chicago Press, 1959. 312p. $12.95pa. ISBN 0-226-17112-4pa.

> Concentrating on Katherine Dunham's childhood, before her career as a dancer/choreographer and her success as an anthropologist who traveled the world to study native dances, her memoirs paint a distressing picture of a dysfunctional family. Born in Chicago in 1909 to a mother of French Canadian and Native American ancestry and a father of West African descent, Dunham had one brother, Albert, Jr. After their mother died, the children were left with aunts while their father, ambitious, yet embittered by his failures, traveled as a salesman. When the father remarried, the family moved to Joliet to open a dry cleaning business. The conflicts between and among the father, the stepmother, and the brother, which Dunham sought to avoid, form the basis of most of the narrative. Recalling her girlhood, Dunham writes brutally and honestly, and, even though set in an earlier time, students will relate to the shy, but perceptive girl who would overcome the obstacles of her youth to find success in her chosen fields. Two black-and-white photographs of Dunham as a child illustrate the book. HCA.

Evers-Williams, Myrlie, and Melinda Blau. **Watch Me Fly: What I Learned on the Way to Becoming the Woman I Was Meant to Be**. Boston: Little, Brown, 1999. 324p. $23.00. ISBN 0-316-25520-3.

> Although Myrlie Evers-Williams insists her memoir is not about her husband, Medgar Evers, or the NAACP, there is plenty about him in it. There is also plenty about living, learning from the past, single parenting, the Black glass ceiling, creating a successful relationship, and aging. Born in the deep South, Evers-Williams married NAACP employee Medgar Evers, who was assassinated in Jackson, Mississippi, during the Civil Rights years of the 1960s, and Evers-Williams spent the next thirty years bringing the killer to justice. To raise her three children, she returned to college and rose through a series of jobs, ending as chair of the NAACP in 1995. Unfortunately, her term was disrupted by scandal. As a person who has had to start over several times (she lost another partner to cancer), Evers-Williams is well qualified to give advice, but hers comes wrapped in story. Read it for history or to learn from one who has been there. Black-and-white photographs and an index are included. HCA.

Giddings, Paula. **When and Where I Enter: The Impact of Black Women on Race and Sex in America**. 2d ed. New York: Morrow, 1984. 408p. $14.00pa. ISBN 0-688-14650-3pa.

> Based on extensive research into primary sources and using the words of Black women wherever possible, Paula Giddings illuminates their unique history grounded in double discrimination, both racial and sexual. Giddings sees Black women as the "linchpin" between the movements for civil rights and women's rights in the twentieth century. In her book, she covers all major movements and personalities from the seventeenth century to the present. Ida B. Wells-Barnett, Mary McLeod Bethune, the Black club

movement, Black women and suffrage, the Student Nonviolent Coordinating Committee, and Black feminists all receive extended treatment. Giddings's book, with its notes, sources, and index, is more topical than Darlene Clark Hine and Kathleen Thompson's *A Shining Thread of Hope*, which is more comprehensive as well as illustrated. Both books offer extensive quotations, but Giddings maintains her thesis of "impact." The books do not duplicate each other, and libraries may want to own both as important sources by noted researchers. HCA.

Hall, Wade. **Passing for Black: The Life and Careers of Mae Street Kidd**. Lexington: University Press of Kentucky, 1997. 193p. $24.95; $14.00pa. ISBN 0-8131-1996-0; 0-8131-0948-5pa.

> Mae Street Kidd lived a remarkable life. Born in 1904 outside Louisville, in Millersburg, Kentucky, Kidd did not know her white father and never spoke to him, although he was pointed out to her once at the post office. Raised as a Black, attending Black schools, Kidd did not make an issue of her race or of her light skin; she just worked hard. When she was seventeen, Kidd began to sell insurance, surpassing records for the Mammoth Life and Accident Insurance Company. Kidd joined the Red Cross and served overseas during World War II. At age sixty-four, she was elected to the Kentucky General Assembly where she sponsored a bill to ratify the Thirteenth, Fourteenth, and Fifteenth Amendments to the United States Constitution, as a symbolic act to free the slaves and give them citizenship rights. Her many accomplishments will be inspiring for many. The book is studded with black-and-white photographs and includes an index. HCA.

Hine, Darlene Clark, Elsa Barkley Brown, Rosalyn Terborg-Penn, eds. **Black Women in America: An Historical Encyclopedia**. 2 vols. Bloomington: Indiana University Press, 1993. 1530p. (Blacks in the Diaspora). $49.95pa. ISBN 0-253-32775-Xpa.

> Containing 804 articles on women, organizations, and topics related to Black women's history, *Black Women in America* comes as close to being a comprehensive encyclopedia as any book on the market. Created by three distinguished scholars with the help of an editorial board and hundreds of contributors, the book's tone is scholarly, yet accessible. The volumes contain many features to aide in research: a reader's guide leads users through the organization of the book; abbreviations to frequently used sources are listed; non-biographical articles are cataloged separately; and biographical entries are sorted according to professions. In addition, a full chronology, a bibliography of basic sources, and a complete index are appended. The entries themselves run from several paragraphs to several pages, but each enjoys a complete bibliography, exhibiting the depth of scholarship afforded to each article. Cross references lead the reader to various forms of a person's name. The book includes notes on all the collaborators and over 450 carefully chosen, clear photographs. The paperback edition of this basic reference is sturdy and produced at a price every school and library can afford. MHCA.

Hine, Darlene Clark, and Kathleen Thompson. **A Shining Thread of Hope: The History of Black Women in America**. New York: Broadway, 1998. 355p. $27.50; $14.00pa. ISBN 0-7679-0110-X; 0-7679-0111-8pa.

> Darlene Clark Hine and Kathleen Thompson offer the best one-volume history of Black women in America. Covering the seventeenth through twentieth centuries in a chronological arrangement, the authors discuss both free and slave women as well as the important organizations and movements. The book is notable for its use of many quotations from Black women throughout and for highlighting the themes of community, education, dignity, and triumph. Three sections of sharp black-and-white photographs with complete captions are chosen to represent topics such as the westward movement and Black women on the stage. Notes, a bibliography, and an index complete an excellent source appropriate for all audiences. MHCA.

Hine, Darlene Clark, and Kathleen Thompson, eds. **Facts On File Encyclopedia of Black Women in America**. 11 vols. New York: Facts On File, 1997. $329.45. ISBN 0-8160-3424-9.

> The *Facts On File Encyclopedia of Black Women in America* takes the basic information in *Black Women in America*, divides it topically, takes on an introductory essay that provides an excellent overview of the subject, and adds approximately 200 articles to expand the content considerably. With its use of larger print in volumes that run between 200 and 300 hundred pages, the set is aimed at school audiences. The volumes include The Early Years, 1619–1899; Literature; Dance, Sports, and Visual Arts; Business and Professions; Music; Education; Religion and Community; Law and Government; Theater Arts and Entertainment; Social Activism; and Science, Health, and Medicine. Although each article is signed, the contributors' notes and the comprehensive bibliographies used in *Black Women in America* have been dropped. Instead, a general bibliography is available at the end of each volume. Bold-faced notations in the text indicate an article in the set on that subject. Each volume contains notes on how to use the book, many black-and-white photographs, a subject-specific chronology, contents of the set listed by volume and by alphabetical entry, and a volume index. A master index and occupations index are available in the science volume. Schools may want to consider this well-put-together set for reference use. MHA.

hooks, bell. **Bone Black: Memories of Girlhood**. New York: Henry Holt, 1996. 183p. $20.00; $11.95pa. ISBN 0-8050-4145-1; 0-8050-5512-6pa.

> bell hooks, who is a respected intellectual and Black feminist, reveals her roots in Hopkinsville, Kentucky, in over sixty short, chronologically arranged vignettes. Like every girl, she sometimes feels lonely and different, and, as the rebellious child among seven children, she is markedly the outsider. Although hooks grows up in a loving family and respects her elders, she witnesses incidents of racism and knows fear, and she is candid about her sexual explorations in chapters written in both first and third person. Women, especially teenagers, will identify with hooks's coming-of-age. HCA.

Hunt, Annie Mae. **I Am Annie Mae: An Extraordinary Woman in Her Own Words, the Personal Story of a Black Texas Woman**. Edited by Ruthe Winegarten. Austin: University of Texas Press, 1983. 152p. $13.95pa. ISBN 0-292-79099-6pa.

> Annie Mae Hunt was born in Texas in 1909, the granddaughter of a slave. In this oral history, edited by Ruthe Winegarten, the essence of Hunt comes through as she tells about her life and the lives of her mother and grandmother, three generations of her family. Grandmother Tildy, born a slave around 1846, was a midwife and the mother of sixteen children; she lived on 1,500 acres given to her by the family that owned her for having born a child by their son. Hunt's mother, Callie, was born in 1889. When she was in her thirties, the man she was living with spoke out of turn to a white man and ran away, but Callie and her daughter suffered severe beatings in retaliation, and Hunt bore the physical scars from this incident throughout her life. Although Hunt never received more than a fifth grade education, she pulled herself up through hard work, entrepreneurship, and politics. Hunt bought a house and worked for herself. After she volunteered for the Democratic Party, she was able to attend President Carter's inauguration. In her memoirs, Hunt considers all the important issues of the day, including women's rights, religion, and family. Her story is interesting in itself, told in short chapters and illustrated with family photographs and documents, but it also illustrates southern Black life from the time of slavery. For more than personal reading, the book can be used as primary source material in history classes. HCA.

Lerner, Gerda, ed. **Black Women in White America: A Documentary History**. New York: Vintage, 1972. 630p. $16.00pa. ISBN 0-679-74314-6pa.

> A great service has been provided by Gerda Lerner in collecting around 150 primary sources on Black women in history. Although the offering is only representative of what is available, the book should find a place in all schools and libraries. Susie King Taylor, Septima Clark, Charlotte Hawkins Brown, Mary McLeod Bethune, Mary Church Terrell, Daisy Bates, Shirley Chisholm, and Pauli Murray are some of the important figures whose writings are included. The documents come from the nineteenth and twentieth centuries and cover slavery, education, Black women's "lot," work, resistance, politics, prejudice, improvement organizations, racial pride, and images of womanhood. Lerner introduces each piece and provides title, author, and date, if available. Bibliographical notes are provided, but no index. This important collection will be used in research and as supplementary material for history classes. HCA.

Nelson, Jill. **Volunteer Slavery: My Authentic Negro Experience**. New York: Penguin, 1993. 244p. $12.95pa. ISBN 0-14-023716-Xpa.

> From the first page to the last, Jill Nelson's voice jumps off the page, biting and funny. Nelson's narrative begins in April 1986 as she enters her job interview with Ben Bradlee, editor of the *Washington Post*. Nelson is under

consideration as a writer for a new Sunday magazine, and immediately she knows the score. The *Post*, in a predominately Black city, needs her, a Black female, as a token. She takes the job anyway. Through the next four years she struggles with diplomacy and invisibility at work, with a teenage daughter at home, and with a series of short-lived relationships. Her Juneteenth is the day she quits. Nelson's caustically humorous book represents the stories of all men and women who work for corporate America, and will appeal to a wide audience. HCA.

Plowden, Martha Ward. **Famous Firsts of Black Women**. Gretna, LA: Pelican, 1993. 155p. $15.95. ISBN 0-88289-973-2.

> Twenty women who have achieved "firsts" are documented in Martha Plowden's book. From the arts and sports to business and politics, the women come from Colonial times and the present. Besides many well-known names, some of the women include poet Gwendolyn Brooks, actress Diahann Carroll, ambassador Patricia Roberts Harris, teacher Elizabeth Duncan Koontz, and sculptor Edmonia Lewis. Several of the entries are short, only a few pages long, and each is illustrated by Ronald Jones. Suggestions for further reading complete the book, which can be used for independent reading or for research. MH.

Smith, Jessie Carney, ed. **Notable Black American Women**. Detroit: Gale, 1992. 1334p. $105.75. ISBN 0-8103-4749-0.

Smith, Jessie Carney, ed. **Notable Black American Women: Book II**. Detroit: Gale, 1996. 775p. $105.75. ISBN 0-8103-9177-5.

> *Notable Black American Women* contains biographies of 800 women, 500 in the first volume and 300 in the second volume, chosen to represent a wide range of geographical, historical, and professional interests. The alphabetically arranged entries are generally longer and more scholarly in tone than those found in *Black Women in America*. Featuring direct quotations, the entries are signed by the author and append a list of references from articles, books, and archival collections. Other features of the volumes include a listing by area of endeavor or occupation and a large subject index. The contributors are listed, but no information about them is presented, and only occasional portraits are included. The second volume includes a list of women from the first volume and indexes them by name only, but it adds a geographical index. Many libraries will want to make Jessie Smith's volumes available in their reference collections. HCA.

Smith, Jessie Carney, ed. **Powerful Black Women**. Detroit: Visible Ink, 1996. 423p. $18.95pa. ISBN 0-7876-0882-3pa.

> A selection of less than 100 of the 800 women's biographies recorded in *Notable Black American Women* are reprinted here, making them available to a wider audience at a lower price. Although not necessarily the best-known

personalities, the approximately seventy women selected are interesting and represent a wide range of endeavors. The book has an improved format with wide margins, captions, and portraits of each subject. The reference lists have been retained, but moved to the back of the book, and a forward by Camille Cosby has been added. A large subject index completes the attractive volume, which should find a place in many homes, classrooms, and libraries. MHCA.

Non-Book Material

African American Women Writers of the 19th Century. 1999. New York Public Library, Schomburg Center for Research in Black Culture, 515 Malcolm X Boulevard, New York, NY 10037-1801. 212-491-2200. E-mail: DigitalSchomburg@nypl.org.URL: http://digital.nypl.org/Schomburg /writers_aa19/toc.html.

The Digital Schomburg is made up of two parts: the fifty-two texts of the *African American Women Writers of the Nineteenth Century* collection, and various images of nineteenth-century African Americans from various divisions of the New York Public Library, including the Schomburg Center. The texts have been carefully transferred to hypertext format, and they are interlinked to the images to form a truly electronic book, searchable and with immediate access to visuals. Authors included in the collection are: Phillis Wheatley, Charlotte Forten Grimké, Harriet Jacobs, Elizabeth Keckley, and Anna Julia Cooper. Besides these familiar names, a number of lesser-known female slave narratives are a part of the collection. The *African American Women Writers of the Nineteenth Century* Web site offers researchers opportunities that never before existed in the manipulation and study of rare books. Educators and students of the Black experience, whether in history or in literature, should look to the Schomburg collection. HCA.

Great Black Women: Achievers Against the Odds. Produced by Valerie F. Whitmore. 52 min. Films for the Humanities and Sciences, 1987. Videocassette. $89.95.

Great Black Women is an excellent choice of film for use during African American History Month. Narrated by Tanya Hart, the film portrays Black women throughout history who overcame obstacles of gender and race, as well as other personal problems, to become well-known in a variety of fields, including media and the arts, politics, sports, and business. It is hard to keep track of all who are mentioned in the film, but some of the distinguished women include Natalie Cole, Fannie Lou Hamer, Valerie Briscoe-Hooks, Whoopi Goldberg, Debbie Allen, Shirley Chisholm, Felicia Rishad, Naomi Sims, Mother Hale, and Maya Angelou. With its rich collection of women, the video could introduce the study of Black history or biography in schools. MHCA.

Guts, Gumption, and Go-Ahead: Annie Mae Hunt Remembers. Produced and directed by Cynthia Salzman Mondell and Allen Mondell. 24 min. Media Projects, 1992. Videocassette. Purchase $95.00; Rental $50.00.

> Irma Hall is the actress who portrays Annie Mae Hunt in this memoir of the granddaughter of a hardworking slave, Tildy (depicted by Donna Hightower), who passed her indomitable spirit to her grandchild. In this sensitive film, cut with archival photographs and film covering the Civil War and Ku Klux Klan through the Civil Rights era and Carter's presidency, the history of the family from Grandma Tildy to Annie Mae is reported. The history is not a happy one and many cruelties are recounted in a straightforward, but not graphic, way. In leaving her husband to move to Dallas during the Depression, Hunt begins to take control of her life. She supports her children through cooking, cleaning, and washing until it occurs to her to work for herself. With earnings from selling beauty products and from sewing, she buys land, builds a house, and works for political causes. After working in Carter's campaign, she rides a bus to Washington to attend his inauguration. The film offers a realistic picture of three generations of Black women who worked hard, achieving small rewards. Hunt, herself, gives the introduction to the film, which is based on the book *I Am Annie Mae*, edited by Ruthe Winegarten. The video can be used in multicultural and in social studies classes as a testimonial of slavery. MHCA.

Happy Birthday Mrs. Craig. Produced and directed by Richard Kaplan. 55 min. Filmakers Library, 1971. Videocassette. Purchase $295.00; Rental $75.00.

> A celebration of the life of Lulu Sandler Craig, the film is narrated by her great-granddaughter a year after a family reunion was held on Craig's one-hundredth birthday. Craig was born in 1868 to parents who were freed from slavery during the Civil War. The family moved to an all-Black colony, Nicodemus, Kansas. When the town was bypassed by the railroad, the family moved on to homestead on the plains of eastern Colorado near Manzanola. Here, Craig had a long teaching career and raised eight children. In the movie, the bright and articulate Craig, as well as four additional generations of her family, are seen in their homes and in still photographs from the time of the Civil War. Craig remembers the Indians in Kansas, going to school with George Washington Carver, and President Grant's second term (the first time her father voted). The family commemorates its veterans for service in the Civil War, World War I, World War II, Korea, and Vietnam. They also discuss Black power, the Black Panthers, racial problems, and *Soul on Ice,* which is topical and timely for the 1970 film. Although younger students may giggle at the hairstyles and clothes, the film gives an excellent sense of history. The pride of this family shines in a production useful in Black history and genealogy studies. MHCA.

Women of Hope: African Americans Who Made a Difference. Bread and Roses Cultural Project, 1994. Posters $59.95; Study Guide $12.95; Educational Discount $39.95 for both.

Framed in bright colors, *African Americans Who Made a Difference* portrays twelve prominent women both contemporary and historical, including Septima P. Clark, Fannie Lou Hamer, Toni Morrison, the Delany sisters, Marian Wright Edelman, Mae C. Jemison, and six others. Most of the women are shown in photographs, but a few artists' portraits are included on the posters, which are in both color and black and white. Each poster includes a quotation from the subject, some of whom are shown in their work environments as writers, crusaders, scientists, artists, and educators. The study guide, which presents full-page biographies, is bilingual (Spanish and English) and includes a myriad of activities useful for middle school students and above. The posters can be purchased and displayed individually or in groups in classrooms, libraries, or offices, especially during African American History Month in February. Teachers will want to employ the posters in conjunction with the most-useful study guide. The *Women of Hope* series from the Bread and Roses Cultural Project includes worthy sets on women from all cultural groups. MHCA.

Asian Americans

Books

Chow, Claire S. **Leaving Deep Water: The Lives of Asian American Women at the Crossroads of Two Cultures**. New York: Dutton, 1998. 302p. $24.95. ISBN 0-525-94075-8.

> Claire Chow's book is built upon over 100 interviews with women of Asian descent who comment on their life experiences. The variety of responses is surprising to Chow who, as a family counselor, is interested in the cultural adjustment Asian American women make as children and adolescents as well as in their family relationships. Opening each chapter with her own experience, Chow covers a variety of social issues: racism, discrimination, stereotyping, ethnicity, and identity. An individual chapter relates immigration stories. Chow's book will be used for personal study by women of color and to present issues for class discussion in sociology and women's history classes. HCA.

Kingston, Maxine Hong. **The Woman Warrior: Memoirs of a Girlhood Among Ghosts**. New York: Vintage, 1976. 243p. $11.00pa. ISBN 0-679-72188-6pa.

> The ghosts Maxine Hong Kingston grew up among are of two types. There are the spirit ghosts who dwell in her mother's "talk-stories" of China, which fill Maxine's mother's days now that she runs a laundromat in Stockton, California, reduced from her former role as healer in China. Ghosts are also the way the immigrant population refers to anyone who is not Chinese, and Kingston is markedly surrounded by ghosts in school. In exploring her position as a woman oppressed by traditional Chinese values, untrusted because,

American born, she is not fully Chinese, yet lacking a place in society, Kingston is drawn to the stories of Chinese women warriors; her narrative becomes a rich mixture of autobiography, legend, and history that spans an ocean and a generation. HCA.

Lee, Mary Paik. **Quiet Odyssey: A Pioneer Korean Woman in America**. Edited by Sucheng Chan. Seattle: University of Washington Press, 1990. 201p. $14.95pa. ISBN 0-295-96969-5pa.

Mary Paik Lee's autobiography is considered quite rare. Immigrating to America as a child in 1906, Lee was one of less than forty Korean-born children residing along the West Coast in the early days of the century. The reasons for this stem from both sides of the ocean. Korea closed emigration after a failed experiment, and the United States passed the 1924 immigration law that drastically reduced the numbers of people coming from Asia. Written from her San Francisco home when she is eighty-five years old, Lee's story tells how, because their well-to-do Christian family was threatened by the invasion of Japan, her family left Korea for Hawaii in 1905 when she was a baby. Within a year they had moved on to California, where they engaged in farming in several locations throughout the state, constantly trying to make ends meet. Lee, a forthright, caring woman, continued this work after her marriage. Sucheng Chan, who edited the text, provides historical background about Korea and the California agricultural industry. Black-and-white photographs and maps are included. HCA.

Ling, Huping. **Surviving on the Gold Mountain: A History of Chinese American Women and Their Lives**. Albany: State University of New York Press, 1998. 252p. $19.95pa. ISBN 0-7914-3864-3pa.

In her comprehensive history of Chinese women's experience in America, Huping Ling divides the text into three parts, covering the early immigration and exclusion period from the 1840s to 1943, the postwar experience from 1943 to 1965, and contemporary women from 1965 through the 1990s. Using tables, documents, and photographs, Ling concludes that social and economic conditions led Chinese women to immigrate, but, once in the United States, their family structure changed as they engaged, with their husbands, in wage earning and decision making for their families. Their process of assimilation was slower, and they remained separate in society until after World War II. Although they participated in organizations within their own communities, it took even more time before Chinese women became visible and active in mainstream politics. The book includes notes, bibliography, and an index. MHCA.

Nakano, Mei T. **Japanese American Women: Three Generations, 1890–1990**. Berkeley: Mina Press, 1990. 256p. $14.95pa. ISBN 0-942610-06-7pa.

The history of the Issei, Nisei, and Sansei, first-, second-, and third-generation Japanese women, is accounted for in Mei T. Nakano's book. Because of early immigration patterns, Japanese women fell into these three distinct generations. Many of the pioneering Issei moved to America as picture brides and for adventure, and they were often insulated from racism in ways that their daughters, the Nisei, who were relocated during World War II, were not. The Nisei, as the transition group, lived dual lives, speaking two languages. The more assimilated Sansei spoke only English, began to marry outside their ethnic community, and built careers. *Japanese American Women* includes the memoir "Okaasan," written by Grace Shibata about her first-generation mother. Many black-and-white photographs are used in the text, and a bibliography and an index are included. MHCA.

Sone, Monica. **Nisei Daughter**. Seattle: University of Washington Press, 1979. 238p. $14.95pa. ISBN 0-295-95688-7pa.

> *Nisei Daughter* begins when Monica Sone is six years old, living with her family in the Carrollton Hotel on the waterfront in Seattle, Washington. She realizes for the first time that she is Japanese when her parents determine to send her to extra classes at Japanese school after elementary school everyday. Because her father runs the hotel, Sone has contact with white visitors; and spending time with her mother helps her understands the Japanese language fairly well. Both these aspects of her upbringing help Sone to paint her childhood in Seattle in the prewar years, before her family is removed to Camp Harmony in Puyallup, Washington, after the bombing of Pearl Harbor. Later, they are sent farther to Camp Minidoka in Idaho, but Sone and her brother and sister apply to leave the camp for college and jobs in the East. Their parents, who have managed to retain the hotel, are later released. Published in 1953, Sone's is the first account of relocation written by a Nisei. Students will use the book for personal reading and for research. MHCA.

Uchida, Yoshiko. **The Invisible Thread**. New York: Beech Tree, 1991. 136p. $4.95pa. ISBN 0-688-13703-2pa.

> Yoshiko Uchida has written many books for children and young adults, using Japanese folktales and her own Japanese-American background as material. *The Invisible Thread* was her memoir of her childhood in Berkeley, California, and of her family's removal to the Topaz relocation camp in Utah during World War II. Twice her parents had taken Uchida and her sister to visit Japan, where Uchida felt like an outsider. As a result of their travels, her father, who worked in imports, was accused of spying and was sent to a prison camp in Montana; the rest of the family went to Utah. Uchida remembered the bad and the good about camp life: the dust storms, going to school, and Christmas in camp. She was released when she received a full graduate fellowship to study education at Smith College. Believing that Sansei, third-generation Japanese, as well as all Americans, must remember these events, Uchida has written several accounts of her experiences at Topaz, both fiction and nonfiction. *The Invisible Thread* includes a section of black-and-white photographs of Uchida and her family. MH.

Wong, Jade Snow. **Fifth Chinese Daughter**. Seattle: University of Washington Press, 1989. 246p. $13.95pa. ISBN 0-295-96826-5pa.

> First published in 1945, *Fifth Chinese Daughter* is the autobiography of Jade Snow Wong as she grew up in San Francisco's Chinatown before World War II. As a member of a very traditional household, Wong speaks only Chinese at home, respects her elders by handing them objects with both hands, and knows her place as the fifth daughter of Wong Hong. Written when she is twenty-four, the memoir tells about the important events in her life. Against the opposition of her parents, Wong goes to college and starts a small ceramics business, although in the end her father admits that this is the independence he wished for her. Decorated with scenes drawn by Kathryn Uhl, the autobiography will be useful in multicultural studies. MHCA.

Yung, Judy. **Unbound Feet: A Social History of Chinese Women in San Francisco**. Berkeley: University of California Press, 1995. 395p. $16.95pa. ISBN 0-520-08867-0pa.

> A second-generation Chinese American and native San Franciscan, Judy Yung provides a complete history of first- and second-generation Chinese women in the city from the nineteenth century to 1945. Yung characterizes the nineteenth century as a period of "bound feet," in which women were restricted to domestic life because of the physical impairments of foot-binding and patriarchal control. After 1902, she identifies increasing freedom and involvement in community organizations, including religious, social, and nationalistic groups. Second-generation women took on a bicultural identity, living a segregated social existence up until World War II; however, the Great Depression and the world war created opportunity for Chinese women through job possibilities, community involvement, and the expansion of family roles. Yung's extensive research comes from government documents, the archives of Christian and Chinese women's organizations, Chinese and English newspapers, and oral histories. While utilizing 350 archived oral histories, Yung also interviewed thirty-two elderly Chinese men and women from the first and second generations especially for this book, and each chapter contains extensive quotations. Black-and-white photographs are included throughout the text, and an appendix presents tables giving population, immigration, nativity, marriage, literacy, and occupational data. Additionally, notes, a glossary of names with their Chinese characters, a bibliography, and an index are included. HCA.

Non-Book Material

Asian American Women of Hope. Bread and Roses Cultural Project, 1998. Posters $59.95; Study Guide $10.00; Educational Discount $39.95 for both.

> Twelve pastel-toned posters with a forty-eight-page study guide make up the *Asian American Women of Hope* set. The women chosen represent the

Indian, Philippine, Chinese, Japanese, Vietnamese, Korean, and Hmong cultures, and they are active as organizers, attorneys, politicians, writers, physicians, and artists. Among the subjects are Maya Lin, Patsy T. Mink, Maxine Hong Kingston, and Yuri Kochiyama. Names and pictures are prominent on the posters, which also feature a short quotation by each subject. A full-page biography of each woman is included in the study guide, which also features activities on names, the history of exclusion, colonialism, and organization. Literature, articles, a time line, a quiz, and a resource guide round out the well-presented guide, offering lots of possibilities for teachers. The posters can be purchased individually, but teachers will want the set with the study guide, which can be used in multicultural curriculums or as part of Asian American History Month in May. MHCA.

Sewing Woman. Produced and directed by Arthur Dong. 14 min. National Asian American Telecommunications Association, 1982. Videocassette. $135.00.

"I'm just a sewing woman," begins the story of Zem Ping Dong, who was a garment worker in Chinatown for over thirty years. In China, Dong was the first (and only) daughter of a poor family, given to a husband at the age of thirteen. Because of hard times, her husband immigrated to the United States, where he was drafted, serving in Europe in World War II. When Dong came to the United States after the war, she had to disown her son and remarry her husband. It was several years before the first son could rejoin his parents, who, by then, had three other children. The family found work easily, and they gained material possessions and status in the community, hosting a huge traditional American wedding along with the Chinese rituals and banquet for their son. *Sewing Woman* is narrated in English by Lisa Lu over Dong's Chinese recitation, for Dong learned only enough English to be naturalized and then promptly forgot it. Filmed in black and white, with contemporary and historical footage as well as family pictures, the film is available with Chinese subtitles. Although short, *Sewing Woman* achieves a major impact as it covers a number of timely issues for history, sociology, and multicultural classes. An excellent study guide is included. MHCA.

Yuri Kochiyama: Passion for Justice. Produced and directed by Patricia Saunders and Rea Tajiri. 57 min. Women Make Movies, 1994. Videocassette. Purchase $250.00; Rental $75.00.

Yuri Kochiyama, who lived in Harlem for over forty years, has been a major activist in a number of causes, including the Civil Rights movement, educational reform, the antiwar movement, the Japanese American compensation movement, and the Puerto Rican liberation movement. Her goals were opposing polarization and promoting understanding among people. Born on the West Coast, Kochiyama's father died in a federal penitentiary, where he was placed after Pearl Harbor when the rest of the family was interned at Jerome, Arkansas. After the war, Kochiyama moved to Harlem, where she was welcomed into many causes as one who was knowledgeable and could speak with conviction. Kochiyama knew Malcolm X; she held his head as he died, and his daughter was interviewed in the video. Kochiyama's activism included participating in the takeover of the Statue of Liberty; this resulted in President Carter's freeing the members of the Puerto Rican liberation movement who had been imprisoned for over twenty years since their attack on Congress in 1954. In 1988, she helped to win compensation and apology for Japanese Americans interned during World War II. A remarkable woman, Kochiyama's story is told through interviews and film clips. The video illustrates the range of political movements during the 1960s and how they addressed racism, injustice, and inequality. HCA.

European Americans

Books

Ets, Marie Hall. **Rosa: The Life of an Italian Immigrant**. 2d ed. Madison: University of Wisconsin Press, 1970. 254p. (Wisconsin Studies in American Autobiography). $16.95pa. ISBN 0-299-16254-0pa.

> Mrs. C., as the maid was known, met sociologist Marie Hall Ets in the Chicago Commons settlement house in 1918. They bonded immediately because Ets was fond of Rosa Cavalleri's storytelling ability, and over the years, Ets listened to Mrs. C.'s life story and wrote the biography of the illiterate Italian immigrant woman. Most of the story took place in Italy, where Cavalleri grew up in the silk-making region not far from Milan; there, she learned the oral tradition in barns where the people gathered with the animals on winter nights to keep warm. Cavalleri was abandoned by her mother on the night she was born and was given to a foster mother to raise. She was bound to an arranged marriage, but her husband left the village to work in the iron mines of Missouri; he sent for his wife in 1884, when she was sixteen. In an unassisted birth, Cavalleri bore her abusive older husband a child; but when he tried to force her into prostitution, she escaped, married a kinder man, and settled in Chicago, where she became associated with the settlement house. Cavalleri's life contains typical elements of many immigrant stories, yet it is atypical in that it was recorded. The combination of her absorbing experiences and the writing, which encompasses Cavalleri's indomitable spirit and the inflections of her voice makes for a compelling tale. HCA.

Halsell, Grace. **In Their Shoes**. Fort Worth: Texas Christian University Press, 1996. 252p. $24.95; $14.95pa. ISBN 0-87565-161-5; 0-87565-170-4pa.

> Grace Halsell lived a fascinating life, traveling all over the world as a writer and reporter. Born in west Texas in 1923 to a thirty-year-old mother, and a sixty-three-year-old father who told her stories of the old days on the Chisholm Trail, Halsell grew up with a great sense of adventure. She rode in the rodeo before beginning her journalistic career, in which she interviewed

Hollywood stars and worked for President Lyndon B. Johnson in the White House. Her most interesting work pertained to her "undercover" assignments, in which she disguised herself to associate with and describe an invisible group. Halsell took a drug to darken her skin so that she could work as a Black maid in Mississippi; became Bessie Yellowhair, a Navajo nanny in Los Angeles; and crossed the Mexican boarder three times as an illegal alien. Her memoir, which contains a section of black-and-white photographs, moves from one adventure to another, and can be used in multicultural studies and for biography reading assignments. HCA.

Non-Book Material

Women's Studies. 1998. University of Pennsylvania, Van Pelt-Dietrich Library, Schoenberg Center for Electronic Text and Image, 3420 Walnut Street, Philadelphia, PA 19104-6206. 215-898-7088. E-mail: Nancy Shawcros, Curator, shawcros@pobox.upenn.edu. URL: http://www.library.upenn.edu /etext/diaries/.

Diaries of five women representing Connecticut, Pennsylvania, and New York, and dating from 1850 to 1909, have been digitized and made available online by the University of Pennsylvania, which plans to make more of its collection available in the future. The *Women's Studies* site also includes the manuscript of a cookbook, including medicinal recipes, and a link to the archives of Black singer Marian Anderson, which is also owned by UPenn. The collection will be of special interest to those in the Northeast and those looking for nineteenth-century material. HCA.

Jewish Americans

Books

Antin, Mary. **The Promised Land**. New York: Penguin, 1997. 305p. $10.95pa. ISBN 0-14-018985-8pa.

First published in 1912, *The Promised Land* was Mary Antin's memoir of her immigration to Boston in 1891. Antin spent her childhood to the age of ten in Polotzk, Russia, where she lived a divided life, realizing a different world outside of her Jewish settlement racked by pogroms. Her memories of those early years were remarkably clear, filling half of her book. In America, where her father brought the family, Antin again felt life was disconnected as the family moved from place to place in the south end of Boston. Enrolled in the public schools, a teacher started her in a writing and publishing career by managing to publish one of Antin's compositions. Her works were mostly autobiographical, and she spent a few years as a Progressive lecturer. *The Promised Land* was critically and popularly successful during its time, due to its remarkable images and wit, and it remains an important account of the immigrant experience. Illustrated with black-and-white photographs, the book also contains a glossary of Yiddish words and suggestions for further reading. This edition introduces a critical essay by Werner Sollors and appends Antin's essay, published in the *New York Times Book Review*, on how she came to write her memoir. MHCA.

Antler, Joyce. **The Journey Home: How Jewish Women Shaped Modern America**. New York: Schocken, 1997. 410p. $16.00pa. ISBN 0-8052-1101-2pa.

The Journey Home is Joyce Antler's combination of history and the biographical accounts of over fifty Jewish women, mainly from the twentieth century. After a prologue that introduces the activities and status of four late-nineteenth-century women, Antler divides the book into three sections covering the periods 1890–1930, 1930–1960, and 1960–1996. Within each period, several women are grouped within the topics of immigration, reform, labor, popular culture, the professions, theater, and feminism. Antler also reflects on the Jewish homeland and women's identity with their religion. The important figures of the century are included: Emma Lazarus, Mary Antin, Maud Nathan, Emma Goldman, Rose Schneiderman, Fanny Brice, Gertrude Stein, Ethel Rosenberg, Bella Abzug, Grace Paley, and many more; however, by placing the women within the context of twentieth-century history and in their congruity as women of faith, the author conceives a larger picture. Antler's excellent overview of Jewish women's contributions contains a short section of black-and-white photographs, notes, and an index. HCA.

Calof, Rachel. **Rachel Calof's Story: Jewish Homesteader on the Northern Plains**. Edited by J. Sanford Rikoon. Bloomington: Indiana University Press, 1995. 158p. $25.00; $12.95pa. ISBN 0-253-32942-6; 0-253-20986-2pa.

When Rachel Calof was sixty years old, she wrote on linen tablets in Yiddish her experience in immigrating from Russia to North Dakota and her life on the homestead for over twenty years. In 1894, when she was eighteen years old, Calof landed at Ellis Island and traveled on to Devils Lake. She married Abraham Calof, whom she had never met because their marriage was arranged, and lived with her in-laws in a dirt-floored shack, which they shared with the farm animals. They carved out a living and raised nine children, often losing more than they gained through droughts, hailstorms, and blizzards. Calof's memoir, which contains black-and-white photographs, was translated by members of her family, and her son added an epilogue about her later life. Two appendices explain Jewish farm settlements and comment upon Calof's life in the perspective of collective history. An index is included in this narrative recounting brutal times. HCA.

Cohen, Rose. Out of the Shadow: A Russian Jewish Girlhood on the Lower East Side. Ithaca, NY: Cornell University Press, 1995. 313p. (Documents in American Social History). $39.95; $15.95pa. ISBN 0-8014-3156-5; 0-8014-8268-2pa.

In *Out of the Shadow,* first published in 1918, Rose Cohen wrote about her family's immigration from the shtetls of Russia to the tenements of the Lower East Side of New York City. Born in 1880 in Belarus, Cohen and an aunt followed her tailor father to New York after he had saved for two years for their passage. The rest of the family joined them the following year. During that time, teenager Cohen worked in the garment sweatshops, where the union movement was growing. When the depression of 1893 struck, Cohen took work as a maid to provide income for the family. During an illness, Cohen was visited by nurse Lillian Wald, who introduced her to the settlement house on Henry Street, providing her with opportunities outside the Jewish neighborhood and a view of a different life. To better herself, Cohen participated in educational opportunities and wrote her memoirs, published before she was forty. She did not live long afterwards, and the facts of her later life and her death are clouded. Her book, noted for its portraits of life in the Lower East Side and containing several photographs as well as black-and-white scenes by artist Walter Jack Duncan, will be used in history and women's studies classes. MHCA.

Glanz, Rudolf. The Jewish Woman in America: Two Female Immigrant Generations, 1820–1929. Vol. 2, **The German Jewish Woman**. New York: KTAV, 1976. 213p. $35.00. ISBN 0-87068-461-2.

Rudolf Glanz recognizes two migrations of Jewish women, the Russians and the Germans. He characterizes the German Jewish immigration as paralleling westward migration, and the establishment of the merchant class in small communities where women created a different social order from that in the old world. In this volume, he discusses family life, social life, fashion, education, and involvement in the women's rights movement along with other topics. His review is scholarly, using many quotations from primary sources. A few black-and-white photographs, cartoons, and documents are used throughout the book, and notes and an index are included. CA.

Hyman, Paula E. Gender and Assimilation in Modern Jewish History: The Roles and Representation of Women. Seattle: University of Washington Press, 1995. 197p. (Samuel and Althea Stroum Lectures in Jewish Studies). $14.95pa. ISBN 0-295-97426-5pa.

In her gender study, Paula Hyman distinguishes between the Western and Eastern societies of Jews, focusing on the Western tradition born in Germany, France, and England, where political and social changes were confronted and a more egalitarian spirit was transmitted to the United States in migration. By the end of the nineteenth century, common gender roles were established in society, and men and women assumed different modes of assimilation. Men created a number of representations of women in response to their own dilemmas of assimilation, leaving women as the primary transmitters of Jewish culture. A bibliography and an index are included. CA.

Levy, Harriet Lane. **920 O'Farrell Street: A Jewish Girlhood in Old San Francisco**. Berkeley: Heyday, 1996. 196p. $12.95pa. ISBN 0-930588-91-6pa.

Taking a room-by-room approach in her writing, Harriet Levy describes the household in which she grew up in San Francisco in the second half of the nineteenth century. Using her wit and love of language, Levy revives the prescriptions of the Victorian Jewish home with great clarity, including descriptions of maids, cooks, Chinese laundrymen, the family, and the neighbors. Levy attended the University of California at Berkeley and wrote with Frank Norris and Jack London before relocating to Paris, where she moved in the social circles of Gertrude Stein and Henri Matisse. Her account of her youth, which re-creates a time long gone, was published in 1937, when she was seventy years old. HCA.

Marcus, Jacob R. **The American Jewish Woman, 1654–1980**. New York: KTAV, 1981. 231p. $19.95. ISBN 0-87068-751-4.

After a brief review of the male Jew in America, Jacob Marcus turns to the history of Jewish women. The account begins in 1654, when Dutch Jews were forced to leave Brazil and travel to New Amsterdam in current New York. Marcus covers the Colonial and Revolutionary periods, followed by larger chapters covering the periods of 1819 to 1892 with the rise of women's associations, 1893 to 1919 and involvement in welfare work and immigration, 1920 to 1962, an era of growth, and 1963–1980, the era of women's revolt. In each section Marcus profiles individual women within the historical context, using a conversational style. His coverage of twentieth-century feminism is particularly notable in this fine overview suitable for school and reference use. Black-and-white illustrations, bibliographical notes, and an index are included. MHCA.

Marcus, Jacob R. **The American Jewish Woman: A Documentary History**. New York: KTAV, 1981. 1047p. $45.00. ISBN 0-87068-752-2.

Meant to accompany *The American Jewish Women, 1654–1980*, Jacob Marcus has collected close to 200 documents recording the experience of Jewish women in America in religious practice, abolitionism, love and marriage, education, suffrage, social reform, the labor movement, birth control, diet, lesbianism, politics, and women's rights. Small-town life and city life from all over the country are accounted for, and Marcus introduces each document, giving its historical background. The documents begin in 1737 with a letter from Abigail Franks of New York to her son in London, and conclude with a 1980 reflection by a Christian woman on her time spent on a kibbutz. Thirty-nine portraits of Jewish women, notes, and an index are included in an important volume that many libraries will want to own. HCA.

Non-Book Material

Jewish Women's Archive. 1999. 68 Harvard Street, Brookline, MA 02445. 617-232-2258; fax 617-975-0109. E-mail: jwarchive@rcn.com. URL: http://www.jwa.org/Jwa-1999/index.htm.

> Dedicated to finding, recording, and making available the history of Jewish women in North America, the *Jewish Women's Archive* is organized around three areas: resources, exhibits, and the virtual archive. Resources offer information about events, educational materials, news, speakers and performers, books, and related Web sites. Exhibits are mounted yearly and feature biographical and documentary material about three women. The virtual archive contains the same archival material that is included in the exhibits. Women included so far are Rebecca Gratz, Emma Lazarus, Molly Picon, Justine W. Polier, Hannah G. Solomon, and Lillian Wald. Offering a professional look and ease of use, this site will continue to expand. MHCA.

Latinas

Books

Martin, Patricia Preciado. **Songs My Mother Sang to Me: An Oral History of Mexican American Women**. Tucson: University of Arizona Press, 1992. 224p. $17.95pa. ISBN 0-8165-1329-5pa.

> *Songs My Mother Sang to Me* is a collection of oral histories of ten elderly Mexican American women representing broad experiences in the agrarian country south of Tuscon. Their interviews show that, although they grew up in ranching country, many later moving into the city, they maintained great respect for the land, their families, their communities, and their religion. Accompanied by several black-and-white photographs, the interviews include a song, a poem, or a prayer from each woman. Patricia Martin has done a great service in preserving this special history, which will be of interest in the Southwest as well as in schools where Spanish is taught. HCA.

Mirandé, Alfredo, and Evangelina Enríquez. **La Chicana: The Mexican-American Woman**. Chicago: University of Chicago Press, 1979. 283p. $13.95pa. ISBN 0-226-53160-0pa.

> A team of professors from the University of California at Riverside has put together a history of Mexican American women from the time of the Aztecs through the rise of the feminist movement, including the topics of family, work and education, and literary images. The literature chapter covers the Chicana in the writing of American and Mexican men and women, giving the broadest possible view. The authors note the "triple oppression" of Chicanas: as women, as victims of colonization, and as inheritors of the machismo culture. The book is sparsely illustrated in black-and-white, including several

graphs. Notes, a glossary, a bibliography, and an index are appended to this comprehensive treatment of an often-ignored culture. HCA.

Ortiz Cofer, Judith. **Silent Dancing: A Partial Remembrance of a Puerto Rican Childhood**. Houston: Arte Publico, 1990. 167p. $9.50pa. ISBN 1-55885-015-5pa.

The author of two books of poetry and a novel, Judith Ortiz Cofer looks back on her youth in thirteen vignettes interspersed with her poems. Ortiz Cofer attended school in the United States, but returned to Puerto Rico during the summer or when her father, who enlisted in the U.S. Navy, went to sea. In the United States, Ortiz Cofer had to act as spokesperson for her mother in a neighborhood where they did not know anyone, and in Puerto Rico she was vigilantly watched over by a pervasive extended family. These conflicting roles and the constant movement between the two countries augmented her cultural identity crisis. Ortiz Cofer learned the oral tradition from her Puerto Rican grandmother, Mamá, who entertained her with many stories. The spoken quality used in describing island customs is part of the book's charm. The essays and poems can be used individually in literature classes, but the memoir as a whole will entice many readers. MHCA.

Ruiz, Vicki L. **From Out of the Shadows: Mexican Women in Twentieth-Century America**. New York: Oxford University Press, 1998. 240p. $30.00; $15.95pa. ISBN 0-19-511483-3; 0-19-513099-5pa.

Historian Vicki Ruiz shows the participation of Mexican women in the twentieth-century history of the Southwest as farm workers, entertainers, labor activists, feminists, community volunteers, and municipal leaders, using the themes of public and private life and cultural identity in each of her chapters. Mexican women who came to this country, some living in locations for generations before the United States was created, adapted their culture to their new situation while at the same time adopting cultural elements of the United States. For instance, in the 1920s, girls rebelled as flappers but required chaperones when they went out. Mexican women were active members of labor unions and political organizations, striving to better their work and living conditions, and they participated in their own unique feminist movement. In the later part of the twentieth century, they gained cultural recognition through community leadership and organization. An appendix provides statistical data on occupations, education, and income; and notes, a bibliography, and an index are included. As Ruiz acknowledges, the history of Latina women is particularly obscure, and, in helping to bring it to light, her book deserves a place in many libraries. HCA.

Santiago, Esmeralda. **Almost a Woman**. Reading, MA: Perseus, 1998. 313p. $24.00. ISBN 0-7382-0043-3.

A continuation of her first book *When I Was Puerto Rican*, Esmeralda Santiago's *Almost a Woman* begins in Brooklyn during the 1960s, where Santiago arrives at the age of thirteen. The oldest of a family of eleven children, who live in a three-room apartment, Santiago learns English, attends the Performing Arts High School, and accompanies her mother to the welfare office to translate. Her mother, overly protective Mami, allows her daughter to accompany her to all-night dance halls, but not to go out with boys until she is twenty years old. When Santiago begins to date, she pursues and is pursued by a divergent string of men, none of them her perfect match. Santiago struggles with humor and love to find acceptance in a new land, to accept herself, and to discover a measure of independence from her beloved Mami. Students will empathize with the feelings of this young woman. HCA.

Non-Book Material

Adelante Mujeres! Produced by the National Women's History Project. 30 min. National Women's History Project, 1992. Videocassette. $49.95.

Beginning with the arrival of the Spanish on the North American continent, *Adelante Mujeres!* is a comprehensive and chronological view of Latina women in the United States. The film covers life on the frontier, the separation from Mexico, migrations, the Mexican Revolution, the world wars, assimilation pressures, the Depression, and cultural organizations. Traditional women's roles in the family, in the church, as healers, and as preservers of the culture are juxtaposed with the more liberal legal and social rights that Latina women enjoyed. Many historical women are introduced or recognized, including María Betancour, Eulalia Arrila de Pérez, Jovita Idar, Concha Ortiz y Pino, Luisa Moreno, and Dolores Huerta. Backed by ethnic music, the film is narrated on and off camera by Maria Cuevas and includes an estimable collection of color and black-and-white archival photographs, many previously unpublished. Because the narration goes by briskly, teachers and students will appreciate that the script is included in the booklet accompanying the film. The video, a unique and well-presented creation, will find a variety of uses in schools as part of social studies, women's history, and multicultural curriculums. MHCA.

Chicana Studies. 1999. University of California at Riverside, 900 University Avenue, Riverside, CA 92521. 909-787-1012. E-mail: Romelia Salinas, salinas@clnet.ucr.edu. URL: http://clnet.ucr.edu/women/womenHP.html.

The *Chicana Studies* Web page offers links to Latina profiles; history; a listserv; and other Web sites, organizations, and networks. Although the site does not offer a huge amount of information at this time, the page is well set up to accommodate growth. Because information on Latina women is limited, researchers will appreciate this site. MHCA.

Women of Hope: Latinas Abriendo Camino. Directed by Robert Rosenberg. 29 min. Films for the Humanities and Sciences, 1996. Videocassette. $99.00.

Women of Hope: Latinas Abriendo Camino. Photographed by Idaljiza Liz-Lepiorz. Designed by Judi Orlick. Films for the Humanities and Sciences, 1995. Posters and study guide. $59.00.

Twelve groundbreaking Latina women are introduced in a busy and fast-moving video production. The film's introduction features three of the women defining the terms *Chicana* and *Latina*. In the first section, which rarely shows a single image, and is more likely to show two or three, several of the subjects discuss their childhoods. The images include color and black-and-white photographs and film ranging from historical events to family chronicles. These early sections are not well captioned, and it is only in the second, main section of the film that each woman is introduced, identified, and discussed. The use of multiple images continues with well-selected, upbeat Latin music running under the narrative. Some of the women speak part of their narration in Spanish, and sometimes subtitles translate the words, but on a few occasions there is no translation. The women selected for the film, most of them immigrants, come from varied backgrounds and occupations, having achieved success in fields ranging from the arts to the hard sciences, and from the social sciences to politics. The list of subjects includes Julia Alvarez, writer; Sandra Cisneros, writer; Miriam Colon, actor; Amalia Mesa-Bains, artist; Tania León, conductor; Adriana Ocampo, planetary geologist; Ana Sol Gutiérrez, aeronautical engineer; Helen Rodríguez-Trias, physician; Antonia Pantoja, educator; Dolores Huerta, labor leader, Antonia Hernández, civil rights lawyer; and Nydia Velázquez, member of Congress. In the final section of the film, the women discuss the future, transmitting considerable wisdom that may bypass the audience because of the speed of the production.

The posters and study guide make it possible to engage and extend the introduction provided in the video. The eighteen-by-twenty-four-inch posters feature a large (twelve-by-eighteen-inch) photograph and an inspiring quotation from each woman as well as her occupation and homeland. The posters feature sepia and muted colors and generally show the subjects in their work situations. The posters can be used alone to introduce Latina women and to inspire and motivate students. The study guide draws the production together: Each woman acquires a full-page biography in Spanish and English. Thirteen classroom lessons use the lives and words of the women of hope to explore issues of ethnicity centered around the themes of names, art, language, history, stereotypes, identity, family, labor, health, mentors, and change. Complete activities use documents and artifacts drawn from the writing of Sandra Cisneros, the border art of Amalia Mesa-Bains, and the publications of the United Farm Workers of America, among others, which are included. The study guide concludes with three pages of resources. *Women of Hope* offers a wide range of opportunities for Spanish, multicultural, history, art, literature, and sociology classes. MHCA.

Native Americans

Books

Albers, Patricia, and Beatrice Medicine. **The Hidden Half: Studies of
Plains Indian Women**. Lanham, MD: University Press of America, 1983.
280p. $56.00; $24.50pa. ISBN 0-8191-2956-9; 0-8191-2957-7pa.

> *The Hidden Half* contains papers presented at the 1977 symposium "The
> Role and Status of Women in Plains Indian Cultures" held at the Plains
> Conference in Lincoln, Nebraska. The symposium reviewed past work on
> the role and status of Plains Indian women and reassessed that work under
> the light of new scholarship. The articles, case studies from field research,
> are mainly historical and concern women in the period before their removal
> to reservations, although two essays deal with women on the reservations.
> Some of the topics include nineteenth-century observations of northern
> plains women, sex task differentiation among the Hidatsa, plains women's
> arts and crafts, Sioux star quilts, gender in the Lakota culture, and sex role
> alternatives for plains women. Each paper contains documentation in a collec-
> tion that will be used in the study of the history of Native American women
> of the plains. CA.

Broker, Ignatia. **Night Flying Woman: An Ojibway Narrative**. St. Paul:
Minnesota Historical Society Press, 1983. 135p. $9.50pa. ISBN 0-87351-
167-0pa.

> The history of Ni-bo-wi-se-gwe, also known as Oona and Night Flying Woman,
> is the focus of this narrative expressed in the manner of the oral tradition
> by Ignatia Broker. Broker is Oona's granddaughter, and so the multigen-
> erational story also illustrates the Ojibway myth that five generations will
> complete a circle of those who live in the traditional ways, and those who
> move away from those beliefs. The majority of the story takes place in the
> late 1800s, when Oona is born during a solar eclipse and receives her name
> and the gifts traditionally given to babies. The tribe has already been removed
> into Minnesota, and they are now being called onto reservations. When
> Oona is five years old, her clan elects to hide deep in the northern woods
> rather than go to the reservation. It is here that Oona becomes a dreamer,
> recognized as one who can foretell the future. Within a few years the hiding
> fails, the clan is forced onto the White Earth Reservation, and a time of
> great change begins. It is Oona's mother who accepts many of the white
> customs, goods, and Christianity, helping the rest of the tribe adjust to the new
> life. The traditional ways of the Ojibway people are so carefully described
> that the reader feels as confused as the tribe members as they try to incor-
> porate old traditions into new rituals. The book ends with Oona, now an old
> woman, telling the stories of her people to her descendants; this cycles the book
> back to the prologue, in which Ignatia Broker describes life in Minneapolis
> (where she moved at the beginning of World War II), her role as an activist,

urged by many to tell the stories of the Ojibway, and how in her generation she returns to many of the native traditions. It is the spirit of the Ojibway that gives the book its strength and its peace. The book's forward outlines the federal laws affecting the tribe from the 1800s, and a glossary presents Native words. MHCA.

Crow Dog, Mary, and Richard Erdoes. **Lakota Woman**. New York: Harper-Perennial, 1990. 263p. $13.00pa. ISBN 0-06-097389-7pa.

In the first chapter of her book, Mary Crow Dog recites the litany of her troubled life. Born on the Rosebud Reservation in South Dakota, Crow Dog could drink a pint of whiskey by the time she was ten, and by age fifteen she was raped. She entered the American Indian Movement (AIM) in the late 1960s, and gave birth to a son during the siege of Wounded Knee in 1973. After Wounded Knee, she married Lakota spiritual leader Leonard Crow Dog, one of the leaders of the Wounded Knee uprising who helped to revive some of the traditional Lakota ceremonies such as the Ghost Dance and Sun Dance. The book documents the living conditions on the reservations, provides an inside look at the history of AIM, and records traditional Lakota culture. Including a section of black-and-white photographs, *Lakota Woman* will find a variety of uses, as biography and as history, in schools and libraries. MHCA.

Curtis, Edward S. **Heart of the Circle: Photographs by Edward S. Curtis of Native American Women**. Edited by Sara Day. San Francisco: Pomegranate, 1997. 128p. $34.95pa. ISBN 0-7649-0006-4pa.

When Edward Curtis found his calling in photographing Native peoples beginning in 1900, he devoted the rest of his life to it. In all, he completed twenty volumes on almost eighty tribes living west of the Mississippi from the Arctic to the Mexican border. *Heart of the Circle* reproduces over 100 photographs Curtis took of Native American women. The photographs are grouped geographically: Plains and Subarctic, Southwest, California and Great Basin, Plateau, Northwest Coast, and the Arctic, and a number of boxed sections highlight specific tribes. Pat Durkin wrote the introduction, which includes reflections from Native women and a full history of Curtis's work, and Alan Bisbort and Sara Day provide the informative captions. *Heart of the Circle* will be useful for research, both through the text and by way of the photographs themselves; it will also be valuable in art classes. MHCA.

Ferris, Jeri. **Native American Doctor: The Story of Susan LaFlesche Picotte**. Minneapolis: Carolrhoda, 1991. 87p. $23.93. ISBN 0-87614-443-1.

Susan LaFlesche Picotte was the daughter of Iron Eye who, as chief of the Omaha in the last half of the nineteenth century, believed his people should be educated and assimilated into white society. As a result, he sent his children to missionary school and to college. Two of his children, Francis and Susette, toured the country speaking about the problems of Native people, and Susan attended medical school, returning to the reservation as the first Native doctor. Although she lived to be only fifty years old, she served the medical needs of all the people in the reservation area and worked as an intermediary with the federal government for the betterment of the Omaha people. Jeri Ferris places Picotte in the context of the times, using black-and-white photographs and maps. Although the Omaha culture is not made entirely clear, Picotte's life is well told. Notes, a bibliography, and an index are appended to a biography suitable for younger readers. MH.

Flood, Renée Sansom. **Lost Bird of Wounded Knee: Spirit of the Lakota**. New York: Da Capo, 1995. 384p. $15.95pa. ISBN 0-306-80822-6pa.

Surviving for four days under the frozen corpse of her mother after the battle of Wounded Knee, Zintkala Nuni, or Lost Bird, was discovered and adopted by General Leonard W. Colby. Colby, a lawyer who served as assistant attorney general of the United States, wanted the child to be a bridge to the Native American tribes with whom his law firm was seeking business, but he exploited and abused the child. His wife, noted suffragist and newspaper editor Clara B. Colby, divorced him and raised the child in a distracted and patronizing manner. Zintkala Nuni, lost between two worlds, suffered through a series of misfortunes before dying at the age of twenty-nine. Although author Renée Flood chanced upon the story of Lost Bird by accident, she was compelled to uncover it, having served as a social worker who removed Native American children from their homes and placed them in foster care. After she found Zintkala Nuni's grave in California, the Lakota people arranged for a reburial with the victims of Wounded Knee on the Pine Ridge Reservation. Flood has written a complete history, uncovering letters and documents from the girl and the adoptive parents, who are both fully profiled. A section of black-and-white photographs, notes, a bibliography, and an index are included in a book that tells a heartrending story. HCA.

Green, Rayna. **Women in American Indian Society**. New York: Chelsea House, 1992. 111p. (Indians of North America). $19.95; $9.95pa. ISBN 1-55546-734-2; 0-7910-0401-5pa.

Employed by the Smithsonian Institution and of Cherokee ancestry, Dr. Rayna Green is well qualified to examine Native women in history. She begins by reviewing the myths created after the first European contact and how they were perpetuated; she then moves on to the traditional roles of women. Following a chronological arrangement, Green examines the invasion of the Americas, the changes brought about by European contact, reservation life, early women involved in reform movements, and contemporary women leaders. A color picture section depicts current artwork from a number of tribes, and black-and-white illustrations and poetry from Native authors are used throughout the book. A bibliography, a glossary, and an index are appended to a useful research book. MHA.

Hungry Wolf, Beverly. **The Ways of My Grandmothers**. New York: Quill, 1980. 256p. $12.00pa. ISBN 0-688-00471-7pa.

Written as a tribute to her grandmothers and to preserve her native culture, Beverly Hungry Wolf provides a mix of customs in her book; she covers the oral history of her grandmothers and older relatives, retells traditional myths and legends, and describes the cultural ways of the Blackfoot people. Hungry Wolf grew up on the Blood Indian Reserve, speaking the Blackfoot language. Educated in Catholic school, she was acculturated away from Native traditions until her mother and husband encouraged her to return. Along with the history and legend, her book mixes oral tradition and memory to create a cultural manual covering such varied topics as birth control, herbs, recipes, camping, dress, and crafts. Containing black-and-white photographs, drawings, and an index, the book will find a variety of uses. MHCA.

Mankiller, Wilma, and Michael Wallis. **Mankiller: A Chief and Her People**. New York: St. Martin's, 1993. 292p. $13.95pa. ISBN 0-312-11393-5pa.

In alternating chapters, Wilma Mankiller and Michael Wallis tell the story of Mankiller's life and the story of the Cherokee Nation. Mankiller was raised in Oklahoma on Mankiller Flats, land allotted to her grandfather by the federal government, until her family was relocated to California when she was ten. During the 1960s, she became politically active, participating in the takeover of Alcatraz Island. After suffering several medical problems, Mankiller assumed the leadership of the Cherokee Nation in 1985, one of the first women to chair a Native American tribe. As for the Cherokee Nation, they were a strong southern tribe who tried to assimilate, even creating their own written language, unsuccessfully, before being removed to Oklahoma along the Trail of Tears 1838. With each chapter introduced with a Cherokee legend and many documents and quotations included, the dual tales provide a much larger context than either could alone, making the book useful as both biography and history. The well-written book, containing two sections of black-and-white photographs, a chronology, a bibliography, and an index, should find a large audience. HCA.

Mountain Wolf Woman. **Mountain Wolf Woman, Sister of Crashing Thunder: The Autobiography of a Winnebago Indian**. Edited by Nancy Oestreich Lurie. Ann Arbor: University of Michigan Press, 1961. 142p. $14.95pa. ISBN 0-472-06109-7pa.

Nancy Lurie became the niece of Mountain Wolf Woman when she was adopted by Mitchell Redcloud, Sr., during his final illness. Lurie first met her aunt in 1945 while doing fieldwork with the Winnebago community in Black River Falls, Wisconsin. Another anthropologist, Paul Radin, had written the story of Mountain Wolf Woman's brother, Crashing Thunder, in 1920. Lurie asked her aunt for permission to record her autobiography, and Mountain Wolf Woman agreed, but it was not until 1958 that they could sit down together to accomplish the task. Mountain Wolf Woman was born in 1884 and was of the generation of Native Americans who acculturated. After attending school for a few years, where she was baptized as a Christian, she was forced by her brother into a marriage. This happened around the turn of the twentieth century when she was still in her teens. When she left her first husband, who was not her choice, she married another man, moved to Nebraska, and entered the peyote culture. Returning to Black River Falls with her family of eight surviving children, Mountain Wolf Woman became a part of the Winnebago community there, dispensing Native medicines. Lurie presents the story of Mountain Wolf Woman's life just as it was told to her, adding abundant notation on the culture gained from her years studying the Winnebago, making the book useful both as an autobiography and in cultural studies. A foreword by anthropologist Ruth Underhill, a section of black-and-white photographs, a map, a pronunciation guide, and notes are included. HCA.

Peterson, Susan. **The Living Tradition of Maria Martinez**. New York: Kodansha, 1989. 300p. $45.00pa. ISBN 0-87011-497-2pa.

Glossy color and black-and-white photographs are the highlight of Susan Peterson's study of San Ildefonso pueblo potter Maria Martinez and her techniques. Martinez was born in the late 1880s. As a child, her aunt taught her to make traditional pueblo pottery during a period when the craft was declining. After Martinez married, she and her husband, Julian, worked for archaeologist Edgar Lee Hewitt, studying the designs on the pot shards he unearthed. The couple experimented until they were able to re-create the black-on-black firing technique of the ancient Anasazi people. As tourism in the West increased and the black San Ildefonso pots became popular souvenirs, the Martinez family engaged in a small industry, Maria shaping the clay and Julian decorating it. Photographs, both historical and contemporary, portray all aspects of pot making, from digging the clay to firing, and include many images of ceramic pieces with their Native designs. Notes on the photographic plates are appended as well as a brief history on black pottery, a genealogical chart, a glossary, a bibliography, and an index. The book will be useful in art, anthropology, and multicultural classes. MHCA.

Rappaport, Doreen. **The Flight of Red Bird: The Life of Zitkala-Sa**. New York: Dial, 1997. 186p. $15.99. ISBN 0-8037-1438-6.

Gertrude Bonnin was born on the Yankton Reservation in South Dakota in 1876, the same year as the Battle of Little Big Horn. To reflect her Native identity, she renamed herself Zitkala-Sa, or Red Bird, when she was in her twenties. She embarked upon a life of service to Indian tribes throughout the United States. Zitkala-Sa spent her youth traveling to boarding schools as far away as Indiana. She became a teacher, working in similar boarding schools and on reservations; but Zitkala-Sa lived during the height of the Native American reform movement, heightened by the publication of Helen Hunt Jackson's *Century of Dishonor* and spurred by the Dawes Act, which split up Native lands. Zitkala-Sa shared her knowledge of her culture by publishing Native tales, and she worked for the betterment of all tribes as an activist, investigator, lecturer, and writer. She lived in Washington, D.C., where she lobbied for Native American rights. Doreen Rappaport uses

Zitkala-Sa's own words to tell most of her story, and two typefaces distinguish the voices of subject and author. Black-and-white photographs are scattered throughout the text, and a chronology, a glossary, a source list, a bibliography, and an index are included. The book is complete and unique and should serve a variety of audiences. MHCA.

Sonneborn, Liz. **A to Z of Native American Women**. New York: Facts on File, 1998. 228p. (Encyclopedia of Women). $27.95. ISBN 0-8160-3580-6.

A to Z of Native American Women contains the biographies of over 100 women of North America from all times. Ranging from one to several pages, many of the articles include a black-and-white illustration, and all the articles provide suggestions for further reading, including primary sources from the women themselves where available. Liz Sonneborn furnishes an introductory essay accompanied by a map of traditional tribal locations. Cross references between Anglo and Native names are provided as well as a bibliography of recommended sources, and general, professional, tribal, and chronological indexes. *A to Z* will be a helpful book for many schools and libraries in locating Native women. MHCA.

Time-Life Books, eds. **The Woman's Way**. Alexandria, VA: Time-Life, 1995. 184p. (American Indians). $24.95. ISBN 0-8094-9729-8.

Containing many special sections and color and black-and-white reproductions of Native artwork both historical and modern, *The Woman's Way* is an overview of the role of female Native Americans in history, in religion, and in the life cycle of the tribe. The book opens with a series of photographs of Native women from many tribes, many by Edward Curtis, representing different life stages. These precede the first chapter, which is also about the life cycles of women. Some of the special sections show body ornamentation, mythologies of women from different tribes, houses, food gathering, and healing arts. Crafts are another important topic in the book which includes a bibliography and index. With its attractive format, the book will be used both for browsing and research. MHCA.

Wall, Steve. **Wisdom's Daughters: Conversations with Women Elders of Native America**. Edited by Harvey Arden. New York: HarperPerennial, 1993. 302p. $17.00pa. ISBN 0-06-092561-2pa.

Steve Wall crosses the country to interview thirteen "clan mothers, faith keepers, mothers, and grandmothers" from ten Native American tribes including the Tewa, Northern Cheyenne, Seminole, Ojibway, Seneca, Mohawk, and other clans. His respectful purpose is to record their words of wisdom, and Wall reports the words much as they are spoken, using many headings. The subjects, shifting from current events such as AIDS and gambling to ancient myth and legend, emphasize the themes of family, concern for the environment, and loss of culture. Many black-and-white photographs of the elders in their homes, with their families, and at recreation are interspersed throughout the interviews. *Wisdom's Daughters* will be appreciated for browsing, for personal reading, or for gifts. HCA.

Wilder, Edna. **Once Upon an Eskimo Time**. Anchorage: Alaska Northwest, 1987. 183p. $12.95pa. ISBN 0-88240-274-9pa.

Once Upon an Eskimo Time is the story of Edna Wilder's mother, whose Eskimo name was Nedercook. Nedercook was believed to have lived for about 121 years, from 1858 to 1979, having been born and raised in the little village of Rocky Point in Norton Sound, south of Nome. The book covers one year in the life of the village when Nedercook is about ten years old and before her first contact with outside society. Much of the story has to do with food gathering, mostly hunting and fishing, because survival depended upon a steady supply of food; however, the book also covers the festivals, stories, and legends of the village, and the numerous songs that Nedercook remembers from her youth. *Once Upon an Eskimo Time* is beautifully illustrated with pencil sketches by Dorothy Mayhew, and the book will be used for personal reading at all levels. MHCA.

Non-Book Material

More Than Words. Produced and directed by Laura Bliss Spaan. 58 min. Cinema Guild, 1995. Videocassette. Purchase $295.00; Rental $95.00.

Marie Smith is the last Eyak Indian to speak her native language. This video follows her as she accompanies her niece from Anchorage, Alaska, to her Native location on Prince William Sound, where she participates in several ceremonies. Smith, whose Native name means "a voice that draws you," explains how the Eyak language was lost when Native children were punished for speaking that tongue in school. A number of other interesting narratives come together in the film. One concerns a niece, who, because she was adopted as a baby had never met her mother; she reestablishes contact with the Eyak tribe through an anthropologist, Frederica de Laguna, who studied the culture in the 1930s. As one who has studied the tribe's history, which she narrates in the film, de Laguna comes to Prince William Sound as an interested observer of the tribe's ceremonies. Finally, the only other living speaker of the Eyak language, Michael Krauss, a linguist who recorded the native tongue as a teacher at the University of Fairbanks, joins the occasion to speak Eyak with Smith. The tribal descendants hold a potlatch ceremony, which has not been performed in over eighty years, and the customs associated with it have been forgotten. There is always choice in culture, de Laguna reassures the descendents; although the future of the Eyak will not be the same as it was in the past, it will be their own. In reviving their traditions, Smith names all the descendants in the native tongue at the potlatch ceremony, and tribal artifacts are displayed. The day after the formal ceremony, the group travels to the site of their original villages, where they plant a tree, symbolizing their rebirth. Although mainly shot in color on location, the film contains some black-and-white photos and film clips. The video will be useful in social studies classes. HCA.

Mountain Wolf Woman, 1884–1960. Produced and directed by Jocelyn Riley. 17 min. Her Own Words, 1990. Videocassette. $95.00.

In this short video, Naomi Russell narrates the biography of her Winnebago grandmother, Mountain Wolf Woman. Russell's voice is excellent for the first-person narration given over still black-and-white and color photographs of artifacts, crafts, costumes, documents, landscapes, and photographs of the family. The film includes several traditional Winnebago songs sung by women that add to the texture. Born in Wisconsin, Mountain Wolf Woman's education at mission school was interrupted when her brother arranged her marriage. After the birth of two children, Mountain Wolf Woman left this jealous husband to marry a man of her own choosing. She bore nine more children while living in various locations around the Midwest, and eventually settled permanently in Wisconsin. The story moves at a fast clip, but more details are available in Nancy Oestreich Lurie's 1961 book by the same name, published by the University of Michigan Press. The film has regional interest and applications for multicultural studies. A useful resource guide is available for $45.00. MHCA.

The Reindeer Queen: The Story of Sinrock Mary. Produced by Maria Brooks. 28 min. Filmakers Library, 1992. Videocassette. Purchase $195.00; Rental $55.00.

The story of Sinrock Mary, a native Alaskan born in 1857, also recounts Alaska's history. Mary was ten years old when Russia sold Alaska to the United States. She learned to speak Russian and English as well as several Native dialects. Because of her language skills, she was hired as an interpreter and traveled to Russia to negotiate the import of reindeer to begin an industry for Eskimos. In treatment paralleling that of indigenous people all over the United States, government agents first oversaw the reindeer herds and leased them to missionaries. Mary and her husband, Charlie, had to complain before they finally received animals to raise. Charlie was duped into moving the herd to the Bering Sea to feed nonexistent starving whalers; the trip took two years and finally killed him. When the gold rush began, miners stole the reindeer for pack animals. Mary fought Charlie's brothers and others for the right to own and control the herd. Although Mary developed the largest herd in Alaska and trained many adopted children to work the animals, the economy and racism kept her from becoming successful. Depression struck as the gold rush ended, and, just as the industry prepared to challenge the beef market in the lower forty-eight states, laws were passed that prevented Eskimos from selling to whites. When the Reindeer Act finally enforced the exclusive right of the Eskimos to own the reindeer, the herd had declined through overgrazing, starvation, and lack of care. The Great Depression had begun, and all hope of a market for the meat was lost, concluding a story that is familiar except for the Alaskan setting. The film is well constructed, using interviews with Mary's children, old black-and-white photographs, excellent historical research, and clear narration. *The Reindeer Queen* can be used in sociology, geography, or history classes. It will, of course, claim regional attention. MHCA.

Wilma P. Mankiller: Woman of Power. Produced and directed by Mary Scott. 29 min. Women Make Movies, 1992. Videocassette. Purchase $250.00; Rental $60.00.

In 1987, Wilma P. Mankiller was elected the twenty-first chief of the Cherokee Nation, overseeing government, economic, and social development for a fourteen-county region in eastern Oklahoma. In this video, Mankiller is followed through a typical day. She talks about the cultural and spiritual values of the tribe, about her goals for her term in office, and about being a woman in a position of power. Mankiller brought self-government to the tribe and established its first judicial system in ninety years. About a half dozen tribal members are interviewed, both those who favor and those who oppose the leader's policies. Mankiller's mother is one of those interviewed, bringing insight into her family background and the obstacles she has overcome. The video is filmed in color and includes early black-and-white family photographs and some color photographs of Cherokee art. A well-presented, interesting production, the video will have regional interest and be useful in women's studies, government, and other classes. MHCA.

Chapter 3

The Province of Women

The Arts

Books

Basinger, Jeanine. **A Woman's View: How Hollywood Spoke to Women, 1930–1960**. Hanover, NH: Wesleyan University Press, 1993. 528p. $22.95pa. ISBN 0-8195-6291-2pa.

Portraying the complex images of women in Hollywood movies during the 1930s, 1940s, and 1950s, and the messages they sent, is the object of Jeanine Basinger's book. This was the era of the "woman's film," a huge genre where a star was placed at the center of the film, temporarily liberated, and, in the end, knew that simply being a woman was her true job. Played by such notables as Joan Crawford, Greta Garbo, Ginger Rogers, Bette Davis, Greer Garson, and Doris Day, the heroines acted independently in unrealistic plots before being brought back into their traditional roles as women. The author uses copious film track quotations and numerous lists to discuss dozens of stars, scores of movies, fashion and glamour, social roles of women and men, as well as marriage, motherhood, and work. Basinger does an excellent job of analyzing and explaining the fairly complex material while maintaining an interesting writing style. Her book, which is illustrated throughout with black-and-white photographs from films, will be useful in media studies and women's studies to describe the effect of the movies on women during that era and in later times. An appendix lists the major box-office stars, and a bibliography and an index of names and film titles are included. HCA.

Chicago, Judy. **The Dinner Party**. New York: Penguin, 1996. $24.95pa. ISBN 0-14-024437-9pa.

Judy Chicago is an artist who between 1974 and 1979, with the help of scores of other people, created an epic work of art dedicated to the history of women. *The Dinner Party* describes the creation of this multimedia project, which consists of a triangular table, forty-eight feet on each side, set for thirty-nine women who chronicle history from creation to the end of World War II. Each place setting includes an elaborately embroidered runner and a porcelain plate that represent the life and times of each woman. The table is set on a heritage floor of triangular white tiles inscribed with the names of 999 additional women. The work is monumental not only for the artistry of the traditional women's crafts that went into it but also for the research that found the women who are included. The names of many of these women were not then, and are not now, household words. *The Dinner Party* tells the women's stories and explains the symbolism of the work. This updated edition also tells the story of the controversy surrounding the piece, of its immense popularity, and of its travels and trials since its 1979 initial installation in the San Francisco Museum of Modern Art. The book, which is illustrated with black-and-white and color photographs, is useful for art classes and projects, for humanities and social studies classes, and for teachers looking for women to include in their curriculums. HCA.

Dickerson, James. **Women on Top: The Quiet Revolution That's Rocking the American Music Industry**. New York: Billboard, 1998. 256p. $21.95. ISBN 0-8230-8489-2.

> Noting that in 1996, for the first time since the inception of the popular music industry with the rise of Elvis Presley, women on the Top 20 music charts out-performed men in an industry that had never particularly catered to or promoted women. Journalist James Dickerson depicts women in the music industry, not just the performers, but women behind the scenes working as executives and publicists, from the 1950s through the 1990s. Chapters covering female music artists over the last five decades are headed by an honor roll of those who made the Top 20 list. Additional headings delineate topical coverage and star profiles ranging from one to several pages and high-lighted by full page black-and-white portraits. The book, which appends music charts, notes, a bibliography, and an index, is a great overview of women in popular music and also a browser's delight. MHCA.

Dudden, Faye E. **Women in the American Theatre: Actresses and Audiences, 1790–1870**. New Haven, CT: Yale University Press, 1994. 260p. $35.00; $16.00pa. ISBN 0-300-05636-2; 0-300-07058-6pa.

> The early years of American theater, a time of either "transformation or objec-tification" for women, is the concern of Faye E. Dudden. In her study, Dudden profiles Fanny Kemble, the first true stage star; Thomas Hamblin, who commercialized the theater; Charlotte Cushman, the greatest actress of the nineteenth century; and Laura Keene, an actress turned manager who pioneered new ideas but failed to make a living. Early theater in the United States offered opportunity to women as actresses and in small business, but, as the theater became more commercial, promoting visual rather than aural experiences, women risked exploitation. As theater expanded, it seg-mented, appealing to audiences based on race, class, and gender. By mid-century, theater entertainment was an economically viable enterprise, was managed by males, was promoted to well-behaved, mostly male audiences, and incorporated a female star system. The industry focused attention on the female body, shaping media objectification to this day, and, as women had been pushed out of the management side of the business, it is impossible to know what a female-inspired theater could have become. Dudder's interest-ing thesis is well researched and presented, including black-and-white illus-trations, notes, a selected bibliography, and an index. It will be useful in drama and women's studies courses. HCA.

Duncan, Isadora. **My Life**. New York: W. W. Norton, 1928. 359p. $14.00pa. ISBN 0-8714-0158-4pa.

> Isadora Duncan was raised unconventionally and continued in this vein throughout her life. A native of San Francisco, whose divorced mother

struggled to support the children, she attended only a few years of public school before pursuing her interest in dance by giving classes. Duncan spent her childhood immersed in the arts and imagination, developing, from her mother's teachings, independence, agnosticism, and asceticism. As a dancer, she created new interpretations, both with and without musical accompaniment, which she performed all over the world. Her work was built upon love of nature, rejection of convention, and veneration of classical forms. She was most appreciated abroad, and after the turn of the twentieth century spent most of her time there. Duncan suffered the grief of bearing three children, all of whom died in childhood, by three men. She had one marriage, to a fourth man, which ended in divorce. Duncan's life ended unusually when a scarf, a symbol of the flowing costume for which she was known, caught in a spoked automobile wheel and broke her neck. Her autobiography, written in 1927, does not cover the last six years of her life, but does give voice to a woman of dominion. HCA.

Echols, Alice. Scars of Sweet Paradise: The Life and Times of Janis Joplin. New York: Metropolitan, 1999. 408p. $26.00. ISBN 0-8050-5387-5.

Written by 1960s historian Alice Echols, *Scars of Sweet Paradise* places Janis Joplin within the context of the social upheaval of her era, creating more than a mere biography. Echols's skills are evident, and, after almost thirty years, she interviews numerous people who knew Joplin as friends, lovers, and musicians. Joplin grew up in Port Arthur, Texas, as a perfect daughter and hard-working student turned rebel. She attended the University of Texas, but migrated to San Francisco in the early 1960s, where she sang in clubs and became addicted to drugs. By the time she returned to San Francisco, after recovering from her addiction in her hometown, the hippie culture had transformed the city; Joplin, as part of Big Brother and the Holding Company, along with bands such as Jefferson Airplane and the Grateful Dead, were a big part of the music scene. *Cheap Thrills*, the first album for Joplin and the Holding Company, was number one for eight weeks, but Joplin split from the group to work solo. Insecure about her success, she was vulnerable about her bad-girl, running-with-the-boys image, but, with a totally free look that was ahead of its time, there was no place for Joplin in prefeminist society. She continued to abuse drugs and alcohol, and bounced through several bands, before dying of an overdose in 1970. Echols shows Joplin in much more detail than her image as a casualty of the rock movement portrays. *Scars of Sweet Paradise,* illustrated with three sections of black-and-white photographs, includes an update section on those who knew Joplin, a discography, notes, and an index. Teens continue to be fascinated by the rock legend with the huge voice, and the book will find as big an audience as the singer did. HCA.

Frank, Gerold. **Judy**. New York: Da Capo, 1975. 654p. $19.95pa. ISBN 0-306-80894-3pa.

Although Gerold Frank met Judy Garland before her death to discuss his writing her biography, Garland had never been able to tell her life story; and in the last year of her life, before her death from an overdose of sleeping pills in 1969, it still did not happen; however, Frank had access to Garland's papers, documents, and photos, and the complete cooperation of her family in creating his book. He interviewed over 200 people, including Garland's sister, children, and husbands, to tell the full story of the actress and singer, who made such films as *The Wizard of Oz* and *A Star is Born*, and whose voice captivated her audiences on concert tours and on television. Garland began as a vaudeville star promoted by a pushy mother; she became a child star at MGM studios, where she was exploited. Living a troubled life, Garland married five times and bore three children by two husbands. She abused alcohol and drugs, which caused her poor decisions, suicide attempts, and nervous breakdowns. During her adult life, her weight shifted from less than 100 pounds to over 150 pounds, and it once took an entire day to clean her up for a television performance. Still, fans loved Garland for her total performance, and Frank alleges that many of the stories Garland told about herself were part of her performance. He sets out to correct all previous misconceptions in *Judy*, which contains two sections of black-and-white photographs and an index. The book will appeal to biography readers and all who love Hollywood glitz. HCA.

Freedman, Russell. **Martha Graham: A Dancer's Life**. New York: Clarion, 1998. 175p. $18.00. ISBN 0-395-74655-8.

Martha Graham revolutionized modern dance by showing great emotion in the stories her dances revealed. Born in Pittsburgh in 1894, Graham studied under Ruth St. Denis before forming her own company. Graham, temperamental and egotistical, created new roles, movements, and performances, developing modern dance into a nouveau art form. Married at the age of fifty-four to a member of her company, Graham continued to dance until she was seventy-five, and even then she continued to teach. Russell Freedman's book is filled with black-and-white photographs of the dancer, who thought herself plain, although her face, with its deep-set eyes, is dramatic. Notes, a bibliography, and an index accompany the text. MHA.

Gaar, Gillian G. **She's a Rebel: The History of Women in Rock and Roll**. Seattle: Seal, 1992. 467p. $16.95pa. ISBN 1-878067-08-7pa.

From "Big Mama" Thornton, Peggy Jones, and the Chantels through k.d. lang, Janet Jackson, and Queen Latifah, journalist Gillian Gaar covers women in rock and roll. Using extensive interviews with rock stars as well as with women in the music industry, Gaar reports how women have always participated in rock, although they have not held the same status as male performers. The book is arranged chronologically, with substantial coverage of the over seventy women and groups presented. Two sections containing over sixty black-and-white photographs grace the book, which includes a preface by Yoko Ono, a bibliography, and general, song title, and album title indices. Including more detail than Dickerson's *Women on Top*, the book makes a nice addition to rock music collections and will be useful for research and personal reading. HCA.

Golden, Eve. **Vamp: The Rise and Fall of Theda Bara**. Vestal, NY: Emprise, 1996. 274p. $19.95pa. ISBN 1-879511-32-0pa.

> Making her debut as the vamp in the film *A Fool There Was* in 1915, Theda Bara became the epitome of that role, appearing in over thirty films over the next five years. The first product of the Hollywood star system, Bara, who hailed from Ohio and whose real name was Theodosia Goodman, had a persona invented for her. Supposedly, she was born under the Sphinx, the child of a French actress and an Italian sculptor. The real facts about Bara were obscured during her day, and because only one of Bara's films survives, tracing her is difficult; however, Eve Golden recreates Bara's life with humor. Many black-and-white photographs survive and fill the book, including one of Bara wearing the famous Cleopatra snake bra. Bara's acting ability may have transcended her stereotyped roles, but she is remembered as a fantasy character in the silent film age. A filmography, a bibliography, and an index complete the book, which will be enjoyed by film buffs and biography readers. HCA.

Grossman, Barbara W. **Funny Woman: The Life and Times of Fanny Brice**. Bloomington: Indiana University Press, 1991. 287p. $37.50; $16.95pa. ISBN 0-253-32653-2; 0-253-20762-2pa.

> Treating Fanny Brice with respect and admiration, Barbara Grossman embarks on an investigative journey to portray the real comedian rather than the show business myth that emerged over a career spanning forty years. Grossman fully admits that tracing Brice was not an easy task. Much of the ephemeral material about her early career was gone, and Brice's children declined to contribute to this biography. Grossman used newspapers, magazines, documents, and interviews with contemporaries to flesh out the picture of Brice, who grew up singing in her family's bars and went on to a versatile career in burlesque, vaudeville, musical revues, film, and radio. Brice appeared in nine *Ziegfeld Follies* between 1910 and 1936, and she headlined a vaudeville show at the Palace Theatre in New York in 1923. Her best-known role was Baby Snooks, on the radio; however, Brice's life was not all happiness and a steady rise to stardom. She married and divorced three times and was unsuccessful as a dramatic actress. Grossman's book will set Brice's life apart from Barbra Streisand's portrayal of her in *Funny Girl*. Including a section of black-and-white photographs, this readable account will be enjoyed by biography readers and used in theater collections. Notes, a bibliography, and an index are included. HCA.

Heller, Jules, and Nancy G. Heller, eds. **North American Women Artists of the Twentieth Century: A Biographical Dictionary**. New York: Garland, 1995. 612p. $135.00; $34.95pa. ISBN 0-8240-6049-0; 0-8153-2584-3pa.

For their compilation, the Hellers, both art professors, have gathered women artists from Canada, the United States, and Mexico who worked in all types of mediums and were born before 1960. Even with its narrow twentieth-century focus, the book contains around 1,500 entries, which are listed alphabetically and include birth and death dates of the artist, major medium of work, and a bibliography. The entries vary in the information they provide: Some contain both biographical and professional information, but some include only a list of professional exhibits, awards, and grants. For well-known artists, where plentiful biographical information exists in other sources, the editors have chosen to exclude that information here. Besides the Hellers, over 100 contributors from all three countries represented in the guide have provided articles. The editors hope that their multinational approach will inspire interest and understanding among the nations represented as well as provide a single source for needed but hard-to-find information. Over 100 full-page, black-and-white, glossy photographs are included in three sections. The illustrations are arranged alphabetically by the artist's name and list title, date, medium, size, and location of the work; however, the plates are not cross referenced in the text or the index. The index is superfluous because it repeats the alphabetical arrangement of the text. Many libraries and art departments will welcome this source, which brings together information on contemporary women artists. HCA.

Holiday, Billie, and William Dufty. **Lady Sings the Blues**. New York: Penguin, 1992. 199p. $11.95pa. ISBN 0-14-006762-0pa.

Lady Sings the Blues is Billie Holiday's own story of her life told with sorrow, remorse, and sarcasm. Holiday was born to a thirteen-year-old single mother around 1915 in Baltimore, Maryland. Although her parents married when she was three, they did not stay together. Holiday's mother left to work in New York, leaving Holiday to be raised by relatives. She began to work when she was ten, running errands for a neighborhood madam. It was through this relationship that she first heard the blues, which she would make her own. Holiday finished her education in the fifth grade and joined her mother in New York, where she danced in Harlem nightclubs and began her singing career. As a club performer, recording artist, and actress, Holiday was well known for her unique voice and musical interpretation of the blues, both in the United States and abroad, between the 1930s and the 1950s. Unfortunately, her career was fraught with the double curse of prejudice and addiction. Traveling, sometimes with white bands, during the Jim Crow period in the South was taxing to Holiday, who faced many incidents of racial discrimination. She had used marijuana as a child, and moved on to cocaine and heroin. She was arrested and rehabilitated multiple times, and, by the end of her career, the ravages of drug and alcohol addiction were evident in her voice and demeanor. Holiday was portrayed by Diana

Ross in the 1972 film *Lady Sings the Blues,* which was based on this book. Although some have questioned the chronology presented in her autobiography, readers will appreciate the authentic voice of a woman who rose to greatness and fell to the depths of despair. MHCA.

Leaming, Barbara. **Marilyn Monroe**. New York: Crown, 1998. 464p. $27.50. ISBN 0-517-70260-6.

Barbara Leaming makes movie star Marilyn Monroe come so much alive that one can almost smell her in this sympathetic portrait based on primary source material. Leaming plunges into Monroe's career in 1951 in the middle of her studio contract disputes, weaving the unhappy events of her youth into several chapters. Her childhood abandonment and family history of mental problems probably affected the course of her life, but Monroe can also be considered a self-made woman who did what it took to achieve success. To accomplish the end she desired, she took modeling and acting lessons, divorced her first husband, and fought the studios. Leaming concentrates on Monroe's film career, marriages, and series of lovers, showing a continuous downward spiral. Sexuality was a major part of Monroe's allure, and, although she thrived on it, it was also used against her. Leaming's biography is well written, sensitive, and factual, and because the Monroe myth has not gone away even decades after her death at age thirty-six in 1962, the book will appeal to many readers. Two carefully chosen sections of black-and-white photographs complement the text, and notes on the sources and an index are included. HCA.

Leider, Emily Wortis. **Becoming Mae West**. New York: Farrar, Straus & Giroux, 1997. 431p. $30.00. ISBN 0-374-10959-1.

Concentrating on the first half of Mae West's life, Emily Leider describes in detail how the actress and comedian created herself and the trouble she got into while doing it. Born in Brooklyn in 1893, Mae West started acting as Baby Mae at the age of five, guided by her mother. Moving from burlesque to vaudeville to the stage, West continually built her character using material she wrote herself. She was arrested on an obscenity charge in 1927 for her role in her own play, *Sex*. Always pushing the limit, West went to Hollywood in the 1930s and brought audiences back to theaters during the Depression in a series of movies, including *Night After Night*, *I'm No Angel*, and *Belle of the Nineties*. Unfortunately, she ran afoul of the Hays Office, charged with maintaining decency in the movie industry, and her career declined, although she remained a cultural icon. Leider's book contains three sections of black-and-white photographs, notes, an essay on sources, and an index. Told with wit and clarity, the book makes great reading. HCA.

Lieb, Sandra R. **Mother of the Blues: A Study of Ma Rainey**. Amherst: University of Massachusetts Press, 1981. 226p. $17.95pa. ISBN 0-87023-394-7pa.

Although only one chapter in Sandra Lieb's study contains biographical material, it is the most documentation hitherto collected on "mother of the blues" Ma Rainey, or Gertrude Pridgett. Rainey, born in 1886, was a minstrel show performer, comedian, dancer, and singer who, during the 1920s, popularized "classic blues," performed almost exclusively by females. Rainey excelled as a songwriter and recorder, but much of her material, made for Paramount records, was lost when the company went bankrupt in the 1930s. In addition, Rainey retired at an early age, making her lesser-known than other blues singers who became popular later. Lieb analyzes Rainey's expressive style and the themes of both her love songs and her comic and cynical songs. The book has several tables detailing her blues rhythms along with black-and-white photographs and a discography. Appendices classify Rainey's recordings, detail a lost song, and list her recordings. Additionally, notes, a bibliography, and general and song title indices are provided. With many lyrics included, *Mother of the Blues* is a must for blues music collections. HCA.

Lisle, Laurie. **Portrait of an Artist: A Biography of Georgia O'Keeffe**. New York: Washington Square, 1986. 496p. $14.00pa. ISBN 0-671-01666-0pa.

Although Georgia O'Keeffe was born in Wisconsin and attended school in Chicago and New York, it was the light and landscape of New Mexico that she loved best. She first visited the state in 1929, and moved there permanently after her husband, photographer and owner of the 291 Gallery in New York, Alfred Stieglitz, died. While O'Keeffe's huge flower pictures are memorable, her best-known works are her western landscapes and paintings of natural objects. Lisle's complete biography, which is suitable for biography and art collections, includes a section of black-and-white photographs as well as a genealogy, sources, a bibliography, and an index. HCA.

Lynn, Loretta, and George Vecsey. **Loretta Lynn: Coal Miner's Daughter**. New York: Da Capo, 1976. 204p. $14.95pa. ISBN 0-306-80680-0pa.

Country music star Loretta Lynn insisted that her autobiography should sound like her by keeping her idioms while retelling her life without covering anything up. Her story began in Butcher Holler, Kentucky, where she was born into extreme poverty. She married Doolittle Lynn before she was fourteen years old and bore four children. Lynn got her break when she sang at the Grand Ole Opry in Nashville, Tennessee, and she rose to stardom in the growing country music industry. In 1972, Lynn was the first female to be named Entertainer of the Year by the Country Music Association. Her travel and concert schedule was grueling, keeping her away from home and late-born twin daughters. Readers will appreciate Lynn's plain-spoken rags-to-riches story, which includes a section of black-and-white photographs with detailed captions, and an index. MHCA.

Mathews, Nancy Mowll. **Mary Cassatt: A Life**. New Haven, CT: Yale University Press, 1994. 383p. $18.00pa. ISBN 0-300-07754-8pa.

> In a detailed biography, Nancy Mathews portrays the inner forces that compelled Mary Cassatt, as a woman, to pursue an international career in art during the Victorian age. Born in Philadelphia, Cassatt knew by the time she was fifteen that she wanted to be an artist. After studying at Pennsylvania Academy of the Fine Arts, she went to Paris for further education, where she was befriended by Edgar Degas and joined the ranks of the experimental impressionists. For sixty years Cassatt lived abroad surrounded by her extended family; she never married. She took as her primary subject mothers and their children, and it is through these luminous paintings that she is chiefly identified today. Recognized abroad, but little appreciated in the United States during her day, Cassatt was continuously driven to improve her technique. Mathews' book is spread with black-and-white illustrations, including many of Cassatt's works. Notes, a bibliography, and an index are included in this well-researched, finely written study. HCA.

Meyer, Susan E. **Mary Cassatt**. New York: Harry N. Abrams, 1990. 92p. (First Impressions). $19.95. ISBN 0-8109-3154-0.

> Color reproductions of Mary Cassatt's artwork, including two foldout pages, are the highlight of Susan Meyer's biography. Cassatt, as one of the only female impressionists, advanced her career in France during the late nineteenth century. Working in pastel, oil, and gouache, Cassett is remembered for her mother-and-child portraits in natural, unposed settings. Full-page and double-page color reproductions allow readers to see Cassatt's brush strokes and use of color. Although the biographical information is utilitarian, art students will find this more visually appealing book preferable to Nancy Mathews's longer biography, *Mary Cassatt: A Life*. A list of illustrations and an index is appended. MHCA.

Moutoussamy-Ashe, Jeanne. **Viewfinders: Black Women Photographers**. New York: Writers and Readers, 1993. 201p. $39.95; $19.95pa. ISBN 0-86316-159-6; 0-86316-158-8pa.

> As a photographer herself, Jeanne Moutoussamy-Ashe felt compelled to discover Black women photographers, a fairly rare breed about whom much information has been lost, and to bring their stories into the broader history of photography. In some instances, only the name and period are known about a photographer; however, the author includes each woman she uncovered in the hope that more information may be forthcoming in the future. The book is divided into five parts, covering periods from 1839 to 1985, with between one and thirteen women included in each section. The sections are introduced by a historical overview reviewing photographic advancements and Black achievements within the context of American history. Wherever possible, a photograph of the photographer and samples of her work are included, and many advertisements for commercial studios illustrate the book. The most notable photographers are Eslanda Cardoza Goode

Robeson, the wife of Paul Robeson, and Louise Martin, who provided photographic coverage of Dr. Martin Luther King, Jr.'s funeral in 1968. Appendices provide capsule biographies and bibliographic sources, and list the women by time period and geographic locations. Notes, a bibliography, and an index are included in a volume that brings together information never before assembled. *Viewfinders* is an important resource for photographic, art, and multicultural collections. MHCA.

O'Dair, Barbara, ed. **Trouble Girls: The Rolling Stone Book of Women in Rock**. New York: Random, 1997. 608p. $25.00pa. ISBN 0-679-76874-2pa.

Trouble Girls is an eclectic mix of essays, ranging in style from the time line and the list to the personal, aimed at presenting the characteristics and approaches of women in the popular music industry. Each contributor decided how to advance her subject, and, although the book was to be biographical and critical, as might be expected there is an overlap between themes and chapters. The book takes a chronological approach, dividing the material into six chapters beginning with pioneers such as Ma Rainey, Billie Holiday, and Patsy Cline and stretching to the millennium with Neneh Cherry and Polly Jean Harvey. *Trouble Girls* has the broadest coverage among the books on the subject, covering the blues, gospel, country, girl groups, folksingers, songwriters, fans, women on the technical end of music production, punk, hip-hop, women in bands, and other topics. Besides the topical coverage, there are many sketches of individual performers, which contain at least one black-and-white portrait, a discography, and often a hits chart. Barbara O'Dair provides the general and chapter introductions to the well-indexed book, which contains notes on the contributors and a great bibliography divided by subject. With its up-to-date contents, the book should have wide appeal in libraries serving young people. MHCA.

Sova, Dawn B. **Women in Hollywood: From Vamp to Studio Head**. New York: Fromm International, 1998. 225p. $24.00. ISBN 0-88064-232-7.

Dawn Sova outlines how, in the early days of Hollywood, and even in pre-Hollywood days, women held many roles in the film industry, as writers, directors, and producers; however, as the studio system became entrenched, women steadily lost influence, and it took ninety years for them to regain the positions they had once held. Although Mary Pickford had founded a studio and Lois Weber was paid $5,000 a week to direct in 1918, it was not until the 1980s and later that Sherry Lansing headed 20th Century Fox; Barbra Streisand became a director; and Jessica Lange, Goldie Hawn, and Sally Field formed their own production companies. Taking a decade-by-decade approach, Dawn Sova portrays all the women who worked in Hollywood, including the stars who are highlighted in all their glory in full-page, black-and-white publicity photographs. Appendices list Academy Awards and top star moneymakers; a bibliography and an index are included. For browsing and research, *Women in Hollywood* will find a wide audience. MHCA.

Tallchief, Maria, and Larry Kaplan. **Maria Tallchief: America's Prima Ballerina**. New York: Henry Holt, 1997. 351p. $27.50. ISBN 0-8050-3302-5.

> The daughter of an Osage Indian father and a Scotch-Irish mother, Maria Tallchief grew up in Oklahoma, but she made a huge impact on American ballet when she arrived in New York in 1942 at the age of seventeen. When she joined the Ballet Russe, she caught the attention of choreographer George Balanchine, whom she married. As the prima ballerina for the rising New York City Ballet company, Tallchief starred in roles Balanchine created for her in *Firebird*, *Swan Lake*, *Orpheus*, and the *Nutcracker*. Tallchief invokes the internal world of professional ballet with its pressures of practice, performance, and injury, but she also recreates her own relationship struggles with several men, including Rudolf Nureyev, besides her three husbands. Balanchine was a huge personality, and Tallchief treats his genius with veneration, while approaching her own talent and achievements with modesty. *Maria Tallchief*, with its three sections of stunning black-and-white photographs and index, will be enjoyed in performance arts and biography collections. MHCA.

Welch, Catherine A. **Margaret Bourke-White: Racing with a Dream**. Minneapolis: Carolrhoda, 1998. 104p. $23.93. ISBN 1-57505-049-8.

> Margaret Bourke-White became one of the first women to enjoy a successful career as a photographer. Born to unorthodox parents in 1904, Bourke-White learned the meaning of curiosity, hard work, and courage. She studied herpetology and photography at a number of colleges, and, after graduation, the amateur had a large enough portfolio to become an independent commercial photographer. Traveling all over the United States and abroad photographing industrial sites and the dust bowl, Bourke-White's style developed and changed. Her big break came on November 23, 1936, when her photograph of the Fort Peck Dam graced the initial cover of *Life* magazine. She continued to shoot photo essays for *Life* during World War II, when she was appointed the first woman war photographer for the U.S. Army Air Forces; her assignments included visiting the front and photographing the Buchenwald concentration camp. From the 1950s until her death in 1971, Bourke-White fought the effects of Parkinson's disease, which hindered further development of her career. Illustrated with many black-and-white photographs, including Bourke-White's works, the biography contains notes, a bibliography, and an index. MH.

Whitfield, Eileen. **Pickford: The Woman Who Made Hollywood**. Lexington: University Press of Kentucky, 1997. 441p. $25.00. ISBN 0-8131-2045-4.

> As Hollywood's first movie icon, Mary Pickford made close to 200 films in a career that began in her childhood and spanned vaudeville, the theater, silent movies, and talkies. Not only did she act, she wrote, produced, and founded United Artists with her husband, Douglas Fairbanks; Charlie Chaplin; and D. W. Griffith. A shrewd businesswoman, Pickford made her fortune in Hollywood, but became reclusive in her declining years. Once "America's

Sweetheart" and "Little Mary," few people would recognize a picture of the great actress today. Unfortunately, many of her films have been destroyed through deterioration of the old nitrate stock, but Pickford bears some responsibility for the loss of her legacy. Recognizing that silent films would not last, and fearing that future generations would laugh at her silent performances, Pickford refused to allow her films to be preserved until it was too late. Although modern audiences still admire the performances of her contemporary, Charlie Chaplin, the visual record of Pickford has been lost and her acting reputation with it. Eileen Whitfield, in her complete biography, with two sections of black-and-white photographs, notes, a bibliography, a filmography, and an index, restores Pickford to a place she deserves as both an actress and entrepreneur. HCA.

Wyman, Carolyn. **Ella Fitzgerald: Jazz Singer Supreme**. New York: Franklin Watts, 1993. 128p. (Impact Biography). $23.60; $6.95pa. ISBN 0-531-13031-2; 0-531-15679-6pa.

Jazz singer Ella Fitzgerald won an amateur contest at the Harlem Opera House to begin her music career, which spanned fifty years. Fitzgerald was one of the youngest big band leaders, a woman conducting an all-male group. Beginning in the 1930s, she worked with most of the notable music personalities of the day, including Chick Webb, Count Basie, Duke Ellington, Dizzy Gillespie, and Nat King Cole. Although admired as a performer, Fitzgerald had to endure travel through the segregated South, where Black performers could not stay in every hotel or eat in every restaurant. The biography contains a section of black-and-white photographs, notes, a discography, a bibliography, and an index. MHA.

Non-Book Material

American Quilt Study Group. 1998. Thirty-fifth and Holdrege Street, East Campus Loop, P.O. Box 4737, Lincoln, NE 68504-0737. 402-472-5361; fax 402-472-5428. E-mail: AQSG2@unl.edu. URL: http://catsis.weber.edu/aqsg/.

Founded in 1980, the American Quilt Study Group is an international organization of over 1,000 members, founded to promote and preserve research on quilt makers, quilts, and quilt-making. With headquarters at the University of Nebraska, the organization offers publications, a research library, and a yearly seminar. HCA.

Dorothea Lange. 13 min. Films for the Humanities and Sciences, 1988. (Against the Odds). Videocassette. $69.95.

The famous Depression-era photograph of a poor woman staring, her face etched with worry, is the visual that opens this short film on the life of photographer Dorothea Lange. A black-and-white film interview with Lange, made before her death in 1965, is used throughout the video so that much of the narration is in her own words. Born in 1895, Lange was crippled by polio as a child, but she used her eyes to "live a visual life." She trained as a portrait photographer and opened her own studio in San Francisco. A trip to the desert opened up documentary photography for Lange, whose photographic record of Great Depression conditions helped to shape government policy. Lange preferred the close-up, and she felt that her lameness opened the way for her to photograph ordinary people. Before her death, Lange was recognized with an exhibit of her work at the Museum of Modern Art in New York City. Those participating in art programs will note with appreciation that her photographic works are framed within the video, making them stand out. Many of these photographs are widely known today, and the video brings the creator into focus. MHCA.

Georgia O'Keeffe Museum. 1999. 217 Johnson Street, Santa Fe, NM 87501. 505-995-0785. E-mail: main@okeeffemuseum.org. URL: http://www.okeeffemuseum.org.

The Georgia O'Keeffe Museum opened in Santa Fe in 1997 some eighty years after O'Keeffe first visited New Mexico. O'Keeffe loved the light and shapes of New Mexico, and the works she painted there are among her most memorable. An artist from childhood, O'Keeffe married New York photographer and gallery owner Alfred Stieglitz. She moved to New Mexico after his death and remained a resident. Online exhibitions, biographical information, and program information are offered at the museum's Web site, which is useful for research. Art teachers will want to bookmark this site. MHCA.

Literature

Books

Angelou, Maya. **I Know Why the Caged Bird Sings**. New York: Bantam, 1969. 246p. $12.00pa. ISBN 0-553-38001-Xpa.

I Know Why the Caged Bird Sings is Maya Angelou's memoir of her youth during the 1930s in Stamps, Arkansas, where, until she gets back on her feet, her divorced mother sends Angelou and her brother, Bailey, to be raised by their grandmother. With a new boyfriend, mother retrieves Maya and Bailey and takes them to St. Louis, where Maya is raped by the boyfriend. Maya refuses to speak for five years, but she observes all that goes on around her back in Stamps. It is Mrs. Bertha Flowers, a Black aristocrat, who helps Maya to heal and regain her speech. Angelou's future as a poet can be heard in the rich language of the narrative, and students will identify with the broken-home situation of the two children in this female coming-of-age story. HCA.

Bair, Deirdre. **Anaïs Nin: A Biography**. New York: Penguin, 1995. 654p. $16.95pa. ISBN 0-14-025525-7pa.

> Noted biographer Deirdre Bair was the first to have full access to the sixty-nine volumes (250,000 pages) of the diary of Anaïs Nin housed at the University of California at Los Angeles. Bair was surprised by the strong reactions of Nin's acquaintances interviewed for the book, reactions that had to do with Nin's constant reinvention of herself, self-absorption, obsession with sex, and invention of facts. Nin, born in Paris, married once and loved scores during her ostentatious life, which she lived amid the major personalities of the mid-twentieth century. Besides her carefully written diary, Nin was a fiction writer who dabbled in the surreal and who is described by Bair as a "*major* minor writer . . . the armature onto which the clay of greatness is thrown." Bair, who cut her manuscript to less than a third of its original length, portrays Nin neither as truth nor lie but as a complicated woman, ahead of her time, who opened the discourse of selfhood, sexuality, and psychoanalysis in the twentieth century. The book contains black-and-white photographs, notes, and an index. CA.

Conn, Peter. **Pearl S. Buck: A Cultural Biography**. Cambridge: Cambridge University Press, 1996. 468p. $29.95; $17.95pa. ISBN 0-521-56080-2; 0-521-63989-1pa.

> As one of only two American women (along with Toni Morrison) to win the Nobel Prize for Literature, Pearl S. Buck is not a household name. Peter Conn illustrates how Buck, whose opinions and topics were undervalued in her own time, has been delegated a back seat in history. Buck was born in the United States of missionary parents who returned to China with their baby. She spent half her life there, growing up bilingual and ill at ease in both cultures. While writing in a range of genres, Buck's most popular fiction was about Chinese and women characters including *The Good Earth*, winner of the Pulitzer Prize in 1932. An expert on China and an author who brought Chinese voices into American literature, she championed Civil Rights and feminist and children's causes, and she opened Welcome House, an international adoption agency. Buck's life was composed of good writing and good works kept down by anti-Asian sentiment and the McCarthy hearings. Conn's book, which includes black-and-white photographs, notes, and an index, looks at the history of both the United States and China in a very readable account about a remarkable woman. HCA.

Cuthbertson, Ken. **Nobody Said Not to Go: The Life, Loves, and Adventures of Emily Hahn**. Boston: Faber and Faber, 1998. 383p. $29.95. ISBN 0-571-19950-X.

> Although Emily (Mickey) Hahn received a degree in mining engineering, it was not a field she could enter in the 1920s. Instead, she became a traveler, adventurer, and writer, author of over fifty books of biography, nonfiction, fiction, humor, and travel, along with hundreds of articles, short stories, and poems. Hahn wrote for the *New Yorker* for eight decades, but she also

crossed the United States to work as a Harvey Girl in Taos, walked solo across central Africa, participated in Red Cross work in the Belgian Congo, served as a concubine to a Chinese poet in Shanghai, became an opium addict, bore an illegitimate child to a British Secret Service officer in Hong Kong, and promoted environmental and wildlife preservation. Hahn never chose the easy path and was never fearful of life's consequences; she remained independent and active. Hahn's excellence in writing was recognized when she was elected to the American Academy of Arts and Letters. Ken Cuthbertson became interested in portraying Hahn when he met her while working on another project; he brings her to life in a book that includes black-and-white photographs, notes, a bibliography, and an index. Make room on the biography shelves for a page-turner. HCA.

Herrmann, Dorothy. **Anne Morrow Lindbergh: A Gift for Life**. New York: Penguin, 1993. 382p. $14.95pa. ISBN 0-14-023238-9pa.

Educated at Smith College, Anne Morrow Lindbergh was a shy and studious young woman who did not know what to say to solo transatlantic aviator Charles Lindbergh when she met him. This was, however, what drew him to her. The couple were married for forty-five years, enduring fame, the kidnapping and murder of a son, and political disfavor. Lindbergh learned to fly, and stood by her husband in his isolationist stance before World War II, and she earned her own reputation as a respected and revered writer of such books as *Gift from the Sea* and *Dearly Beloved*. Although the famous couple sealed their papers and rejected all offers to chronicle their lives, Dorothy Herrmann attempts to explain gaps in Lindbergh's life not covered in her autobiographical writings as well as to give a more complete look at her as a writer. Herrmann's book, for use in literature and biography collections, contains two sections of black-and-white photographs, a list of Lindbergh's works, notes, a selected bibliography, and an index. HCA.

Holtz, William. **The Ghost in the Little House: A Life of Rose Wilder Lane**. Columbia: University of Missouri Press, 1993. 425p. (Missouri Biography). $29.95; $19.95pa. ISBN 0-8262-0887-8; 0-8262-1015-5pa.

William Holtz presents the complete life of Rose Wilder Lane, Laura Ingalls Wilder's daughter; attempting to prove that Lane was the ghost writer of her mother's *Little House* books. Although Lane hid this during her lifetime, she left a written record, which Holtz employs to tell of the troubled relationship between the two. Although Lane grew up in the little house on the prairie and moved throughout the Midwest with her parents, she was very much a woman of the twentieth century. As a writer, the author of *Let the Hurricane Roar;* a political analyst; and world traveler, she deserves to be remembered in her own right. Biography readers, as well as those who enjoy juvenile writer Wilder, will be curious about the book, which contains a black-and-white photograph section, an appendix showing Lane's editing of the *Little House* manuscripts, notes, and an index. HCA.

Hurston, Zora Neale. **Dust Tracks on a Road: An Autobiography**. New York: HarperCollins, 1996. $22.50; $13.50pa. ISBN 0-06-016726-2; 0-06-092168-4pa.

> Published in 1942, *Dust Tracks on a Road* was Zora Neale Hurston's account of her own life. The Hurston family moved to the all Black town of Eatonville, Florida when Zora was very young. When she was away at school, her mother died and her father remarried, splitting the family. With no roots, Hurston seemed doomed to life as a domestic; but she persisted in her education and attended Barnard College, where she studied anthropology under Franz Boas. Hurston, who loved to listen to stories as a child, collected folklore in the South, in Jamaica, and in Haiti, and published several books based on her research, including *Mules and Men* and *Tell My Horse*; however, Hurston had an equally important career as a writer of fiction and participant in the Harlem Renaissance in the 1920s; *Their Eyes Were Watching God* was her masterpiece. Unfortunately, Hurston did not receive recognition commensurate with her achievement during her lifetime; she always wanted for money, and she died poor, resting in an unmarked grave until rediscovered by Alice Walker. Hurston was secretive in a number of ways about her life, and her autobiography must not be viewed as a full account, but rather as the story she wanted to tell. HCA.

Johnston, Norma. **Louisa May: The World and Works of Louisa May Alcott**. New York: Beech Tree, 1991. 239p. $4.95pa. ISBN 0-688-12696-0pa.

> Although she worked as an actress, editor, teacher, and nurse, Louisa May Alcott was chiefly a writer, excelling in Victorian adolescent, domestic fiction based on her powers of observation. The author was constantly struggling to support her poor family, which she headed for most of her adult life. Alcott was a nurse during the Civil War and wrote about her experiences in *Hospital Sketches*. The book was well accepted, but Alcott had been spinning out various types of tales for some time, writing thrillers, poems, and juvenile pieces under several pseudonyms. When her best-selling novel, *Little Women*, was published in 1868 and 1869, the fictional March family closely paralleled the Alcott family. The success of the book somewhat relieved family economic pressures, but Alcott persevered at writing all her life, publishing nearly 300 pieces. Norma Johnston's biography contains black-and-white photographs and portraits, suggestions for further reading, and an index. MHA.

Kochersberger, Robert C., Jr., ed. **More Than a Muckraker: Ida Tarbell's Lifetime in Journalism**. Knoxville: University of Tennessee Press, 1994. 242p. $19.50pa. ISBN 0-87049-934-3pa.

> Editor Robert Kochersberger has brought together a careful selection of twenty-five pieces of Ida Tarbell's writing. In his introduction, he provides the biography of the woman Teddy Roosevelt considered a muckraker, but, in the broader view, Tarbell can be considered the woman who pioneered investigative journalism based on scientific research. Trained as a biologist at Allegheny College, where she was the sole female in her class and one of

four on campus, Tarbell was born too soon to realize a career in biology, but she detested the alternative, teaching. As a writer, Tarbell was accomplished in biography, in the essay, and in investigative reports. Although best known for her exposé of the Standard Oil Company, which brought about antitrust reforms, Tarbell wrote widely. Included in the book are biographical pieces on Manon Phlipon Roland and Abraham Lincoln, reports on such business practices as tariff protections and mine safety, essays on her first airplane ride and Prohibition, and radio addresses on working in later life. Tarbell's most ambivalent writing concerned women's issues. Although choosing to remain single, Tarbell supported women's place in the home in *The Business of Being a Woman*, yet, in many other writings, she promoted women in a variety of fields and positions. Besides notes, a bibliography, and an index, Kochersberger includes an appendix explaining Chautauqua, for which Tarbell wrote and lectured in later life. Tarbell's work remains vital today, and journalism students will appreciate having the collection available for comparison against current investigative reports. HCA.

Kramer, Barbara. **Amy Tan: Author of *The Joy Luck Club***. Springfield, NJ: Enslow, 1996. 112p. (People to Know). $19.95. ISBN 0-89490-699-2.

Although Amy Tan denied her Chinese heritage as a youth, her embrace of her past boosted her to the best-seller list with all three of her novels, *The Joy Luck Club, The Kitchen God's Wife*, and *The Hundred Secret Senses*. Barbara Kramer's biography, including full-page, black-and-white photographs, discusses Tan's childhood, career as a writer, autobiographical strains, and fear of the publication of her second book. Quotations from interviews and reviews are used throughout the book, which includes a chronology, notes, a bibliography, and an index. MH.

Lisandrelli, Elaine Slivinski. **Maya Angelou: More Than a Poet**. Springfield, NJ: Enslow, 1996. 128p. (African-American Biographies). $19.95. ISBN 0-89490-684-4.

More Than a Poet opens with Maya Angelou reading her uplifting poem "On the Pulse of Morning" at the 1993 inauguration of President William Jefferson Clinton; Elaine Lisandrelli shows Angelou as one who has overcome the obstacles of poverty, race, physical attack, and single motherhood to live a varied life as a singer, dancer, actress, writer, and champion of her race. Drawing on Angelou's five books of autobiography, Lisandrelli gives a full portrait of the writer and includes quotations, black-and-white photographs of people and places, a chronology, notes, a bibliography, and an index. Students who read *I Know Why the Caged Bird Sings* in school will appreciate the book's portrayal of Angelou's later life, struggles, and successes. MH.

Lyons, Mary E. **Sorrow's Kitchen: The Life and Folklore of Zora Neale Hurston**. New York: Scribner's, 1990. 144p. $15.00. ISBN 0-684-19198-9.

Folklorist and novelist Zora Neale Hurston brought the authentic voice of Black experience to print at a time when the reading public was not yet ready to accept it. Now her work is enthusiastically appreciated, but Hurston did not live to enjoy these rewards; she died poor in her birth state of Florida. Although she had always loved stories, Hurston studied anthropology under Franz Boas and collected Black folklore in the South for her own studies and for the Library of Congress. Hurston also traveled to Jamaica and Haiti to document voodoo practices. She was part of the Harlem Renaissance, best known for her fiction *Their Eyes Were Watching God*, although she was not as celebrated as many of the male authors. Lyons's book does an admirable job of portraying Hurston as a woman of enthusiasm, even though Lyons admits that Hurston was not truthful in everything she reported about her life and often tried to please white patrons rather than be true to what she felt was right. *Sorrow's Kitchen* includes selections from Hurston's writing in every chapter as well as black-and-white photographs, notes, suggested readings, a bibliography, and an index. MH.

Marks, Jason. **Around the World in 72 Days**. Pittsburgh: Sterling, 1999. 185p. $6.95pa. ISBN 1-56315-103-0pa.

The race between reporters Nellie Bly (Elizabeth Cochrane), of the *New York World*, and Elizabeth Bisland, of the monthly magazine *Cosmopolitan*, to beat the record of Jules Verne's fictional character Phineas Fogg in traveling around the world in less than eighty days is brought to life by author Jason Marks. Beginning in November 1889, Bly headed east and Bisland headed west on whirlwind world tours recorded in journals and reported in their respective periodicals. Making good use of the primary source record, Marks tells the stories in alternating chapters. Bly had thought up this stunt herself and was anxiously awaiting the call to travel, but Bisland, who valued her privacy, hated the idea but was compelled to go by her publisher, who was looking for a circulation boost. Bisland completed the trip in seventy-six days and published a book *In Seven Stages: A Flying Trip Around the World*. Always the better-known of the two, Bly won the race in seventy-two days and wrote her own book. Mark's travelogue encompasses the biographical details of the two opposites, the complexities of women traveling alone in the late Victorian period, and the pressures from the media hosts, who were pouring large amounts of money into the venture. *Around the World in 72 Days*, including a section of black-and-white photographs, is an enjoyable read with insights into women's place in journalism in an earlier time. MHCA.

McKissack, Patricia C., and Fredrick L. McKissack. **Young, Black, and Determined: A Biography of Lorraine Hansberry**. New York: Holiday House, 1998. 152p. $18.95. ISBN 0-8234-1300-4.

As the first Black women to mount a Broadway play and receive the New York Drama Critics Circle Award, Lorraine Hansberry wrote of events close to her life. When she was in grade school, her parents moved to a white section of Chicago, where her father challenged their eviction in court, winning a battle to eliminate housing discrimination. Once these proceedings were over, their Chicago home was visited by such figures as

W. E. B. DuBois and James Baldwin. After some college and art school courses, Hansberry moved to New York, where she wrote for Paul Robeson's journal, *Freedom*. All of these intellectual and political influences came together in her first play, *A Raisin in the Sun*, the story of a Black Chicago family trying to move up and fulfill their dreams. Hansberry wrote several more plays before her early death from cancer. The husband she divorced, but named as her literary executor, went on to create a book and play of Hansberry's collected writing, *To Be Young, Gifted, and Black*. The McKissacks' biography is based on Hansberry's writing, which is quoted throughout, and interviews with friends and family. The authors place Hansberry within the rising Civil Rights movement, especially in their time line. The well-written book includes clear black-and-white photographs, a bibliography, and an index. MHA.

Mills, Kay. **A Place in the News: From the Women's Pages to the Front Page**. New York: Columbia University Press, 1990. 378p. $19.50pa. ISBN 0-231-07417-4pa.

Veteran journalist and editorial writer Kay Mills maintains an attitude in her history of women in newspaper work. As one on the front lines of equality since the 1960s, Mills is familiar with discrimination in the industry, and her reprisal is to end each chapter with "Everyday Indignities," a capsule telling some way of doing business that excluded or demeaned women reporters. Although briefly surveying women reporters from Colonial times, Mills's focus is on the twentieth century, the growth of women reporters from the 1930s, and their attainments in the last twenty years. Mills interviewed over 150 women from newspapers around the country for *A Place in the News;* their profiles are used throughout the text, which is not overly centered on famous names. She hypothesizes on how the newspaper business and news coverage might be different if women ran the show: making news assignments as well as covering events. Journalism courses will want to own this account, which contains a section of black-and-white photographs, notes, and an index. HCA.

Mirriam-Goldberg, Caryn. **Sandra Cisneros: Latina Writer and Activist**. Springfield, NJ: Enslow, 1998. 112p. $19.95. ISBN 0-7660-1045-7.

Although only in her forties, Sandra Cisneros has built her reputation as a writer. Born in Chicago to a Mexican father and Mexican American mother, the family often traveled to her father's native home for extended visits. Although not a great student and from a poor family, Cisneros set her sights on college, and she attended Loyola University and the creative writing program at the University of Iowa, from which she received an M.F.A. Soon afterwards, she began to publish her work, including her best-known book, *The House on Mango Street*, which is taught in many schools. A creative person, Cisneros also cares about young people, who will find her story inspiring. Black-and-white photographs, maps, a chronology, notes, suggestions for further reading, and an index accompany the text. MH.

Price-Groff, Claire. **Extraordinary Women Journalists**. New York: Children's, 1997. 272p. (Extraordinary People). $37.00; $16.95pa. ISBN 0-516-20474-2; 0-516-26242-4pa.

> Almost fifty American women journalists are profiled in interesting capsule biographies in Claire Price-Groff's book. Acknowledging that making the selection of the truly "extraordinary" was difficult, Price-Groff includes an appendix describing sixty-four additional women, and she groups some women together in entries on Colonial, suffrage, African American, gossip, and feminist journalists. The biographies of women from the seventeenth century to the present range from three to five pages and usually include a black-and-white portrait or other illustration along with a quotation. Many journalistic fields are presented, from columnists to critics and from photo-journalists to television panelists. Besides a glossary and index, the book includes sources of further information in books, from organizations and through Internet sites. The author provides exciting anecdotes and historical context so that readers learn more than just biographical details in a book that will be used for research material and for independent reading. MH.

Schockley, Ann Allen. **Afro-American Women Writers, 1746–1933: An Anthology and Critical Guide**. Boston: G. K. Hall, 1988. 465p. $45.00. ISBN 0-8161-8823-8.

> Librarian Ann Schockley has collected historical, biographical, and biblio-graphical information as well as sample writings of forty Black women writers from Colonial times through the Harlem Renaissance. She divides her book into four parts covering the Colonial period to the Civil War, Reconstruction to the end of the nineteenth century, turn of the twentieth century to the Harlem Renaissance, and the New Negro Movement, or Harlem Renais-sance, from 1924 to 1933. Because only two writers of the later movement published before 1933, Schockley appends biographical sketches of Harlem Renaissance women who published later; another appendix lists selected sources on writers from 1900 to 1933. Schockley's introduction is a good his-toriography of her subject, and each section of the book begins with a historical overview and a chronology of the contents. The entry on each woman includes a footnoted biography, a selected list of primary and secondary source material, and selections from the subject's poetry, biography, essays, short stories, fiction, or autobiographical writing. The book is intended for use as a supple-mental text, but it can also be used in literature, multicultural, and women's studies classes as well as for reference and research. HCA.

Stendhal, Renate, ed. **Gertrude Stein in Words and Pictures: A Photo-biography**. Chapel Hill, NC: Algonquin Books of Chapel Hill, 1994. 286p. $19.95pa. ISBN 0-945575-99-8pa.

> The "mother of modernism," Gertrude Stein desperately wanted to be remembered for her writing, but she is more renowned for her influence on cutting-edge artists and writers who attended her salons in Paris after the turn of the twentieth century. Born in Pennsylvania, Stein lived in Austria,

France, and California before attending Radcliffe and Johns Hopkins University Medical School. Giving up medicine for art, she settled in Paris, where she lived out her life, writing daily and socializing widely. Editor Renate Stendhal theorizes that the hundreds of photographs Stein posed for during her life probably held hidden symbolism and messages in the same way her writing did. Stendhal chose 360 photographs, over 100 of them published for the first time, and matched them with quotations from Stein's writing and the work of those who knew her. The combination sheds new light on Stein as a presence and influence. Divided into nine chapters, each begins with a chronology of Stein's life in the period and includes multiple black-and-white photographs, documents, and artwork, accompanied by succinct captions and quotations. The sources for the quotes as well as for the photo and text credits are appended. A bibliography and index accompany the publication, which will be useful in literature and art collections. HCA.

Whitelaw, Nancy. **Let's Go! Let's Publish! Katharine Graham and the Washington Post**. Greensboro: Morgan Reynolds, 1999. 112p. (Makers of the Media). $18.95. ISBN 1-883846-37-4.

Publisher Katharine Graham's story, which illustrates the development and politics of a major newspaper for over a century, is one of personal triumph over adversities. As a child, Graham felt unworthy of her high-powered family, a feeling that was intensified by an overbearing and troubled husband. When her manic-depressive husband died in 1963, Graham stepped into his role as publisher of the *Washington Post* and head of its media empire. These were interesting news days: Graham printed the Pentagon Papers, the government's secret account of the Vietnam War, despite a suit by the U.S. government to suppress them, and she broke the Watergate story, which lead to the resignation of President Richard Nixon. Leading the *Post* for over thirty years, from the time she was in her mid-forties, Graham maintained its position as a top newspaper and earned many publishing honors. Besides black-and-white photographs, a time line, a glossary, a bibliography, notes, and an index, *Let's Go! Let's Publish!* also contains an appendix of milestones in journalism history, making the book useful as report material. MH.

Whitelaw, Nancy. **They Wrote Their Own Headlines: American Women Journalists**. Greensboro: Morgan Reynolds, 1994. 142p. (World Writers). $17.95. ISBN 1-883846-06-4.

Seven pioneer women representing varied fields of journalism are portrayed in Nancy Whitelaw's collective biography. Listed chronologically by date of birth, the women include muckraker Ida M. Tarbell, foreign correspondent Dorothy Thompson, photographer Margaret Bourke-White, White House reporter Alice Dunnigan, advice columnist Ann Landers, television journalist Charlayne Hunter-Gault, and the first women to win a Pulitzer Prize, war correspondent Marguerite Higgins. Each biography contains a full-page, black-and-white portrait of the subject and a bibliography of her books.

Appended to the book, which offers useful report information, are a glossary, an index, and a selected bibliography. MH.

Yannuzzi, Della A. **Zora Neale Hurston: Southern Storyteller**. Springfield, NJ: Enslow, 1996. 104p. (African-American Biographies). $19.95. ISBN 0-89490-685-2.

In a biography suitable for middle school readers, Della Yannuzzi portrays Zora Neale Hurston as a person who worked hard all her life but who failed in the end to achieve financial gain or notoriety. Hurston had a stubborn streak behind her drive, and because of this she lost friends, one of them Langston Hughes, a fellow writer in the Harlem Renaissance, and she died alone. To support herself, Hurston accepted help from wealthy patrons and wrote to their specifications instead of her own. Unrecognized in her own time, Hurston's legacy lies in her collections of folklore and in her novels—one being *Their Eyes Were Watching God*— which she wrote in popular vernaculars and set in all-Black communities. Yannuzzi's biography contains full-page black-and-white photographs, a chronology, notes, suggestions for further reading, and an index. M.

Non-Book Material

As I Remember It: A Portrait of Dorothy West. Produced and directed by Salem Mekuria. 56 min. Women Make Movies, 1991. Videocassette. Purchase $295.00; Rental $90.00.

Interviewed during her seventy-sixth year, Dorothy West looks back at her upbringing as a middle-class Black in the early years of the twentieth century, her life as a writer, and her involvement in the Harlem Renaissance. The child of a freed slave turned successful produce dealer on Martha's Vineyard, West had a comfortable childhood living with several brothers and sisters who passed for white. Several magazines aimed at creating audiences and opportunities for Black writers were being founded, and in 1926 West entered a contest sponsored by one of these magazines in which she tied for second place with Zora Neale Hurston. After going to New York to accept the award, West moved to Harlem to become a part of the cultural revival taking place there. As West explains in her interview, the women of the Harlem Renaissance lived in the shadow of the men. There were many fine female writers who, even until recently, went unrecognized. Although the Harlem Renaissance ended in the late 1920s, West tried twice to create literary magazines that would keep it going, but each one was unsuccessful. West's own masterpiece, *The Living Is Easy*, the story of a middle-class Black family ruled by an ambivalent mother, was not completed and published until the 1940s. Far from the political sentiments of other Black writers of the time, West could be called the predecessor of Terry McMillan and other current writers who focus on the everyday experiences of Black life. The film features an extensive interview with West, who continues an active life on Martha's

Vineyard and writes for the local paper. Black-and-white photographs, and color and black-and-white film are used to illustrate the video. More than a portrait of the author, the film interprets racial conditions during the first half of the twentieth century and, as such, can be used in history, literature, and multicultural courses. HCA.

Renascence: Edna St. Vincent Millay, Poet. Produced and directed by Vanessa Barth. 60 min. Films for the Humanities and Sciences, 1993. Videocassette. Purchase $89.95; Rental $75.00.

Including fifteen poems by Edna St. Vincent Millay, *Renascence* relates the poet's life through commentary by scholars, the poet's own letters and works, dramatization, and black-and-white family photos and film clips. Several of Millay's major poems are read and analyzed, including the title piece "Renascence," which was written at age twenty and showed Millay's early genius. She was born and raised in Maine by a mother who divorced and worked to support three daughters, providing them with as much music and literature as she could. The publication of "Renascence" earned Millay a benefactor, who arranged to send her to Vassar. An established poet by the time she left school, Millay settled in Greenwich Village and worked with playwright Floyd Dell, whose quotes about Millay are scattered throughout the film. Millay fell in love, and her second published collection of poems contained love sonnets. Bored with New York, Millay traveled through Europe for several years. Here she realized how much she missed home and her mother. She wrote *The Harp Weaver and Other Poems* as a tribute to her mother, a work that earned the Pulitzer Prize in 1923. When Millay returned to the United States, she met the man she would marry. They settled in upstate New York and on a Maine island, where Millay's later work reflected these natural settings and political themes. The poet abhorred the executions of Sacco and Vanzetti in 1927, and she deplored the course of world events, which she wrote about in propaganda-like poems in *The Buck and the Snow* and *Make Bright the Arrows*. She suffered from depression and a nervous breakdown. Over the course of her lifetime her poems showed three major themes, the importance of nature, the pain and healing of love, and the unfortunate and unmendable course of human events, and she remained the "independent poet goddess." The film presents a good analysis and is recommended for use in American literature and poetry courses. HCA.

Politics

Books

Braden, Maria. **Women Politicians and the Media**. Lexington: University Press of Kentucky, 1996. 235p. $29.95; $14.95pa. ISBN 0-8131-1970-7; 0-8131-0869-1pa.

> While acknowledging how the media has changed since women got the vote in 1920, Maria Braden allows that women have always been held to a political standard different from that of men; the media has focused on women's images and made clear its skepticism about their ability to perform. In many ways, journalists are locked into tradition, transmitting it unconsciously. Braden's chronological overview of women in politics uses interviews, portraits, and quotations to depict women politician's treatment by the press. Extended treatment is given to Jeannette Rankin, Helen Gahagan Douglas, Clare Boothe Luce, Margaret Chase Smith, Bella Abzug, Geraldine Ferraro, Elizabeth Holtzman, and Ann Richards. The Equal Rights Amendment, the perspectives of women reporters, and the history of women in presidential politics, including Victoria Woodhull, Margaret Chase Smith, and Shirley Chisholm, are also covered. *Women Politicians and the Media*, which includes black-and-white photographs, notes, a bibliography, and an index, will be used in women's history, political science, and media courses. MHCA.

Burkett, Elinor. **The Right Women: A Journey Through the Heart of Conservative America**. New York: Scribner, 1998. 288p. $23.00; $14.00pa. ISBN 0-684-83308-5; 0-684-85202-0pa.

> After crossing America in the aftermath of the 1994 elections, which brought a flurry of conservative women to office, journalist Elinor Burkett proposes some ideas about those who elected them. Burkett admits to never having talked to women who did not self-identify as feminists, and with this admission comes the realization of the arrogance of feminism, one possible reason it has alienated many women. Burkett interviews a wide range of conservative women: young and old; Republicans, Libertarians, and Muslims; militia members and mothers. She finds that the institution of feminism itself seems too remote, that having it all comes at too high a price, and that men are not seen as the enemy. In the 1990s, women are acting independently in forming new relationships with social institutions so that they can configure their lives in ways that make sense to them. In this way, the crux of feminism is carried forward in the individual decisions women make in seeking self-fulfillment in their lives. *The Right Women* does not promote a political agenda, but, in an intriguing examination, takes a closer look at women's reality in the 1990s. HCA.

Byman, Jeremy. **Madam Secretary: The Story of Madeleine Albright**. Greensboro: Morgan Reynolds, 1998. 96p. (Notable Americans). $18.95. ISBN 1-883846-23-4.

> Forced out of Czechoslovakia before World War II when the rest of their extended family were killed by Nazis, Madeleine Korbel Albright and her family moved to Denver after the war, where she attended school and matriculated to Wellesley College. After raising a family and completing a doctorate degree, Albright entered politics and worked for President Jimmy Carter on the staff of the National Security Council. During the Reagan years, Albright worked for a think tank and taught until President Bill Clinton called upon her to serve as ambassador to the United Nations and as secretary of state, the first woman to hold this post. This short biography illustrates Albright's life and career with black-and-white photographs, a time line, a bibliography, and an index. MH.

Conway, M. Margaret, David W. Ahern, Gertrude A. Steuernagel, Earlean McCarrick, and Robert H. Jerry II. **Women and Public Policy: A Revolution in Progress**. Washington, DC: Congressional Quarterly, 1995. 213p. $22.95pa. ISBN 0-87187-923-9pa.

> *Woman and Public Policy* traces the dual relationship between the effects of changing culture on policy and changing policy on culture. The authors offer chapters covering the issues of education; health care; employment; economic equity in credit, housing and retirement; insurance; family law; child care; and the criminal justice system. Each chapter begins with a vignette to illustrate discriminatory practice, and ends with notes, a chronology, and suggestions for further reading. Several charts and graphs illustrate the *Women and Public Policy*, which also includes an index. It will be useful in government and women's studies courses and for debate. HCA.

Fireside, Bryna J. **Is There a Woman in the House . . . or Senate?** Morton Grove, IL: Albert Whitman, 1994. 144p. $14.95. ISBN 0-8075-3662-8.

> In profiling ten women who served in the House or Senate, Bryna Fireside began with her heroine, Jeannette Rankin, the first woman to serve in the House of Representatives, in 1917. She then chose nine contemporary figures to interview, representing a wide range of geographic areas, religions, and racial backgrounds. The six Democrats and four Republicans, nine of whom she personally interviewed, include Rankin, Margaret Chase Smith, Shirley Chisholm, Bella Abzug, Barbara Jordan, Patricia Schroeder, Millicent Fenwick, Barbara Mikulski, Nancy Kassebaum, and Geraldine Ferraro. In profiling their childhoods, political careers, and causes, Fireside uses a variety of photographs, taken in both childhood and adulthood, of the subjects with their families and at work. The book begins with a section explaining how Congress works and concludes with the author's explanation of her method of selecting the politicians. A selected bibliography and an index are included in a volume that will be useful for reports. MH.

Gordon, Linda. **Pitied but Not Entitled: Single Mothers and the History of Welfare, 1890–1935**. New York: Free Press, 1994. 433p. $22.95. ISBN 0-02-912485-9.

>   Whereas "welfare" formerly had a pleasant connotation, it now has a negative meaning associated with poverty and enforced taxation. The shift in meaning came about between 1890, at the beginning of the reform period, and 1935, when the Social Security Act, which covered unemployment compensation, public health, aid to the blind, and public assistance to the elderly and to dependent children, was passed. The welfare system was founded on the basis of exclusion; it stratified in the years after 1935 based on the principals of "needs, earnings, and rights." Generally, help was available to those who needed it the least and trickled down to minorities, dependent children, and the truly poor. Linda Gordon traces the development of the welfare system from its roots in the maternalistic reform movement and the development of social research, through the consideration of welfare models including the family wage, and up to the passage of the congressional bill, which incorporated all forms of welfare. Gordon discusses settlement houses, the Children's Bureau, Black women's clubs, the Depression, and the New Deal, as well as the perspectives each brought to the building of the institution of welfare. Each chapter is introduced with a historical photograph or cartoon, and an appendix lists welfare reform leaders, Black, white, male, and female. Notes and an index are included in a study that is pivotal to the understanding of contemporary welfare systems. HCA.

Gould, Lewis L., ed. **American First Ladies: Their Lives and Their Legacy**. New York: Garland, 1996. 686p. $100.00; $25.95pa. ISBN 0-8153-1479-5; 0-8153-2585-1pa.

>   Defining a first lady as one who has been married to a president during his term of office, Gould includes only thirty-eight women in his collection of biographical essays with bibliographic notes. From Martha Washington to Hillary Rodham Clinton, the development of the role of first lady unrolls. Several wives, Anna Harrison, Letitia Tyler, Margaret Taylor, and Jane Pierce, played little public role, while Eleanor Roosevelt redefined the office. The bibliographic essays contain important information for researchers, noting any writings by a first lady, the location of her papers, memoirs by family or friends, biographies of herself and of her husband, and other relevant sources. A black-and-white portrait accompanies each article; the exception is Margaret Taylor, for whom no known portrait exists. Appendices list the Siena College First Lady Polls for 1982 and 1993, which rank presidential spouses on ten categories, along with a list of the presidents and those who served them as first ladies, whether as spouse or in another relationship. Notes on the contributors and a detailed index round out the well-presented and useful book. HCA.

Kaptur, Marcy. **Women of Congress: A Twentieth-Century Odyssey**.
Washington, DC: Congressional Quarterly, 1996. 256p. $29.50. ISBN
0-87187-989-1.

> Marcy Kaptur, representative from the Ninth District in Ohio since 1982,
> profiles fifteen congressional women. Dividing her book into three parts,
> Kaptur includes Jeannette Rankin, the first woman in the House, and two
> others in section one, covering 1917 to World War II. Section two tells about
> Margaret Chase Smith and six others in the years between World War II
> and the 1960s, and Shirley Chisholm and four others are included in the
> modern era. Besides the familiar personalities mentioned, Kaptur portrays
> lesser-known figures in portraits that discuss biographical details, families,
> motivating issues, and legislative records. Along with the introduction,
> which discusses women and women's issues in Congress, each chapter begins
> with a historical overview. Black-and-white portraits are placed through-
> out the book, and an additional section of black-and-white illustrations of
> the women of Congress is included. Wonderful tables lay out all the women of
> Congress chronologically, alphabetically, by longevity, and by state. Selected
> readings and an index complete this careful study, which provides in-depth
> material for more serious students. HCA.

Morin, Isobel V. **Women of the U.S. Congress**. Minneapolis: Oliver, 1994.
160p. (Profiles). $16.95. ISBN 1-881508-12-9.

> Seven congresswomen are framed in Isobel Morin's simple overview, from
> the first representative, Jeannette Rankin, in 1917, to Senator Barbara
> Mikulski, who is still serving. The women in between include Margaret
> Chase Smith, Helen Gahagan Douglas, Shirley Chisholm, Barbara Jordan,
> and Nancy Kassebaum. The biographies are anecdotal, illustrating the areas
> of interest of each legislator. Besides her introduction, which outlines
> women's involvement in federal elections since the passage of the Nine-
> teenth Amendment in 1920, Morin concludes with a chapter explaining the
> phenomenon of the 1992 election in which 117 women ran for Congress,
> more than in any previous election. Morin includes a nice selection of
> black-and-white photographs in her *Women of the U.S. Congress,* more
> than appear in the other books reviewed in this section. A chronological list
> of all women who have served in Congress, a bibliography, and an index are
> appended to a book that will be useful for reports. MH.

Morin, Isobel V. **Women Who Reformed Politics**. Minneapolis: Oliver,
1994. 160p. (Profiles). $16.95. ISBN 1-881508-16-1.

> No elected officials are included among eight women who spearheaded
> various reform movements from ante-bellum times to the present. The
> women included in *Women Who Reformed Politics* are abolitionist Abby
> Kelley Foster, temperance crusader Frances Willard, antilynching cam-
> paigner Ida Wells-Barnett, suffragist Carrie Chapman Catt, political boss
> Molly Dewson, Civil Rights activists Pauli Murray and Fannie Lou Hamer,
> and feminist Gloria Steinem. Their biographies are complete and interesting,

containing many black-and-white illustrations. A time line reports the major reform movements in U.S. history, and a bibliography and an index are appended. *Women Who Reformed Politics* will make enjoyable independent reading and serve as research material. MH.

Schultz, Jeffrey D., and Laura van Assendelft, eds. **Encyclopedia of Women in American Politics**. Phoenix: Oryx, 1999. 354p. (American Political Landscape). $116.88. ISBN 1-57356-131-2.

> *Encyclopedia of Women in American Politics* is a one-volume source covering Colonial times to the present. Using an alphabetical arrangement, the encyclopedia lists over 700 entries, including "every woman who has served in a political capacity," important events, court cases, and issues. More than fifty scholars contributed entries, each of which has a bibliography and cross-references. Former White House Bureau Chief for United Press International, Helen Thomas, writes the forward, Karen O'Connor presents a historical overview for the introduction, and appendices present speeches and documents; lists of women who served in Congress, as governors, as first ladies, and as cabinet members; political organizations; and a time line from the year 1848. A detailed index finishes the publication, which makes an excellent reference source for libraries serving government, women's studies, or American history courses. MHCA.

Truman, Margaret. **First Ladies**. New York: Fawcett Columbine, 1995. 368p. $12.95pa. ISBN 0-449-22323-Xpa.

> The joy of Margaret Truman's volume on first ladies is that it is a conversational view of a very few women who hold a special position, rather than a reference guide filled with dates and political connections. The reader becomes acquainted with those included as individuals through the anecdotes told about them. Truman, daughter of a first lady, does not opt for chronological arrangement; rather she presents the women topically, so that Julia Grant and Mamie Eisenhower are grouped together as generals' wives, and Mary Todd Lincoln and Florence Kling Harding appear next to each other as the worst first ladies. All the twentieth-century wives are fully covered, and many but not all of the first ladies are included. Truman's book, with its scattered portraits and index, will enrich research assignments. MHCA.

Non-Book Material

American Association of University Women. 1999. 1111 Sixteenth Street NW, Washington, DC 20036. 800-326-AAUW; fax 202-872-1425. E-mail: info@aauw.org. URL: http://www.aauw.org/home.html.

> The American Association of University Women is a political and philanthropic organization with interests in promoting education and equity. From their Web site, they track issues and make their research available, including their extensive research on the gender gap in education, which is

published in *The AAUW Report: How Schools Shortchange Girls* (1992). Information about AAUW's fellowships, grants, and awards to women can be accessed here, as well as the voting record of the current Congress. Government and teacher education classes will want to be familiar with this site. HCA.

The Feminist Majority Foundation Online. 1999. 1600 Wilson Boulevard, Suite 801, Arlington, VA 22209. 703-522-2214; fax 703-522-2219. E-mail: femmaj@feminist.org. URL: http://www.feminist.org/.

Founded in 1987 by Eleanor Smeal and other women, the Feminist Majority pledges to empower and to win equality for women. That a majority of women identify themselves as feminists is reflected in the group's name. The organization is made up of two wings: the Feminist Majority, working on public policy advocacy; and the Feminist Majority Foundation, active in research and public education. Their searchable Web site is international in scope and contains news, research, and further links. It is a good place to gather information with a woman-centered viewpoint for debates or other projects. HCA.

The League of Women Voters: A Voice for Citizens, a Force for Change. 1999. 1730 M Street NW, Washington, DC 20036-4508. 800-249-1965; fax 202-429-0854. E-mail: lwv@lwv.org. URL: http://lwv.org/.

The League of Women Voters was created in 1919 by a motion Carrie Chapman Catt put before the National American Woman Suffrage Association to reorganize into a new structure reflecting a different focus after the passing of the Nineteenth Amendment. Since its inception, the League has worked to ensure informed and active participation in government and civic concerns by all people at all levels of government. Their Web site presents their eighty-year history of political involvement and many quotes by famous League participants, although this section of information is not easy to find unless actively sought. The Web site contains links to other political and women's issues sites, as well as the League's local affiliates. Government classes and individuals researching the history of this group should be drawn here. HCA.

National Organization for Women. 1998. 1000 Sixteenth Street NW, Washington, DC 20036. 202-331-0066; fax 202-785-8576. E-mail: now@now.org. URL: http://www.now.org/.

An organization of activist feminists since its founding in 1966, the National Organization for Women works toward economic equality for women, the Equal Rights Amendment to the Constitution, reproductive freedom, lesbian rights, an end to sexual harassment and violence against women, and the termination of racism. The NOW Web site documents the group's history and contains background and position information on the issues they support. The site is searchable for ease in locating information and includes links to feminist indexes, government resources, and political news on the World

Wide Web. Government classes and students searching for debate positions will find the location useful. HCA.

National Woman's Party. 1998. Sewall-Belmont House, 144 Constitution Avenue NE, Washington, DC 20002. 202-546-3989; fax 202-546-3997. E-mail: lteuwen@natwomanparty.org. URL: http://www.natwomanparty.org/.

> Operating out of a national historic landmark, the Sewall-Belmont House in Washington, D.C., the National Woman's Party was founded by Alice Paul in 1916. It was Paul who pursued more militant tactics in the struggle for the vote by having party members picket the White House and go on hunger strikes. Paul was the author of the Equal Rights Amendment, penned in 1923, which the National Woman's Party continues to promote. The Sewall-Belmont House was purchased for the NWP in 1926 by million-aire Alva Belmont, who succeeded Alice Paul, in 1921, as chair of the party. The Capitol Hill mansion has belonged to the party since the time of Belmont's gift. The NWP has a library at the Sewall-Belmont House, and presents the history of the movement and related links on their Web site. MHCA.

Secretary of State Madeleine Korbel Albright. U.S. Department of State, 2201 C Street NW, Washington, DC 20520. 202-647-4000; fax 202-647-7120. E-mail: secretary@state.gov. URL: http://secretary.state.gov/index.html.

> A quote from the secretary of state and her portrait introduce the homepage for Madeleine Korbel Albright. Further links to the news story from which the quote was taken, other quotes, the secretary's travel schedule, biographical information, and highlights of her interests complete the site, which links back to the Department of State's homepage. Albright, confirmed unanimously by the Senate in 1997, is the first female to head the Department of State. Nominated by President Clinton, Albright's background in international affairs has led her to hold a variety of government posts, in-cluding that of representative to the United Nations. Albright speaks four languages and has a career background in teaching and research. Her *60 Minutes* interview and questions students have sent to her are also included at this searchable site, which is suitable for research. MHCA.

Women's International League for Peace and Freedom. n.d. 1213 Race Street, Philadelphia, PA 19107. 215-563-7110; fax 215-563-5527. E-mail: wilpf@wilpf.org. URL: http://www.wilpf.org/.

> Jane Addams served as the first president to the Women's International League for Peace and Freedom after it organized in The Hague in 1915 to suggest ways to end World War I. The WILPF has existed since that time to promote equality for all people, to guarantee basic human rights, to address basic human needs, to end violence, and to promote world disarmament and peace. The history of the group and a time line are available on their Web site, which also outlines their programs, resources, and action agendas. Contact information to local chapters is listed. MHCA.

Religion

Books

Allen, Paula Gunn. **Grandmothers of the Light: A Medicine Woman's Sourcebook**. Boston: Beacon, 1991. 246p. $14.00pa. ISBN 0-8070-8103-5pa.

> A scholar of Laguna Pueblo and Sioux heritage, Paula Gunn Allen collected twenty-one stories of Native American mythology, which embody women as supernatural beings. The stories reveal the goddesses, recount the uses of ritual magic both long ago and today, and explain how human women relate to the supernaturals. Allen believes that stories connect people to the "universe of medicine . . . or sacred power"; she has included stories that she uses personally as spiritual guides. The book is divided into three parts: "Cosmogyny: The Goddesses," "Ritual Magic and Aspects of the Goddesses," and "Myth, Magic, and Medicine in the Modern World." Essays introduce the book and each section, and, in a postscript, Allen acknowledges the commonalties in spirituality among eleven tribes representing all the geographical regions of North America: Chippewa, Aztec, Cherokee, Navajo, Karok, and others. A glossary and bibliography are appended. *Grandmothers of the Light* will be used in comparative religion classes and multicultural studies. HCA.

Blumhofer, Edith L. **Aimee Semple McPherson: Everybody's Sister**. Grand Rapids, MI: William B. Eerdmans, 1993. 431p. (Library of Religious Biography). $16.00pa. ISBN 0-8028-0155-2pa.

> Using previously unavailable documents from Aimee Semple McPherson's own Church of the Foursquare Gospel, biographer Edith Blumhofer presents the fullest portrait yet written of the evangelist who took up white dress and blue cape and was known simply as Sister. McPherson was born in Ontario, and, while still in her infancy, she was dedicated to God's work by her mother, a member of the Salvation Army. At the age of seventeen, McPherson was converted at a Pentecostal revival, and two years later the church made her a preacher. She remained in this denomination for the rest of her life, converting many new members through revivals, publications, and good works. With a flair for publicity and self-promotion and a belief in faith healing, McPherson preached old-time Bible theology with a fundamental interpretation. When she moved her burgeoning following to California in 1918, the ascent of her ministry began. She traveled in the United States and abroad, holding huge revivals, and she built the Angelus Temple in Los Angeles; however, the evangelist was not without controversy. McPherson was widowed once and divorced twice; she was at odds with her mother, who ran the administrative functions of her church; and her daughter disassociated from the family. McPherson faced a string of lawsuits over her business affairs and libelous statements, but her most controversial action came when she disappeared from a swimming beach in 1926, surfacing a month later in Mexico, claiming that she had been kidnapped.

McPherson worked enormously hard, but the work and controversy took a toll; she suffered mental breakdowns and died of an overdose of sleeping pills in 1944. Immensely popular in her day, she left an established empire of Pentecostal churches to her son. Full of the dramatic incidents people love, McPherson's biography will be popular reading. HCA.

Brekus, Catherine A. **Strangers and Pilgrims: Female Preaching in America, 1740–1845**. Chapel Hill: University of North Carolina Press, 1998. 466p. (Gender and American Culture). $49.95; $17.95pa. ISBN 0-8078-2441-0; 0-8078-4745-3pa.

Catherine Brekus uncovers over 100 female evangelical preachers who influenced the revivals of the first and second Great Awakenings in the eighteenth and early nineteenth centuries. Although popular during their time, these women have since been forgotten for two reasons: They were too conservative to be remembered by woman's rights activists, and they were too radical to be remembered by church history. Thus, both groups ignored them, and had they not written their own memoirs, they would be truly lost. Brekus searched these memoirs, memoirs of clergymen, religious periodicals, and church manuscript collections in her research. Because of opposition towards female preachers and because of the changing role of women during the period, a tradition of female evangelism was never established, and women sermonizers in each century have had to reestablish themselves because they did not know the history of their predecessors. Black-and-white illustrations are included throughout the text, which also includes a list of all the female preachers, notes, a bibliography, and an index. Brekus's book will be important where religious studies are part of the curriculum. HCA.

Coles, Robert. **Dorothy Day: A Radical Devotion**. Reading, MA: Perseus, 1987. 182p. (Radcliffe Biography). $16.50pa. ISBN 0-201-07974-7pa.

More a conversation than a biography, Robert Coles's work calls upon notes and tape recordings he made of discussions with Dorothy Day to explore themes in her life. Although the biographical facts of Day's life as an activist who converted to Catholicism and lived out her life in voluntary poverty helping the poor and supporting righteous causes are present, Coles focuses on Day's idealism, conversion, relationship to the church, politicism, and commitment. Day co-founded the Catholic Worker Movement, dedicated to helping the poor through hospitality houses across the country, and wrote a column for the *Catholic Worker* newspaper. Particularly interesting to those seeking inspiration is the final chapter in which Coles traces saints, theologians, and novelists whom Day considered illuminating. Readers will appreciate the long passages from Day's own words in a portrait that contains notes, a bibliography and an index. HCA.

Gill, Gillian. **Mary Baker Eddy**. Reading, MA: Perseus, 1998. 713p. $35.00. ISBN 0-7382-0042-5.

Given more access to records of the Church of Christ Scientist than any previous researcher, Gillian Gill centers her extensive biography of the first sixty years of the life of Mary Baker Eddy, church founder, as well as her private life, public image, and intellectual achievements. Eddy's attainment as the only woman to create a major religion, the intellectual legacy she left in her publications, as well as the economic empire she built from a base of penury must be remembered beyond the speculation, accusations, counteraccusations, and lawsuits that filled the last third of her life until her death at eighty-nine. Eddy's church was built around her belief that the mind was greater than the body, expressed in her book *Science and Health*. Eddy, who suffered nervous hysteria, was healed by mesmerist Phineas Parkhusrt Quimby, who believed in mental healing. She would later be accused of plagiarizing him. Soon after Quimby's death, Eddy had a breakthrough experience to which she attributed the birth of Christian Science. A fall left her incapacitated; however, after several days, she rose from bed, healed through reading the Bible. During hectic and uncomfortable years, Eddy worked out her spiritual philosophy and taught it to disciples with zeal. Her strength was as a teacher, but because of an ever-changing series of alliances with men and women who would betray her, lead her astray, or break with her philosophies, Eddy retired from active participation in the church and retreated to Concord, New Hampshire. Even in seclusion, Eddy had to defend herself from attacks, by her son and by Joseph Pulitzer's New York *World*, which charged her with mental incompetence. When the new Mother Church was built in Boston, Eddy did not attend the dedication, and she only visited the city four times after her removal. It was only two years before her death that she insisted upon the founding of a daily newspaper, the *Christian Science Monitor*; after her death, the church organization was maintained in the way she had desired. While disparaged constantly, Eddy's life was remarkable, and readers will find her a worthy subject. The book contains three sections of black-and-white photographs, a chronology, observations on the research, reviews of the important published books on the subject, notes, and an index. CA.

Keller, Rosemary Skinner, and Rosemary Radford Ruether, eds. **In Our Own Voices: Four Centuries of American Women's Religious Writing**. New York: HarperSanFrancisco, 1995. 542p. $20.00pa. ISBN 0-06-063292-5pa.

Ten chapters cover the diversity of American religious experience since the seventeenth century and women's place within it. Rosemary Keller provides the general introduction on gender and culture within American religion, and the historical context of each individual chapter is composed by an expert. These preludes are followed by a grouping of black-and-white illustrations of most of the women whose voices follow. Between five and twenty documents are included in each chapter, covering Catholic women, Protestant laywomen, Jewish women, Black women, Evangelical women, Protestant women in social reform, women and ordination, Utopian societies, American Indian women, and growing pluralism. Included are the writings of Mother Jones, Toni Morrison, Elizabeth Cady Stanton, Anne Hutchinson, Sister Blandina Segale, Starhawk, and many other renowned and obscure women. The book is a treasure trove of primary sources for history and religion and should be invaluable in cultural studies. A list of contributors, notes, and an index are included. HCA

Kent, Deborah. **Dorothy Day: Friend to the Forgotten**. Grand Rapids, MI: William B. Eerdmans, 1996. 146p. $15.00; $8.00pa. ISBN 0-8028-5117-7; 0-8028-5100-2pa.

An activist who supported social causes throughout the twentieth century from woman suffrage to peace, Dorothy Day lived as an example of the religion to which she converted. Born in New York, Day attended the University of Illinois, where she became attuned to social injustice and poverty and joined the Socialist party. She left school, moved to New York, and became a reporter, working against military conscription and for woman suffrage. Day was arrested with the suffragists picketing in front of the White House and sentenced to thirty days in the Occoquan workhouse, where she joined the hunger strike in further protest. Through a common law marriage, Day bore a daughter, Tamar, an experience that brought about her conversion to Catholicism in 1927; soon afterward, Day helped found the Catholic Worker movement. For the rest of her life, until her death in 1980, Day participated in the movement as a writer, a worker in the hospitality houses, and a resident of the work farms. She did not give up her activism, but joined in protests supporting conscientious objectors, opposed nuclear weapons, endorsed Civil Rights, and denounced the Vietnam War; she was arrested a number of times for civil disobedience. Day's faith and conviction led her to live her life in voluntary poverty, and young people will find her example inspiring. Deborah Kent's biography contains a section of black-and-white photographs, source notes, suggestions for further reading, and an index. MHA

Nadell, Pamela S. **Women Who Would Be Rabbis: A History of Women's Ordination, 1889–1985**. Boston: Beacon, 1998. 300p. $30.00. ISBN 0-8070-3648-X.

Presenting the often obscured and overlooked 100-year, history of women soliciting to become Jewish religious leaders, Pamela Nadell looks beyond the culminating event of the ordination of Sally Priesand in 1972. A century ago, Jewish women and men began discussing the possibility of women rabbis, a discussion that continues today. Nadell examines temple records, newspapers, letters, and the 1889 short story by Mary M. Cohen to uncover the history of women's admission to theological schools; and the changes in thought and custom of both society and the Jewish religion that led to women's participation. All branches of Judaism in the United States are considered: Reform, Reconstructionist, Conservative, and Orthodox. A section of black-and-white photographs, notes, and an index are included in this fine study. HCA.

Reis, Elizabeth, ed. **Spellbound: Women and Witchcraft in America**. Wilmington, DE: SR Books, 1998. 276p. $45.00; $16.95pa. ISBN 0-8420-2576-6; 0-8420-2577-4pa.

Giving the broad overview of women's connection to witchcraft in America, editor Elizabeth Reis uncovers new material on gender and ethnic-based persecution and presents an unexplored perspective of women's seeking female-centered spiritualism. In twelve essays, contributors cover the history of witchcraft from Colonial times to the modern Goddess religion. Although each essay brings new insights, witchcraft between the early and modern periods is neglected in the work; all the essays covering the middle centuries connect witchcraft to race. Two articles look at witchcraft as a part of Native American religion in the Iroquois and Seneca tribes in New York in cases occurring in 1821 and 1930. Two other papers look at witchcraft among African American women: Sojourner Truth, and hoodooism practiced in churches in New Orleans. Five essays deal with Colonial witchcraft; three portray aspects of the Goddess religion. Among these, Starhawk embraces witchcraft and reveals some of its practices; Cynthia Eller looks more broadly at those who do not employ witchcraft but borrow from different cultures as part of neopagan belief; and Linda Jencson betrays the hidden misogynistic practices in Goddess worship. Witchcraft, while disturbing to society, has been practiced across centuries and cultures for a number of reasons. *Spellbound*, with it diffuse perspective, will be used in women's, multicultural, and religious studies, and in history courses where spirituality in America is traced. Reis provides an introduction, suggested readings, and notes about the contributors. HCA.

Sisters, Servants of the Immaculate Heart of Mary, Monroe, Michigan. **Building Sisterhood: A Feminist History of the Sisters, Servants of the Immaculate Heart of Mary**. Syracuse: Syracuse University Press, 1997. 392p. (Women and Gender in North American Religions). $49.95; $24.95pa. ISBN 0-8156-2737-8; 0-8156-2741-6pa.

Beginning in the late 1980s the Sisters of the Servants of the Immaculate Heart of Mary (I.H.M.) order in Monroe, Michigan, began to explore how they could reexamine their history with a feminist perspective. Meeting in 1990, the group drew up a set of seventeen "Working Assumptions for the Claiming Our Roots Project," which are appended to the book. Covering history, feminist history, and the process and product they wanted to create, the list could serve as a model to any historian or group engaging in a collective procedure. Sixteen members of the I.H.M. order and two nonmembers brought together the history of the group, the daily life of the sisters, their relationship to the Catholic church in terms of authority, leadership and governance, and their educational mission. Margaret Susan Thompson, a historian and scholar of Catholic women, provided the introduction and context for each section of the book. The book, including an extensive bibliography and index, presents well-researched scholarship, and it will interest a range of readers, from those interested in the religious perspective to those interested in the feminist perspective. HCA.

Stoltzfus, Louise. **Amish Women: Lives and Stories**. Intercourse, PA: Good Books, 1994. 123p. $14.95; $8.95pa. ISBN 1-56148-129-7; 1-56148-228-5pa.

Framed by chapters relating her own experience as an Amish woman in Lancaster, Pennsylvania, Louis Stoltzfus introduces ten Amish women. Stoltzfus relates a range of life experiences, from those of her grandmothers and mother to those of women she did not know, emphasizing their Amish traditions in plainness, cooking, farm life, family, children, and religion. Through tragedy and world travel, the women show intelligence and creativity. Several pencil drawings illustrate the text that imitates Amish ways in its brevity. MHCA.

Warner, Wayne. **Kathryn Kuhlman: The Woman Behind the Miracles**. Ann Arbor, MI: Servant, 1993. 283p. $10.99pa. ISBN 0-89283-794-2pa.

Kathryn Kuhlman was a woman evangelist following in the footsteps of Aimee Semple McPherson. Born in Concordia, Missouri, with roots in the Methodist and Baptist denominations, Kuhlman moved on to Pentecostalism and became an independent charismatic and faith healer (although she hated the label) who attracted a broad range of believers. Kuhlman preached for forty-eight years, never losing her appeal and always demanding proof of a healing before publicizing it in her network of books, television and radio programs, and religious services presented all over the United States. In the long line of American evangelists, Kuhlman's story deserves a place; it is told here in a conversational tone with documentation by Wayne Warner. A section of black-and-white photographs (small in size) are included in a center section, and a note about the Kathryn Kuhlman Foundation is appended. MHCA.

Yohn, Susan M. **A Contest of Faiths: Missionary Women and Pluralism in the American Southwest**. Ithaca, NY: Cornell University Press, 1995. 266p. $45.00; $17.95pa. ISBN 0-8014-2964-1; 0-8014-8273-9pa.

Between 1867 and 1924, the Woman's Board of Home Missions of the Presbyterian Church sent women missionaries to northern New Mexico, into the largely Hispanic Catholic population, with the purpose of creating better citizens through education and conversion. While Susan Yohn's book traces the rise of female missionaries during the reform period and the motivations of women who joined in the work, it also identifies a number of contests that eventually led to a change in the nature of the work. The first contest was between the church and the women who were assuming formerly male-dominated roles, but an additional contest emerged between the white and Hispanic cultures in New Mexico. Eventually, the women missionaries came to appreciate the things they learned from the native population and to express the value of cultural pluralism. Realizing that their Hispanic clients did not seek conversion, the women missionaries downplayed their religious mission and put more effort toward education, which the population wanted. With the change in roles, the missionaries became more like social workers and the field required more professional training, thus changing the voluntary nature of the work for which the women had offered themselves. Containing a map, scattered black-and-white photographs, a bibliography, and an index, Yohn's study will be useful in sociology, religious, and women's studies. HCA.

Science and Technology

Books

Altman, Linda Jacobs. **Women Inventors**. New York: Facts on File, 1997. 118p. (American Profiles). $17.95. ISBN 0-8160-3385-4.

> Ten women inventors representing a myriad of products from the nineteenth and twentieth centuries are presented in this installment of the American Profiles series. As with other books in the series, each entry includes black-and-white illustrations, a timeline, suggestions for further reading, and a complete index, enhancing the research value of the book. The inventors profiled here include Amanda Theodosia Jones and her vacuum canning process; Carrie Everson, who devised an oil flotation mining technique in the gold fields of Colorado; Sara Josephine Baker, a doctor who developed safety and health care products for children; Madam C. J. Walker, an entrepreneur who created a line of hair care products for African American women; Ida Rosenthal, the inventor of the brassiere; Katharine Blodgett, who devised the military smoke screen; Elizabeth Hazen and Rachel Brown, patentees of the antifungal drug Nystatin; Bette Graham, who developed and marketed Liquid Paper; and the designer of the Barbie doll, Ruth Handler. Libraries will find *Women Inventors* valuable report material. MH.

Bonta, Marcia Myers, ed. **American Women Afield: Writings by Pioneering Women Naturalists**. College Station: Texas A & M University Press, 1995. 248p. (Louise Lindsey Merrick Natural Environment). $15.95pa. ISBN 0-89096-634-6pa.

> Marcia Bonta has colllected the eclectic writings of twenty-five women naturalists from the nineteenth and early twentieth centuries. Representing the fields of botany, entomology, ornithology, and ecology, the women were in many respects pioneers, collecting field notes from locations ranging from their front yards to the Amazon River valley and publishing in both popular and scholarly journals. Both the articles and the black-and-white illustrations give an idea of the rigors of the fieldwork; women had to defy Victorian custom and travel by horse-and-buggy and on foot to observation

sites. The book begins with the author of *Rural Hours,* Susan Fenimore Cooper (daughter of James), who was born in 1813, and ends with pioneer ecologist Rachel Carson, born in 1907. Editor Marcia Bonta has gleaned a formidable collection of entries, presenting biographical information and one or more selections from the published works of each naturalist. *American Women Afield,* which includes a selected bibliography to the book as well as to each entry, will be useful in writing classes to show the range of technical writing, and in science classes. HCA.

Bragg, Janet Harmon, and Marjorie M. Kriz. **Soaring Above Setbacks: The Autobiography of Janet Harmon Bragg, African American Aviator.** Washington, DC: Smithsonian Institution Press, 1996. 120p. $19.95; $12.95pa. ISBN 1-56098-458-9; 1-56098-755-3pa.

Born in Georgia, Janet Harmon Bragg received a nursing degree from Spelman College, and, finding there was no commitment to health care for the African American population in the South, she moved to Chicago. There, in the 1930s, she entered the Aeronautical University to learn to fly. She became the first Black woman to hold a commercial pilot's license, and she helped to build an airport and hanger with the Challenger Air Pilots' Association. Bragg owned three nursing homes on the south side of Chicago, mentored Ethiopian students studying in the United States (which gained her an invitation from Emperor Haile Selassie to visit that country), and was honored by the Smithsonian Institution for her achievements in aviation. Bragg's autobiography uncovers the history of Black people in the early days of aviation and recounts a remarkable life. A section of black-and-white photographs and an index are included as well as an appendix in which friends and colleagues remember the aviator. MHCA.

Butler, Susan. **East to the Dawn: The Life of Amelia Earhart.** Reading, MA: Addison-Wesley, 1997. 489p. $27.50. ISBN 0-201-31144-5.

A lifelong interest in Amelia Earhart compelled Susan Butler to search again for primary source documentation on the aviator. She uncovered an unpublished biographical manuscript by Earhart's close friend, Janet Mabie, and interviewed those who knew the pilot. The result is an extensive portrait of a beloved woman who was lost in the Pacific attempting to be the first to circumnavigate the globe; she died at thirty-nine. Butler portrays Earhart as a child and family member, as a rising star in aviation, as a married woman, and as a champion of women's rights who gave her time to charitable causes and promoted equal education. Less than thirty-five pages of the book are devoted to the failed round-the-world trip, and the author concludes, without perpetuating rumors or adding to speculation, that the pilot was simply lost at sea. Butler's book is the most definitive portrait of Earhart as a person, not as a myth. It contains two sections of black-and-white photographs, notes, a bibliography, and an index. HCA.

Camp, Carole Ann. **Sally Ride: First American Woman in Space**. Springfield, NJ: Enslow, 1997. 104p. (People to Know). $19.95. ISBN 0-89490-829-4.

> In 1983, Sally Ride became the first American woman to travel to space, as a flight engineer on the space shuttle *Challenger*. Carole Camp's biography concentrates mostly on Ride's NASA career: recruitment, training, two space missions, and an administrative job. The book does a good job of answering students' questions about life in space, and most of the black-and-white photographs depict Ride in her role of astronaut. Although Ride's childhood, education, and career as a physicist and teacher after leaving NASA are included, the book would benefit from more illustrations covering these aspects of Ride's life. The book will fulfill research requests and includes a chronology, notes, suggestions for further reading, and an index. MH.

Ehrenreich, Barbara, and Deirdre English. **Complaints and Disorders: The Sexual Politics of Sickness**. New York: Feminist Press, 1973. 94p. $6.95pa. ISBN 0-912670-20-7pa.

> Journalists Barbara Ehrenreich and Deirdre English look at women's illnesses, influenced by the male-dominated medical system that became institutionalized in the late nineteenth century. Because women's medical care, the understanding and control of the female body, birth control, abortion, and childbirth are key to women's complete participation in society, the way the medical establishment views women's health is significant to the roles they can assume. The authors reconstruct medical treatment to women in the upper class, including the topics of invalidism, the establishment of medical reputation, and knowledge about both physical and mental health, as well as sickness in the working classes, the threat of disease-carrying immigrants, venereal disease, and the rise of public health services and birth control. The authors conclude with comments on how past medical practice continues to affect women's health issues today. Although the conclusion may be slightly outdated, the historical information is enlightening and will provide fodder for interesting research topics. Illustrated with copious black-and-white illustrations, both period and modern, the book includes a bibliography. HCA.

Fine, Edith Hope. **Barbara McClintock: Nobel Prize Geneticist**. Springfield, NJ: Enslow, 1998. 128p. (People to Know). $19.95. ISBN 0-89490-983-5.

> Born in 1902, Barbara McClintock was educated at Cornell and pursued a career as a research scientist, a rarity for women at the time. She had identified chromosomes in several species a decade before James Watson and Francis Crick announced the structure of DNA. Her most famous work explained "jumping genes," or transposons, which changed positions on chromosomes, but it was not until late in her career that she was honored for her genetic discoveries. She was the first woman to receive the National Medal of Science and the first woman to receive an unshared Nobel Prize for Physiology or Medicine. McClintock's joy in work, willingness to share with others, and good humor are all evident in Edith Fine's biography. Although

McClintock was involved in high-level research, Fine makes it accessible to the reader in text and with diagrams. Also included are black-and-white photographs, a chronology, notes, a glossary, suggestions for further reading, and an index. MH.

Goldstein, Donald M., and Katherine V. Dillon. **Amelia: The Centennial Biography of an Aviation Pioneer**. Washington, DC: Brassey's, 1997. 321p. $24.95. ISBN 1-57488-134-5.

For those who wish to continue to theorize about Amelia Earhart's disappearance in 1937, the full rundown on all rumors and speculation is contained in *Amelia*, where over 115 pages are given to the topic. The authors capitalize on the unpublished, independent research of retired Navy Captain Laurence F. Safford, who looked into reports that a Navy high-frequency direction finder was installed in 1937 on Howland Island, Earhart's destination when she disappeared. Additionally, the authors call upon information from Georgia businessman John F. Luttrell, who used technical data in an effort to determine the location of the pilot's plane. While Earhart's childhood and career are covered, the authors' interest is obviously in the round-the-world flight attempt, which makes the book preferable for research, although no definitive answers are included. Two sections of black-and-white photographs, notes, a glossary, a bibliography, and an index are included. HCA.

Gormley, Beatrice. **Maria Mitchell: The Soul of an Astronomer**. Grand Rapids, MI: William B. Eerdmans, 1995. 123p. $8.00pa. ISBN 0-8028-5099-5pa.

When she was twenty-nine years old, Maria Mitchell discovered a comet and won a gold medal; the year was 1847. Raised a Quaker in Nantucket, Massachusetts, Mitchell received higher education and forged a reputation as a professor of astronomy at Vassar College; before she retired, she trained her own successor. While deeply religious, seeing God's hand in all his natural works, Mitchell believed in woman's rights and women's education, and she used her position to promote these causes. Beatrice Gormley uses quotations from Mitchell and a section of black-and-white illustrations to interpret the astronomer in a book that includes source notes, suggestions for further reading, and an index. As a personality, Mitchell is well worth knowing and will make an interesting addition to biography and science collections. MH.

Haynsworth, Leslie, and David Toomey. **Amelia Earhart's Daughters: The Wild and Glorious Story of American Women Aviators from World War II to the Dawn of the Space Age**. New York: Morrow, 1998. 322p. $24.00. ISBN 0-688-15233-3.

Amelia Earhart's Daughters describes two episodes in the history of women in aviation. The first part of the book covers women aviators who served as Women's Airforce Service Pilots (WASPs) in World War II, transporting various types of planes from manufacturers to air bases. Pilots Jacqueline

Cochran and Nancy Harkness Love along with General Henry "Hap" Arnold were primarily responsible for setting up the service and for seeing that the women received military status. A transitional portion of the book traces pilots Jacqueline Cochran and Jerrie Cobb in the years 1943 through 1959, when it was nearly impossible for women pilots to work. The later part of the book presents the history of the thirteen women NASA tested on a preliminary basis for astronaut training in 1961. As one of those tested, Cobb carried the case for inclusion to Capitol Hill, where it was debated by Congress; but NASA never accepted the women, even though they had proved themselves ready for training. The thirteen women are all profiled here and their subsequent careers are related. The book is framed by the 1995 launch of space shuttle *Discovery*, piloted by Lieutenant Colonel Eileen Collins, which the women astronaut candidates from the 1960s were invited to watch. Although not the complete history the title implies, the two events are fully covered and the focus on the several personalities lends a compelling element to the story. Eight pages of black-and-white photographs, a selected bibliography, and an index are included. MHCA.

Kent, Jacqueline C. **Women in Medicine**. Minneapolis: Oliver, 1998. 160p. (Profiles). $16.95. ISBN 1-881508-46-3.

Although the introduction and time line outline women's participation in medicine throughout history, the chapters present eight American women doctors, including Susan La Flesche Picotte, May Edward Chinn, and Dorothy Lavinia Brown. Presenting an overview of obstacles and achievements from the nineteenth century the other doctors include: Elizabeth Blackwell, the first woman to graduate from medical school; Mary Edwards Walker, who had to fight for the right to perform surgery on Union troops in the Civil War, spent time in a Confederate prison, and received the Congressional Medal of Honor; Helen Brooke Taussig, who pioneered heart bypass surgery to save "blue babies;" Alma Dea Morani, who helped perfect plastic surgery; and Virginia Apgar, who developed a way of rating the condition of newborns. Representing many ethnic groups, these women proved their ability to advance health care. *Women in Medicine* is illustrated throughout with black-and-white illustrations and includes a bibliography and an index. MH.

Kline, Nancy. **Elizabeth Blackwell: A Doctor's Triumph**. Berkeley: Conari, 1997. 190p. (Barnard Biography). $6.95pa. ISBN 1-57324-057-5pa.

America's first woman doctor, Elizabeth Blackwell, graduated from Geneva Medical School in New York in 1849. Two years of effort had gone into her campaign to enter medical training, and she found out that her acceptance was a fluke; her application had been put to a vote of the all-male student body, who believed it was a prank from a rival school. Blackwell needed determination to achieve her career goal, but she came from independent and progressive thinkers; the Blackwell family was committed to abolition and woman's rights, and her sister, Emily, would later join her as a physician.

Blackwell, who trained nurses during the Civil War, opened her own practice, started an infirmary, and founded a medical school for women in New York. After the medical school was established, Blackwell returned to the country of her birth, England, to live out her life, writing on her specialty, hygiene, and attending to reform causes. A chronology, a selected bibliography, and an index accompany the narrative, which includes quotations from Blackwell's personal journal and letters. MH.

Lear, Linda. **Rachel Carson: Witness for Nature**. New York: Henry Holt, 1997. 634p. $35.00; $17.95pa. ISBN 0-8050-3427-7; 0-8050-3428-5pa.

Credited with opening the environmental movement, Rachel Carson was somewhat of an oddity for her time. Serving as a government scientist in the 1940s, Carson grew up in Springdale, Pennsylvania, with a love of nature and a conviction she would be a writer. After attending Pennsylvania College for Women, she became a biologist and editor with the U.S. Bureau of Fisheries. In 1951, she published *The Sea Around Us*, winner of the National Book Award, to show the ocean as a living thing rather than just scenery. Concerned about the effects of the pesticide DDT, Carson launched an investigation and wrote *Silent Spring* in 1962; she revealed that, despite the chemical companies' promises, DDT was killing many birds and insects and causing harm to ecosystems. Carson testified before Congress on the issue, inspiring a change in government policy towards protection of the environment. Lear's biography, researched over ten years, fully portrays Carson, a private person, for the first time. The book includes two sections of black-and-white photographs, cartoons, notes, a bibliography, and an index. The inspiring account should be available in serious science and environmental collections as well as to biography readers. HCA.

Macdonald, Anne L. **Feminine Ingenuity: Women and Invention in America**. New York: Ballantine, 1992. 514p. $14.00pa. ISBN 0-345-38314-1pa.

A patent holder herself, Anne Macdonald limits her book on American women inventors to those who applied for and received patents. An ongoing debate over Katherine Greene's part in the invention of the cotton gin, which is documented only through oral stories because her name does not appear on the patent, helped to forge this decision. The history begins in 1809 with Mary Kies's patent on a straw weaving process used to make hats. Using descriptions of inventions and their inventors, Macdonald portrays the parallel history of woman's rights, for only through the right to own their property and control their earnings could women advance as inventors. While women created products for use within their own sphere in the home, they also thought up products for the fields of medicine, military science, manufacturing, and industry. Notable chapters cover the Woman's Pavilion at the 1876 Centennial Exposition, and dress reform. Using quotations from various documents as well as numerous black-and-white illustrations and portraits, Macdonald writes in an upbeat, witty style, making her book both an enjoyable read and a research treasure. MHCA.

Malone, Mary. **Maya Lin: Architect and Artist**. Springfield, NJ: Enslow, 1995. 112p. (People to Know). $19.95. ISBN 0-89490-499-X.

> When Maya Lin was a senior at Yale University, she entered a national competition to create a memorial to the Vietnam War veterans. Her project, one in 1,421 entries, won the contest and the hearts of all Americans, despite some initial skepticism of the black marble wall's unique design. Lin went on to receive advanced training in architecture and to design the Civil Rights Memorial in Montgomery, Alabama; the topiary landscape at the Coliseum in Charlotte, North Carolina; and the ceiling clock in Penn Station in New York City. The perceptive and creative artist, now in her forties, is well profiled in Mary Malone's biography, which includes a chronology, notes, suggestions for further reading, and an index. Students will enjoy the presentation which, includes black-and-white illustrations, including many of the designs discussed. MH.

Mead, Margaret. **Blackberry Winter: My Earlier Years**. New York: Kodansha, 1972. 305p. $15.00pa. ISBN 1-56836-069-Xpa.

> A few years before her death in 1978, anthropologist Margaret Mead looked back on her own life through the lens of her career spent studying sex roles and families in eight world cultures. The first daughter of a university professor and an activist mother, Mead was educated by her paternal grandmother, a former school principal. She attended DePauw and Barnard and became the protégé of Franz Boas, departing for Samoa at the age of twenty-three on a field study. Her reports, including *Coming of Age in Samoa*, became popular reading. Mead served as curator at the American Museum of Natural History in New York for most of her career, traveling on other field studies and writing copiously. She married and divorced three times and had one child, Mary Catherine Bateson. Although the book concludes with her early years of motherhood, Mead looks back as a grandmother, in the last two chapters, on the three generations of parenting and child raising with which she is familiar and considers the changes in American families caused by divorce and single parenting. Mead's secure place as the world's most popular anthropologist and her unique worldview of families give special insights to her own story. HCA.

Rich, Doris L. **Queen Bess: Daredevil Aviator**. Washington, DC: Smithsonian Institution Press, 1993. 153p. $18.95; $13.95pa. ISBN 1-56098-265-9; 1-56098-618-2pa.

> Bessie Coleman was the first Black woman to earn a pilot's license, in 1921, but she had to go to Europe for her training because no school in the United States would enroll a person of African American descent, especially a woman. Born in Texas to a poor family, Coleman made her way up in the world as a manicurist in Chicago. She saved and borrowed enough money to travel to Europe for flight training, and, once she had her pilot's license, she flew in air shows as a brilliant stunt pilot, intent on earning enough to start her own flight school. Her goal was never achieved when, in 1926,

during a practice run, she fell from an airplane and died. While Coleman was recognized in the Black community during the 1920s, it took another sixty years for her achievements to be universally appreciated. Mae Jemison, writing in an afterword, admits to feeling cheated because, until she became an astronaut, she did not know of Coleman. Doris Rich's tirelessly researched biography, which will appeal to many readers, includes notes, a bibliography, and an index. MHCA.

Rossiter, Margaret W. **Women Scientists in America: Before Affirmative Action, 1940–1972**. Baltimore: Johns Hopkins University Press, 1995. 584p. $39.95; $17.95pa. ISBN 0-8018-4893-8; 0-8018-5711-2pa.

> Looking at the participation of women in the sciences from 1940 through 1972, Margaret Rossiter paints an unhappy picture. Even during the expanding years of science, even with a need for workers created by World War II and the Cold War, and even with more women than ever being trained in the sciences, women were invisible and undervalued. Colleges used nepotism rules to refuse women employment, and in government and industry the same attitudes that prevailed in society at large kept women out of jobs or marginalized them at work. Although home economics was created as a woman's field, women's organizations did not recognize and react against discrimination. It was not until the advent of affirmative action, later in the 1970s, that these patterns changed. Two sections of black-and-white photographs, as well as profuse tables, illustrate part two of Rossiter's highly researched study, which also includes notes, a long bibliography, and a complete index. HCA.

Vare, Ethlie Ann, and Greg Ptacek. **Women Inventors and Their Discoveries**. Minneapolis: Oliver, 1993. 160p. $18.75. ISBN 1-881508-06-4.

> Ranging from the eighteenth to the twentieth century, ten women inventors are profiled in Ethlie Vare and Greg Ptacek's book. Presented in roughly chronological order, the profiles each contain several black-and-white illustrations. Among those introduced are Elizabeth Lucas Pinckney, who invented indigo dye on her family's South Carolina plantation; Martha Coston, who developed the night signal flare for military use; Fannie Farmer, who standardized recipes into a cookbook; and Stephanie Kwolek, who designed the bulletproof, flameproof fabric, Kevlar. Also profiled are Nobel Prize geneticist, Barbara McClintock; Navy admiral and computer programmer, Grace Hopper; and Barbie doll designer, Ruth Handler, who also writes the book's forward. A bibliography and an index are appended to this useful report material. MH.

Veglahn, Nancy J. **Women Scientists**. New York: Facts on File, 1991. 134p. (American Profiles). $19.95. ISBN 0-8160-2482-0.

> Eleven American women scientists, historical and contemporary, representing the fields of botany, astronomy, medicine, physics, biochemistry, anthropology, genetics, and biology are included in Nancy Veglahn's collection.

Placed chronologically according to date of birth, the biographical and professional profiles include at least two black-and-white illustrations, a chronology, and suggestions for further reading. The scientists, who have received many honors and awards and have served at many prestigious universities include Alice Eastwood, Nettie Maria Stevens, Annie Jump Cannon, Alice Hamilton, Edith Quimby, Margaret Mead, Rachel Carson, and Mildred Dresselhaus, as well as the Nobel Prize winners Gerty Cori, Barbara McClintock, and Rosalyn Yalow. A brief introduction covering women's involvement in science in American history and an index are included in a book that will be useful for reports. MH.

Yount, Lisa. **Women Aviators**. New York: Facts on File, 1995. 144p. (American Profiles). $19.95. ISBN 0-8160-3062-6.

From the 1910s, women have been a part of the development of aviation in barnstorming, record setting, military service, space flight, and piloting experimental aircraft. *Women Aviators* profiles eleven women from throughout the twentieth century, including Katherine Stinson, Bessie Coleman, Amelia Earhart, Anne Morrow Lindbergh, Jacqueline Cochran, Jerrie Cobb, Sally Ride, Jeana L. Yeager, and others. Each entry is accompanied by a time line and suggestions for further reading, and the book is indexed and illustrated with black-and-white photographs. *Women Aviators* provides exciting reading material and valuable report information. MH.

Non-Book Material

Amelia Earhart: Queen of the Air. Produced by Laura Verklan. 50 min. A & E, 1996. (A & E Biography). Videocassette. $19.95.

Using extensive black-and-white film of Earhart, including newsreel footage and interviews, this video biography produces an excellent portrayal of one of the first female aviators. The film includes interviews with Earhart's sister, Muriel Morrissey; cousin, Nancy Morse; biographer, Doris Rich; historian, Susan Ware; and fellow aviator, Eleanor Smith. Earhart's childhood and family life are traced, but the emphasis is on the 1920s and 1930s, when Earhart broke air records. One year after Charles Lindbergh's solo Atlantic crossing, Earhart became the first female to fly across the Atlantic. She was unhappy with her designation as "Lady Lindy" because she was well aware that she was only part of the crew on that flight, which was promoted by publisher G. P. Putnam. Putman continued to promote and to court Earhart, who, despite some misgivings, eventually married him. In 1932, Earhart, who was fearless in the air, made her own solo Atlantic crossing, followed in 1935 by a solo Pacific trip from Honolulu to Los Angeles. Her last trip came in 1937 when she attempted to circumnavigate the equator. By necessity, the trip included a navigator, but it ended in disaster when the team failed to locate and land on tiny Howland Island in the Pacific. Many theories on Earhart's disappearance have been put forth, but the film does not dwell on them. Using the recording of Earhart's last radio message, it promotes the theory that the team ran out of fuel and downed in the Pacific, where they died, their bodies were never found. Although flying is the focus, Earhart's other activities as a feminist and promoter of social causes are also covered. She is portrayed as a complex person who was, perhaps, used on some occasions. Students will be fascinated by Amelia Earhart, and this biography can be used for individual research as well as for classroom use in history and aviation classes. MHCA.

Margaret Mead: An Observer Observed. Directed by Virginia Yans-McLaughlin. 85 min. Filmakers Library, 1996. Videocassette. Purchase $350.00; Rental $85.00.

Margaret Mead was the best-known female anthropologist, appealing to a popular audience throughout her career. This film, told through archival film and still photographs, interviews, and dramatic reenactments, skillfully recreates Mead's career and the controversies that surrounded her. When Mead finished her graduate work at Columbia in the 1920s, she set off to test the modern theories of her mentor, Franz Boas. Boas believed that all cultures were worthy and that there was not one high Western culture. Each time Mead went into the field, she developed a well-articulated problem to study; on her first assignment in Samoa, the question was whether adolescence was painful in all societies. She concluded in *Coming of Age in Samoa* that adolescent angst was a learned behavior. The book discussed pre-marital sex among Samoan girls, a topic unmentionable at the time. The topic, as well as Mead's being a young woman traveling in uncharted territory alone, made Mead the subject of much discussion. She followed her first adventure with two other trips to the South Seas to study belief systems of children in *Growing Up in New Guinea* and gender differences in *Sex and Temperament in Three Primitive Societies*. As the first to study the role of women in any society, Mead, as usual, had picked a study topic that was fascinating to the general public and connected with issues of the time. She chose to write for popular magazines rather than for academic journals. Mead married and divorced three times when divorce was not socially acceptable. She had one daughter, Mary Catherine Bateson, who comments extensively about her mother in the video. In her later years, after publishing thirty-five books, Mead was a favorite guest on television talk shows. After her death in 1978, her Samoan work was criticized as inaccurate, the assumptions of a naive young woman. The fact remains that Mead was a pioneer in anthropological fieldwork, she did what she wanted to do with her life, and she enjoyed a long and successful career that opened new opportunities for women. HCA.

Mary Jane Colter: The Desert View. Produced and directed by Jennifer Lee. 54 min. Lucerne Media, 1996. Videocassette. Purchase $145.00; Rental $60.00.

Unrecognized during her own time, Mary Elizabeth Jane Colter is now known as a unique architect and designer. Inspired by Sioux ledger book drawings given to her as a child, and promising to support her family after the death of her father, Colter became an architect near the turn of the twentieth century, when few women were employed in that field. She could not, in fact, sign building documents as the designer. Colter went to work for the Fred Harvey Company, designing hotels and restaurants along the Santa Fe Railroad through the Southwest to bolster the rudimentary tourist trade. She worked for Harvey for forty years. Her best-known works were constructed at the Grand Canyon (including the Hopi House), where six of her designs are listed on the National Register of Historic Places. Colter studied the indigenous cultures of the Southwest and designed her buildings to grow out of natural settings, incorporating the history of each location. Her Grand Canyon structures feature unique and historic natural elements, including petroglyphs and rock from all the strata in the canyon, although it is no longer permissible to remove these natural and man-made objects from their original locations. Filmed mostly at the Grand Canyon and including interviews with park rangers and other locals, the video includes film and still photographs of Colter and her buildings. There is narration from Colter's writings, including a published book. *Mary Jane Colter*, which can be used in art courses, introduces audiences to a personality worthy of consideration for her singular architectural achievements, as well as entertaining audiences with stunning views of the American Southwest. MHCA.

The Ninety-Nines: International Organization of Women Pilots. 1999.
Box 965, 7100 Terminal Drive, Oklahoma City, OK 73159-0965.
800-994-1929; fax 405-685-7985. E-mail: 99s@ninety-nines.org. URL:
http://www.ninety-nines.org/.

A large Web page featuring lots of history is offered by the Ninety-Nines, a group of one less than 100 licensed female pilots founded in 1929 for mutual support and the advancement of aviation. Amelia Earhart was a founding member. Not only the past, but the present and future of women in aviation are presented on the page. The group offers membership, yearly fly-ins, a monthly magazine, scholarships, and information useful to student researchers. MHCA.

WISE: Archives of Women in Science and Engineering. 1998. Iowa
State University, 403 Parks Library, Ames, IA 50011-2140. 515-294-6648;
fax 515-294-5525. E-mail: Tanya Zanish-Belcher, Curator,
tzanish@iastate.edu. URL: http://www.lib.iastate.edu/spcl/wise/wise.html.

Iowa State University hosts an excellent site celebrating women in science. The university is actively seeking the papers of organizations or women involved in science and engineering either avocationally or as a career. The Web site lists archival collections, rare books, secondary sources, teaching resources, and related links, making it a great place to start research. Iowa State is also taking oral histories of women scientists and mounting virtual exhibits. The well-laid-out, attractive page is easy to use, even for younger students. MHCA.

Women of NASA. 1999. NASA Ames Research Center, Moffet Field, CA 94035. 650-604-5000. URL: http://quest.arc.nasa.gov/women/intro.html.

> NASA developed this Web site to encourage girls to consider careers in math, science, and technology. The site profiles many different women who work for NASA in a variety of capacities, not just the astronauts. Each week the site features one woman employee in an interactive chat session. Teaching activities and resources round out the site. Teachers in the hard sciences will applaud NASA's efforts in making their specialists available in the classroom on such a regular basis. MH.

Women of Science at the MBL. 1996. Marine Biological Laboratory, 7 MBL Street, Woods Hole, MA 02543. 508-548-3705; fax 508-540-6902. URL: http://www.mbl.edu/html/WOMEN/intro.html.

> A timeline is used to present a baker's dozen of women scientists who studied at the Marine Biological Laboratory (MBL) between 1850 and 1930. Because women had raised half of the money necessary to establish the institution, the MBL encouraged the enrollment of women, especially for advanced training for teaching in high schools and colleges. Approximately one-third of the students in advanced science classes were women from all over the country, including Gertrude Stein and Barbara McClintock. Biographical, bibliographical, and other links are available for each woman, and each subject is illustrated with at least one photograph. The site is an excellent source for school research projects on women in the sciences. MHCA.

Women Space Pioneers. Produced by Elliott H. Haimoff and Scott Stillman. 26 min. Churchill Media, 1994. Videocassette. $149.95.

> Narrated by Nichelle Nichols, Star Trek's Lieutenant Uhuru, this is the story of the recruitment, training and flights of NASA's first eight women astronauts. At the beginning of the space program there was no discussion of using women in space. A number of changes in the 1970s made it possible to recruit women for space duty. Thirty-five new astronauts were accepted into the space program in 1978; of these six were women. Two more women began training in 1980. All of these women had exceptional credentials, including advanced educational degrees, and with backgrounds ranging from medicine to engineering and from oceanography to biochemistry. As the women began a four-year training period, they faced opposition from astronauts who were already in line to fly. It was not until the seventh flight of the space shuttle that Dr. Sally Ride was chosen to operate the shuttle arm, becoming the first American woman in space. The video features interviews with all the women astronauts, various male astronauts, and three former directors of NASA, including the first woman director, Dr. Carolyn Huntoon. Film clips of training, of blast-off, and of flights add interest to the film. The video features women who trained and flew later, including Mae Jemison and Eileen Collins, a shuttle pilot. Although a fine tribute to NASA women Sally Ride, Judith Resnik, Kathryn Sullivan, Anna Fisher, Margaret Rhea Seddon, Shannon Lucid, Bonnie Dunbar, and Ellen Ochoa,

the film, made for the Johnson Space Center's 1995 tribute to the first women astronauts, takes a narrow view. Downplaying all controversy, it does not mention that affirmative action forced NASA to recruit women, that Judith Resnik died in the Challenger accident, or that Jerrie Cobb, who was considered for training in the 1960s, never saw space. Still, the film is well put together and will be enjoyed by many audiences. MHCA.

Sexuality, Reproduction, and Identity

Books

Borst, Charlotte G. **Catching Babies: The Professionalization of Child-birth, 1870–1920**. Cambridge, MA: Harvard University Press, 1995. 254p. $41.50. ISBN 0-674-10262-2.

By studying birth certificates, health department records, state licenses, and censuses, Charlotte Borst concluded that rising medical professionalism led to the decline of midwifery between 1870 and 1920 in four Wisconsin counties: Trempealeau, Price, Dane, and Milwaukee. While the training and skill of medical professionals was increasing during this period, returning young doctors to their communities as emissaries of a new type of science, midwives were not changing, and practitioners continued to be middle-class women. The decline of midwives was often portrayed as a misogynist plot of the medical profession, but it was more the case that the women put themselves out of business by failing to keep up with consumer demand for higher skills, appreciated by pregnant women who were choosing physicians to attend the births of their children. Borst's book is filled with charts and graphs visually illustrating her findings about education and demographics. An appendix explains Borst's quantitative sources, and notes and an index are included. CA.

Brodie, Janet Farrell. **Contraception and Abortion in Nineteenth-Century America**. Ithaca, NY: Cornell University Press, 1994. 373p. $17.95pa. ISBN 0-8014-8433-2pa.

In reviewing the period between 1830 and 1870, historian Janet Brodie concludes that a surprising array of birth control devices and information were available to people in various economic classes and areas of the country; however, Brodie maintains that it took more than just knowledge, it took desire to limit family size. The combination of the two factors brought about the drastic lowering of the birth rate during the middle years of the nineteenth century among white families. Although contraception and abortion methods had been kept secret, it was the expanding market economy of Jacksonian America and entrepreneurial business practice that made information more available. Still, by the 1870s, the knowledge had become criminalized with the passage of the Comstock law, which made it a crime to distribute birth control information. Brodie uncovered documentation of the trade in contraceptive literature and devices mostly from advertising, business, and credit records from Colonial times. Two sections of black-and-white portraits and reproductions of period literature are included in the book along with notes, a selected bibliography, and an index. Although *Contraception and Abortion* sheds new light on the Victorian era, it also gives meaningful historical context to current struggles with these issues. HCA.

Brumberg, Joan Jacobs. **The Body Project: An Intimate History of American Girls**. New York: Random, 1997. 267p. $25.00; $13.00pa. ISBN 0-679-40297-7; 0-679-73529-1pa.

By studying the diaries of girls written between the 1830s and the 1990s, Joan Brumberg is able to identify changes in the way adolescent girls feel about their bodies. Victorian girls emphasized good deeds, moral development, and spirituality, and were not encouraged to dwell on their looks or material possessions; they contrast greatly to twentieth-century girls, who not only mature earlier, but, under extreme societal pressure, take on the body as a project for feeding (or not), exercising, and decorating. Contemporary girls grow up with fewer social protections, leaving them with little adult support and at risk to a number of pressures. Brumberg uses a variety of evidence, including an outstanding collection of photographs and advertisements, to show how mother-daughter bonds have loosened over time and how science and the mass media have created an ideal physique. Brumberg elaborates on accelerated development, menstruation, skin, sexuality, the body as project, and the need for girl advocacy. Giving the historical context of these topics presents a unique perspective in an important book that includes notes and an index. MHCA.

Chen, Constance M. **"The Sex Side of Life:" Mary Ware Dennett's Pioneering Battle for Birth Control and Sex Education**. New York: New Press, 1996. 374p. $25.00; $15.00pa. ISBN 1-56584-132-8; 1-56584-133-6pa.

Trained as an artist at the school of the Boston Museum of Fine Arts, Mary Ware Dennett entered into all the reform efforts at the turn of the twentieth century: suffrage, pacifism, and birth control. Constance Chen centers her biography around three major battles in Dennett's life. When Dennett's husband was lured away by another woman with the promise of "free love," she fought a bitter custody battle for her two sons. Her next battle was with Margaret Sanger, another birth control advocate, over who should have access to birth control information. Although Dennett maintained that everyone needed access to reliable facts, Sanger promoted a "doctors only" policy that eventually won favor, giving the medical establishment sole control over the dissemination of birth control information. Dennett's final battle came over the sex education essay she wrote for her sons and published as a pamphlet, "The Sex Side of Life." In violation of the Comstock law, which prohibited the mailing of so-called obscene material, Dennett was arrested, tried, and fined. Because Dennett was a little-known figure in the history of birth control and sex education, there have been many misconceptions about her life; Chen corrects these in her biography. Appendices reproduce the Comstock Act, Dennett's sex education pamphlet, and letters addressed to the court during the obscenity trial. Along with these documents, a section of black-and-white photographs, notes, a selected bibliography, and an index are included. Dennett's story is valuable for both health and legal studies. HCA.

Faderman, Lillian. **Odd Girls and Twilight Lovers: A History of Lesbian Life in Twentieth-Century America**. New York: Penguin, 1991. 373p. $14.95pa. ISBN 0-14-017122-3pa.

In *Odd Girls and Twilight Lovers,* Lillian Faderman carefully details the evolution of lesbianism from the "romantic friendships" of the late Victorian era through the diversity characteristic of the late twentieth century. Faderman calls upon a variety of sources, including archives, journals, literature, and personal interviews, and includes many quotations in presenting this history. Believing that lesbian identity was not possible until a culture had been created around it, Faderman reveals how the building of that culture began in the 1920s when sexologists conceptualized lesbians. Since the 1920s, lesbianism has evolved, passing through a number of stages: from early repression through more openness during World War II to a complete shutdown during the McCarthy era; the creation of a number of subcultures in the postwar decades; and a revolution with demands for civil rights and a place in society in the late twentieth century. Faderman theorizes that lesbian culture could not grow until women were able to support themselves economically and to interact with other women in gender-specific colleges, on sports teams, in army units, and in social clubs. The author portrays women from many races and classes in providing the broadest possible look at lesbian life and the social, political, and economic conditions under which it developed in the twentieth century. Faderman's well-researched and important book includes two sections of black-and-white illustrations, notes, and an index. Although the lesbian movement may be controversial in many communities, the ability to look at its history is significant in bringing this section of the population into a more neutral societal position. HCA.

Faderman, Lillian. **To Believe in Women: What Lesbians Have Done for America—A History**. Boston: Houghton Mifflin, 1999. 434p. $30.00. ISBN 0-395-85010-X.

Although nineteenth-century women did not know the word "lesbian," a number of those who were at the forefront of the important movements that won rights and opportunities for women lived in primary relationships with another woman; these often lasted for twenty years or more. Historian Lillian Faderman documents these relationships through letters and journals and believes that the arrangements freed these women to pursue education, careers, and causes that would not have been possible had they engaged in heterosexual relationships. The author chronicles notable leaders from the fields of suffrage, reform, education, and the professions to make her case. Faderman is a leading scholar in lesbian studies and has written four other books on the subject; her impeccable work will be an aid to research for many students. *To Believe in Women* contains two sections of black-and-white photographs of the subjects discussed, notes, and an index. HCA.

Formanek-Brunell, Miriam. **Made to Play House: Dolls and the Commercialization of American Girlhood, 1830–1930**. New Haven, CT: Yale University Press, 1993. 233p. $32.50. ISBN 0-300-05072-0.

Miriam Formanek-Brunell looks at dolls in terms of both the creation of female identity and the creation of a business to accommodate an attendant rising commercial culture. Although both men and women made dolls, they made them very differently. With more business skill, men took over the doll industry, developing mechanical types of dolls with an emphasis on materials and gadgetry. Women tended to build doll businesses out of their homes and with their relatives, creating softer dolls more in tune with their perceptions of children's needs. Women did not market exclusively to females, and several women fabricated dolls around social reform themes. More than the businesses themselves, the gender image projected by male- and female-made dolls was different, and the play associated with dolls also changed over time. *Made to Play House* is filled with black-and-white photographs of advertisements, dolls, children playing, and manufacturing processes. Formanek-Brunell uses such sources as magazines, literature, patents, and dolls themselves in constructing her history of the industry since its inception. The broad-ranging book, which includes notes and an index, will find use in business courses, in gender studies, and in sociology classes. HCA.

Hodes, Martha. **White Women, Black Men: Illicit Sex in the Nineteenth-Century South**. New Haven, CT: Yale University Press, 1997. 338p. $30.00. ISBN 0-300-06970-7.

Although rare, relationships between white women and Black men were tolerated in the ante-bellum South. It was after emancipation that biracial relationships became much more taboo and evoked incidents of violence as couples were targeted by the Ku Klux Klan, who feared the ascendancy of Black men. Before the Civil War, these relationships were considered local affairs, and Martha Hodes uses a variety of documents from court and legislative bodies to present cases of marriage, rape, and adultery. The author records that violence against both partners escalated after the war, when the affairs became politicized. Notes, a bibliography, and an index are included in this carefully researched book. *White Women, Black Men* will be useful in the study of the history of race relations. HCA.

Kaplan, Laura. **The Story of Jane: The Legendary Underground Feminist Abortion Service**. Chicago: University of Chicago Press, 1995. 314p. $14.95pa. ISBN 0-226-42421-9pa.

Laura Kaplan was herself a member of Jane, or the Abortion Counseling Service of Women's Liberation, although she came to the group late, about halfway through its brief four-year history. The group was formed among women in Chicago to fulfill a need, that is, to provide abortions before the Supreme Court decision *Roe vs. Wade* legalized the procedure in 1973. Advertising in local newspapers simply as "Jane," the group initially counseled women and referred them to doctors who would perform the procedure. Because the group received so many calls, they needed a physician with whom they could work closely. When the members discovered that their practitioner had no medical credentials, they understood that it was possible for them to perform the procedure themselves, thus empowering themselves and their clients. Empowerment is a major theme of Kaplan's collective memoir, gathered from interviews with many of the over 100 women who participated in the group. Jane served approximately 12,000 women over a four-year period. As feminists, the members believed in participatory medicine, something that was not available at the time; however, within their organization, information did not flow as freely as it did to their own clients, causing internal problems. Because of the illegal nature of the organization and the work it performed, which mandated that very few records be kept, Jane's unique history has never been widely known. Some members still do not care to be identified, and all participants mentioned in the book are identified by pseudonym. *The Story of Jane* is an important piece of women's medical history to be placed on the continuum of women's full participation in health care as midwives in Colonial times to their roles as consumers of health care after the professionalization of male-dominated medical practice in the twentieth century. Jane helped turn the pendulum back. The powerful narrative, which includes a bibliography, a list of resources, and an index, can be used in history, health, and feminist studies. HCA.

Kennedy, Elizabeth Lapovsky, and Madeline D. Davis. **Boots of Leather, Slippers of Gold: The History of a Lesbian Community**. New York: Penguin, 1993. 434p. $15.95pa. ISBN 0-14-023550-7pa.

In a thirteen-year study, researchers Elizabeth Kennedy and Madeline Davis collected the oral histories of forty-five lesbians of Buffalo, New York, to chronicle the history of that lesbian community from the 1930s through the 1960s. Focusing on bar culture, race, class, allocation of public space, sexuality, relationships, and identity, the authors show the complexity of the community as it evolved over approximately forty years and then place the history into the context of current politics. In their search for respect, the Buffalo lesbians overcame intolerance and violence, and the book quotes extensively from their interviews. Although many lesbian communities are being identified today, *Boots of Leather, Slippers of Gold*, which includes black-and-white photographs, a map, notes, a general index, and an index of narrators, will pave the way in the re-creation of other local histories. HCA.

McCann, Carole R. **Birth Control Politics in the United States, 1916–1945**. Ithaca, NY: Cornell University Press, 1994. 242p. $32.50. ISBN 0-8014-2490-9.

Although Margaret Sanger founded the birth control movement on the feminist argument that women should be able to control their own bodies, over the thirty-year period in which contraception became legal and widely available to women in 800 nation-wide clinics, the original argument was lost and supplanted with others. Carole McCann develops the process by which this came about, beginning with the failure of feminist groups to embrace the cause of birth control. The medical establishment took over dispensing contraception, making it necessary to have a legitimate need for birth control. An economic reason for "child spacing" was created to encourage parents to limit their families to the number of children they could support; a social need was established through eugenics, or "racial betterment," which played on fear of the rising immigrant population. During the 1930s, Sanger formed coalitions with African Americans to promote birth control using these same arguments, racist in connotation. McCann's study, which includes a chronology, a bibliography, and an index, gives a clearer picture of birth control in the years before the development of the pill, and it has implications for many areas of study. HCA.

Middlebrook, Diane Wood. **Suits Me: The Double Life of Billy Tipton**. Boston: Houghton Mifflin, 1998. 326p. $25.00. ISBN 0-395-65489-0.

Author Diane Middlebrook was approached by Kitty Tipton Oakes, the last of Billy Tipton's five wives, to research his life and write his biography. Tipton was born Dorothy Lucille Tipton, but, from the time he was nineteen until his death at age seventy-four, he lived a male persona. Although Tipton left no documentation explaining his sex change, Middlebrook reasons that his desire to be a jazz musician may have been an influence. The author's intimate portrayal of the show business world adds color to the book. Tipton traveled and performed as a pianist, a saxophonist, and a band leader for years before settling in Seattle and running an entertainment agency. His birth gender was revealed only when he died in 1989, and the author's task was to find and interview those who knew Tipton in the hope of understanding his choices. Through access to his papers, his friends, and his family, Middlebrook is able to be frank about Tipton's deception in all areas of his life. Only one wife, who found out accidentally, ever suspected that he was a woman. Tipton's interesting case study could be used in sociology classes. Black-and-white maps and photographs, a family tree, notes, references, and an index are included. HCA.

Mohr, James C. **Abortion in America: The Origins and Evolution of National Policy, 1800–1900**. New York: Oxford University Press, 1978. 331p. $11.95pa. ISBN 0-19-502616-6pa.

Although the focus of the abortion debate today is on social and religious policy, in the nineteenth century discussions centered around medicine, when laws regarding abortion changed dramatically. In 1800 there were no statutes on the subject of abortion; the practice was based on common law, which did not recognize the existence of the fetus until it quickened during the fourth or fifth month of pregnancy. During the century, abortion increasingly came into the public view, more abortions were performed, and those seeking abortions were "white, married, Protestant, native-born women of the middle and upper classes." At this same time, doctors were seeking to centralize control of medical procedures, and, in reaction to nativist pressures and their own desire for a professional image, medical groups lobbied for legislation regulating abortion so that by the end of the century increasingly prescriptive laws existed in all jurisdictions. These laws would stand for almost a century until the Roe vs. Wade Supreme Court decision of 1973. James Mohr's historical study of the changes in abortion policy, containing quotations, black-and-white illustrations, notes, and an index, will bring a broader perspective into any discussion of the topic. HCA.

National Museum and Archive of Lesbian and Gay History, comps. **The Lesbian Almanac**. New York: Berkley, 1996. 534p. $16.95pa. ISBN 0-425-15301-0pa.

The Lesbian Almanac contains a huge amount of information on lesbian history, culture, and organizations. The almanac begins with a comprehensive time line of lesbian history in North America, followed by a listing of notable lesbians, lesbian quotations, lesbian slang, and statistics. The majority of the book presents all types of topical information pertaining to lesbians in art, business, education, health, literature, the military, politics, religion, sexuality, sports, and other areas. A section of AIDS information and directories to community centers, organizations, and resources round out the book. One caution: For most of the historical information, no source is cited, and users of the almanac may want to verify reliability because some errors are present. Still, the book is a great source and should be made widely available. MHCA.

Peiss, Kathy. **Hope in a Jar: The Making of America's Beauty Culture**. New York: Henry Holt, 1998. 334p. $15.95pa. ISBN 0-8050-5551-7pa.

Native American women knew plants that would treat skin problems, and from Colonial times women had beauty recipes. During the nineteenth century, society judged beauty through manners, morals, and behavior, rather than by physical appearance; but although the painted woman had negative connotations, all that would change in the next century. Around the beginning of the twentieth century, the beauty culture opened a place in business for such women as Madame C. J. Walker, Elizabeth Arden, and Helena Rubinstein, even though this position was later taken over by men. Not just commerce, beauty culture was "a system of meaning," and advertising created a changing image urging women to make-up and keep up. During World War

II, the use of lipstick to look attractive was promoted as a woman's patriotic duty, but later, in the 1960s, cosmetics were viewed as tools of male oppression, and feminists opted for a more natural look. Remnants of that argument persist today, but historian Kathy Peiss presents the history of beauty culture without making judgments, which she leaves to the reader. *Hope in a Jar,* which provides plenty of fodder for research papers, includes copiousness black-and-white illustrations, including cartoons and advertisements; notes and an index. MHCA.

Rose, Al. **Storyville, New Orleans: Being an Authentic, Illustrated Account of the Notorious Red-Light District**. Tuscaloosa: University of Alabama Press, 1974. 225p. $19.95pa. ISBN 0-8173-4403-9pa.

Storyville was a legally established district for prostitution in the city of New Orleans between 1898 and 1917 until it was closed down by the U.S. Department of the Navy. Storyville was adjacent to the French Quarter, running northeast of Canal Street; however, after it was shut down, the street names in the area were changed. Al Rose, a New Orleans native, attempts to recreate the history of Storyville from ransacked library collections and government archives. He collects enough advertising, publications, interviews, city ordinances, and photographs, particularly those by photographer Ernest Bellocq, to put together an account of the area physically as well as to document the people, the businesses, the houses of ill repute, the local press, and the jazz performers, including Jelly Roll Morton, associated with the area. The book contains some nude photographs, but, typical of the area itself, many of the pictures have been damaged in some way. Rose begins with an account of how the area was established, and includes the city documents that were associated with the incorporation and tested its legality. Of many interviews conducted, Rose includes seven, from both male and female residents, as the most representative. Appended are a directory of Storyville's jazz musicians, several newspaper stories, a bibliographical note, and an index. *Storyville* is not a book for everyone, but it is an authentic history of particular lifestyles at the turn of the century in a great southern city. CA.

Wertz, Richard W., and Dorothy C. Wertz. **Lying-in: A History of Childbirth in America**. Rev. ed. New Haven, CT: Yale University Press, 1989. 322p. $19.00pa. ISBN 0-300-04087-3pa.

Childbirth has changed in America since Colonial times when it was considered a social occasion conducted by a midwife. Although midwives were common throughout the nineteenth century, they were replaced by doctors, hospitals, and a variety of medical technologies. As the science of obstetrics developed, doctors had to overcome women's modesty, high mortality rates, pain, and puerperal fever by developing instruments, drugs, and treatments for women in labor. No sooner had hospital births become the established norm than women began to question their lack of involvement in the birth process; thus natural childbirth, lay midwives, birthing centers, and home birth became options to what had become a highly impersonal experience.

Lying-in was written in 1977 as the first social and cultural history of child-birth. Although other histories were written after that time, the authors believe their conclusions stand, and they updated the book with a new chapter, covering new medical technologies from the 1980s. The history, with its black-and-white illustrations, a bibliography, and an index, will be useful for a variety of researchers and readers. HCA.

Non-Book Material

Jane: An Abortion Service. Produced and directed by Kate Kirtz and Nell Lundy. 58 min. Women Make Movies, 1996. Videocassette. Purchase $245.00; Rental $90.00.

> *Jane: An Abortion Service* brings to light a little-known chapter in history and lets it shine through the perspective of its time. In the late 1960s and early 1970s, when abortion was illegal, a group of women in Chicago organized themselves to provide abortion information and counseling. The legal system, economics, and opportunity soon compelled a group of over 100 women to provide safe, illegal abortions to women in the Chicago area. They advertised in the newspapers under the name of Jane. Women who called for pregnancy advice were counseled and, if they wanted it, provided with an inexpensive, local abortion. There was never a medical complication in the approximately 12,000 abortions provided over five years. The service was eventually raided by the police, who had, apparently, been aware of it all along. Because no one would testify against Jane, and because the Roe vs. Wade decision—making abortion legal—was handed down during the trial, all charges were dismissed. The filmmakers interview women involved with Jane both as practitioners and as clients. Some are identified fully, some only partially, and some are disguised as they answer questions about Jane and their experiences in the feminist movement. Black-and-white film clips elucidate the history of the period: the 1968 Democratic National Convention in Chicago, the legalization of abortion in New York, and the era's antiwar and women's rights protests. The film is a fascinating piece of history that should be viewed as a historical account, not as a political piece in current abortion arguments. Although women's classical roles in medicine and as healers are not discussed in the film, it nevertheless makes a good companion piece to *A Midwife's Tale* for health programming or for women's studies. HCA.

The Lesbian History Project: Links to Lesbian History on the Internet. 1996. E-mail: Yolanda Retter, retter@skat.usc.edu. URL: http://www-lib.usc.edu/~retter/main.html.

> *The Lesbian History Project* promotes the visibility of lesbian history by maintaining a record of links to information, accomplishments, and related subjects. Archives and collections are the focus of the linked sites, which include journals, dissertations, bibliographies, interviews, pictures, and news. Researchers will appreciate this very simple listing. HCA.

Margaret Sanger. Produced by Bruce Alfred and Holly Ornstein Carter. 87 min. Films for the Humanities and Sciences, 1998. Videocassette. Purchase $149.00; Rental $75.00.

Portraying her admirable as well as her abominable sides, *Margaret Sanger* offers a carefully researched, fully-fleshed portrait of the twentieth century's main birth control advocate. The film incorporates black-and-white photographs and film; documents; and interviews with historians, friends, and relatives of Sanger. Alexander Sanger, who carries on his grandmother's crusade, offers insight throughout the film. Born to Irish immigrant parents of Corning, New York in 1879, Sanger was intimately familiar with the problems of too many children. Her mother had eighteen pregnancies in twenty-two years, of which Margaret was the youngest girl of eleven surviving children. Her sisters sent her through school, but she married, had three children, and recovered from an attack of tuberculosis before becoming a visiting nurse. When she worked with maternity cases among New York's immigrant population in the early years of the twentieth century, birth control information and products were illegal. It was at this time that Sanger turned radical, joining the Socialist party and participating in strikes. Although she knew postal inspection laws made it illegal to distribute birth control information, Sanger published a sixteen-page pamphlet on how to use the pessary. She then left the country before ordering its release. She stayed away two years, but when her husband was arrested for distributing the pamphlet, she came home, partly to capitalize on the publicity his trial was generating. Soon after reuniting with her abandoned children, her daughter, Peggy, became ill and died. Public outrage at prosecuting a bereaved mother prompted the dropping of charges against her regarding the distribution of the birth control pamphlet. Sanger was not finished with the issue and soon opened the first birth control clinic in America. She was arrested ten days later and served a thirty-day sentence. She opened another clinic and illegally imported diaphragms from Europe. Changes came when Sanger was remarried to a man with money available to help the cause. New tactics were employed that changed the laws so that birth control information could be provided and products could be dispensed to married women who were desperate to prevent pregnancy. Sanger traveled all over the world promoting birth control, especially in Japan, where she enjoyed great popularity. During the 1920s, she began to speak on the controversial subject of eugenics, the use of birth control to prevent the passing on of certain racial and genetic characteristics. Considered racist in many circles, eugenics added to Sanger's controversial reputation. Still, Sanger knew that a simple, inexpensive form of birth control was a necessity, and in the 1950s she began the search for a scientist and for the money to fulfill this need. With financial backing from Katherine McCormick, she employed Gregory Pinkus, who developed the pill, changing forever women's options and control over their reproductive rights. After suffering with TB and related health problems for most of her life, Sanger died at the age of eighty-seven in 1966, ending a lifelong, single-minded career that overcame opposition from the church, the government, and the medical establishment. Her amazing story on film can be used for group study or as the basis of individual research. HCA.

Mazer Collection: The June L. Mazer Lesbian Collection. 1998. 310-659-2478. E-mail: mazercoll@earthlink.net. URL: http://www.lesbian.org/mazer/.

Founded in Oakland in 1981 and originally called the West Coast Lesbian Collections, the assortment of art, manuscripts, books, recordings, periodicals, photographs, games, papers, and clothing was renamed for activist June L. Mazer after her death. The Mazer Collection is dedicated to gathering and preserving materials by and about lesbians. As with any archive, the organization offers programs, exhibits, speakers, and a newsletter. These same services are available on their Web page, which also outlines the holdings in the collection: 2,300 books, 550 periodicals, unpublished papers, audio and videotapes, and other items. The introduction to the site is written by historian Lillian Faderman. Although the materials are not available online, researchers will appreciate knowing where to find them. HCA.

Miss America Organization Community Hall. 1998. P.O. Box 119, Atlantic City, NJ 08404. 609-345-7571; fax 609-347-6079. E-mail: feedback @missamerica.org. URL: http://missamerica.org/communityhall/commhall.htm.

The *Miss America Organization Community Hall* creates a place for women to discuss contemporary social topics. Web surfers will relish the history of the Miss America pageant, presented by decades with illustrations. The history covers the major events of Miss America, but, as might be expected, ignores controversy. The site is fun to visit, but the abbreviated history somewhat limits its research value, although it remains one of the few sources available on Miss America. MHCA.

Miss . . . or Myth? Produced by Geoffrey Dunn, Mark Schwartz, and Clarie Rubach. 60 min. Cinema Guild, 1986. Videocassette. Purchase $350.00; Rental $100.00.

After a brief presentation on the history of the Miss America pageant, *Miss . . . or Myth?* presents a balanced account of all the issues surrounding beauty contests, including the objectification of women, body image, scholarships, sexism, racism, corporate sponsorship, eating disorders, and perfectionism. The discussion of these issues is centered around the 1985 Miss California pageant. Since 1979, this beauty contest, held in Santa Cruz, had been protested by up to 1,000 feminists, who staged the alternative "Myth America" parade and protest across the street from the official event. Scenes from both the protest and the contest are included as well as black-and-white film footage from early Miss California and Miss America pageants. Numerous people are interviewed in the film: pageant officials, former Miss Americas, state winners, citizens of Santa Cruz, professors, and protesters, including former model Ann Simonton. Several of the protesters are victims of sexual assault and are living with the ramifications of those significant, life-altering events. The filmmakers have no political agenda; they present the issues fairly, carefully juxtaposing comments from each side, which makes the film a great discussion starter. The video can be used in sociology and women's studies classes, or with groups looking for interesting debate material. Beauty contests are a part of our culture, but no historical book material is currently in print on the topic. HCA.

Sports and Recreation

Books

Anema, Durlynn. **Harriet Chalmers Adams: Explorer and Adventurer**. Greensboro: Morgan Reynolds, 1997. 112p. (Notable Americans). $18.95. ISBN 1-883846-18-8.

> With a family heritage of overland migration and a childhood of exploring mining claims with her father, Harriet Chalmers Adams loved to travel. During her life she covered over 100,000 miles, principally on the American continents, but also to all the lands ever controlled by Spain and Portugal as well as to other locations around the globe. As an expert on Latin American culture, Adams became an accurate writer and popular lecturer. Starting in 1907, she wrote and photographed for the National Geographic Society and lectured in their annual programs. Adams traveled both alone and with her husband by all manner of conveyance, from mule to dugout canoe. When she sustained a back injury from a fall in the Balearic Islands, she was told she would never walk again, but, after a two-year recovery, she got up and embarked on a seven-month tour through Europe, Africa, and the Near East. Adams's vivacious character and many adventures will charm readers in a biography that includes black-and-white photographs, maps, a bibliography, and an index. MH.

Blum, Arlene. **Annapurna: A Woman's Place**. San Francisco: Sierra Club, 1980. 256p. $16.00pa. ISBN 1-57805-022-7pa.

> In 1978, Arlene Blum was part of the American Women's Himalayan Expedition to Annapurna, one of fifteen mountains in the world above 26,000 feet. As with any ascent of this magnitude, the organization and support was monumental; arriving at a point high on the mountain from which a summit attempt can be made, after traveling to Nepal, trekking into the Himalayas, establishing a series of base camps, and portaging supplies and equipment to an extremely high altitude, was a formidable task. Beyond the personal fortitude to take on this task, the unknowns of personal health, weather, and local Sherpa support were variables beyond control. Although members of the women's team reached the summit, two climbers were lost in this supported by National Geographic Society expedition. Blum's tale, drawing upon the diaries of the other twelve team members, is an intense account of the expedition from beginning to end. Studded with

both black-and-white photographs and maps, and including a section of color photographs, readers become familiar with both the climbing team and the Sherpas. Maurice Herzog, the first to summit Annapurna, provides a forward, and Blum's introduction gives a history of mountaineering women. A bibliography and an index are included in this poignant recollection. MHCA.

Cayleff, Susan E. **Babe: The Life and Legend of Babe Didrikson Zaharias**. Urbana: University of Illinois Press, 1995. 327p. (Women in American History). (Sport and Society). $29.95; $14.95pa. ISBN 0-252-01793-5; 0-252-06593-Xpa.

While Babe Didrikson Zaharias grew up playing neighborhood baseball and high school basketball, most of the sports she engaged in so successfully she learned as an adult. She was the winner of two Olympic gold medals in track and field; she had a huge career in golf; and she was one of the founders of the Ladies Professional Golf Association. Although Zaharias wrote an autobiography shortly before her death from cancer in 1956, Susan Cayleff's portrayal presents new information, focusing on the facts of Zaharias's life and the myths the sports star created in order to live within societal norms during the midcentury and cover her lesbian relationship. Cayleff interviewed Betty Dodd, golfer and Zaharias's partner, who was candid about the relationship after the death of Zaharias's husband, George. Given the type of life she was forced to lead and her athletic achievements, without the benefits of modern training and conditioning often given from childhood, Zaharias's attainments are all the more remarkable. As one of the early women's sports stars, she paved the way for women to participate more fully in amateur and professional athletics. A section of black-and-white photographs, an introduction covering the history of women in sports, notes, and an index are included. HCA.

Kaufman, Polly Welts. **National Parks and the Woman's Voice: A History**. Albuquerque: University of New Mexico Press, 1996. 305p. $18.95pa. ISBN 0-8263-1870-3pa.

Dividing her book into two sections, the pioneers and the modern sisters, Polly Kaufman portrays all the ways in which women have participated in National Park history. Beginning as travelers and explorers, women went on to advocate for the establishment of National Parks. From the early days, women served as park rangers, with Clare Marie Hodges serving as the first woman ranger in Yosemite in 1918, although more of these jobs went to women later when men turned away from historical interpretation. A very important role was played by wives of park employees, who filled vital roles in the understaffed parks, lobbied for better living conditions, and built communities and amenities around the parks. Although women continue to fulfill many of these same roles today, they also fill more paid positions as rangers, superintendents, and managers. Kaufman's account opens up what has traditionally been considered a man's world with lively history and good information for researchers, including two sections of black-and-white photographs, notes, a bibliographic essay, and an index. HCA.

Macy, Sue. **A Whole New Ball Game: The Story of the All-American Girls Professional Baseball League**. New York: Henry Holt, 1993. 140p. $14.95; $4.99pa. ISBN 0-8050-1942-1; 0-140-37423-0pa.

When Sue Macy began her research on the All-American Girls Professional Baseball League in 1981, a magazine article and an unpublished master's degree thesis were all that existed beyond the newspapers and magazines of the 1940s and 1950s and the memorabilia of the team members themselves. The League had virtually vanished from history, and it took the work of the players to have it recognized with a permanent display in the National Baseball Hall of Fame in Cooperstown, New York in 1988. In writing *A Whole New Ball Game*, Macy researched everywhere she could, and interviewed many of the former players. A girls' baseball league was the brainchild of Philip K. Wrigley as a way to keep professional baseball active during World War II, when many men served overseas and the men and women left at home worked harder than ever in the war effort. The league began in 1943 and lasted until 1954, when changing economics and changing social mores retired the game. Throughout the tenure of the league, the players adhered to strict rules of conduct, attending charm school to ensure that they acted like ladies. This fun book is illustrated with black-and-white photographs and documents, and includes team rules and statistics, a chronology, source information, a bibliography, and an index. Macy has done baseball a service by filling in the historical record on women's participation in the sport. MHA.

Macy, Sue. **Winning Ways: A Photohistory of American Women in Sports**. New York: Henry Holt, 1996. 217p. $15.95; $5.99pa. ISBN 0-8050-4147-8; 0-590-76336-9pa.

Sue Macy writes an extremely readable book that traces the history of American women in sports from the 1800s to the 1990s. The book is more than a mere history because it traces the changes in fashions and attitudes toward women through two centuries. In the nineteenth century, women were often discouraged from exercising, and their corsets and layers of clothes did not make activity easy. Throughout the years, women continually had to overcome obstacles so that they could fully participate in sports. Women were not invited to enter the Boston Marathon until 1972, and girls could not join Little League baseball until lawsuits were filed in 1974. Many of the women who were groundbreakers in sports, such as Ora Mae Washington, an early tennis champion, and Ann Meyers, who signed a contract to play basketball with the NBA, have been largely overlooked. Besides a chronology, a list of resources, and an index, the book is filled with wonderful black-and-white photographs as well as some documents. The juxtaposition of old and new photographs in the last chapter speaks volumes. *Winning Ways* belongs in every library, for no other sports history melds the social and historical so well. Readers will be surprised by what they learn. MHA.

Oglesby, Carole A., et al., eds. **Encyclopedia of Women and Sport in America**. Phoenix: Oryx, 1998. 360p. $65.00. ISBN 0-89774-993-6.

> With over eighty contributors and six editors, the *Encyclopedia of Women and Sport in America* is somewhat uneven, and, as with any attempt at this type of coverage, it is not comprehensive, although it includes over forty sports and 140 biographies of both well-known and obscure women, some marked with a special "boundary breaker" symbol. A myriad of other topics are covered as well, including multicultural involvement, organizations, career information, sports psychology, and media image tips. Although contact information for organizations is not included, nor any Internet Web sites, the hall of fame section does include mailing addresses. The encyclopedia's strength lies in its putting so much information together between two covers. The alphabetical arrangement contains cross references, and a table of contents and index help in identifying topics and names. Some entries contain a list of references; suggested readings broken down by sport and a selected bibliography are appended. The book is convenient to use, and many libraries will want to own it. MHCA.

Plowden, Martha Ward. **Olympic Black Women**. Gretna, LA: Pelican, 1996. 174p. $16.95. ISBN 1-56554-080-8.

> Bringing together information rare in any other source, Martha Plowden profiles twenty-five African American women who have participated in the Olympics since 1932. The sketches, covering the likes of Evelyn Ashford, Alice Coachman, Gail Devers, Jackie Joyner-Kersee, and Wilma Rudolph, range from one to four pages, and are headed by the sport in which the athlete participated and her dates. A portrait by artist Ronald Jones accompanies each sketch. Introductions cover the histories of African American women in the Olympics, the ancient Olympics, and the modern Olympics; appendices list athletic organizations, all Black women who have represented the United States in Olympic competition, the sites of the modern Olympics, a glossary, and suggestions for further reading. The book should be popular during African American History Month and for report material. MH.

VanDerveer, Tara, and Joan Ryan. **Shooting from the Outside: How a Coach and Her Olympic Team Transformed Women's Basketball**. New York: Avon, 1997. 259p. $23.00; $12.50pa. ISBN 0-380-97588-2; 0-380-79498-5pa.

> Coach of the 1996 Olympic gold-medal winning women's basketball team, Tara VanDerveer spent a year with the twelve-woman squad, playing sixty undefeated games. The book chronicles the way the personalities of the players came together to create a winning tradition that opened the door for a professional women's basketball league. The book also provides a history of the rise of women's sports through the lens of VanDerveer's career. VanDerveer surmounted times when women's sports received no respect; played collegiate ball; became a three-time National Coach of the Year, and coached Stanford to two NCAA championships. The book, which contains a

center section of black-and-white photographs, is a dramatic sports story that will be enjoyed by many readers. MHCA.

Woolum, Janet. **Outstanding Women Athletes: Who They Are and How They Influenced Sports in America**. 2d ed. Phoenix: Oryx, 1998. 412p. $54.95. ISBN 1-57356-120-7.

> *Outstanding Women Athletes* is a great compendium of reference material that every library will want to own. It begins with a history of women's sports in America from Colonial times to 1997, including a time line of milestones. Women's participation in the modern Olympics from 1896 is outlined for both summer and winter games, detailing the highlights of the games, number of women participants, and new events for women. Eighty-six individual biographies, each including a portrait and, where available, suggested readings, profile important women from a range of sports, including the standards as well as sled-dog racing, wheelchair athletes, mountain biking, bowling, auto racing, mountain climbing, rodeo, and bullfighting, among others. An appendix presents the alphabetically arranged entries by sport. A new section has been added to the second edition, which profiles both individuals and groups in ten outstanding women's teams from the All-American Girls Professional Baseball League through the 1996 Olympic teams. A selected bibliography and a directory of organizations listed by sport are included as well as all Olympic gold medalists, selected national award winners and champions, National Collegiate Athletic Association champions for Division I, selected reference sources, and an index. Beyond its reference uses, readers will enjoy browsing through *Outstanding Women Athletes* just to see what's there. MHCA.

Non-Book Material

Althea Gibson. Produced and directed by Carol Clarke and Paul Van der Grift. 60 min. Thunderhead Productions, 1998. Videocassette. $95.00.

> Althea Gibson was a sports superstar at a time when there were no female sports superstars, let alone Black female superstars. Born in South Carolina to sharecropper parents who made seventy-five dollars in a year for their entire cotton crop, Gibson and her family moved to Harlem to escape poverty just as the Depression struck. Gibson grew into a tough tomboy who would ride the subway all night or stay at the Children's Home to avoid going home to her father. She learned to play tennis on the street through the Police Athletic League. Throughout her career, many people, both white and Black, went out of their way to help and support her, through personal loans and gifts, with housing and education, and in athletic clubs and organizations. Gibson was the first African American woman to win the Wimbledon tennis championship in 1957 and 1958. After her successful tennis career, she became a professional golfer, overcoming racial prejudice in opening both of these sports to people of color. Gibson also had a beautiful voice and musical talent. She recorded a vocal album, and most of the music used throughout the video is

of her singing. The film is a fine tribute to an inspiring sports pioneer, using both black-and-white and color film and newsclips. Gibson appears in segments recorded in a 1984 interview, and Maya Angelou is the narrator. MHCA.

"I'll Ride That Horse!" Montana Women Bronc Riders. Produced and directed by Doris Loeser. 27 min. Women Make Movies, 1994. Videocassette. Purchase $195.00; Rental $65.00.

A film made for Montana Public Television presents the history of women rodeo bronc riders, beginning with Fannie Sperry Steele, the lady champion of the 1913 Calgary Stampede and the role model and predecessor to a number of Montana women who enjoyed careers in the rodeo. Her successors include four Montana women who were raised in the saddle in the open landscape. With their ranching backgrounds, they were not afraid to ride any horse at any rodeo. Alice Greenough, Margie Greenough, Marge Brander, and Bobby Kramer are interviewed about their lives and seen working on their ranches; they all participated in rodeos from the 1920s to the 1950s. The film includes black-and-white photographs, and color and black-and-white film. As the women tell it, injuries brought about the end of women's bronc riding in the rodeos, but this engaging video recalls its not widely known past. The film will have special appeal in regional and western history collections. MHCA.

She Lives to Ride. Produced and directed by Alice Stone. 56 min. Women Make Movies, 1994. Videocassette. Purchase $295.00; Rental $90.00.

She Lives to Ride accomplishes two goals: It presents over eighty years of women's participation in motorcycle riding, and it profiles five contemporary women involved in the sport for a variety of reasons. As far back as World War I, the Van Buren sisters motorcycled across the United States raising money for the war effort. Their two-month trip included the first motorcycle ascent of Pike's Peak and an arrest for wearing pants in public. Other early women riders, and Hollywood portrayals of women bikers, are interspersed throughout the film between interviews with Jo Giovannoni, Dot Robinson, Becky Brown, Jacqui Sturgess, and Amy Berry, who range in age from their thirties to their eighties and who ride in all-women, lesbian, and Black bikers groups. The women's interests and professions outside of biking show the range of women who enjoy riding. Bikers will love this well-made, inclusive production filmed in color with historic black-and-white footage, but it will also be enjoyed by a larger audience. HCA.

Work

Books

Baxandall, Rosalyn, and Linda Gordon, eds. **America's Working Women: A Documentary History, 1600 to the Present**. Rev. ed. New York: W. W. Norton, 1995. 356p. $14.95pa. ISBN 0-393-31262-3pa.

> Nearly doubling the number of documents in the 1976 edition, *America's Working Women* includes the voices of various classes, races, and ethnic groups in presenting the history of women as part of the working class, in unpaid labor within families, and in continuing traditional female occupations. From descriptions of corn-grinding, servitude, union organizing, and prostitution to themes of harassment, housework, and undervalued jobs, the editors have chosen documents from a wide variety of writing, including diaries, magazines, histories, songs, and fiction. The book is divided into seven chronological chapters, each introducing a time period. Each document has a heading, although it does not necessarily identify the writer and source; they are, however, identified in an appendix. Two sections of black-and-white photographs are included as well as an index. Teachers will be impressed with the range of material included, which can be used in a variety of settings. MHCA.

Boydston, Jeanne. **Home and Work: Housework, Wages, and the Ideology of Labor in the Early Republic**. New York: Oxford University Press, 1990. 222p. $17.95pa. ISBN 0-19-508561-2pa.

> Set in New York and New England, Jeanne Boydston surveys the changes that occurred in women's housework between the Colonial period and the Civil War. This was the period where home manufacture, when women's work had obvious impact on the family, gave way to industrialization and the rise of the consumer culture. Women became the dependents of wage earning partners as the visibility of the work they performed disappeared. While tracing the changes chronologically over this period, Boydston also closely analyzes the nature of housework and its importance to the economy. Boydston's is one of the most scholarly studies of housework, and includes numerous quotations from primary sources, notes, a bibliography, and an index. HCA.

Branch, Muriel Miller, and Dorothy Marie Rice. **Pennies to Dollars: The Story of Maggie Lena Walker**. North Haven, CT: Linnet, 1997. 100p. $17.95; $13.95pa. ISBN 0-208-02453-0; 0-208-02455-7pa.

> Maggie Lena Walker, the daughter of a former slave and a white abolitionist, was born out of wedlock. Growing up in Richmond, Virginia, Walker volunteered for, and later ran, a charity organization, the Independent Order of St. Luke. In working to improve herself, Walker taught school and learned

accounting, which enabled her to start a small penny savings bank for Blacks. Her bank later merged to become the Consolidated Bank and Trust Company, and she became chair of the board of directors. Her life was not without hardship: She battled disability and lost a husband at the hands of her son. Containing black-and-white photographs and an index, this short biography is suitable for younger readers. MH.

Byerly, Victoria. **Hard Times Cotton Mill Girls: Personal Histories of Womanhood and Poverty in the South**. Ithaca, NY: ILR Press, 1986. 223p. $14.95pa. ISBN 0-87546-129-8pa.

Victoria Byerly, a former textile worker, collected the oral histories of twenty Black and white women who worked in the North Carolina textile mills. As the fourth generation of her family to go to the mills, Byerly was familiar with the work, but a college scholarship set her free. She returned to collect the stories of women connected by poverty, gender, region, and their work. Byerly organized the stories around the themes of transition from farm to factory; transition from childhood to work; transition to marriage and motherhood while working; adjustments for Black women in a white mill town; and labor-organizing activities. Black-and-white portraits of locations and of most of the women interviewed are included, along with an index, in this intimate account of the lives of working women. HCA.

Cowan, Ruth Schwartz. **More Work for Mother: The Ironies of Household Technology from the Open Hearth to the Microwave**. New York: Basic, 1983. 257p. $17.00pa. ISBN 0-465-04732-7pa.

Ruth Cowan shows how and why women spend more time at housework than they did in the nineteenth century. While still living the agrarian life, men and women spent equal time working; now, at the turn of the millennium, the majority of housework falls to women. Cowan believes this came about as part of both a capitalistic and a patriarchal conspiracy. Advertising for laundry detergents raised expectations for clean clothes, which generated more laundry for mother. When men went to work to gain cash wages to pay for gas and electricity, they gave up a chore and no longer chopped wood to heat the wood stove; women, however, still cooked, and Cowan sees this same pattern in the food, clothing, and health care systems of the twentieth century. Alternative methods of production for family needs aimed at decreasing women's workload, such as commercial laundries, cooperative food services, and servants, interfered with family privacy and never took hold. Classism increased household work for women because a variety of food, clean clothing, and neat homes were associated with the better-off, and women were willing to work to attain this. *More Work for Mother* includes four picture essays on the evolution of housework, laundry, transportation systems, and the contrast between rich and poor. Everyone who works within the home should find some part of Cowan's study of interest. It will be useful in sociology and history classes. A bibliography and an index are appended. HCA.

Disher, Sharon Hanley. **First Class: Women Join the Ranks at the Naval Academy**. Annapolis: Naval Institute Press, 1998. 362p. $29.95. ISBN 1-55750-165-3.

> In 1976, Sharon Hanley Disher was one of eighty-one young women to join the first sexually integrated class at the Naval Academy. Twelve years later, at Homecoming, she heard stories reminiscent of the treatment her class had received, and she wondered why conditions had not progressed more. Although she felt certain another of her female classmates would write a book, it never happened, and because the women of her class felt it was important that their story be told, she embarked on the process of collecting journals and letters and interviewing the fifty-four other women who graduated with her (a list of them is included). Some of her classmates had experiences they wanted to share, some refused to talk at all, and some gave permission to be included in the book, which they later recanted. Disher's narrative reads more like a novel. In fact, one of the two women she follows from induction to graduation is a composite character. These women, still teenagers when the book opens, faced harassment, eating disorders, date rape, and mental and physical challenges. Still, Disher supports the Navy, and does not regret her ten-year career after Annapolis. *First Class* makes an exciting read for teens, especially those considering military careers. HCA.

Eisenberg, Susan. **We'll Call You If We Need You: Experiences of Women Working Construction**. Ithaca, NY: ILR Press, 1998. 217p. $25.00. ISBN 0-8014-3360-6.

> In 1978, President Jimmy Carter established hiring goals for women in the construction trades and created timetables to meet these goals on federally funded construction projects. By 1998, 25 percent of workers were to be women, an objective that has obviously not been accomplished: Women workers grew to about 2 percent of the work force and stayed at that level. Master electrician and poet Susan Eisenberg interviews thirty women who entered the field as carpenters, electricians, ironworkers, painters, and plumbers during the affirmative action period, and they candidly portray the reasons their numbers have not grown. Eisenberg organizes the oral histories around a building theme from constructing the concrete footings and how women entered their profession, to a "punch list" of what still needs to be done to break down gender barriers. A few of Eisenberg's poems and a number of black-and-white photographs appear throughout the book, which also includes an appendix profiling those interviewed. The book will be an eye-opener in career collections. MHCA.

Fitch, Noel Riley. **Appetite for Life: The Biography of Julia Child**. New York: Doubleday, 1997. 569p. $29.95; $15.00pa. ISBN 0-385-48335-X; 0-385-49383-5pa.

> Beyond a biography, Noel Fitch's study of epicurean Julia Child is also a history of the culinary arts in the second half of the twentieth century.

Readers come away from the book feeling they know the tall, fun-loving chef, now in her eighties, as well as knowing much more about food. A free-wheeling California girl, Child attended Smith College and then began to look for something interesting enough to occupy her time. She went to the Far East as a civilian attached to the Office of Strategic Services in World War II, where she met her husband of almost fifty years, Paul Child. After their marriage, they lived for a time in Europe, where Julia studied French cooking. The rest is history: the publication of her book *Mastering the Art of French Cooking*, her many television shows, and her rise as the recognized expert on all epicurean subjects. In trying to be comprehensive, Fitch, who had access to all Child's diaries and letters, does occasionally bog down; yet, a respectful portrait of the cook emerges, a woman who entered a male world in the middle of the twentieth century and turned it around, becoming a quirky cultural icon at the same time. HCA.

Garza, Hedda. **Barred from the Bar: A History of Women in the Legal Profession**. New York: Franklin Watts, 1996. 224p. $23.60; $9.00pa. ISBN 0-531-11265-9; 0-531-15795-4pa.

After an overview of women's involvement in law and politics in American history before the Civil War, Hedda Garza goes on to show how women's active involvement in the legal profession is generally a twentieth-century phenomena. The first practicing woman lawyer, Myra Bradwell, passed the bar exam with honors in 1869, but had to petition the Supreme Court after she was denied admittance to the Illinois bar. Women made slow progress in the legal profession, both in gaining admission to law schools and in being admitted to the bar, and their numbers remained low in the profession, especially if they were women of color. It was not until 1981 that Sandra Day O'Connor was appointed to the Supreme Court, followed in 1994 by Ruth Bader Ginsburg, who had been one of nine women among 500 students entering Harvard law school in 1956. Garza's book, which will be useful in both civics and career studies, is filled with many interesting anecdotes and is accompanied by black-and-white photographs, notes, a bibliography, and an index. MHCA.

Goodsell, Willystine, ed. **Pioneers of Women's Education in the United States: Emma Willard, Catherine [sic] Beecher, Mary Lyon**. New York: Ams, l970. 311p. $32.50. ISBN 0-404-02864-0.

First published in 1931, Willystine Goodsell wrote a brief introduction about the education of women in the United States, followed by biographical portraits of three pioneer promoters of women's education along with several selections from each one's writings. Emma Willard opened the Troy Female Seminary in 1821, developing teaching methods and writing her own textbooks. Selections from her textbooks as well as her address "Plan for Improving Female Education" are included. Although Catharine Beecher strongly believed in woman's place in the domestic sphere, she also believed in women's education and in women as teachers. She recruited teachers for frontier schools through her organization, the American Woman's Educational Association, founded in 1852. Four of Beecher's letters, essays, and speeches on education are included. Three of Mary Lyon's papers describe her plan for the Mount Holyoke Female Seminary, which she opened in 1837 in South Hadley, Massachusetts. Goodsell's compilation of the lives and works of these early teachers is still an important work. The book includes a black-and-white portrait of each woman and an index. HCA.

Jeffrey, Laura S. **Great American Businesswomen**. Springfield, NJ: Enslow, 1996. 112p. (Collective Biographies). $19.95. ISBN 0-89490-706-9.

Ten businesswomen of the twentieth century, notable in a number of fields, are profiled in short biographies that include a portrait and at least one other illustration. Some of these women created a place for themselves in existing fields, like economic advisor Alice Rivlin, Wall Street analyst Elaine Garzarelli, talk show moderator Oprah Winfrey, and food expert Debbi Fields. Others created unique niches, for instance, Eileen Ford and her modeling agency, Maggie Walker and her bank for African Americans, Madam C. J. Walker and her hair-care products for Blacks, and Ruth Handler and her Barbie doll. Finally, several women took over ably when their husbands died, as in the cases of Olive Ann Beech and her aviation company, and Katharine Graham at the *Washington Post*. Notes and an index are included in a book that will be useful as report material. MH.

Kessler-Harris, Alice. **Out to Work: A History of Wage-Earning Women in the United States**. Oxford: Oxford University Press, 1982. 400p. $13.95pa. ISBN 0-19-503353-1pa.

Following the record of women in the labor force from Colonial times through 1980, historian Alice Kessler-Harris blends the history of women's household work with women's wage-earning work. Both have been tied to economic cycles, social progress, self-perception, and visions of the family. Women's ability to care for the changing home is one of the great debates of American history, placing women at a disadvantage in the workforce and reinforcing a system of patriarchy. Although women have been denied opportunity and kept at the low end of the workforce, they have also been the recipients of protective legislation that may or may not have been to their benefit. As the consumer culture grew, work became a necessity rather than an option, creating the tensions surrounding housework that produced the women's movement in the 1960s. In demonstrating how the basic debate between women's work in the home and women's wage-earning work has gone on for centuries, Kessler-Harris brings in different classes, races, and ethnic groups. With three historical divisions and several accompanying sections of black-and-white illustrations, the book's chronological progression also includes substantial notes and an index. This important work should be part of history and economic collections. HCA.

Kessler-Harris, Alice. **Women Have Always Worked: A Historical Overview**. New York: Feminist Press, 1981. 193p. (Women's Lives / Women's Work). $12.95pa. ISBN 0-912670-67-3pa.

> Organized around five themes, Alice Kessler-Harris presents an overview of women in unpaid and paid work in American history. The author considers the meaning of work to women, household labor, wage labor, work in social causes, and changes in the workforce. Each section has a chronological perspective and contains two double-page, black-and-white photo spreads. The book spans American history from Colonial times through the 1970s, an excellent introduction to the topic. Notes and an index are appended. MHCA.

Kwolek-Folland, Angel. **Incorporating Women: A History of Women and Business in the United States**. New York: Twayne, 1998. 275p. (Twayne's Evolution of Modern Business). $29.95. ISBN 0-8057-4519-X.

> From the days when Ojibwa women dealt with fur traders, women in the United States have always been in business. They have participated as entrepreneurs, as family members, as professionals, and as workers, and author Angel Kwolek-Folland tries to focus on these varied roles, as well as upon race and class, in her chronological history. Her aim is not merely to add women to business history, but to reconceptualize the nature of economic activity. Using charts, Kwolek-Folland traces women in business from Colonial times, when they were not considered independent of their husbands to their recognition as individuals at the end of the nineteenth century to their appointments as heads of large corporations in the 1990s. Women's role in business, while always characterized by inequity, has constantly evolved as times have changed; and women's traditional sphere has allowed for the definition of a gendered business niche in which women could prosper. Notes, a bibliographic essay, and an index round out Kwolek-Folland's overview. HCA.

Levinson, Nancy Smiler. **She's Been Working on the Railroad**. New York: Lodestar, 1997. 104p. $16.99. ISBN 0-525-67545-0.

> Railroad work has traditionally been considered men's work, but Nancy Levinson's book does much to reconstruct that history to include women. Beginning in the 1870s, *She's Been Working on the Railroad* profiles individuals and trends in rail work through the 1990s, portraying women who acted as telegraph operators, station managers, railroad presidents, rail car designers, waitresses, and nurses, and moving into jobs in the rail yards, in maintenance, and on trains as engineers and operators. Levinson shows that women faced resistance to their employment even during war times, when they were needed as workers. Many black-and-white photographs of women working and of memorabilia are provided by photographer and railroad buff Shirley Burman. The book, including several boxed sections on special topics, a glossary, notes, suggestions for further reading, and an index, will update library collections on transportation. MHA.

Moore, Marat. **Women in the Mines: Stories of Life and Work**. New York: Twayne, 1996. 337p. (Twayne's Oral History). $32.95. ISBN 0-8057-7834-9.

The oral histories of several generations of female miners are collected in Marat Moore's *Women in the Mines*. After an introductory overview of women in mining, the first part of the book presents the stories of eight women during the first half of the twentieth century through World War II. Beginning with Helen Krmpotich, who was present at the 1914 Ludlow massacre in Colorado, the narratives include women who started jobs in their teens, worked with their fathers, labored in family operations, or entered the mines during World War II. The rest of the book chronicles women who took higher-paying mine jobs during the affirmative action period of the 1970s. They discuss how and why they came to mining, what obstacles they faced, their place in the union, their leadership during layoffs, and the current decline in numbers of female miners. Twenty-four of the sixty-eight women originally interviewed for the project are included in the book, although, both groups are listed. Numerous photographs taken by the author, a miner and journalist, illustrate the book. Appendices include a collection of early mining documents pertaining to women and a chart of hiring statistics; notes, a bibliography, and an index are also included. *Women in the Mines* is a necessity in mining regions, and in other areas it will add perspective to labor collections. HCA.

Morris, Juddi. **The Harvey Girls: The Women Who Civilized the West**. New York: Walker, 1994. 101p. $8.95pa. ISBN 0-8027-7520-9pa.

Fred Harvey thought that rail passengers should eat good meals in comfortable settings. Working for the Santa Fe Railroad, starting in the 1870s, Harvey located a string of restaurants across the southwestern United States, and staffed them with young women, the Harvey Girls, recruited from all across the country. When they were trained, they performed according to Harvey's high expectations for service and reliability. The girls signed contracts agreeing to live in dorms and go where they were needed. They were paid a wage, room and board, and given a rail pass, and they thrived until the decline of the railroads in the 1950s. Morris interviewed former Harvey Girls; their comments are included in her fun narrative, which will be enjoyed by those who remember the Harvey restaurants. Black-and-white photographs, notes, a bibliography, and an index are included. Although the book concentrates more on the twentieth century than the early years, students can use this study in considering women's roles in the West. MHA.

Pile, Robert B. **Women Business Leaders**. Minneapolis: Oliver, 1995. 160p. (Profiles). $16.95. ISBN 1-881508-24-2.

Eight contemporary women in business are portrayed by Robert Pile in enthusiastic profiles that include quotations. The only household name is Mary Kay Ash, of cosmetics fame, but the other women represent a wide variety of interests; the women are Helen Boehm, art sculpture manufacturing; Leeann Chin, food service; Ellen Terry, real estate; Ella Musolino-Alber, women's tennis promotion; Louise Woerner, health care; Masako Boissonnault, interior design; and Marilyn Hamilton, wheelchair manufacturing. The subjects have generally had high-profile, public careers, and they are pictured at work and with a variety of famous people, lending interest to the biographies for a wide range of students. An appendix lists over thirty other important businesswomen, and a bibliography and an index are included. MH.

Weiler, Kathleen. **Country Schoolwomen: Teaching in Rural California, 1850–1950**. Stanford: Stanford University Press, 1998. 339p. $49.50. ISBN 0-8047-3004-0.

The dual purpose of *Country Schoolwomen* is to reveal the lives of rural women teachers and to understand how they felt about their experiences. Kathleen Weiler, a relation to several of these teachers, uses various sources, education documents, census and school records, autobiographies, and oral histories, to explore the framework of rural teaching, progressing from a national to a local perspective. Beginning with an overview of women teachers in American history, Weiler moves to an exploration of how gender shaped California's education institutions. The author looks at schooling in Kings and Tulare counties and, finally, the lives and careers of the female teachers who worked there in the late nineteenth and early twentieth centuries. Weiler concludes that teaching allowed women independence, respect, and economic security. In addition, they were free from the constant authority and control of men superiors and of state or federal guidelines until after World War II, when schools were consolidated and sexual politics took over. After World War II, women teachers helped to maintain a culture of racism. While Weiler's findings are surprising in some ways, they help to give a more accurate view of a profession well known to most people. A section of black-and-white photographs, tables, notes, a bibliography, and an index are included in this scholarly study. CA.

Wheaton, Elizabeth. **Myra Bradwell: First Woman Lawyer**. Greensboro: Morgan Reynolds, 1997. 95p. (Notable Americans). $18.95. ISBN 1-883846-17-X.

Although Myra Bradwell was the first woman admitted to the bar to actually practice law after a prolonged struggle to attain the status, she was not, technically, the first woman lawyer. Bradwell grew up in an abolitionist family who opposed her marriage to James Bradwell. She studied law under the tutelage of her husband, who became a judge and rose in Illinois politics, and, with him, she started a legal newspaper and printing business. Although this incident is not mentioned in the book, her newspaper followed the case of an Iowa woman, Arabella Mansfield, who was admitted to the bar in that state but never practiced law. Bradwell passed the bar exam, but she was turned down in her petition to be admitted to the bar by the Illinois Supreme Court. It was twenty years before the Court reversed its decision. In the meantime, the Bradwell home and businesses were wiped out in the Chicago fire, and Bradwell made a name for herself in the suffrage cause by demanding the release of Mary Todd Lincoln from an insane asylum, and by bringing the 1893 World's Columbian Exposition to Chicago. Wheaton's is a pleasant account of Bradwell, with black-and-white illustrations, a time line, notes, a bibliography, and an index, suitable for younger students. MH.

Non-Book Material

Breaking Boundaries! The 11th Berkshire Conference on the History of Women. n.d. URL: http://www-berks.aas.duke.edu/.

The Berkshire Conference was founded in the 1930s as a vehicle for women historians to network with each other; it holds a major conference, the Big Berks, triannually. Beyond the presentation of the conference's details, the Web site presents the history of the Berkshire Conference, including some historical photographs. Anyone interested in women's history is welcome to join the group, and membership fees are low. Yearly prizes are awarded for the best book and best article by women historians, and these are listed on the Web site. CA.

Business and Professional Women/USA: A Leading Advocate for Working Women. 1998. 2012 Massachusetts Avenue NW, Washington, DC 20036. 202-293-1100; fax 202-861-0298. URL: http://www.bpwusa.org/.

Business and Professional Women was founded in 1919 as part of the World War I effort when the federal government recognized the need to organize skilled women. The Web site features an extensive page on their history, including a photo exhibit. As advocates for working women, the organization strives to achieve workplace equity through a variety of activities. Vocational teachers will want to be aware of this site. MHCA.

Five College Archives Digital Access Project. 1999. Five Colleges, Inc., 97 Spring Street, Amherst, MA 01002-2324. 413-256-8316; fax 413-256-0249. E-mail: clio@clio.fivecolleges.edu. URL: http://clio.fivecolleges.edu/.

Amherst College, Hampshire College, Mount Holyoke College, Smith College, and the University of Massachusetts have joined forces to digitize archival records and manuscript collections relating to women's education at these institutions, thus making available some of the oldest records on women's involvement in higher education. Founded by Mary Lyon in 1837, Mount Holyoke is recognized as the first women's college. Sophia Smith provided in her will for the establishment of Smith College, which opened in 1871. Both institutions are a part of the Seven Sisters, private liberal arts colleges founded in the nineteenth century for the education of women. The Five Colleges project makes available over 24,000 documents, manuscripts, and publications, including some graphical material and motion picture footage. Neatly organized, the Web page allows investigators to search all the institutions. The links relate mostly to digitization projects, not to other women's history sites. The site will be of topical and regional interest. HCA.

The Maids: A Documentary. Produced and directed by Muriel Jackson. 28 min. Women Make Movies, 1985. Videocassette. Purchase $225.00; Rental $60.00.

Beginning after the Civil War, African American women did most of the domestic work in the South and predominated in the field in other areas of the country. Household service provided these women with a means of supporting themselves, and, in many cases, was the only work available to them. During the 1960s, rising public assistance and the nature of domestic work influenced Black women to move away from the field. In 1973, Dorothy Bolden led the National Domestic Workers of America in winning government protection and benefits for workers in this field. In *The Maids*, Bolden is interviewed, as well as several people who began cleaning services in the early 1970s. They discuss the stigmas of the work as well as racism and sexism in the field. Although the documentary seems to be Georgia-based, it is well balanced and contributes to labor history, women's studies, and African American studies. HCA.

Mine Eyes Have Seen the Glory: The Women's Army Corps. Produced and directed by Paul Hansen. 30 min. Chip Taylor Communications, 1997. Videocassette. $166.65.

A little broader than covering just the Women's Army Corps, *Mine Eyes Have Seen the Glory* actually presents a history of women in the armed forces, packing a lot of information into a half hour. The time before World War II is covered briefly because in 1942, Congress passed legislation establishing the Women's Army Auxiliary Corps recognizing that women were needed in the war effort and that their service would free men for combat duty. They were enlisted, outfitted, and trained for the only four jobs they were permitted: clerk, typist, driver, and cook. General George Marshall realized that women needed status and benefits if enlistment goals were to be filled. A 1943 bill created the Women's Army Corps, allowing for more training and service overseas, but excluding combat duty. Over 100,000 women served in all the different theaters of World War II, and they have continued to serve in all military actions since that time in all the branches of the military. The Women's Army Corps was disbanded in 1974 as women became a part of the regular army. About a dozen veterans are interviewed for this film, which includes a rich display of film clips and black-and-white photographs, carefully arranged and well researched. Public libraries should consider *Mine Eyes Have Seen the Glory* for use with veterans groups. MHCA.

Railroad Women. Produced by Dorothy Velasco and Sharon Genasci. 30 min. Women Make Movies, 1988. Videocassette. Purchase $195.00; Rental $50.00.

Illustrated with black-and-white photographs and pictures from railroad and historical archives as well as color film, *Railroad Women* delivers the history of women in railroading from the middle of the nineteenth century through the present. Some fine folk music is included in this film, which interviews five lively women who started railroad careers during World War II as well as two interesting contemporary women railroad workers. Women's first rail jobs included delivering mail, cleaning stations, selling food, and entertaining passengers with gambling games in the cars. Both world wars created jobs with the railroads, which were generally more lucrative than other types of employment. While realizing they were outside the mainstream of women's work, all the women interviewed enjoyed their jobs. The film can be used in schools where transportation or careers are units of study, but it will have a broader appeal to general audiences, and it will be of regional interest in the Northwest, where the film is set. MHCA.

Women Veterans: A History of Their Past, Information for the Present. 1996. E-mail: captbarb@aug.com. URL: http://userpages.aug.com/captbarb/.

The best site for information about women in the United States military is the project of Captain Barbara A. Wilson, USAF (Ret.). Students will appreciate this interactive site, which features a quiz and many pictures. Veterans and researchers will like the comprehensive nature of the site and the number of links to other information. All of the wars from the Revolution to Operation Desert Fox are covered as well as topics such as prisoners of war, spies, medals, and monuments. Posters, music, a bibliography, and a time line are just some of the additional features. Wilson has done an excellent job, obviously putting hours of research into her page. Public libraries may want to feature it in November for Veteran's Day. MHCA.

Historiography of Women in the United States

Women have always been a part of the historical record both as participants and as chroniclers. Women made history, but they also chronicled it in diaries, letters, travel journals, biographies, and research studies. There are many different reasons why women wrote history. No doubt many women wanted to leave a written record of their personal experiences. Sometimes women recognized the historic significance of their work and wanted to document it. Other times women had an interest in a particular topic and resolved to write about it. Later, individuals, both men and women, recognized the absence of women in history and set about to remedy the situation. During the last half of the twentieth century, interest, scholarship, and publication in the field exploded. Several outstanding women's historians, with original thought and extensive research, added greatly to the body of work that makes up women's history and the theory and methodology surrounding it. Archives were established, and women's history was celebrated through a number of events. The record of women's history available at the end of the twentieth century was created for many reasons.

There was always a written record of women in history, but because females had been so hidden in the historical record, it was felt that the sources to document the involvement of women did not exist. This was never true. Rather, a combination of factors, including patriarchal social structure, lack of education for women, and limits on women's influence, caused women's writings and contributions to be ignored. For years, women writers were viewed as amateurs who used dramatic, moralistic, or superficial topics. Although much of women's writing enjoyed great popularity in its day, because it was not considered serious, it was lost, forgotten, and undervalued (Smith 1998). Men wrote books and texts in which they chose to view history by the standards they felt were important (Beard 1946). Women were considered part of man, and thus their history was the same as men's. The official record was of diplomatic, military, political, and economic history, rather than of social or domestic history. Recognition of the existence of documentation discovering the role of women made possible the growth of women's history as a field of study.

It is important to know the historiography of women because the past affects the present. Understanding what information was available in the past and why it was created has a bearing on what is created now or may be created in the future. Although American women have generally been missing from history for most of the nation's past, there were writers, historians, and publications dealing exclusively with the realm of women's involvement in the affairs of the nation, although many went unrecognized until recent times. Whether the earlier chroniclers were considered amateur or professional, they made possible a more comprehensive, realistic view of the past. The important women's historians, the chronological progression of women's history, and the milestones in the history of women help to complete the historical record.

Women in the Colonial and Revolutionary Periods

In the historiography of women, Colonial women, as a group, have been widely studied. A variety of methods characterized the recording of early women, ranging from the oral tradition to women writers who deliberately focused on the experience of women. Research on the Colonials was conducted by Alice Morse Earle, a nineteenth-century authority, and other historians in the 1930s. A record of their involvement exists in diaries and letters, but the problem with studying Colonial women was that, as individuals, they were hard to trace. Under the Blackstone Commentaries, English common law imported to the New World, women legally disappeared when they married. They became one with their husbands, with all property and legal documents held in the husband's name. Legal and court documents hold few clues, and other forms of documentation had to be used to establish a history of America's first settlers. Similar problems existed in recording Native American women. Language barriers and their undervalued culture with no written tradition put them in the same league as white women in terms of their invisibility in history, and their culture continued to be passed on only through the oral tradition.

Where written language existed, diaries and journals were one way women recorded history, but, even early in the republic, a few women were formally identified as historians. One such woman was Hannah Adams, who received education at home because she suffered ill health throughout childhood. Her poor health made her timid, although she gained many influential friends around Boston; they helped her with her publications, gave her access to sources, and promoted her work. All of this was helpful, for writing was her only means of providing a small income. Known for her meticulous research and use of multiple sources, Adams's main subjects were religion and New England. Her best-known work, *A Memoir of Miss Hannah Adams, Written by Herself*, was published posthumously in 1832 (James, James, and Boyer 1971, 1:9–11). "Written by herself" became a phrase associated with women's writing as a way of conveying the authenticity of the female author. Disclaimers were frequently found on women's writing because women did not have access to education. Colonial poet Phillis Wheatley was examined by a committee of men who testified to the genuineness of her work so that it could be published.

Although the authority of the female pen was in no way established and recognized, women wrote accounts of the American Revolution as participants in the events of their times. Mercy Otis Warren published a three-volume narrative called *History of the Rise, Progress, and Termination of the American Revolution* in 1805. Containing much the same information as other histories of the time, the books were remarkable for including Warren's own perspective on the events and people she knew personally.

Her volumes remain in print, giving a female view of those unsettled times. Born in Barnstable, Massachusetts, Mercy Otis was not formally educated; however, she was able to gain some knowledge at home through listening to her brother's tutors and sitting through political discussions. Her father, John Otis, was a judge in the county court and a leader in the community. Mercy Otis married James Warren of Plymouth, who was a member of the state legislature. Her home became a meeting place for patriots, among them John Adams, and the propaganda Warren wrote for the cause was published in the newspapers. Unfortunately, when family circumstances fell on hard times after the war, Warren's appeals to John Adams for assistance went unanswered, causing her to treat him unkindly in her history. Both Abigail and John Adams had encouraged Warren to write history; a heated exchange of letters about the slight took place until the two sides were reconciled in 1812. Still, Adams complained that "History is not the Province of the Ladies" (Norton 1980; Scanlon and Cosner 1996; Warren 1989).

Although Adams advised women away from writing history, his counsel was not heeded by Elizabeth Fries Lummis Ellet. A published writer living in New York in the middle of the nineteenth century, Ellet, who had been educated at a girl's school, wanted to provide a record of women's part in the American Revolution. She realized no such account existed, even in Warren's history. Ellet wrote three volumes titled *The Women of the American Revolution,* published between 1848 and 1850. The works were based on letters and interviews with the descendants of over 160 renowned and unknown women who lived through the war. Ellet was a careful researcher. The material that did not fit into the Revolution manuscript was published later as *Domestic History of the American Revolution*. Continuing in this vein, Ellet collected other stories, publishing *Pioneer Women of the West* in 1852 and *Queens of American Society* in 1867 (Scanlon and Cosner 1996; Smith 1998).

The distinctions between Hannah Adams, Mercy Otis Warren, and Elizabeth Fries Lummis Ellet were clear. Adams was a writer who found that she could make a living from researching and writing history. Warren was a woman historian who had no particular interest in women's involvement in the Revolution, except for her own experience. Ellet was the first women's historian because she recognized that women's roles needed to be recorded, and she focused on them exclusively. Even from earliest times, women's history was written in a variety of models, making a record of events and people available to future generations.

Early Biographical Collections

After Ellet's pioneering work in recording the lives of women in the Revolution, the history of women continued to be documented. In fact, Ellet's idea of compiling biographies about women became popular. The number of women writing history increased, and, during the nineteenth century, a number of biographical collections on women were produced. Because women were rarely allowed in the universities or the professions, the authors were considered amateurs. The advent of the professional woman historian was still to come; however, education and many other issues concerning the advancement of women would come to a head during this century. With multiple causes, such as abolition, suffrage, and reform progressing throughout the century, each writer supported or opposed the issues of the day according to her own beliefs and reflected such in her writing.

Lydia Maria Child was an example of those who juggled the issues during the nineteenth century. Child, who was educated at a seminary for females, and may be best remembered for her Thanksgiving ballad, which opens "Over the river and through the woods," was a major abolitionist, but not a suffragist. She began her career by publishing, in 1835, the two volume biographical collection *The History of the Condition of Women in Various Ages and Nations*. The work was not highly regarded in later years because it was thought to contain errors. As an ardent abolitionist, Child put her best efforts toward that cause. She edited and wrote the introduction to the original edition of *Incidents in the Life of a Slave Girl* by Harriet Jacobs, published in 1861. In her introduction, Child acknowledged how unpopular her bringing the female slave narrative to print might be. The sales of her other writings were affected by her political stance, forcing Child to live on a decreased income (Jacobs 1988; Karcher 1994).

As the influential editor of *Godey's Lady's Book* for forty years beginning in 1837, Sarah Josepha Buell Hale was a strong supporter of education for women, but she believed that a woman's place was in the home, not in politics; to this end, she filled her magazine with recipes, advice, fashion, and literature to help edify the female reader. She learned about literature through reading along at home with her brother, who attended Dartmouth College. Hale was the author or editor of over fifty books, including the 1835 *Woman's Record*, an encyclopedia of 2,500 biographical entries. One of Hale's criteria for selection into the *Record* was high moral character. Her ethics, as represented in her publications, were typical of the Victorian age (Keenan 1996).

Phebe Ann Coffin Hanaford was another collector of female biographies and the author of *Women of the Century* in 1876, a popular book that was reissued in 1882 under the title *Daughters of America*. Hanaford was educated in public and private schools, began writing at the age of thirteen, and received advanced training from a local minister. She was ordained and preached for a good portion of her life. Her interest in women's history, evident in her biographical compilation, corresponded to her support for suffrage, and she helped to organize the American Woman Suffrage Association (James, James, and Boyer 1971, 2:126–27).

Other suffragists collected female biographies. In 1893, Frances Willard and Mary A. Livermore joined forces to edit an illustrated compilation of over 1,500 life stories called *A Woman of the Century*. Although the pair were editors in name only, their names added influence to a book that was outstanding for its careful selection of entries, fluent writing style, and reliability. Willard and Livermore were both well known. Willard was a college graduate and the founder of the Woman's Christian Temperance Union. Livermore, whose education came from female seminary and teaching, gained notoriety working for the Sanitation Commission during the Civil War. She went on to edit the *Woman's Journal*, a long-lived suffrage publication (James, James, and Boyer 1971, 2:410–13; 3:613–19).

Collections of female biographies did not disappear after the nineteenth century. John William Leonard edited *Women's Who's Who of America* in 1914–1915, and Mabel Ward Cameron and others edited the three volumes of *Biographical Cyclopedia of American Women* published between 1924 and 1928. Although the later book lacked the accuracy and selection criteria of Willard and Livermore's volume (James, James, and Boyer 1971, 1:x), many of these volumes would become more important to women's history later. Biographical collections were established as a genre, one step in creating women's historiography.

Suffrage Historians

Although focused on the attainment of rights for women in the later half of the nineteenth century, the suffragists seemed to foresee the historic value of their work and felt an obligation to record it. They did not merely collect female biographies, they chronicled a movement. Susan B. Anthony saved every scrap of paper from her work, including manuscripts, bills, minutes, and all of her own correspondence. These documents were the basis of the six volumes of *The History of Woman Suffrage,* edited by Anthony along with Elizabeth Cady Stanton, Matilda Joslyn Gage, and, later, Ida Husted Harper. The books, published between 1881 and 1922, required all of these editors. The first three volumes of the history took over ten years to complete, for, at first, Cady Stanton and Anthony thought a 100-page pamphlet would suffice to tell the story. As they began to go through their material, they realized that a booklet would never adequately cover the movement, and the project was dropped for a time. When taken up again in 1880, the first volume ran over 800 pages, covering only the years 1848 to 1861. Their work was written entirely by hand, each document being copied for inclusion. Anthony and Cady Stanton lived together for seven months while working on the history. Anthony selected the documents and Cady Stanton wrote the introductory descriptions, which had to be kept short. Their account tended to be more esoteric than analytical, with the major focus being the National Woman Suffrage Association, especially after the split in the movement in 1869. Lucy Stone was asked to provide a history of the American Woman Suffrage Association, the competing organization after the split, which she refused to do; she noted that it was impossible to write a history of suffrage until the vote had been won. The authors would have failed to include any reference to the AWSA if Harriot Stanton Blatch, Cady Stanton's daughter and an important participant in the suffrage movement, had not objected and written the chapter herself. Anthony invested large sums of money to have the history published; she then gave it away to libraries. The history, each volume of which was nearly 1,000 pages, was completed by the other editors after the deaths of Cady Stanton and Anthony and the passage of the Nineteenth Amendment (Banner 1980; Sherr 1995).

The History of Woman Suffrage remains the definitive text on the early suffrage movement, though not the only account. Paulina Wright Davis, another early suffragist and editor of *Una*, one of the first periodicals on the subject of woman's rights, wrote *A History of the National Woman's Rights Movement*, which was published in 1871 (Smith 1998). Other suffrage newspapers were published, including the *Lily*, edited by Amelia Bloomer; the long-lived *Woman's Journal*, edited by Mary Livermore and Lucy Stone; and the *Revolution*, edited by Susan B. Anthony and Elizabeth Cady Stanton. All these publications added to the record of the suffrage movement.

In the second generation of suffragists, those who saw the passage of the Nineteenth Amendment, Carrie Chapman Catt chose to chronicle the movement. Catt, who was hand-chosen by Susan B. Anthony to be her successor in the leadership of the reunited National American Woman Suffrage Association, co-authored *Woman Suffrage and Politics* with Nettie Rogers Shuler, Catt's own choice for corresponding secretary in the NAWSA. The book, written in 1923, covers the suffrage movement through the passage of the Nineteenth Amendment in 1920 (James, James, and Boyer 1971, 1:209–13; 3:287).

The two oldest women's history archives were founded with the records of the suffragists. Prior to the suffrage movement, a few carelessly kept archival collections were housed with individuals or underfunded nonprofit groups rather than at universities (Smith 1998). The major suffrage archives were established at Radcliffe College and Smith College (Lerner 1981). The basis of the Radcliffe archives was Maud Wood Park's collection on woman's rights, donated to the college in 1943. Park was a Boston suffragist who graduated from Radcliffe, founded the first chapter of the College Equal Suffrage League, and traveled the country to found other chapters. In 1920, she became the first president of the League of Women Voters. Park's records, joined by other materials, grew into the Women's Archives and was renamed the Arthur and Elizabeth Schlesinger Library to honor Professor Arthur M. Schlesinger, Sr., a historian who first noted the absence of women in history, and his wife (Sicherman et al. 1980). Elizabeth Bancroft Schlesinger taught in a one-room school to earn college tuition. After World War II, she wrote articles on women's history, especially for *American Heritage* magazine (Scanlon and Cosner 1996). The Sophia Smith Collection at Smith College was founded in 1942 and named after the college's founder, a spinster who provided in her will for the founding of a women's college in Northhampton, Massachusetts.

While the Schlesinger and the Smith are the largest women's history archives, other collections were built. A private library belonging to Miriam Y. Holden ended up in the Library of Congress. Holden had collected the papers of her friends Alice Paul, Margaret Sanger, Mary Beard, Eugenia Leonard, and Elizabeth Schlesinger, as well as some of her own work done in the National Women's Party, with the idea of forming a national women's history archive (Lerner 1979; Sicherman et al. 1980). Additionally, the Schomburg Center for Research in Black Culture in the New York Public Library, the Negro Collection at Howard University, and the Bethune Museum and Archives hold documents on the history of Black women (Flexner 1959; Scanlon and Cosner 1996). The Schomburg Center, established in the 1920s, houses over 5 million items dating as far back as the eighth century (Jacobs 1988).

While the suffragists were collecting and publishing their papers, the antisuffragists were also furnishing information on their beliefs. The founder of Barnard College, Annie Nathan Meyer, lectured against suffrage, although her views on women were ambivalent. In 1891, she edited *Women's Work in America,* in which she admired the achievements of women in the professions, but her inconsistency towards women's place was a lifetime theme. On the one hand, she supported female education, honored women's attainments, and wrote professionally herself; on the other, she felt women belonged at home (Sicherman et al. 1980).

Ida Minerva Tarbell, the muckraking journalist, became an anti-feminist in her later years. As a girl at home, Tarbell learned about the legal limitations of marriage from Frances Willard, head of the WCTU. Indoctrinated to the cause of woman's rights, Tarbell saw education as a way to escape the narrowness of home and family. She attended Allegheny College as one of only five women in the freshmen class. After teaching and writing, Tarbell began a long and powerful career in journalism. Even with the notoriety for her 1904 exposé *The History of the Standard Oil Company*, Tarbell seemed to regret the feminist decisions she made as a girl and felt a loss from never marrying or having children. In 1911, she penned *The Book of Woman's Power,* followed in 1912 by *The Business of Being a Woman,* in which she expressed her view that home and family were more important than career (Beard 1946; Scanlon and Cosner 1996).

Although the suffragists recorded their work and formed archives from their papers, they were not supported by everyone. The views of those who favored the traditional roles for women were also recorded. Most of these women were amateur writers, lacking advanced education or specialized training. Their personal interests in the causes of the day led them to become a part of the historiography.

Emerging Authorities

In the later half of the nineteenth century, a number of factors caused women's historical writing to intensify. Many reform movements, including suffrage, were in full swing. Easier travel changed the way women viewed the world. Women's clubs were founded, which brought women broader perspectives; local museums and archives were established, giving women new topics and sources on which to write. At this time, several authorities emerged who wrote on various aspects of women's history. It was a step beyond merely compiling biographies or the papers of a cause. High amateurism was the name given to the period, for women were still not receiving advanced education and were often excluded from using university libraries and archives (Smith 1998); however, advanced training or unique knowledge in a narrower field allowed some women to become specialists.

One of the emerging authorities was Caroline Dall, who was considered brilliant enough to be invited to join Margaret Fuller's Boston-based transcendental "conversation" groups in the 1840s. When her husband became a missionary in India, Dall became a suffragist and feminist. She wrote a vindication of famous historical women, *Historical Pictures Retouched*, in 1860. Her major work came in 1867 in *The College, the Market, and the Court: Or Women's Relation to Education, Labor, and Law,* in which she argued that the home did not provide enough stimulation to keep women happy and that employment and legal restrictions based on sex should be removed. A founder the American Social Science Association, Dall's work was research-based, although she had no formal advanced education. Her ideas predated those of both Charlotte Perkins Gilman, whose pleas for female economic independence would come over thirty years later (James, James, and Boyer 1971, 1:428–29), and Betty Friedan, whose model of the unhappy housewife would emerge in the 1950s.

Alice Cunningham Fletcher was another specialist. Unschooled, except for a mentor relationship, she became an ethnologist studying the Native tribes. She joined the Indian reform movement to help pass the 1887 Dawes Act, which returned tribal lands held in common to individual members of each tribe. Fletcher had a long and distinguished career in anthropology, including many scholarly publications and field assignments from various branches of the government as well as President Chester A. Arthur. Fletcher's work documented the matrilineal society of the Iroquois. Lecturing on this topic to an 1888 meeting of the International Council of Women, Fletcher described how tribal women felt better off under native law than under white law because they could own their own homes, belongings, and persons, advantages unknown to married white women at the end of the nineteenth century (Mankiller et al. 1998; Wagner 1996).

Alice Morse Earle was an early expert on Colonial women and their times, and another notable high amateur. Several of her works, which she carefully researched from primary sources by using numerous libraries both in the United States and abroad, remain in print as standards in the field. Recognized as an authority, she received quantities of letters containing all manner of information, sources, and materials. Earle, who was educated in Boston schools, came from a family of great collectors. She began writing at the request of her father, using the family's materials. In 1891, she published *The Sabbath in Puritan New England*; over the next twelve years, she wrote seventeen books and numerous articles on the Colonial past that focused on such topics as childhood, domestic life, and biography. Earle was unique in looking at culture rather than at affairs of state, upon which most historians concentrated (Scanlon and Cosner 1996). Earle's work, in another way, was seen as looking to the past with nostalgia for a sense of identity as new immigrants arrived in the United States (Smith 1998). In either view, by opening up social themes, Earle made a contribution to women's history.

Without formal education, several of the women mentioned can be considered the first women's history specialists because of their interests in limited fields and concentration on the experience of women. They participated in pioneering work in sociology, anthropology, and cultural history, and they were the precursors to women entering the professional fields when higher education opened up to women.

Beginnings of Professionalism

When women began to receive college degrees in the late nineteenth century, the reform movements opened new opportunities. Not only did women become professional historians, they also established the field of social work, starting settlement houses to improve working and living conditions for urban dwellers and immigrants. Social work was considered acceptable for women as they began to forge careers. Because the use of new research techniques was part of this work, women began to use survey methods and to keep more careful records (Smith 1998). Investigation of women's working lives was a major theme for a growing number of women, and research reports added to the historiography of women. Women were entering a variety of fields for the first time, and many pioneers in the vocations, just like the suffragists, wrote histories of women in the professions.

Elizabeth Blackwell was the first woman to earn a medical degree, graduating from Geneva College in upstate New York in 1849. She felt that it was important to chronicle women's early work in her chosen field; she wrote several books on the subject, including *The Influence of Women in the Profession of Medicine* and *Pioneer Work in Opening the Medical Profession to Women* (Cullen-DuPont 1996). Whereas Blackwell represented female doctors, Adelaide Nutting chronicled the nursing profession. Nutting entered the first class of the new Johns Hopkins Hospital Training School for Nurses, staying on to become superintendent of nurses and forging standards for nursing education. She was co-author of the four-volume *History of*

Nursing, published between 1907 and 1912 (James, James, and Boyer 1971, 2:642–44). Lillian Wald and Alice Hamilton entered the field of medicine later than had Blackwell and Nutting; they used their training to advance the field of social work. Wald, with a nursing degree, saw first-hand the needs of immigrant, urban women. She opened the Henry Street settlement in New York City to administer to the health needs of the population. Later, the establishment broadened its mission to administer to all kinds of social needs (Cullen-DuPont 1996). Dr. Hamilton joined Jane Addams at Hull House in Chicago. Hamilton's work, combining laboratory techniques and field study, documented lead poisoning victims in Illinois and compelled a change in state law to protect workers (Sicherman et al. 1980).

The health work going on in the settlement houses was only a fraction of the undertakings. When Jane Addams founded Hull House in Chicago in 1889, immigrants were flooding into the cities. There were no child labor laws, workday laws, housing legislation, or trade union protections. Addams brought together, as residents of Hull House, an array of women who used their newly acquired degrees, modern statistical methods, and field study techniques to report on conditions in such a proficient and learned way as to compel reforms for working women, children, and immigrants. These early social scientists, who wrote reports and published material, included Julia Lathrop, sisters Edith and Grace Abbott, Sophonisba Breckinridge, and Florence Kelley (Lerner 1981; Mankiller et al. 1998).

Other women, outside the settlement house environment, were adding to the body of social research on women during the Progressive era at the turn of the century. Josephine Goldmark investigated women's working hours and the Triangle Shirtwaist Factory Fire. Mary Van Kleeck examined conditions of New York City factory girls (Mankiller et al. 1998), and Helen Sumner Woodbury became a recognized labor expert. Woodbury's interest in labor and social justice led her to graduate school at the University of Wisconsin, where she studied under Frederick Jackson Turner and John R. Commons. As part of a group headed by Commons and sponsored by the U.S. Bureau of Labor Statistics, she wrote *History of Women in Industry in the United States,* which was published in 1910 as volume nine of the *Report on Condition of Woman and Child Wage-Earners in the U.S.* Her dissertation was a major part of the 1918 publication by the same group, *History of Labour in the United States.* Before her interest in labor, Woodbury interrupted her college work to do field study in Colorado, where women had the vote, resulting in the publication of *Equal Suffrage* in 1909 (James, James, and Boyer 1971, 3:650–52).

The field of history was opening to women by the late nineteenth century, and several women were pioneer historians. The first woman to receive a Ph.D. in history was Kate Ernest Levi, who graduated from the University of Wisconsin in 1893. Anna Julia Cooper, author of *A Voice from the South by a Black Woman of the South,* which advocated education for African Americans, became in 1925 the first Black woman granted a Ph.D.

After a full public school teaching career, Cooper received her degree from the Sorbonne when she was sixty-five. Lucy Maynard Salmon was the first history professor hired by Vassar, where she introduced the seminar method. She was charged with introducing amateur, or low, topics, using newspapers and train schedules, which she felt were viable sources for social research, and she published several studies on using such sources. Hired in 1887 with a B.A. and M.A. from the University of Michigan, where she had written a prize-winning dissertation, *History of the Appointing Power of the President*, Salmon gave long service as chair of the history department at Vassar; but she had to muster all her resources to fend off a challenge to this seat by a male colleague. Salmon pioneered research methods in social history, which were considered lowbrow at the time. Another early woman professional historian was Margaret Judson, who attended Harvard in the 1920s. She had to gain permission to use the Harvard Law Library and was required to enter by the back door; one professor refused to teach, consult, or examine her. Judson denied the hardships of her education and told colleagues in the 1970s that they should be less feminist. Caroline Ware, whose dissertation, *The Early New England Cotton Manufacture*, earned three prizes in economics in 1929, tended to break the rules by attending all-male history smokers where, she insisted, she was treated with respect. Upon marriage, Ware kept her own name, which was better known than her husband's. She became a teacher at Vassar in the 1930s (Scanlon and Cosner 1996; Smith 1998).

During the late nineteenth century, women who entered the history profession intruded on a male field and were treated as outcasts. Women who became historians frequently did not marry, could be professionally rebuked for any sort of personal misstep, and were often denied jobs, which were awarded to men instead. The discipline held that only men were capable of the objectivity necessary for interpreting documentary evidence (Smith 1998). Women in academia found that hierarchy and canon-making occurred in the same way as they did in social life (McIntosh 1981, 3), a well-known phenomenon during the era. During their careers and in the historiography, academic women from the turn of the twentieth century were largely ignored.

The field of history became professionalized with the founding of the American Historical Association (AHA) in 1884; however, women faced discrimination here too and were viewed as "storytellers" by many male members (Smith 1998). At its founding, women were included in the membership of the AHA; Lucy Maynard Salmon was an original member of the group. The AHA's first woman president, Nellie Neilson, was not elected until 1940. During the same year, Mildred Thompson of Vassar College presided over an AHA conference workshop on women in history, the first time a session was devoted to this theme. The topic did not change prevailing opinions: In John Higham's 1965 history of the Association, the only woman mentioned was Mary Beard, who appeared in two footnotes (Scott 1988).

As women entered professional fields and began careers, they added to the written record of women's accomplishments through histories and research reports. The research reports, showing the effects of women's participation in higher education, were greatly enhanced by their careful methods and techniques. The nineteenth century yielded much more documentation on women than the previous centuries had, and it was apparent that women would not back away from the new opportunities open to them.

Changes in the Twentieth Century

The first half of the twentieth century was a time of contradictions for women's history. A major milestone was reached with the recognition that women were missing from most historical accounts. Whereas the century began with hope for a changed societal role for women, it yielded to ridicule during the 1940s and 1950s. This change occurred even though research covered more fields of interest and scholarship increased.

While the professions were opening, the socialist revolution was questioning traditional culture and criticizing patriarchal society. Floyd Dell was a socialist, subscribing to Marxist theory and the writings of Friedrich Engels, which criticized the traditional division of labor in the family and noted how the wife and children were slaves to the husband. Dell's 1913 book, *Women As World Builders*, advocated a changed role for women (*Contemporary Authors* 1998; Lerner 1981). As suffrage had not been won when this book was published, and Marxism never found favor in the United States, Dell was more a harbinger of the second wave of feminism that would appear fifty years later.

Once women had the vote, after the passage of the Nineteenth Amendment in 1920, there was a marked change in thinking about women in history. Not only did Dell wonder about their status, but others wondered about their absence. This was first chronicled by the 1922 study by Arthur M. Schlesinger, Sr., *New Viewpoints in American History*. Schlesinger was the first to comment on how women were missing in recorded history. He tried to remedy the absence in his 1933 book, *The Rise of the American City*, by including a separate chapter on women (Lerner 1981). Schlesinger, a professor at Radcliffe College, maintained his interest in women's history, proposing a scholarly collection of biographies, *Notable American Women*, which was published in 1971. The Women's Archives established at Radcliffe was renamed in honor of Schlesinger and his wife, Elizabeth, a writer using women's history themes.

During the 1920s and 1930s, new research topics and new historians added to the field. Several books focused on the history of women in education. Willystine Goodsell, an education professor in Teacher's College at Columbia University, published *The Education of Women: Its Social Background and Its Problems* in 1923, followed a few years later by *Pioneers of Women's Education in the United States: Emma Willard, Catharine Beecher, Mary Lyon*. During this same period, Thomas Woody of the University of Pennsylvania wrote, in two volumes, *A History of Women's Education in the United States*. Woody's work uncovered a number of previously undiscovered women. Additionally, a number of biographies of women educators were published during the 1920s (Lerner 1981).

A revival of interest in Colonial women was evidenced by several major studies in the 1930s. Richard Morris depended on legal sources to uncover the status of Colonial women for *Studies in the History of American Law*, published in 1930. Elizabeth Dexter was the first to deal with Colonial women as workers by studying business directories and newspapers for *Colonial Women of Affairs*. Published in 1931, it showed women holding a variety of jobs and possessing many skills. Dexter, a notable historian, would go on to serve on the advisory board and as a consultant to the first edition of *Notable American Women*. In 1935, Mary S. Benson published *Women in Eighteenth Century America: A Study of Opinion and Social Usage*. By drawing on a wealth of primary source material, Julia Cherry Spruill assembled *Woman's Life and Work in the Southern Colonies* in 1938 (Lerner 1981). All but the first of these books, which illustrated a new depth of scholarship, were published by university presses. By the end of the 1930s, Colonial women were thoroughly uncovered, a preview to what could be accomplished with women of other periods.

It was also during the 1930s that Kate Campbell Hurd-Mead assembled her pioneering histories of women in medicine. A doctor, graduated from Woman's Medical College of Pennsylvania in 1888, Hurd-Mead studied women in the medical professions throughout her career, encouraged by colleagues at the Johns Hopkins Hospital Historical Club. Upon her retirement, her research grew as she traveled the world with her investigations, resulting in *Medical Women of America* in 1933 and *A History of Women in Medicine from the Earliest Times to the Beginning of the Nineteenth Century* in 1938. She planned two more volumes to the later book that remained unfinished at the time of her death (James, James, and Boyer 1971, 2:241–42). Her work added to the medical histories begun by Elizabeth Blackwell and Adelaide Nutting in the previous century.

During the 1940s, while women were going off to work to support the war effort, they faced antagonism in print from Philip Wylie's *A Generation of Vipers*, published in 1942. A best-seller at the time and still in print, *A Generation of Vipers* is a rambling list of everything the author saw wrong with society. One of his objections was to the overplayed, iconoclastic image of the American mother. Wylie's stereotype of mom dominated the 1950s, and his misogynistic essay would reverberate until the end of the century (*Contemporary Authors* 1998; Lerner 1981). The century had begun by reevaluating women's traditional role in the family, but by midcentury that role was being ridiculed.

Women in History

The inconsistencies of the early twentieth century arose because women were still peripheral to history, but there were several historians who would change that. Mary Ritter Beard's *Women As a Force in History*, published in 1946, changed the way women were perceived. Trained in sociology, and overwhelmingly interested in the affairs of her sex, Beard believed that women's contributions were central to all of history, and she was determined never to look upon women as victims. Together, these theories opened up a new era of women's history. Beard believed the representation of women as subservient over the past 100 years had influenced beliefs about the sexes. She felt the women's reform protests of the previous century, while advancing women in some ways, had done a disservice to women in showing their need for special protections in areas such as employment and welfare. With her husband, Charles Austin Beard, she integrated women into a series of books and texts, beginning with *The Rise of American Civilization* in 1927. In these books, Beard did include women in every period of history, the first time such a task had been accomplished. Whereas Arthur Schlesinger had added women as a separate chapter, Beard included them throughout the text. In *Women As a Force in History*, she portrayed women in all times and places as central figures. It was the first history belonging to women; men and political developments were not the focus. Beard originated the concept of women's history and women's studies, declaring that more study was needed to uncover all of women's roles. She tried, without success, to bring women's history into academia by proposing a course in women's studies at Radcliffe (Beard 1946; Lerner 1979; Sicherman et al. 1980). In her 1933 book, *America Through Women's Eyes*, she used women's first-hand accounts to show how history was not necessarily the commonly recorded epic of the great nation. She broke with her husband, who tried to incorporate the history of women into the prevailing historical account of the day. Beard, like other married partners, suffered from becoming part of a husband-wife team: Because it was always assumed the husband did the bulk of the research and writing, he received full credit despite the wife's contribution (Smith 1998). In splintering from her husband, Beard proved to be ahead of her time, and like any harbinger, she was ignored. At the time of her major publications, public opinion was not open to what she had to say; however, her work laid the foundation for what was to come.

It was over a decade before the next landmark in women's history was written by feminist Eleanor Flexner, who documented the suffrage struggle in *Century of Struggle: The Woman's Rights Movement in the United States*. Published in 1959, the book was expansive, covering the history of women in America from the seventeenth century through the passage of the Nineteenth Amendment. Remarkable for its careful research from many manuscript resources, it left questions for the next generation of historians to consider. Like Beard, Flexner was not critically acclaimed during her time, but the book endured and is still in print. Flexner went on to serve as a consultant to both editions of *Notable American Women;* Betty Friedan acknowledged the historian, calling *Century of Struggle* important reading. In the twentieth anniversary edition of *The Feminine Mystique* in 1983, Friedan admonished feminists for constantly re-creating their struggle through not knowing their past (Friedan 1983; Lerner 1981).

The history of women had finally been published, but two studies released the same year as Flexner's *Century of Struggle* showed unfavorable directions in other areas. Mabel Newcomer's *Century of Higher Education for Women* showed that in twenty years women had lost ground in academic life; and Robert W. Smuts's *Women and Work in America* showed that women continued to be undervalued in labor (Lerner 1981).

In 1962, a male historian again noticed the absence of women in history, but David Potter took it one step further than had Arthur Schlesinger. In his essay "National Character," Potter reexamined Frederick Jackson Turner's frontier thesis and theorized that the West did not present possibility for women as it did for men. Opportunity for women expanded in the closing of the frontier and the rise of the city, where a variety of occupations were available for women (Lerner 1981). The idea of Potter's essay, along with the work of Beard and Flexner, prompted other historians to look at traditional history through women's eyes and to reexamine some of the commonly held views.

Feminism Reborn

By the second half of the twentieth century, a model of a revised history, which included women, was established. The door was open to reexamine other areas. One domain ripe for review was the myth of the happy housewife, which Betty Friedan reevaluated in *The Feminine Mystique,* published in 1963. *The Feminine Mystique* challenged the belief that women were content within the domestic domain as wives and mothers by describing the dissatisfaction of educated women at home. The book induced the second wave of feminism, the first wave coming in the period of the push for suffrage; it also freed women to question the role that culture has assigned to them and to seek ways in which they could be more self-fulfilled. The expansion of modern feminism, coupled with the acceptance of social history as a way of looking at the past, fueled interest in women's history and allowed for the boom of new resources in the field during the last quarter of the century (Hartman and Banner 1974; Lerner 1981).

Beyond the rise of feminism, the 1960s saw the ascent of the career of the women's historian who had the greatest impact on the field. Gerda Lerner (1979) created and tested theory, establishing the discipline of women's history. Lerner emigrated from Austria in 1939 and received a Ph.D. from Columbia University in 1966. At the time of her graduation, when some of her professors had told her to study women unobtrusively, she set five goals for herself: to research and write on women's history topics, to prove the existence of women's history sources, to improve the status of women in the history profession, to document student demand for women's history courses, and to design those courses. Lerner refused to work modestly. Beginning her career at the age of forty-six, she felt she had to be productive. Her age gave her confidence, and knowing what she wanted to accomplish helped her to withstand discouragement, pressure, and disapproval from students and professors. She completed her graduation goals and contributed extensively to the field.

Lerner taught at Long Island University, Sarah Lawrence College, and the University of Wisconsin. In 1963, she taught the first class on American women in history since a similar class had been offered at Radcliffe in the 1930s. Her extensive writing included: *The Grimké Sisters from South Carolina: Rebels Against Slavery*, 1967; *The Woman in American History*, 1971; *Black Women in White America: A Documentary History*, 1972; *The Female Experience: An American Documentary*, 1976; *The Majority Find Its Past: Placing Women in History*, 1979, honored by the Berkshire Conference of Women Historians; *Teaching Women's History*, 1981; *The Creation of Patriarchy*, 1986, winner of the Joan Kelly Prize from the American Historical Association; *The Creation of Feminist Consciousness*, 1993; and *Why History Matters: Life and Thought*, 1997. Her books tested her theories as she continued to look further into history for explanations of the creation of the patriarchal society.

Lerner's major theories revolved around the goals she set for herself at the time of her graduation. She insisted that primary source material existed to document women's involvement in all of history. With Anne Firor Scott, Lerner surveyed sites in every state to find thousands of locations holding women's archives (Scanlon and Cosner 1996). Later Lerner postulated that women's experience did not fit into the periods historians typically used in recounting the American epic. These two theories, primary sources and periodization, were the basis of her 1976 book *The Female Experience: An American Documentary*. The book was composed exclusively of selections from documents by and about women, and, rather than being arranged chronologically, it was divided according to women's life stages and topics important to women's lives.

Lerner (1979; 1981), like Mary Beard, faulted the nineteenth- and twentieth-century feminists, up through Flexner, for focusing on oppression. To advance women's history as a discipline, the model of the subjected group had to be discarded. Much of women's history had chronicled the suffrage movement, recording only white women's experience. Lerner believed that expanded research was needed to form a broader history, including that of all classes, races, and ethnic groups. With more research, women's history would eventually force a paradigm shift by looking at history in a more inclusive way. She felt that, by asking questions to elicit information that would bring women and other underrepresented groups into view, a history for all people would be created.

Among the historians to emerge in the post-war years, Lerner certainly had the greatest significance; indeed, she had emerged at a time when women historians were still a rarity. In 1950, only twenty-nine advanced degrees in history were granted to women, 11 percent of degrees. By 1970, the number of degrees had grown to 137, but the percentage had only increased two points. In 1989, 37 percent of Ph.D.s were conferred upon women. During the third quarter of the twentieth century, the number of theses written on social history quadrupled, replacing political history as the main focus of graduate research (Appleby, Hunt, and Jacob 1994). The women's movement and the field of women's history was affecting academia.

A Discipline Emerges

Following the formation of the Kennedy Commission on the Status of Women in 1961 and the founding of the National Organization for Women in 1966, women's history emerged as a distinct discipline with publications, research, organizations, and celebrations of its own. As with any new discipline, definitive, scholarly reference books were needed, and the leading reference source, *Notable American Women (NAW)*, was published in three volumes in 1971. Another volume, *The Modern Period*, followed in 1980. *Notable American Women* brought together distinctive biographical research and writing covering the period 1607 through 1975; it was based mainly on the archival material held in the Schlesinger Library at Radcliffe College. In the extensive research leading to the selection of women to be represented in *NAW*, some of the historical titles created by American women of the past were called into use. Sarah Josepha Hale's *Woman's Record* was consulted, as well as Frances Willard and Mary Livermore's *A Woman of the Century*. Both of these sources held up to the test of time. Arthur M. Schlesinger, who tried to rectify the deplorable lack of women in history in *New Viewpoints in American History* (1922), served as a member of the College Council and chair of the Advisory Board to the Women's Archives. In 1955, he proposed that Radcliffe undertake the biographical project to provide definitive reports on America's great women. A new volume of *NAW*, with an expected publication date around 2003, has been proposed; it will include about 500 women and cover the years 1975 to 2000 (James, James, and Boyer 1971, 1:ix–x; *Notable* 1998, 5).

During the same year as the publication of *Notable American Women*, two other studies looked at the portrayal of women in textbooks. Janice Law Trecker's study, called "Women in U.S. History High School Textbooks," was published in the March 1971 issue of *Social Education*. Generally, Trecker found that women were not represented, and their accomplishments were not acknowledged (McLure and McLure 1977). At the same time, Dolores Barracano Schmidt and Earl Robert Schmidt (1976, 42–54) surveyed twenty-three college history texts. The amount written on women ran from a quarter page in 448 pages to nineteen of 1,256 pages. None of the books ignored women altogether, but their inclusion was minimal. These studies awakened educators and the public to the absence of women in textbooks and influenced publishers to reexamine their material.

In 1973, the first Berkshire Conference on the History of Women was held at Douglass College, Rutgers University. The expected attendance of about 100 was greatly surpassed. After the first meeting, Mary Hartman and Lois Banner (1974), both professors at Douglass College, edited a number of the papers presented, publishing *Clio's Consciousness Raised*. The essays challenged many long-held assumptions about women in history; their notable authors, depth of scholarship, and breadth of topics gained great significance for the collection. At the second Berkshire Conference, held at Radcliffe, attendance doubled, topping 1,000. These conferences were sponsored by the Berkshire Conference of Women Historians, a group founded in the 1930s as a way for women to forge professional connections; the early women professionals were often excluded from male social events and needed their own way to network. The "Big Berk" conferences have met regularly since 1973. Meeting triannually now, they draw several thousand people from all over the world. At the 1996 conference, held at the University of North Carolina, Chapel Hill, classes were canceled during the event, a policy unheard of even during the NCAA basketball championships. The 1999 conference at the University of Rochester, New York, listed over 700 presenters in the program (*Breaking Boundaries!* 1998). The growth of the conferences over the last quarter century testifies to the tremendous appeal of women's history.

By the end of the decade, interest in women's history had grown to a point where a national celebration was envisioned. In the summer of 1979, Gerda Lerner's idea of founding an institute for women leaders was adopted as the Women's History Institute, held at Sarah Lawrence College. Molly Murphy MacGregor, later head of the National Women's History Project, came from California with the idea of a Women's History Week, such as the one celebrated in the Sonoma County schools during March. The March date was chosen to coincide with International Women's Day, a day celebrated in the United States on and off since its 1909 founding as a celebration of peace. When the Institute agreed to help in securing a congressional resolution for a week-long national celebration, the proposal was given to Representative Patricia Schroeder of Colorado. Two years later, in 1981, Senator Orrin Hatch of Utah and Representative Barbara Mikulski of Maryland were the sponsors of the first joint congressional resolution for National Women's History Week. The observance proved popular: In 1987, the National Women's History Project, a California organization formed in 1980 to provide education, materials and information on the topic, asked Congress to expand the celebration to a month. March has been Women's

History Month ever since (Kerber, Kessler-Harris, and Sklar 1995; *National* 1998).

Another event held in 1979 did even more to bring women's history to the public's attention. A major exhibition held at the San Francisco Museum of Modern Art provided the first public showing of Judy Chicago's monumental, intellectual installation based on women in history and called *The Dinner Party*. A multimedia exhibit, *The Dinner Party* consisted of a triangular table set with thirteen places on each forty-eight-foot side. The places had an embroidered runner and a porcelain plate designed to represent a historic woman. The guests were arranged around the table from earliest times (Primordial Goddess) to the end of World War II (Georgia O'Keeffe). The "heritage floor" in the middle of the installation was composed of 2,300 triangular tiles carrying the names of 999 additional women. In all, the piece represented 1,038 women at a time when women's history was widely unknown to the general public. Tremendous research went into documenting all the women represented. With an audience of over 1 million people, *The Dinner Party* made great inroads in bringing historic women into the popular culture (Chicago 1996). The 1970s was the decade of public awareness for women's history in the creation of a major reference work and public celebrations of women's history.

Women's History Boom

By the 1980s, women's history was a growth industry with new types of publications. Capable women's historians, who had grown up with women's history in the 1970s, continued to teach and write. They were joined by many other scholars in filling out the historical record by creating and examining theories that would integrate what was still a new field of study. Although not all-inclusive, some of the major work was being done by the following historians. The list recognizes each individual's work in the field of women's history only.

- Lois Banner earned advanced degrees from Columbia University. She was the author or editor of *Women in Modern America: A Brief History*, 1974; *Clio's Consciousness Raised: New Perspectives on the History of Women*, 1974; and *Elizabeth Cady Stanton: A Radical for Woman's Rights*, 1980.

- With advanced degrees from Columbia University and teaching service at Duke University, William H. Chafe was the author of *The American Woman: Her Changing Social, Political, and Economic Roles, 1920–1970*, 1972, revised as *Paradox of Change: American Women in the Twentieth Century*, 1991; *Women and Equality: Changing Patterns in American Culture*, 1977; and *The Road to Equality: American Women Since*

1962, 1994. Chafe was instrumental in developing theory in women's history.

- A graduate of Cornell and Brandeis, Nancy F. Cott taught at Yale beginning in 1975. One of the founders of the field of women's history, Cott was inspired by her work in the women's movement. Her writings included *Root of Bitterness: Documents of the Social History of American Women*, 1972 and 1996; *The Bonds of Womanhood: "Woman's Sphere" in New England, 1780–1835*, 1977 and 1997; and *A Woman Making History: Mary Ritter Beard Through Her Letters*, 1991. She was also editor of the eleven-volume *Young Oxford History of Women in the United States*, 1995.

- Carl N. Degler served as professor of history at Stanford University after receiving advanced degrees from Columbia University. Degler's contributions to women's history included theoretical development, service on the advisory board to *Notable American Women: The Modern Period*, and writing *At Odds: Women and the Family in America from the Revolution to the Present* in 1980.

- Ellen Carol DuBois received her Ph.D. from Northwestern University and worked at the State University of New York at Buffalo. She wrote extensively on women's history, including *Feminism and Suffrage: The Emergence of an Independent Women's Movement in America, 1848–1869*, 1978; *Elizabeth Cady Stanton, Susan B. Anthony: Correspondence, Writings, Speeches*, 1981; *Eighty Years and More: Elizabeth Cady Stanton Reminiscences 1815–1897*, 1992; co-editor of *Unequal Sisters: A Multicultural Reader in U.S. Women's History*, 1994; and *Harriet Stanton Blatch and the Winning of Woman Suffrage*, 1997.

- Since 1984, Linda Gordon has worked at the University of Wisconsin after receiving degrees from Swarthmore and Yale. Her research topics included birth control, gender and state, and domestic violence. She received nominations in the history category of the National Book Award in 1976 for *Woman's Body, Woman's Right: A Social History of Birth Control in America* and in 1988 for *Heroes of Their Own Lives: The Politics and History of Family Violence, Boston, 1880–1960*, which also won the Joan Kelly Prize for the best book in women's history or theory from the American Historical Association. Additionally, she earned the 1994 Berkshire Prize for the best book in women's history for *Pitied But Not Entitled: Single Mothers and the Origins of Welfare*. Her other contributions included those of co-editor of *America's Working Women: A Documentary History*, 1976 and 1995; editor of *Maternity: Letters from Working Women*, 1979; and editor of *Women and the State: Historical and Theoretical Essays*, 1990.

- Darlene Clark Hine, co-editor of *Black Women in America: An Historical Encyclopedia*, 1994, was a leader in discovering African American women's history. With advanced degrees from Kent State University, Hine has carried on her work at Michigan State University since 1987.

- Professor emeritus at New Mexico State University, Joan M. Jensen's specialty was western women. Her work included co-editing *A Needle, a Bobbin, a Strike: Women Needleworkers in America*, 1985; co-editor of *New Mexico Women: Intercultural Perspectives*, 1986; *Decades of Discontent: The Women's Movement, 1920–1940*, 1987; *Loosening the Bonds: Mid-Atlantic Farm Women, 1750–1850*, 1987; *Promise to the Land: Essays on Rural Women*, 1991; and *One Foot on the Rockies: Women and Creativity in the Modern American West*, 1995. Jensen's degrees were from the University of California at Los Angeles.

- Joan Kelly was trained at Columbia University and served as professor at the City College of New York from 1956 to 1982. She was cofounder, with Gerda Lerner, of the master's program in women's history at Sarah Lawrence College, where Lerner challenged her in 1971 to rethink her field in relation to women. Although Kelly initially felt that she could not find women in the study of the Renaissance, she was ultimately able to include women. Consequently, she developed a teaching method based upon asking key questions that empowered students and guided their work. After her death, an award in her name was given yearly by the American Historical Association for the best book on women's history or theory. Kelly's work was collected in *Women, History and Theory: The Essays of Joan Kelly,* published in 1984.

- A professor at the University of Iowa, Linda K. Kerber earned a Ph.D. from Columbia University. She wrote extensively on women's history topics as the author of *Women of the Republic: Intellect and Ideology in Revolutionary America*, 1980; co-editor of *Women's America: Refocusing the Past*, 1982; author of *The Impact of Women on American Education*, 1983; and "History Will Do It No Justice:" *Women's Lives in Revolutionary America*, 1987; co-editor and contributor to *U.S. History as Women's History: New Feminist Essays*, 1993; and author of *Toward an Intellectual History of Women: Essays*, 1997.

- Born in England, Alice Kessler-Harris earned advanced degrees from Rutgers University, where she also taught. Her work merged the fields of labor and women's history, and, as an expert witness, she testified in the *Equal Opportunity Employment Commission v. Sears Roebuck and Company* case tried before U.S. District Court in 1978. She consulted on *Notable American Women: The Modern Period*. Kessler-Harris was the author of *Women Have Always Worked*, 1980; *Out to Work: A History of Wage-Earning Women in the U.S.*, 1982; and *A Woman's Wage: Historical Meanings and Social Consequences*, 1990.

- Professor emeritus at Boston University, Aileen Kraditor earned her advanced degrees from Columbia University. She was author of *The Ideas of the Woman Suffrage Movement, 1890–1920*, 1965 and 1981.

- With advanced degrees from Harvard and teaching experience at Cornell, Mary Beth Norton credited her interest in women's history to the feminist movement. She was the co-editor of *Women of America: A History*, 1979, and *To Toil the Livelong Day: America's Women at Work, 1790–1980*, 1987. She was the author of *Major Problems in American Women's History*, 1989; and *Liberty's Daughters: The Revolutionary Experience of American Women, 1750–1800*, the winner of the Berkshire Prize in 1981.

- Vicki L. Ruiz was the author of *Cannery Women, Cannery Lives*, 1987; co-editor of *Western Women: Their Land, Their Lives*, 1988; and co-editor of *Unequal Sisters: A Multicultural Reader in U.S. Women's History*, 1994. Currently working at Arizona State University in Tempe, Ruiz earned her degrees from Florida State University and Stanford University.

- Anne Firor Scott, one of the first historians of American women, is a professor emeritus at Duke University. As the only girl in her family, Scott never learned that as a woman she might have limited opportunities, and the idea never occurred to her until one of her University of Georgia professors suggested it. She served on the advisory board to *Notable American Women: The Modern Period*; edited *Jane Addams: Democracy and Social Ethics*, 1964; and *One-Half the People*, 1976; and wrote *The Southern Lady*, 1970; *The American Woman: Who Was She?*, 1970; and *Women in American Life*, 1970.

- Currently serving as the first woman invited to join the Institute for Advanced Studies at Princeton University, which was founded by Albert Einstein, Joan Wallach Scott earned her degree from the University of Wisconsin. Known for employing the postmodern theory of Michel Foucault, Scott analyzed relationships in her books *Women, Work, and Family*, 1978; and *Gender and the Politics of History*, 1988.

- Kathryn Kish Sklar received a National Book Award nomination in 1974 for *Catharine Beecher: A Study of American Domesticity*, which also collected the Berkshire Conference of Women Historians annual prize. She was the editor of *The Writings of Harriet Beecher Stowe*, 1981; *Notes of Sixty Years; The Autobiography of Florence Kelley, 1859–1926*, 1985; and a co-editor and contributor to *Women and Power in American History*, 1990; and *U.S. History as Women's History*, 1995. With degrees from the University of Michigan, Sklar has served as professor at the State University of New York, Binghamton (*Contemporary Authors* 1998; Scanlon and Cosner 1996).

After Gerda Lerner, these men and women were the first generation of modern women's historians, researching to open the field and creating courses and departments within colleges and universities. They mentored the second generation of women's historians, now coming to fruition.

Even with the body of research now available, the historic record of women was not complete; however, by the middle of the 1990s, a number of writers were comfortable using the historical record to create chronologies and time lines, something that had not been attempted before. While providing a start, these books will continue to be appended and expanded as new people and events are uncovered. For now, they show the maturity of the field with their wealth of dates, people, places, and events. The time lines began in 1987 with Judith Freemen Clark's *Almanac of American Women in the Twentieth Century*, but its scope was more limited than those that would come after. *The Women's Chronology: A Year-by-Year Record, from Prehistory to the Present* by James Trager was published in 1994, as well as *Chronology of Women's History* by Kirstin Olsen. Trager's effort took the more standard year-by-year approach, whereas Olsen's used five-year intervals. These books were joined in 1996 by *Timelines of American Women's History* by Sue Heinemann, and *The Timetables of Women's History: A Chronology of the Most Important People and Events in Women's History* by Karen Greenspan. The latter was part of a series of Timetables books published by Simon and Schuster. Several others followed these, so that, by the end of the decade, scholarship had gone beyond the straight chronology with the publication of *The Readers' Companion to U.S. Women's History*, edited by Wilma Mankiller, Gwendolyn Mink, Marysa Navarro, Barbara Smith, and Gloria Steinem, in 1998. Rather than taking the chronological approach, or listing people and events, the editors compiled an alphabetical list of topics important to women's history; they focused on cultural diversity, giving each article broad perspectives. The book was unique in this regard, and thus created a new model in writing.

The chronologies of women's history were not being developed in isolation. During the same period, time lines of achievement were written for all major cultural groups of the United States. *Native Time: A Historical Time Line of Native America* by Lee Frances was published in 1998, following *Timelines of Native American History* by Carl Waldman in 1994 and *Timetables of Native American History* by Susan Hazen-Hammond in 1997. The *Hispanic American Chronology* by Nicolas Kanellos was published in 1995. *Asian American Chronology* by Deborah G. Baron and Susan B. Gall came out in 1996. African Americans were represented in *Black Women in America,* edited by Darlene Clark Hine, Elsa Barkley Brown, and Rosalyn Terborg-Penn in 1993; *Timelines of African-American History* by Tom Cowan in 1994; and *African American Almanac: Day-by-Day Black History* by Kenneth A. Mimms and Leon Thomas Ross in 1997.

American women's history began with the stories of Native American women and the journals of women immigrating to this country, and it continues today. The development of the field into a respected discipline at the end of the twentieth century came about because of men and women who collected, wrote, researched, and reinterpreted. By virtue of the offerings of generations of interested people, women are now recognized for their part in history and can never again be ignored. Because all manner of people have written on the subject for a variety of reasons, this brief historiography cannot include all those who have made contributions. Many scholars have worked at creating theory and at strengthening the field to ensure a good record. The distinguished contributions of the first generations of women's historians demands that the next generation continue to uncover new material and reinterpret the historical record in a way that includes all people.

References

Appleby, Joyce, Lynn Hunt, and Margaret Jacob. 1994. *Telling the Truth About History*. New York: W. W. Norton.

Banner, Lois W. 1980. *Elizabeth Cady Stanton: A Radical for Woman's Rights*. Library of American Biography, ed. Oscar Handlin. N.p.: HarperCollins.

Beard, Mary R. 1946. *Woman as a Force in History: A Study in Traditions and Realities*. New York: Macmillan.

Breaking Boundaries!: The Eleventh Berkshire Conference on the History of Women. 1998. URL: http://www-berks.aas.duke.edu/index.html.

Chicago, Judy. 1996. *The Dinner Party*. New York: Penguin.

Contemporary Authors. 1998. URL: http://www.gale.com/gale/company.html.

Cullen-DuPont, Kathryn. 1996. *The Encyclopedia of Women's History in America*. New York: Da Capo.

Flexner, Eleanor. 1959. *Century of Struggle: The Woman's Rights Movement in the United States*. Cambridge: Belknap Press of Harvard University Press.

Friedan, Betty. 1983. *The Feminine Mystique*. Reprint, with a new introduction and epilogue by the author. New York: Dell.

Hartman, Mary S., and Lois Banner, eds. 1974. *Clio's Consciousness Raised: New Perspectives on the History of Women*. New York: Harper Colophon.

Jacobs, Harriet. 1988. *Incidents in the Life of a Slave Girl*. Edited by Lydia Maria Child with an introduction by Howard Dobson. New York: Oxford University Press.

James, Edward T., Janet Wilson James, and Paul S. Boyer, eds. 1971. *Notable American Women, 1607–1950: A Biographical Dictionary*. 3 vols. Cambridge: Belknap Press of Harvard University Press.

Karcher, Carolyn L. 1994. *The First Woman in the Republic: A Cultural Biography of Lydia Maria Child*. Durham, NC: Duke University Press.

Keenan, Sheila. 1996. *Scholastic Encyclopedia of Women in the United States*. New York: Scholastic Reference.

Kerber, Linda K., Alice Kessler-Harris, and Kathryn Kish Sklar, eds. 1995. *U.S. History as Women's History: New Feminist Essays*. Chapel Hill: University of North Carolina Press.

Lerner, Gerda. 1979. *The Majority Finds Its Past: Placing Women in History*. Oxford: Oxford University Press.

———. 1981. *Teaching Women's History*. Washington, DC: American Historical Association.

Mankiller, Wilma, et al., eds. 1998. *The Reader's Companion to U.S. Women's History*. Boston: Houghton Mifflin.

McIntosh, Peggy. 1981. "The Study of Women: Implications for Reconstructing the Liberal Arts Disciplines." *The Forum for Liberal Education* 4, no. 1 (October): 1–3.

McLure, Gail Thomas, and John W. McLure. 1977. *Women's Studies*. Washington, DC: National Education Association.

National Women's History Project. 1998. URL: http://www.nwhp.org/.

Norton, Mary Beth. 1980. *Liberty's Daughters: The Revolutionary Experience of American Women, 1750–1800.* Ithaca, NY: Cornell University Press.

"*Notable American Women* Vol. 5." 1998. *Women's History Network News* (July): 5.

Scanlon, Jennifer, and Shaaron Cosner. 1996. *American Women Historians, 1700s–1990s: A Biographical Dictionary.* Westport, CT: Greenwood.

Schmidt, Dolores Barracano, and Earl Robert Schmidt. 1976. "The Invisible Woman: The Historian as Professional Magician." In *Liberating Women's History: Theoretical and Critical Essays,* edited by Berenice A. Carroll. Urbana: University of Illinois Press.

Scott, Joan Wallach. 1988. *Gender and the Politics of History.* New York: Columbia University Press.

Sherr, Lynn. 1995. *Failure Is Impossible: Susan B. Anthony in Her Own Words.* New York: Times.

Sicherman, Barbara, et al., eds. 1980. *Notable American Woman, the Modern Period: A Biographical Dictionary.* Cambridge: Belknap Press of Harvard University Press.

Smith, Bonnie G. 1998. *The Gender of History: Men, Women, and Historical Practice.* Cambridge: Harvard University Press.

Wagner, Sally Roesch. 1996. *The Untold Story of the Iroquois Influence on Early Feminists.* Aberdeen, SD: Sky Carrier.

Warren, Mercy Otis. 1989. *History of the Rise, Progress and Termination of the American Revolution, Interspersed with Biographical, Political and Moral Observations.* 2 vols. Edited by Lester H. Cohen. Indianapolis: Liberty Fund.

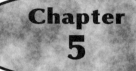

Chapter
5

Women's History
Theory and
Methodology

Theory concerning women's history was not developed until the later half of the twentieth century. Mary Ritter Beard (1946), an early women's historian writing in the late 1940s, believed that women were a "force" in history. She did not believe in portraying women as an oppressed minority, the model up until that time. In the late 1960s, Gerda Lerner added her own ideas to Beard's and developed women's history into an academic discipline. As she led the way in creating theory, she was joined by many other historians so that at the turn of the century the subject has become fully formed; however, as with any academic discipline, it will continue to grow and change. As a maturing discipline, a number of issues specific to women's history were identified for research. Women's history made historical scholarship more complex, especially in attempting to write a comprehensive history of the United States. One of the most consuming questions was how best to fit women's history into the already existing and fully formed field of history. Bringing this new topic into long-established educational institutions posed dilemmas. The struggle to establish itself continued even as teaching methodology that best fit the subject area was developed. There were no easy answers, and what has been done may be replaced with newer models and methods in the future.

Overview of Historical Theory

History went through stages of development over the last 300 years because each age has looked at the past according to its own values and beliefs. Historical theory was first formed during the Enlightenment in the eighteenth century, when the rise of modern science influenced history to develop disciplined methods. At the extreme, historians became scientists searching for repeating patterns in human development. Before this time, history was dominated by fifteen centuries of Christian tradition that infused all accounts with religious dogma. During the Enlightenment, the sciences turned away from God as the center of reason (Appleby, Hunt, and Jacob 1994).

When Europeans came to North America on a quest of discovery, they were fueled by a tradition of intellect and the idea that history was linear. They brought with them patriarchal culture and conviction of one reality and universal knowledge. This tradition continued into the eighteenth century, when interest in broad overview, comparative study, and critical examination of authentic documents furthered history. Government, politics, religion, economics, military matters, and other such concerns chiefly affecting white males were the basis of history. In the New World and elsewhere, history was fueled by nationalism, which kept it focused on the affairs of state (Mankiller et al. 1998).

In the nineteenth century, history was influenced by Leopold von Ranke, a German historian who believed in the use of primary sources and objectivity. Believing absolute truth could be defined by careful research, Ranke originated the seminar method, bringing a group of students together to examine material in a thoughtful way. Historical study moved to the university setting, a male bastion. Highly respected, Ranke became the first honorary member of the American Historical Association when it was founded in 1884 (Smith 1998). History took on a cause-and-effect association, keeping its focus narrow.

In the twentieth century, other views of history came to the forefront. The absolutism of earlier eras gave way to relativism, the idea that history was a creation of time and place influenced by a person's own perceptions. From 1890 until World War II, history pulled apart. Ranke's topics and sources were now considered too limited. Although some historians still believed in excessive documentation based on scientific standards, it was a time of questioning and revision, leading to the birth of modernism (Smith 1998). American modernism was based on the disciplines of sociology and political science and derived from the eighteenth-century belief that reason and science overcame scripture, tradition, and custom. Modernism encompassed universally applicable scientific method, emphasizing free thinking and acting individuals, class struggle, and broad demographic change (Appleby, Hunt, and Jacob 1994).

Frederick Jackson Turner and other historians of the nineteenth century championed a closer relationship between the social sciences and history, but, as nationalism prevailed, this relationship did not develop until after World War II. Charles and Mary Beard, progressives of the 1930s and 1940s, were the first to drop the patriotic focus and write history that included many types of groups. As nationalism faded, it opened the door for the inclusion of women in the historic record (Appleby, Hunt, and Jacob 1994; Mankiller et al. 1998). History was supposed to be about universal truth, not about a particular group of people. Nonetheless, throughout nearly all of American history, issues of class, gender, and race have influenced politics and led to the development in the twentieth century of the mass movements of socialism, feminism, and civil rights (Smith 1998). These pressures mandated that history be more inclusive.

The theories of Karl Marx were another influence that changed the way history was conceived in the twentieth century. By applying class struggle as a framework for inquiry, Marx created a way to reinterpret history. Friedrich Engels expressed Marxist views in his theories on women and families as a class oppressed by husbands in his 1884 book, *The Origin of the Family, Private Property and the State*. Engels established the social character of woman's relation to man. The changes in that relation of concern to him were the transition to patriarchy during the movement from the kin-based society to modern civilization, and the overthrow of patriarchy coming with the advent of socialism. Engels analyzed women's subordination in relation to private property and in relation to the inequality of classes. Marxism proved useful to women's historians as another vehicle for the inclusion of women's experience in the historical record (Kelly 1984; Mankiller et al. 1998; Scott 1988).

The discipline of women's history was formed in the 1960s at the same time postmodernist French historians Michel Foucault and Jacques Derrida began to look at the discontinuities of history and question the idea of historical truth. They felt there were no absolutely authoritative historical accounts, and it was, therefore, impossible to attach universal meaning to historical categories or the relationships among historical classifications. Foucault tried to reexamine knowledge based on associations of power between individuals and groups, using as many pieces of evidence as possible. Derrida developed a method of reading termed *deconstruction;* he believed that a text withheld as much information as it presented. Postmodernism, just like Marxism, paved the way for the study of women's history in a number of ways. First, it allowed for the examination of the kinds of documents that would include women's experience. Second, it introduced the concept of power as a framework for questioning history. Third, it allowed for discussion of peoples other than those who had been the main historical focus. Both postmodernism and Marxism proved useful to the discipline (Appleby, Hunt, and Jacob 1994; Harris and McNamera 1984; Scott 1988).

Adding to the new ways of looking at history were the methodologies of anthropologists and sociologists. Ethno-historians began to look at the meaning and intent of actions, an idea that supported the development of women's history; however, by placing women in a social context, the entire outline of history had to be reconceptualized in a more inclusive way (Harris and McNamera 1984). The growth of social history after World War II reflected the backgrounds and interests of those entering higher education, women, people of color, and descendants of immigrants. Social historians hoped to fill out the established record by showing how limited it had been, but they were criticized for being less objective and ignoring traditional values (Appleby, Hunt, and Jacob 1994). Gradually, a more interdisciplinary and multicultural approach to history allowed for a broader view of the changes in civilization. The experiences of women and ethnic groups were recognized as influences on the historical record, and multicultural women's history was seen as the only way to allow many voices and experiences to be heard. Family history gained importance in uncovering hidden, often ignored, stories of groups outside the power structure (Mankiller et al. 1998; Melosh 1993).

History stands at a crossroads at the beginning of the new millennium. Postmodernism, multiculturalism, and social history are thought to be extreme theories, unlikely to endure. Their counterparts, relativism and traditionalism, will also fade as new historical theories predominate. The hope for the future is in pragmatism and practical realism, with their commitment to a knowable world, belief in provisional knowledge, and advancement of criticism and debate (Appleby, Hunt, and Jacob 1994). Although the fading theories have been a boon to women's history, the discipline should be secure enough to move forward even when interpreted in new ways.

The constantly evolving field of history has no end, nor can historians predict what will interest future generations, nor what new kinds of history will be created. New questions, techniques, and interests are applied to new information. History can be told in many ways, and the interests of different peoples, in different times, changes how the story is interpreted (Bailyn 1994). There will always be history, but whose history and how it is presented will depend, as it always has, on the dominant culture at any given time.

Theories of Women's History

Women's history evolved within the mutable theories of the larger discipline of history, while at the same time being shaped by changing conceptualization within its narrower field. Historian Joan Kelly (1984) identified two goals for the practice: to restore women to history and to restore history to women. Although these goals were laudable, historians still had to develop ways of accomplishing them. When Lerner (1979) began seriously to investigate women's history in the late 1960s, she believed there was no conceptual framework to the discipline. As she saw it, first-generation feminists, those with a political agenda to improve and expand the rights of women, had been the ones to write about women's history. They accomplished this chiefly by collecting biographies and adding up women's contributions. Lerner felt their writing ignored anyone who did not fit into the mold of the progressive nineteenth-century woman, creating a history built on social class that excluded antifeminists, women of color, and the working poor. Early writing tended to focus on a certain subject: first on women as an oppressed group and later exclusively on suffrage. Lerner believed that women's history should emphasize the total female experience, unjudged by male standards. With no competent way to deal with women historically, writing about them was both hindered and limited.

Models of historical writing were inadequate in recording women's history. Literature on women had primarily been squeezed into four small categories: biographies, organizational histories, how-to books, and social histories. These writings were problematic and did not present a complete picture. Biographies tended to fall into the trap of the psychoanalytic model, influenced by Sigmund Freud, where women were examined in relation to their traditional roles as wives and mothers. Histories of women in organizations fell into the contribution model, defining what society had gained from women's involvement. The how-to books, on marriage, child rearing, etiquette, or conduct of life, were aimed at dictating how women should live. Finally, social histories, where women were analyzed in relation to a specific topic or period, failed to give a full picture. All of these writings tended to look at women in restricted ways. Another tendency in writing women's history was to analyze the narrative from the view of external forces, those outside women's sphere of influence. This proclivity sent the message that the subject was not important enough to investigate in its own right (Gordon, Buhle, and Dye 1976, 75–92).

Still another limited model for looking at women, the Victorian cult of domesticity, was popular for a time. In the early work of women's history, it was assumed there was one universal experience. Although the first generation feminists saw gender as the principle factor of oppression of women in the institutions of medicine, education, religion, and government, exclusion from these fields correlated to inclusion in another sphere, domesticity. For a time, women's sphere and female oppression became a women's history paradigm; it promoted the concept of women's officiating in the areas of home, worship, children, schooling, charity, moral reform, temperance, abolition, and suffrage. Among the historians who discovered and expressed the cult of domesticity were Barbara Welter, in *Dimity Convictions: American Woman in the Nineteenth Century*, 1977; Nancy Cott, in *The Bonds of Womanhood: "Woman's Sphere" in New England, 1780–1835*, 1977 and 1997; and Carroll Smith-Rosenberg, in *Disorderly Conduct: Visions of Victorian America*, 1985 (Hewitt 1990, 1–14). The view was inadequate, for it most commonly represented the experience of northern white women, excluding all others. Neither Beard nor Lerner favored the model of oppression, and research on African American women and the rise of multiculturalism proved there never was a universal female experience. Domesticity, although well documented, was too narrow in its focus to be useful to women's history.

Women's sphere had far-ranging significance and became the basis of another theory to capture women's experience where women's situation was limited to production, sexuality, reproduction, and the socialization of children, which was even more limiting than the cult of domesticity. Societal change for women could be brought about only by a change in all four situations, for a change in only one area would be offset by a reaction in another (Mitchell 1976, 385–394). In this model, where change must occur in all four domains, it would seem logical that women's situation could only improve during times of great social upheaval. Only during times of unrest would there be enough momentum in society to affect every area. There is some support for this theory among those who postulate that the greatest advances for women have come during the wars and periods of multiple reform movements such as the Progressive era and the 1960s. Still, limiting theories cannot encompass all the experiences of women over 400 years of American history.

In the 1970s, historian William H. Chafe (1977) used social theory to look at women's experience based on two types of group behavior. Aggregate behavior was defined as unplanned activities based on gender, such as comforting the grieving or taking food to sick friends. Collective behavior consisted of activities based on group self-awareness, where women came together consciously for a purpose, such as rallying for peace. Stages in each type of group behavior could be compared, and Chafe suggested a way of analyzing the continuum: the definition of women as a group in relation to other groups, the level of collective self-awareness of women, the dominate culture's definition of women's sphere, the roles women assume in relation to the normative culture, and the outside conditions that reinforce change in society. Chafe's method, although helpful in framing questions, was probably more useful in sociological fields than in history. Group theory never seriously influenced the study of women's history.

The early theories applied to women's history were too narrow. There seemed to be no framework that was inclusive of all women until the multicultural approach came into the field. Multiculturalism reversed narrower regional tendencies. Writing about the Northeast focused on white women, whereas writing of the Southeast had a more biracial flavor. In both regions, emphasis rested on relationships of power between such groups of women as slaves and mistresses or immigrants and social workers. Multicultural writing was closer to Western writing, where immigration came from many directions: east, west, and south (DuBois and Ruiz 1990); not only did it include the voices of all women by giving them an audience and honoring every experience, it was the most promising framework for examining the varied experiences of women.

Although many early theories were discarded, women's history still had limited approaches and a number of unresolved issues. Lerner (1979) believed many conceptual frameworks would be needed over time in building the field. Drawing on only a third of a century of growth, women's history was still in a developmental phase, and history, in general, continued to grow and change according to new ways of looking at the past. In its short rise, women's history moved from the exclusionary to the inclusive, from a narrow focus to a broader one. Of the several frameworks that failed, only two remained under serious consideration: Lerner's original concept of women's history as the stories of female experience unjudged by patriarchal standards and the model of multiculturalism.

Issues in Women's History

As the discipline of women's history and the various theories surrounding it developed, a number of issues, typical of any new discipline, arose. These issues surrounded how to define women, how to find sources to document fully women's involvement, how to fit women into standard chronological historical periods, and how to integrate women's history into general history. These questions centered on how women's history should be treated as a discipline if, indeed, it could be treated as a discipline at all. Constantly evolving speculation and concepts developed around each issue. It is worth mentioning that each of these topics was identified by Lerner, although others have discussed them, too.

Defining Women

The first issue in women's history asked how women should be defined. What sort of group were they? What definition benefited them? A number of interpretations, including biological, minority, legal, and social, could be given. Certainly, one of the most defining characteristics of women was their physiology. Biological differences decreed that sex be used as a division in society, for only one sex bore children. Sexual characteristics made women highly visible within society in much the same way as it made people of color visible. Carl N. Degler (1975), who was involved in formalizing women's history theory, tried to define women through their unique life cycles by using such categories as "dies before adulthood," "unmarried adult," "married with no children," "widowed with children," etc. In Lerner's 1976 book, *The Female Experience: An American Documentary*, she used life stages as a way of placing women in history, organizing the content around the biological rites of passage. The biological definition of women, although keenly important, did not give the entire picture.

Whether or not women could be considered a minority was another question frequently asked in trying to define them. As Lerner (1979) explained, women were not a minority, for statistically they were the majority of the population; however, they were treated as a minority group. Beyond their sexual definition, their majority status was their other most defining characteristic. Degler (1975) believed that if one used the sociological definition—a minority as a group lacking power—then certainly women fit the definition, and he held women's history to be a form of minority history. The minority issue was confused when census counts were mixed with discussions of treatment within society.

If women were treated as a minority group in society, their legal status was called into question. During almost three quarters of American history, women were one legal entity with their husbands within the institution of marriage as based on the Blackstone Commentaries, English common law that formed the basis of the legal system in the United States. Women's interests were seen as the same as their husbands, or, more broadly, as the same as men's. Although women held a plurality, the patriarchal nature of society never allowed them a position of power. Women were missing from history because historians were men, and men simply overlooked women. History was defined by those aspects of human culture in which men were active: war, politics, and business. Because much of the history of women was interpreted through such external measures as class and economics, women were forced to become the objects of history rather than the subjects (Gordon, Buhle, and Dye 1976, 75–92). It was only in the twentieth century, when women gained more legal rights, that their history began to be uncovered and reported.

Although feminists were intensely interested in women's legal definition, they attempted to define women more socially, as a collective group, because their energy came from organizing in this way. The search to understand their aggregate condition helped them to identify strengths, social importance, and forms of unity throughout history. By identifying themselves as a group, women in the nineteenth century were able to organize around their common feelings, to promote the agendas they believed important, and to create their own history (Gordon, Buhle, and Dye 1976, 75–92). Women felt the power of group organization, but they also acted as individuals in effecting social change (Johansson 1976, 400–430). Group behavior was too limiting a definition for women in the same way that Chafe's attempt at using the sociological model of group behavior was too restrictive as an encompassing theory for women's history.

The cultural role of women was still not clear among the competing definitions. Beyond the biological, minority, legal, and group definitions, there was another way to view women according to their societal positions, past and present. Females were scattered throughout the population, occurring in every other subgroup. They shared in the values of the groups they belonged to, but their experience as women was unique. They come together to act according to special interests, but they were frequently divided by class, race, religion, or other criteria, and they were divided within themselves like no other group. Historically, women were considered subordinate to men, but white women were not subordinate in the same way as other racial or ethnic groups. Although white women had no great power, they were always part of the ruling elite or close to sources of power by virtue of kinship or other relationships. Women were often most closely tied to members of the opposite sex. Some women were exploited, but they were also exploiters, especially of other women. They were dissatisfied with the opportunities available to them, yet they resisted change to their situation. Women were unique in that they moved among many roles within family and society, whereas men were more focused on their economic role (Lerner 1979; 1981). In all ways, women's societal role was full of contradictions.

Women were a group with a unique past and a singular position in society. Among all the ways of defining them, the two characteristics remaining the most stable were their physiological differences and their majority status. The past 100 years was proof that legal status and cultural roles change over time, and women's contradictory cultural role must be examined in relation to thousands of years of patriarchal influence, not just hundreds of years of history in the United States. Because the present affects what of the past is seen as important, history is constantly being reinterpreted (Smith 1976, 368-384), and the definition of women will continuously be molded by the shifting interests of society.

Documenting Women's Experience Through Sources

A second issue for women's history was sources. Many felt women's history could not be developed as a full discipline because documentary sources did not exist; but as the growth in publishing on the topic since the 1970s attests, this is not true. Although for a number of reasons women were more difficult to uncover, with every passing year it becomes less of an issue. In fact, documentation should no longer be considered an issue in women's history.

Before women's property laws were passed in the late nineteenth century, it was hard to find legal records on women. Within the institution of marriage, women had no rights to personal property, could not make a will, and could not be sued. Legal actions concerning women were transacted under their husbands' or fathers' names; thus women were invisible under law. Other sources on women were available in local histories, letters, diaries, records of organizations, magazines, labor files, and government archives. Family documents were also important because families preserved what they felt was significant (Smith 1976, 368–384). After the Civil War and the Great Depression, oral histories proved to be another important way to maintain history. While some of these sources had been considered low or unworthy in the past, the advent of social history as a way of adding to the historical record dissolved some of the prejudice.

The National Archives and Record Administration for the federal government was founded in 1935. Major women's archives, based on the papers of suffrage leaders, were established in the 1940s, but to prove the existence of sources, a survey of women's history repositories was conducted in 1979 with funding from the National Endowment for the Humanities. Known as the Women's History Source Survey, over 3,500 repositories for archival material were located; however, researching women was difficult because many documents were not cataloged in a way that made women accessible. Subject headings and other access points often failed to include women as a topic, and some material was lost in broader subject areas (Lerner 1979; 1981). The advent of searching on computers and the digitization of archival material have made women much more accessible both through faster access to sources and through availability of rare material to more people. Although the archival survey helped to locate records, research for women was still more time-consuming.

So much material has been uncovered that women's history can never be called a fad (McIntosh 1981, 3), nor is it ever likely to disappear. Females were hidden behind their husbands in a cultural view that said they were unimportant. Although their history was buried, it was preserved for those who asked the right questions and conducted thorough searches. As awareness of women's history grew, accessibility was made easier, and convenience in research will likely increase with new developments in computer technology.

Historical Periods

Historical periodization was a third issue for women's history. Lerner asserted that the story of women in history could not be told through the standard method of dividing history into time periods. She broke ground in her 1976 book, *The Female Experience: An American Documentary,* by dividing the material according to women's life stages and other topics of importance to women. Lerner felt developmental turning points were not the same for women as for men. Whereas rights of passage for men might occur in the voting booth or in military service, evolutionary stages for women focused on reproduction and child raising. Because the passage points for women centered around mortality, developments in medicine and health defined changes in their life conditions more than developments in politics and the affairs of state. Women, as the center of the home and as child bearers, were ageless and not linked to time in conventional ways. Historians wanted to write history with a beginning and an end, but the timeless quality of women's lives confused historians. There was no place for women in conventional historical writing.

Lerner was not the only historian thinking about the question of historical periods. David Potter's 1962 essay, "National Character," was the first to focus on how historical events did not weigh equally on men and women by using Frederick Jackson Turner's frontier thesis as an example. Where the opening of the West was seen as a time of great opportunity for men, the same was not true for women. The frontier was a place of restricted roles for women; however, after the closing of the frontier, the rise of cities was a time of advancement for women, with more jobs, positions, and appointments becoming available (Degler 1981).

Another attempt to reorganize history to focus on the feminine was shaped by Kelly (1984), who believed that turning points in history did not influence both sexes equally and that periods were measured according to male standards. In a panel discussion entitled "The Effects of Women's History upon Traditional Historiography" given at the second Berkshire Conference on the History of Women at Radcliffe College in October 1974, Kelly attributed the idea of creating cycles around female life events to Richard Vann. Kelly hoped that periodization would become relational, maintaining the story of changes in major social structure while adding an evaluation of how these changes affected women. The relationships between the sexes, or other groups in society, would become the focus.

Degler (1975) also saw historical periodization as an issue, deliberating on the topic in his speech *"Is There a History of Women?"* He felt that wars were a time of opportunity for women, both economically and socially, for when the social structure was torn apart, advantages could be gained. The opposite was also true: When male opportunity advanced, women withdrew into the background. Degler saw women at the forefront of a number of issues, including temperance, peace, and the abolition of slavery. These issues tended to belong to the sex, with much lower participation by men.

Differences for women and men were confirmed in other areas of historical advancement. The growth of industry and the professions was damaging to women, forcing those who had enjoyed a measure of independence in family management to become economically dependent on others. Instead of making items in the home, women were constrained into consumer roles. In medicine, women were removed from traditional healing roles, restricting their sphere of influence as they became consumers rather than practitioners (Smith 1976, 368–384). Another example was protective legislation, passed in the best interest of women, during the period of industrialization. Special welfare and work legislation may have been partly responsible for the defeat of the Equal Rights Amendment in 1982 by giving the lasting impression that women needed safety nets in these environments (Degler 1981). The need for female protection lingers today, restricting women from full combat participation within the military.

Although periodization was troubling where it concerned women's history, the discipline had not yet advanced to a place where historical periods specific to women could be identified. Lerner's attempt in *The Female Experience* was not wholly successful, for its divisions by life stages read more like a sociological text than a history. Female periodization will require further research and reevaluation of the past, and women's periods may never become a reality, for they would signify a paradigm shift from male-centered to female-centered culture. A more likely development would be the compilation of women's history textbooks, like Beard's (1946) attempts. Women's history periodization, an interesting theme, will continue to intrigue historians.

Integration of Women's History

As a new discipline, women's history must establish a place for itself within the canon of history. The question of whether it should exist as separate course work or be integrated into the canon creates a fourth issue for the discipline. The ideal is for women's history to be completely integrated, a history for everyone, but changes are necessary for this to happen. As more is known about women's history, traditional history has changed to accommodate it. The changes have been developmental, passing through a number of stages. Lerner (1979) articulates four steps to the integration of women's history. In the beginning, women of achievement are identified and added to history as a form of compensation. This stage dwells on personality and fails to take into account women of different classes. Later, the contributions of women are identified, but are judged by the standards of men: what men think women should be. Fitting women into a traditional framework is the object of this stage. Then, women's experience is examined by moving from a male-oriented to a female-oriented outlook, the current stage for most historians. Lerner did not feel this was a good stopping place because women's history must move to a new paradigm, where it is synthesized into all of history. This transformation is the ultimate goal, but it cannot be carried out through the discipline of history alone; it must be interdisciplinary.

Even though there is a continuum for the integration of women's history, patriarchal bias remains a barrier to the integration of women's history. Invisible cultural bias keeps women's history from being seen as important and from being brought into the established historical canon. For synthesis to occur, new standards must be applied which do not judge women on the same scale as men but take into account the social place of each sex in each time period. Generally, historians are unaware of the patriarchal biases in every part of the value system, culture, and language (Lerner 1979). Cultural proclivities are so pervasive that they are transparent or are considered the norm. These attitudes create a barrier to the study of women in history and must be brought into the open and discussed (Johansson 1976, 400–430). Awareness of cultural bias and development of new standards for an inclusive curriculum will advance the integration of women's history.

Other questions slow the synthesis of women's history. Women's history still has a political agenda that keeps it from becoming a natural part of the general history; indeed, a true feminist history might be used as an argument for female advantages (Bailyn 1994). Still, some feminists support women's history as a separate program in the belief that integrated history is certain to be male-dominated. With such widespread disagreement, others (Melosh 1993) question whether integration can ever be achieved. Women's history may be only transitional, a stage in the process of a completely integrated history belonging to some different future culture where sex roles are not as disparate. There is fear that once synthesis occurs, history may be back where it was in the beginning. The past will be viewed through the value system of the dominant culture, and the entire transformation will have been an exercise in futility in its return to the status quo (Searing 1984, 239–252). Women's history has not reached the synthesis stage, and the possibility of a history inclusive of all people is for the future to decide.

Pedagogy of Women's History

Women's history has developed its own teaching methods, including setting up the course work to be more inclusive and student-oriented. Bringing the subject matter into educational institutions has been helped by several recent trends in education. Enough research has been done, especially on gender studies programs, to yield excellent suggestions on how to integrate women's history.

Institutional Integration

Bringing a new discipline into educational institutions is always a challenge because some schools are open to expanding curricula, whereas some resist change. It is reasonable to assume, given the continuing patriarchal nature of society, that women's history will not be taught without some outside insistence. Educational reform to include women's history takes organization and leadership, but, given the current student body, it is obligatory. Half of all students are females, disengaged by a curriculum that focuses on male achievement in such areas as politics and war. Students of color also fail to see themselves reflected in history, literature, or other content. Revised curricula would better prepare all students for today's world. Most school programs were devised to educate Western white, male leaders in a time of Western dominance and economic expansion, a model that no longer exists (McIntosh 1981, 3). There are various models of school reform that outline processes for institutional integration. Although the benefits of a more inclusive curriculum are clear, the roadblocks to the inclusion of women's history should be examined; however enough is known about the processes and pitfalls to make integration smoother.

New scholarship affects educational institutions by changing content and by changing methodologies. When adding women's history, as with any reform effort, schools need to rethink what it is students should know about the history, literature, and social organization of the United States. In reflecting on new content, teachers must analyze their own prejudices and assumptions about scholarship and about their classrooms; and, if necessary, they should be willing to change. Colleagues within institutions can evaluate each other and make positive suggestions for improvement. Administrative support, leadership, and faculty development are all necessary in establishing institutional change (Butler and Walter 1991).

There are several models for educational change. One reform strategy is the top-down model, in which change is mandated from above. Another, the piggy-back model, hinges reform to another effort in the institution. Thus, women's history could be initiated along with other interdisciplinary courses. Finally, there is bottom-up reform, where students or teachers rally for curriculum change (Schmitz 1985).

Using any model of reform, integration of women's history may be hampered by a number of issues. First, some educators believe that history is boring and have no interest in participating in reform efforts. They may be unfamiliar with multicultural women's history and feel threatened by the new content. Second, history is complex and open to interpretation; theory surrounding women's history is in a developmental stage and cannot be outlined in concrete terms, leaving its merit open to debate. Finally, the feeling exists that the advancement of women's history brings with it anti-male bias (*Woman's Place* 1994), and opposition may organize around this idea. Any of these roadblocks can hamper efforts to include women's history in an educational institution.

Whenever a major change comes to an institution, certain steps will help to alleviate resistance. A major component is the planning process, which includes many steps and contacts. Most important, administrative support is necessary, for no program will come to fruition without it. It should be sought early and reestablished often. Leaders for the project should be identified, and they should form a consensus on the short-term goals for integration, remembering that small steps are better than large measures. Meanwhile, a network of people interested in women's history should be developed, and the awareness and knowledge of the faculty towards the subject should be gauged while students are made aware of the new program. It is important that assumptions not be made and that real data be obtained concerning the interest and support of constituent groups. The entire educational climate within the institution should be assessed to assure that no underlying political issues could undermine the reform effort. The new program should be made as visible as possible while new resources are purchased or developed. It is important not to rush the planning phase, for doing this could cause mistakes that might not be overcome later (Schmitz 1985).

When educational reform is carried out, faculty development programs are a key component. Any staff development program should be challenging to the faculty, setting clear expectations as to their level of participation and involvement. Follow-up activities should be specified to ensure high-quality integration activities; communication with all participants after staff development takes place will help further the goals of the project (Schmitz 1985). Integration programs, based on the model above, or on any other model, can help to assure that students receive a more realistic picture of the past.

Although women's history has made tremendous inroads and has grown steadily in the last quarter century, it is evident that most students are not exposed to it in school because it has not yet become a part of public education. Where it is taught in secondary schools, it is often dependent either on one person or on a small group of faculty members who have an interest in the topic and who have introduced and promoted it (Kaub 1984, 165–179). Because of this, women's history courses reflect the peculiarities of the institutions or personalities that created them.

Even with its exceptional scholarship, women's history may be dismissed as separatist; that is, centering on sex and family rather than on politics and economics, and, therefore, not influencing the understanding of important events (Scott 1988). Although textbooks now include more women, rarely does one include a truly balanced treatment, and subtle forms of bias still exist even though social studies curriculum has shifted away from political history towards social history (*AAUW* 1992). The growth of scholarship and publishers' interest in inclusion are promising trends for the future. Established educational patterns cannot be changed without an effort to confront bias where it occurs and to extend content through integration efforts.

Institutional integration is challenging, requiring leadership and continuing efforts to ensure success. Students, teachers, and administrators must all be involved, and a systematic program is needed to ensure a smooth process. Even with good planning, outside influences may derail the process; perseverance is still needed.

Curricula Models

Once women's history is established within an institution, it may go through several curricula models or developmental stages. The ultimate goal is always a transformed and completely integrated curriculum; but, until research fills in the record of women in history, incremental steps are necessary.

Separate course work was an early model of teaching women's history. Although it brought women's history into schools, this model also gave the impression that women's history was supplementary and not important. Later, specialized courses looked at women's history in relation to specific fields of interest. Such topics as family history; sexuality; suffrage; the housewife; or women and work, innovation, religion, education, community, and welfare were covered for shorter periods or infrequently (Lerner 1981). These types of courses allowed educational institutions to offer some content while raising awareness for the new curriculum among constituents.

Integration into the existing curriculum may also be addressed in steps ranging from the womanless curriculum to the recognition of a few accomplished women, the recognition of women's issues, and the study of women and minorities' daily lives; and to a reconstructed, inclusive history (McIntosh 1983). Using incremental stages keeps women's history from becoming just an add-on. All models of curriculum integration share certain similarities and anticipate the same objective, moving to the next stage on the way to a transformed history that belongs to everyone.

While moving along the integration continuum, women's history faces the additional problem of being mainstreamed into all disciplines, of becoming interdisciplinary while at the same time trying to keep its independence and honor its uniqueness (Merritt 1984, 253–262). Women's history is interdisciplinary by its very nature because women have been involved in all aspects of civilization, including the sciences and technology; the arts and literature; and the social sciences. This interdisciplinary obstacle is inherent to education where knowledge is divided into distinct units. Teaching a discipline across numerous content areas has never been an easy task. Fortunately, women's history enters academia at the same time that computers and writing have become examples of subjects taught across the curriculum, and these interdisciplinary models help to create an environment beneficial to integrating women in history (Schuster and Van Dyne 1985). Just as promoting computers as tools for accomplishing tasks and improving written expression in all disciplines is educationally advantageous, so women's history can be received on the same basis; that is, as a way to engage students and improve motivation through inclusiveness. Faculties who have joined together to gain computer skills or to learn to improve writing should also be able to see the benefit of interdisciplinary in-service activities on women's history, and they should be less resistant to this type of cross-disciplinary staff development.

There is no single effective curriculum model for women's history. Stand-alone classes, special units, integration, and interdisciplinary approaches have all been tried. For women's history, working out the balance among these elements is the challenge of the twenty-first century, and it is possible that a variety of teaching models will continue to exist for some time to come.

Teaching Methods

A number of specific teaching methods have grown up around women's history. The goal of the discipline is to transform history by promoting pluralism and avoiding universal distinctions. Women's history teaches only differences unless connections are identified. Respect is part of the reconstruction of history and is one of the discipline's strengths. Women's history is built on the understanding that gender, race, class, ethnicity, and gender orientation form the basis of cultural identity, and the discipline must promote scholarship and methodology that is not sexist, racist, classist, ethnocentric, or heterosexist. Research must also seek to understand power relationships and to avoid being seen as superficial. Women's history must examine and test paradigms as they occur in the learning environment; transformation of history will never take place without such considerations (Butler and Walter 1991).

Multiculturalism has come to be associated with women's history. History without a multicultural focus not only becomes distorted but promotes stereotypes and allows for alienation, disinterest, and the creation of barriers among people. Stressing multiculturalism gives a more authentic view of history and expands the themes available. When students can identify with history, they feel empowered, self-confident, and encouraged to form partnerships with other students (*Woman's Place* 1994). Honoring all contributions, not only those of women, but the experiences of all cultural groups, changes history and the way history is understood. Students' responses to history broaden when they are aware of the reactions of others; indeed, the understanding and valuing of others' experiences enriches each person (Schuster and Van Dyne 1985). Both an inclusive focus and a multicultural approach have been the strengths of women's history.

Strategies to ensure an inclusive focus have been developed in the women's history classroom, where the learning process tends to become a part of the curriculum (Schmitz 1985). This phenomena is partly a result of the unfinished nature of women's history. Not all the answers are available yet; but finding the answers is an important investigative technique because teachers and students become co-learners. The teacher's overriding philosophy should be to ensure a focus on women by always assuming that women have made a contribution to all fields and to all periods of history. To bring women into the discussion, or to give perspective to a position, teachers should frame and ask questions that elicit meaningful answers. The way a question is asked can give shape to the way history is viewed (*Woman's Place* 1994).

Lerner (1979) believed that the right questions would elicit the distinctive information needed to bring women into focus. She established a set of questions for use in the history classroom in the 1981 pamphlet, *Teaching Women's History*, published by the American Historical Association. The questions were generic enough to extend to all disciplines or topics, and all teachers committed to expanding class content to include women and cultural groups could use them. They focused on establishing gender, race, class, ethnicity, or sexual orientation as forms of analysis.

1. Where and who are the missing women?

2. What did they contribute to American history?

3. What did women do while the men were doing what the textbook tells us was important?

4. How did women live? What did they do?

5. What have women contributed to abolitionism, to reform, to the progressive movement, to the labor movement?

6. How did women define the issue?

7. How was it different for women?

8. What was the female experience?

9. How is gender defined in a given period?

10. Who defined women's sexual lives? Who controlled women's sexuality and how was it controlled?

11. How do the relations between the sexes affect the social and economic relations of the sexes in society?

12. What kind of paid work did women do in industrial society and what were their working conditions? What was the impact of industrialization on women?

13. What was the effect on women's labor force participation of their cultural indoctrination to homemaking and motherhood as their primary function?

14. What motivates women's decisions as workers?

15. What would history be like if it were seen through the eyes of women and ordered by values which they define?

16. How did women respond to their subordinate status and what were the consequences of these responses?

17. How did individual feminist consciousness develop into collective consciousness, and how was it manifested?

18. How did women see their world? How did they relate to other women?

19. What has been the experience of women of different classes, races, and religious and ethnic groups in terms of the above questions? How can the differences and similarities be explained?

A variety of other teaching methods focusing on the student have become associated with women's history. One technique is that of using windows and mirrors to expand and reflect history. Windows broaden history and give new viewpoints. Mirrors help in reflecting on one's own background and place in history (*Woman's Place* 1994). Windows and mirrors validate and include students' personal experiences, committing them to take responsibility for their own learning (Schuster and Van Dyne 1985). Autobiographies, biographies, family histories, life cycles, personal timelines, and oral histories are methods associated with the student focus, connecting the student to the past. As part of the student focus, teachers should not be afraid to correct distorted, stereotyped, inaccurate, or biased information when it is encountered. This may involve crossing material out of textbooks, tearing up articles, discussing issues, or debating speakers. These acts can be very empowering to students who often feel the printed word is the law.

Still focusing on the student, collective work is also important in teaching women in history. The inclusive approach promotes sharing among the class (Searing 1984, 239–252), using such methods as class discussions, group projects, and paired dialogue. Lerner (1979) feels that cooperative methods come from the strengths of women themselves because they tend to work more in unison, making the reflection of this innate style in classroom practices only natural.

Not only are cooperative methods important, but community outreach to groups (Searing 1984, 239–252) becomes vital as part of the goal of transforming history. Achieving the goal means reaching beyond the classroom, for women's history, with its inclusive mandate, has societal implications beyond its content (Butler and Walter 1991). Community outreach allows for local interviews, guest speakers, and collections of local histories, activities that reinforce students' involvement and their active participation in history.

Inclusive, multicultural, questioning, student-focused, cooperative: All these characterize women's history. These methods are carried out through honoring the experiences of all, which means through inquiry, involvement in the learning process, empowering students, group work, and outreach in the community. Some of these techniques became associated with the discipline from the inherent strengths of women. As women's history continues to mature, these procedures may remain constant, may expand, or may change with the introduction of new ways of teaching.

Women's history is part of the evolution of the field of history itself, and just as in the broader field, theories concerning women's history have developed and changed since its inception. The discipline has a number of issues that are specific to itself, and a number of pedagogical methods have grown to be associated with the field. Generally, women's history is an interdisciplinary, inclusive development, a new field engaged in finding a place for itself within a broader domain.

References

The AAUW Report, How Schools Shortchange Girls: A Study of Major Findings on Girls and Education. 1992. Washington, DC: American Association of University Women Educational Foundation.

Appleby, Joyce, Lynn Hunt, and Margaret Jacob. 1994. *Telling the Truth About History.* New York: W. W. Norton.

Bailyn, Bernard. 1994. *On the Teaching and Writing of History,* edited by Edward Connery Lathem. Hanover, NH: Montgomery Endowment, Dartmouth College.

Beard, Mary R. 1946. *Woman as a Force in History: A Study in Traditions and Realities.* New York: Macmillan.

Butler, Johnnella E., and John C. Walter, eds. 1991. *Transforming the Curriculum: Ethnic Studies and Women's Studies.* Albany: State University of New York Press.

Chafe, William H. 1977. *Women and Equality: Changing Patterns in American Culture.* New York: Oxford University Press.

Degler, Carl N. 1975. *Is There a History of Women?: An Inaugural Lecture Delivered Before the University of Oxford on 14 March 1974*. Oxford: Clarendon.

———. 1981. "What the Women's Movement Has Done to American History." *Soundings* 64, no. 4 (winter): 403–421.

DuBois, Ellen Carol, and Vicki L. Ruiz, eds. 1990. *Unequal Sisters: A Multicultural Reader in U.S. Women's History*. New York: Routledge.

Gordon, Ann D., Mari Jo Buhle, and Nancy Schrom Dye. 1976. "The Problem of Women's History." In *Liberating Women's History: Theoretical and Critical Essays,* edited by Berenice A. Carroll. Urbana, IL: University of Illinois Press.

Harris, Barbara J., and JoAnn K. McNamara, eds. 1984. *Women and the Structure of Society: Selected Research from the Fifth Berkshire Conference on the History of Women*. Durham, NC: Duke University Press.

Hewitt, Nancy. 1990. "Beyond the Search for Sisterhood: American Women's History in the 1980s." In *Unequal Sisters: A Multicultural Reader in U.S. Women's History*, edited by Ellen Carol DuBois and Vicki L. Ruiz. New York: Routledge.

Johansson, Sheila Ryan. 1976. "'Herstory' as History: A New Field or Another Fad?" In *Liberating Women's History: Theoretical and Critical Essays*, edited by Berenice A. Carroll. Urbana, IL: University of Illinois Press.

Kaub, Shirley Jane. 1984. "Women's Studies at the Secondary School Level." In *Women and Education: Equity or Equality?* edited by Elizabeth Fennema and M. Jane Ayer. Berkeley: McCutchan.

Kelly, Joan. 1984. *Women, History, and Theory: The Essays of Joan Kelly*. Chicago: University of Chicago Press.

Lerner, Gerda. 1979. *The Majority Finds Its Past: Placing Women in History*. Oxford: Oxford University Press.

———. 1981. *Teaching Women's History*. Washington, DC: American Historical Association.

———, ed. 1976. *The Female Experience: An American Documentary*. Indianapolis, IN: Bobbs-Merrill.

Mankiller, Wilma, et al., eds. 1998. *The Reader's Companion to U.S. Women's History*. Boston: Houghton Mifflin.

McIntosh, Peggy. 1981. "The Study of Women: Implications for Reconstructing the Liberal Arts Disciplines." *The Forum for Liberal Education* 4, no. 1 (October): 1–3.

———. 1983. *Interactive Phases of Curricular Re-vision: A Feminist Perspective.* Wellesley, MA: Wellesley College Center for Research on Women.

Melosh, Barbara, ed. 1993. *Gender and American History Since 1890.* London: Routledge.

Merritt, Karen. 1984. "Women's Studies: A Discipline Takes Shape." In *Women and Education: Equity or Equality?* edited by Elizabeth Fennema and M. Jane Ayer. Berkeley: McCutchan.

Mitchell, Juliet. 1976. "Four Structures in a Complex Unity." In *Liberating Women's History: Theoretical and Critical Essays*, edited by Berenice A. Carroll. Urbana, IL: University of Illinois Press.

Schmitz, Betty. 1985. *Integrating Women's Studies into the Curriculum: A Guide and Bibliography.* Old Westbury, NY: Feminist Press.

Schuster, Marilyn R., and Susan R. Van Dyne. 1985. *Women's Place in the Academy: Transforming the Liberal Arts Curriculum.* Totowa, NJ: Rowman and Allanheld.

Scott, Joan Wallach. 1988. *Gender and the Politics of History.* New York: Columbia University Press.

Searing, Susan E. 1984. "Studying Women's Studies: A Guide to Archival Research." In *Women and Education: Equity or Equality?* edited by Elizabeth Fennema and M. Jane Ayer. Berkeley: McCutchan.

Smith, Hilda. 1976. "Feminism and the Methodology of Women's History." In *Liberating Women's History: Theoretical and Critical Essays*, edited by Berenice A. Carroll. Urbana, IL: University of Illinois Press.

Smith, Bonnie G. 1998. *The Gender of History: Men, Women, and Historical Practice.* Cambridge: Harvard University Press.

A Woman's Place Is . . . in the Curriculum: Teacher Training Conference [notebook]. 1994. Windsor, CA: National Women's History Project.

Chapter
6

*Transcended
Education*

Although women's history has expanded, entering the curriculum and modifying teaching methods, for most students in most places the patriarchal view continues to dominate education. Educational institutions call for students to adopt an overriding philosophy, but because patriarchy is so much a part of culture, it is an unconscious part of the curriculum. Although people believe that education is benign and neutral, it passes on tradition, and therefore schools play a significant role in perpetuating a male-based society. Margaret Mead explains our immersion in a gendered society with an analogy: If a fish were an anthropologist, the last thing it would discover is water (Sadker and Sadker 1994). Still, schools cannot teach what society does not know (Spender 1982), and cultural shifts enter into the main-stream slowly; thus changes in gendered education will take time.

Throughout the 1990s, prolific research added to the body of knowledge on gender and education to such an extent that it is rapidly becoming a part of the educational vernacular, helping to speed a cultural move to more equitable education. Multiple studies show that girls start out in elementary school with high self-esteem, achieving higher standardized test scores than boys; however, the further girls go in education, the lower their self-esteem and their test scores fall, even when they are receiving higher grades than boys. Beyond societal and media pressure to conform to narrow gender norms, one way this phenomenon can be accounted for is by recognizing how girls are schooled in a gendered environment that ignores their strengths, belittles them as educational citizens, silences their voices, and forces them to become spectators rather than participants in education over prolonged periods. For girls, entering school is like entering an institution where they will silently watch from their desks as boys act, discuss, and demand teachers' attention. They will learn an alien curriculum in which they do not see their own sex reflected in the materials. As a result of unconscious and invisible pressures, adolescent girls risk depression and a number of destructive behaviors. Although girls compete with boys in school, this competition continues in higher education and in the job market with no guarantee of change, and girls frequently fail to take high-level math and science classes, thus lowering their lifetime wage-earning capacity (Sadker and Sadker 1994). No wonder they lose interest as the years roll by. Women have never received gender-equal education, and, for the most part, they suffer their loses in silence under the pressure of societal norms that leave them relatively invisible.

Men have never received gender-equal education either, and they also suffer. Although boys receive most of the teacher's attention, are well-represented in textbooks, score highest on standardized tests, receive most scholarship dollars, and seem to be on their way to good jobs with high salaries, they are also most often at the bottom of their classes, they are more often diagnosed as learning-disabled, and they are more likely to flunk a course or fail to be promoted. Boys are risk-takers, inclined towards accidents, suicide, and homicide. They compete against each other in class, but, as only one can come out on top, many others are set up for disappointment. There is only one acceptable role for men in society: athlete. Boys are socialized to this role early and strongly, but, even when it is apparent that so many aspirations cannot become reality, boys strongly resist broader roles (Sadker and Sadker 1994). Additionally, boys are the primary victims of violence in schools, where they are also the majority of the mentally ill and substance-abusing students. They comprise two thirds of the special education students, and, once entered into special education classes, their problems are harder to alleviate. Boys drop out of schools at four times the rate of girls, make up 90 percent of school discipline problems, are less often honored as valedictorians and salutatorians, and are less likely to go on to college. Girls score lower on achievement tests, but boys get poorer grades, especially in reading, where boys rank as much as a year and a half behind girls (Gurian 1998).

Even though girls and boys face problems within educational institutions, all recent educational studies emphasize the improvement to be gained by students when schools adopt gender-fair curricula. Continuing the traditional patriarchal-based model hurts everybody. It is critical that attention be paid to the needs of all students if they are to achieve educational success as well as success in society and gender equity is a criteria that must be linked to a focus on race, culture, socioeconomic status, abilities, and sexual orientation (*Growing Smart* 1995). Although women's history and muticulturalism are inclusive curricula, they will never influence students if school reform does not include new research on inclusiveness. Without gender equity, all students suffer, but women are perceived as second-class students; this ensures that women's history and other cultural studies will always be tacked onto subjects rather than become part of a transformed curriculum.

Curriculum revision must take place within the broader sphere of societal change so that everyone can benefit. At the start of the new millennium, schools cannot show promising results without reassessing the way society has changed. The nearly two-decade long, stumbling search for educational reform has not substantially changed an institution that was invented to serve Western white males, even though it is now called on to serve both sexes and multiple cultural groups. Reform efforts must use current research to create more equitable delivery and more meaningful content, and to re-create the institution itself. Change must begin with awareness and move to retraining, revision, and constant reevaluation. Transcended education moves within the realm of possibility when equality is the goal.

Transcended Research

Gender research accelerated in the 1980s, and today an excellent picture of the relationship between gender and education is available. Much of this research contains careful documentation and can give schools a much clearer picture of how to proceed in reform efforts. In many fields of study, such as history, medicine, education, and psychology, males had always been the research subjects; this changed when the research of Carol Gilligan (1993) challenged the pattern. As a teacher of psychology, Gilligan discovered that research in her field was almost solely based on groups of men. In her book, *In a Different Voice: Psychological Theory and Women's Development*, Gilligan revealed that Lawrence Kohlberg's study, from which he created a six-step scale of moral development that placed women's responses at a lower level than men's, was based solely on a male sample. Gilligan hypothesized that psychological research either ignored or did not know how to treat women's voices; indeed, being built around relationships, they had a focus different from that of men. *In a Different Voice* developed the concept of woman's distinctive voice, based on the female way of thinking and the female experience. Gilligan thought failure to see the different reality of women's lives came from the assumption of one social experience, and she encouraged continued research to broaden the understanding of human development. Although Gilligan's work was criticized as quasi-scientific and limited in sampling, she was the first to postulate on psychological gender differences. Whereas Gilligan emphasized response differences, other researchers found more overlap than difference in psychological scores between the sexes (Faludi 1991). Sex differences shown in psychological testing may lie in the interpretation of the researchers, and basic differences in the way men and women think will continue to be studied.

After Gilligan opened the door to reevaluate psychological studies, other research considered the differences. Brain and biochemical research showed differences between the sexes. Male testosterone, a strong hormone, heavily influenced males to be fast-acting, mechanical, and dominant. In these reactions, testosterone cut males off from emotional development. In addition, male brains developed more slowly than female brains and had smaller frontal lobes, the areas that function socially and cognitively. Men tended to objectify because of their lesser brain capacity to deal with emotion. Males also tended to lateralize, or restrict, action to one side of the brain, ignoring stimulation to the other half. By contrast, females had larger corpus callosums, nerves that connect the two sides of the brain and that process emotive data. In MRI scans, female brains showed a faster rate of blood flow, accelerated electrical activity, and use of both sides of the brain (Gurian 1998). The practical applications of such hard science data to education are slow in coming. Although differences in perception, brain function, and body chemistry occur, education has the power to magnify or diminish sex differences (Sadker and Sadker 1994); thus education's role in society becomes even more critical.

Ten years after the release of *In a Different Voice*, which showed how gender was used in psychology, several important works were published spotlighting how girls are served in educational institutions. Each of these studies influenced the next, as the evidence of unequal gender treatment in schools added up. Sexual discrimination was called to the attention of public schools in 1972 by Title IX of the Higher Education Act, which banned sex bias in athletics and other activities in all educational institutions receiving federal aid. Educational reform became a national focus after the 1983 report *A Nation at Risk,* issued by the U.S. Department of Education. In 1992, the American Association of University Women pulled gender and educational reform together in a groundbreaking report, *How Schools Shortchange Girls: A Study of Major Findings on Girls and Education,* which reviewed volumes of research to show how gender made a difference in education—even when gender was ignored as a category for educational reform and was passed over in nearly all the major reform studies of the 1980s. At the same time, in achievement scores, through curriculum design, and in self-esteem levels, girls were not achieving at the same levels as boys. The report raised awareness about inequities in schools while not offering hard solutions.

While the evidence of girl's unequal educational experience was being uncovered, one teacher in San Francisco was creating a classroom unlike any other. It was completely female-focused, from the posters and slogans that hung on the walls to the books taught and the assignments given. The teacher, Judy Logan, (1997) put women at the center of the curriculum in her middle school classes, with confidence that she could teach a womanist curriculum. Logan began slowly, basing her changes on the five-step model for inclusive teaching, which was developed by Peggy McIntosh (1983), the director of the Wellesley College Center for Research on Women. McIntosh saw that traditional curricula was womanless and all white. When change began, a few women and people of color who were exceptional achievers were added to the traditional curriculum. Next, the curriculum focused on issues; women and ethnic groups were considered problems, anomalies, absences, or victims. After this, the daily lives and cultures of women and minorities were considered worthy of study. In the final step, curricula were redefined and restructured to include everyone. When Logan's students were interviewed about what went on in their classes, the girls worried about being the center of discussion all the time and wondered how the boys felt about this. The boys saw the focus on women as no big deal as long as it was interesting. Logan never apologized for including women, knowing that students only resist studying women when they are presented as less important, and she constantly reassured students to prevent win-or-lose situations from developing. With the inclusive classroom climate Logan created, even her assignment for students to portray African American women was successful for everyone (Orenstein 1994).

Logan created the inclusive classroom before three major studies of adolescent girls, self-esteem, and education were published in 1994. One, Peggy Orenstein's *SchoolGirls: Young Women, Self-Esteem, and the Confidence Gap* (1994), dealt with girls in the educational setting, whereas Mary Pipher's *Reviving Ophelia: Saving the Selves of Adolescent Girls* (1994) took a broader, more sociological approach to the topic. Both of these studies showed how girls during adolescence rapidly lost confidence in themselves and became at risk for a variety of consequences, including pregnancy, drug and alcohol abuse, depression, eating disorders, and self-mutilation. The reasons for declining self-esteem ranged from familial, societal, and media pressures to conform to narrow gender norms to the recognition of exclusion from mainstream society. Schools, especially, have given these messages to girls through textbooks, teacher interactions, and a hidden curriculum. The final study, Myra and David Sadker's *Failing at Fairness: How Our Schools Cheat Girls* (1994), brought together a wealth of research, including twenty years of the Sadker's own studies, showing that schools were not gender-equal. The Sadkers covered all aspects of education, including standardized tests, teacher interactions, and same-sex schooling, among other topics. The evidence they accumulated was overwhelming, but they offered hope that schools could change, and that training to effect these changes was not difficult.

A few years after these well-researched studies came into print, Michael Gurian (1998), a therapist and educator, published *A Fine Young Man: What Parents, Mentors and Educators Can Do to Shape Adolescent Boys into Exceptional Men,* which, with its insistence that it was boys who were shortchanged in education, would have been considered a backlash book had the author not argued throughout the work for an equitable treatment of both sexes in schools. Gurian called for the study of male and female development in education courses and for research-based teaching methods to best educate both sexes. *A Fine Young Man* lacked the serious research and documentation of the girl studies, which left its conclusions open to interpretation; however, its theme of equality could not be disputed.

Gurian seemed to be a voice in the wilderness until Susan Faludi, the feminist author of *Backlash* who, in the 1980s, identified societal trends keeping women from achieving the total equality that the women's movement had set out to gain in the 1960s, published a new book, *Stiffed: The Betrayal of the American Man,* in late 1999. The book amassed evidence gathered since World War II of the changing culture for males in the United States, including media pressure to attain a certain image, changing employment demands, and degenerating manhood. Although Faludi viewed the book as extending the "principles of feminism to men," she also saw men in a double bind, caught up in societal change with no traditional adversary to fight back against (Faludi 1999). A redefinition of maleness at the turn of the twenty-first century became a media theme, covering all aspects of society, not just education. That both females and males suffer under the current educational system was well documented, yet the use of current research to change teaching methods, curricula, and reevaluate the school climate could bring about change.

The Three Curricula

The AAUW report (1992) recognizes three school curricula: the classroom curriculum, or the teaching methods; the formal curriculum, or the content of what was taught; and the evaded curriculum, or what was not taught. Each of these sends messages to students. Although the AAUW report, *Failing at Fairness*, and *A Fine Young Man* promote gender equity within the three school curricula, each outlines differences in learning styles inherent to each sex. Girls are more inductive and intuitive, gravitate to small group-learning environments, use more concrete language, and require more realistic teaching. Boys are more deductive; reason more abstractly; prefer large-group learning because of their competitive, independent natures; use more abstract language; and favor symbolic representation coupled with logic and proof (Gurian 1998). The dichotomies set up for the classroom teacher are obvious. In appealing to one set of learners, the other may be shut out, but creativity, adaptability, and constant vigilance within the education community can create a school for everyone.

Classroom As Curriculum

The classroom as curriculum has to do with teaching methods, teacher interactions, and classroom organization. The interactions that occur between students and teachers account for much of what goes on in the classroom, and much of the Sadker's (1994) research concerns teaching interactions. The Sadkers noticed how teachers give four different responses to students in the classroom: 10 percent of responses are praise; 5 percent are criticism; 33 percent are remediation; and 52 percent are acceptance, a sort of neutral acknowledgment. The most helpful responses to students are the first three, for they let students know what they are doing right or wrong and how to correct work. In typical classrooms, boys receive the most of all the helpful types of responses. Girls are most likely to get the acceptance response, or the least amount of feedback, on their work. Feedback is only part of classroom interaction. Both the Sadker's (1994) research and the AAUW report explain how, as girls move on in education, they become silent in the classroom, leaving the class discussion and questioning to the boys. The Sadkers (1994) show the reason for this is that teachers call on boys in much greater numbers. Additionally, teachers allow boys to call out in class, but admonish girls when they do the same thing. Even though girls may require more think time before answering a question, they seldom get it. Classrooms, ruled by tight time constraints, move at such a furious pace that, when they ask a question, teachers seldom wait more than a second for an answer.

Most teachers are surprised to know that they engage in unequal interactive practices. Fortunately, these practices are easily correctable through awareness and training. Doing self-assessments by audio or videotaping classrooms, learning to log those who are called on and how they respond, keeping notes on class discussions, and trading this service with a partner teacher can quickly make a classroom much more equitable. When teachers equalize their interaction with students, girls regain their voices, boys learn to listen more carefully and choose the comments they wish to make, slower students feel more comfortable knowing they will have think time before having to respond, and all students receive the type of feedback that will help them to improve their work.

Teachers need to be aware that gender affects the way students speak. Linguist Deborah Tannen, one of the first to study the speech patterns of women, establishes how their speech patterns differ from those of men in her books *You Just Don't Understand: Women and Men in Conversation* and *Gender and Discourse*. In speaking, women hesitate and make false starts; their voices go up at the end of sentences; and they use qualifiers, tag questions, and apologies as part of what they want to say (Sandler and Hoffman 1992). These speech patterns make girls seem less sure of themselves, and, as a result, they are more often interrupted or ignored, and they easily yield their turn (Benjamin and Irwin-DeVitis 1998). In oral interaction with female students, teachers practice both overt and covert behaviors in showing women they are less worthy of attention. Overtly, teachers may make comments telling girls they lack ability or seriousness in a subject; they may use sexist humor and comments to send harmful messages; and they may speak to girls in patronizing, impatient, or frowning manners. Covertly, teachers may create more eye contact with men, offer them more encouragement, nod and gesture in response to male comments, use a tone of voice that shows more interest in men's comments, hold a posture of attention towards male speakers, group students in ways that favor men, and give men more credit in discussions. As with other interactions, teachers must have an awareness of the speech patterns used by both sexes and attend to their verbal and nonverbal reactions and interactions so that they are gender-neutral in the classroom.

The gender-equitable classroom is not hard to create. It takes, first, a personal knowledge of gender issues and, second, the desire to create a climate of equality. This kind of atmosphere tells students that gender is an acceptable topic and that the teacher is willing to discuss it (Benjamin and Irwin-DeVitis 1998). Teachers must be willing to examine their classroom practices to correct often indiscernible inequitable routines and to improve interactions by making a commitment to open classrooms with participation and respect by all. Teachers should articulate their expectations for class discussions and offer to help anxious students. Students should be called by name, and the same form of address should be used for all students; women and men should be called on directly in proportion to their ratio in the class; and the same types of questions, in the same tone of voice, should be asked to all students. After the teacher has asked a question, the wait time should be five to ten seconds. Dividing the class into quadrants will assure equal participation while avoiding addressing just part of the room. Class participation can be encouraged by polling the class on questions or having the class write the answers to questions. Teachers must ensure that women are not verbally interrupted, and sexist language, extending to any sort of analogies (such as to sports, the military, or fraternities) that exclude some members of the classroom must be avoided (Sandler and Hoffman 1992).

Besides verbal interactions, other procedures affecting gender fall under the heading of the classroom as curriculum. In choosing class-room activities, teachers tend to choose male-oriented instruction. Even as early as kindergarten, the classroom may emphasize impulse control, small-motor development, and language enhancement, skills that girls already know and in which they may, in fact, surpass boys. Although girls at this age could benefit from improving their skills in large muscle devel-opment, often these activities are considered as play; therefore girls are not instructed in them and may not voluntarily choose to engage in them. Girls tend to be educational spectators, often pushed out of activities by more-active boys. They may be physically squeezed out of laboratory, computer, or other hands-on work. Girls need classroom structure that forces them to participate (*AAUW* 1992). Simulations are an excellent method for involv-ing both boys and girls in hands-on, meaningful learning (McLure and McLure 1977). Because girls take a more passive classroom role, teachers may do work for them instead of showing them how to do their own work. This action dismisses and enables them (Sadker and Sadker 1994). In the problem area of math, girls benefit from reading the book and trying some problems before going to class; when this method is used, as opposed to the method of first discussing problems in class, girls perform at the same level as boys (*AAUW* 1992). Because girls use more intuition than abstract reason-ing, they do not make the great leaps in cognition that boys do, and their math and science instruction must be more concrete (Gurian 1998). Females prefer a learning style referred to as "connected knowing," in which they lean on their intuition to empathetically enter a subject; however, this teaching method is not widely used in introducing new topics (*AAUW* 1992). Logan (1997) uses a form of connected knowing, making associations from students' real lives to every new subject introduced. Equalizing classroom activities requires better knowledge of the developmental skills of both sexes and thoughtful lesson planning, but it pays off in increased learning.

Although girls may benefit from working in group settings, these may pose some problems. In the early grades, girls prefer same-sex groups, and overall, girls favor small-group work, whereas boys want to work alone or in large groups (Gurian 1998). Although group work may promote cross-gender or cross-race friendship, boost academic performance, allow for mainstreaming of special-needs students, and help develop mutual class concerns, if not carefully structured, group settings can be dominated by the strongest personalities; because communication problems can then become an obstacle, roles within the group should be rotated regularly to ensure equal participation (*AAUW* 1992). Teachers can help students create groups that address their educational needs and instructional goals (*Growing Smart* 1995).

Altogether, by being aware of research findings, teachers can create classrooms with interactions and activities in which both sexes have an equal opportunity to achieve. There should be a variety of activities that appeal to both active and passive learning styles, ensuring that each student fully participates in the educational process. Students can be given choices in methods of presentation that allow them to demonstrate their strengths. Again, all these suggestions should be carried out in a climate of inclusiveness, with clear expectations for behavior and achievement.

Standard Curriculum

Not only teaching methods must change in order to promote gender equity, the curriculum must also change. Most school material comes from textbooks that transmit cultural values, define reality, and sometimes reinforce myths and stereotypes. In the 1970s and 1980s, surveys of textbooks showed that women were not fairly represented either in narrative or in pictures. The drop in self-esteem for females as they go through school may be attributed to a curriculum lacking female models, giving the impression that girls are less valuable than boys (*AAUW* 1992). Almost a decade after working with publishers to incorporate nonsexist guidelines, the Sadkers (1994) found that little had changed in college-level texts; the guidelines had been forgotten. The National Women's History Project endorses "guerrilla editing" of incorrect information in textbooks (*Woman's Place* 1994). Students are empowered in crossing out, or otherwise changing the written word. The AAUW report (1992) finds some improvement in textbooks, but rarely is there a dual and balanced treatment of women in any field. Their research shows that both sexes benefit academically from the use of nonsexist, multicultural materials. Stereotyping is reduced, more favorable attitudes toward other groups are exhibited, and a wider range of role models is possible. When textbooks fail to provide a broad view, teachers may wish to use several texts or to bring in supplementary material. The AAUW is not surprised to find bias in curriculum materials; only four of thirty-five studies responding to the 1983 U.S. Department of Education report, *A Nation at Risk*, mention gender as a category of students at risk, and less than 1 percent of the text in 138 articles published in nine prominent educational journals between 1983 and 1987 address sex equity. The AAUW asks why reports on restructuring schools that look at student achievement never look at curricula that could be affecting student achievement by excluding women and other cultural groups, thereby giving a skewed look at society and alienating many students.

Along with textbooks, literature needs to be balanced. Teachers must select a variety of characters as role models to students, avoid stereotypes, accommodate male and female interests, and achieve a balance of male and female authors. Discussion of sex roles is necessary even with a balanced literature curriculum in order to establish an open classroom (Benjamin and Irwin-DeVitis 1998). Many times a balance of literature means moving away from what is considered "the canon" in language arts and English classes. Teachers must be willing to drop some standard works, to use multiple texts, and to ensure that boys and girls read widely (*AAUW* 1992). When film, video, and other media presentations are used in language arts classes, they, too, should be analyzed for their sex-role depiction. In dramatic presentations, even in the classics, roles can be gender-adjusted to reflect a more equitable distribution (Sadker and Sadker 1994). Students will make gendered choices in writing, as they do in choosing literature, and differences in communication will be apparent. The teacher's awareness of and willingness to deal with students' choices and differences will help to ensure a gender-equitable classroom.

There are ways for teachers to measure the equity of curricula and textbooks. The AAUW report (1992) outlines the attributes of a gender-fair curriculum: inclusive, accurate, affirmative, representative, integrated, and showing the variations among and within groups. In measuring textbooks, the National Council of Teachers of Foreign Languages presents six forms of sexual bias: the exclusion of girls, stereotyping of both sexes, superficiality of attention to social problems, cultural inaccuracies or exclusions, subordination or degradation of women, and isolation of materials on women. Both lists serve as adequate guides in reviewing materials, and teachers may add to these with other measures learned from working with various textbooks and pieces of literature.

The Evaded Curriculum

The curricula and the teaching make up a major part of what goes on in school; however, there is still another part, the evaded curriculum. Schools can perpetuate inequalities through this hidden curriculum (Weis 1988). Part of the evaded curriculum has to do with subjects that are not taught. These topics send a message to girls and boys about cultural values. Topics such as substance abuse, contraception, sexually transmitted diseases, body image, eating disorders, depression, suicide, expressing emotions, gender and power, and physical and emotional abuse are important, but students never hear about them or have the opportunity to discuss them formally in school (*AAUW* 1992). Media depictions of men and women, which fill the airwaves twenty-four hours a day and are readily available at any newsstand, are another topic that is rarely addressed within educational institutions. To improve equity, school-reform efforts must evaluate school climate by what is not taught and what is taught in both the formal curriculum and teaching methods.

Another part of the evaded curriculum has to do with sexual harassment. Females bear the brunt of sexual harassment that girls begin to experience even in elementary school and that increases throughout their school years. When schools ignore the problems of sexual harassment, they give it tacit approval. The Sadkers (1994) call college campuses dangerous places for women because of the climate that has developed there surrounding male athletic teams and fraternities. It is a climate encompassing violence, another topic of the evaded curriculum. Sexual harassment is a hot political topic. Employees who cannot adjust to more equitable workplaces are usually eliminated from them through zero-tolerance policies, but among school children this solution is not possible. Education, example, and constant vigilance are necessary to raise the next generation with respect.

The hidden curriculum also encompasses what might be called the culture of the school, including its unquestioned practices. Traditionally, schools are run according to what many would call female standards. The expected behavior is quiet and controlled, and males, with large muscle movements and low impulse control, are often at odds within this culture, in jeopardy of being labeled learning-disabled or attention-deficit disordered (*Who Needs* 1999). Unquestionably, gender is a category of classification in school in many ways. Marked by dress, language, and artifacts, gender tends to be more highly visible than race, ethnicity, religion, or social class (Thorne 1993). Schools are such gendered places that many practices become ritualized and go unidentified and unchallenged. For example, the displays on classroom walls are often unremarkable, unless you are a girl looking at male political leaders, scientists, and sports heroes without ever seeing yourself reflected. The same is true for ethnic children who may overwhelmingly see white children depicted in school materials.

Barrie Thorne (1993), who spent several years observing elementary school children, recognizes that they prefer their own sex and seek them out, marking off territory in the classroom, the lunchroom, the playground, and in other school spaces. Classrooms are often divided by gender; when students move between locations in the school building, they often move in gender groups or lines, and classroom contests often pit boys against girls. Playground rituals involve chasing one sex or another and may also involve the passing of "cooties" or some other form of pollution; however, behind many of these school-based rituals are the themes of aggression and power. The Sadkers (1994) point out that boys often take over the best tables in the lunchroom, the entire computer lab, and the most space and best equipment on the playground, leaving the girls on the edges. Often no one even thinks about questioning what is going on; however, teachers can work to challenge and change these common school practices by grouping students according to some criteria other than gender or race, sustaining a culture of cooperation, facilitating access to all activities for all students, and intervening to challenge the dynamics of stereotyping and power (Thorne 1993).

By recognizing the three curricula, schools can act to change procedures and methods that promote one sex or group over another. These changes, which need not be difficult, do take constant application as well as giving up some methods that may be considered traditions, but student achievement will benefit from the alternatives.

Single-Sex Classrooms

With all the evidence of gender inequality, support has reemerged for single-sex schools in recent years because one school curriculum may not be able to meet the needs of boys as well as girls (*AAUW* 1992). Research shows benefits for girls in single-sex schools, where graduates demonstrate higher self-esteem, personal identity, and academic and career achievement. Although research on all-male education is mixed, some showing all-male schools to be better, some showing co-education to be better, and some showing no difference, girls' schools are advantageous even though sexism exists, no matter what the school setting. Schools vary widely in their approach and effectiveness, and any school must be carefully evaluated in relation to a particular student (Sadker and Sadker 1994). Single-sex schools or classes do not comply with Title IX of the Higher Education Act; however, voluntary, short-term single-sex courses may allow schools to remedy some past inequalities and prepare students to enter co-educational classes (*Growing Smart* 1995). With the advances in recent knowledge of developmental differences and educational differences, the Title IX law should be reevaluated to allow schools to group students in ways that will promote the best education for them.

As the school year opened in the fall of 1999, a number of schools were creating single-sex classrooms with the blessings of parents. The emphasis, however, seemed to be on alleviating the social distractions of co-educational institutions; such a reason for creating single-sex classrooms is simplistic and erroneous if gender-specific teaching methods are not employed within those classrooms. And even if single-sex classrooms use current research to teach to the strengths of each sex, common sense dictates that not every boy and every girl conforms to these modes in their learning styles. In transcended education, there must be a way to determine the learning style of each student and to assure that teaching meets the need of every child.

Again and again, this decade's research has shown that an inclusive, multicultural, gender-fair curricula benefits everyone, both boys and girls. To provide the gender-fair curriculum, the AAUW report (1992) recommends awareness in every aspect of schools, not just in history and literature, but even in music, art, and physical education curricula. Attention only to the curriculum will not accomplish gender-equity, either. Teaching methods and school culture must also be addressed to promote fairness everywhere. Inclusive teaching, honoring all, and emphasizing tolerance and classroom cooperation changes the traditional instructional relationship as students direct their own learning while searching for meaning, rather than for right or wrong answers (Orenstein 1994).

Both sexes face enormous societal pressure to conform to certain very narrow norms. They need upstanding and wide-ranging role models as they shape their lives, but traditional history presents only limited role models (*Woman's Place* 1994). In today's world, both men and women make up half the work force, half the citizens, and half the parents. In fact, more women now attend American higher education institutions, comprising 56 percent of students. Within the next decade, women are expected to hold more jobs in business and biology than men (*Who Needs* 1999). Without gender-equal schools, stereotypes are reinforced and the educational experience is less rich for everyone (Sandler and Hoffman 1992). In other words, students are set up to enter marriages and workplaces, carrying on in the same stereotypical and traditional ways. The tired myths of the twentieth century should not influence the twenty-first century.

References

The *AAUW Report: How Schools Shortchange Girls: A Study of Major Findings on Girls and Education*. 1992. Washington, DC: American Association of University Women Educational Foundation.

Benjamin, Beth, and Linda Irwin-DeVitis. 1998. "Censoring Girls' Choices: Continued Gender Bias in English Language Arts Classrooms." *English Journal* (February): 64–72.

Faludi, Susan. 1991. *Backlash: The Undeclared War Against American Women*. New York: Doubleday.

———. 1999. "The Betrayal of the American Man." *Newsweek* (September 13): 48–59.

Gilligan, Carol. 1993. *In a Different Voice: Psychological Theory and Women's Development*. 2d ed. Cambridge: Harvard University Press.

Growing Smart: What's Working for Girls in School, Executive Summary and Action Guide. 1995. Washington, DC: American Association of University Women.

Gurian, Michael. 1998. *A Fine Young Man: What Parents, Mentors and Educators Can Do to Shape Adolescent Boys into Exceptional Men*. New York: Jeremy P. Tarcher/Putnam.

Logan, Judy. 1997. *Teaching Stories*. New York: Kodansha.

McIntosh, Peggy. 1983. *Interactive Phases of Curricular Re-vision: A Feminist Perspective*. Wellesley, MA: Wellesley College Center for Research on Women.

McLure, Gail Thomas, and John W. McLure. 1977. *Women's Studies*. Washington, DC: National Education Association.

Orenstein, Peggy. 1994. *SchoolGirls: Young Women, Self-Esteem, and the Confidence Gap*. New York: Doubleday.

Pipher, Mary. 1994. *Reviving Ophelia: Saving the Selves of Adolescent Girls*. New York: Ballantine.

Sadker, Myra, and David Sadker. 1994. *Failing at Fairness: How Our Schools Cheat Girls*. New York: Touchstone.

Sandler, Bernice Resnick, and Ellen Hoffman. 1992. *Teaching Faculty Members to Be Better Teachers: A Guide to Equitable and Effective Classroom Techniques*. Washington, DC: Association of American Colleges.

Spender, Dale. 1982. *Invisible Women: The Schooling Scandal*. London: Writers and Readers.

Thorne, Barrie. 1993. *Gender Play: Girls and Boys in School*. New Brunswick, NJ: Rutgers University Press.

Weis, Lois, ed. 1988. *Class, Race, and Gender in American Education*. Albany: State University of New York Press.

"Who Needs Men? Addressing the Prospect of a Matrilinear Millennium." 1999. *Harper's* 298, no. 1789 (June): 33–46.

A Woman's Place Is . . . in the Curriculum: Teacher Training Conference [notebook]. 1994. Windsor, CA: National Women's History Project.

Appendix

Audio-Visual Producers

A & E Home Video
19 Gregory Drive
South Burlington, VT 05403
800-423-1212

Ambrose Video Publishing
24 W. 44th Street, Suite 2100
New York, NY 10036
800-526-4663

An American Nurse at War, Inc.
5 Colby Street
Keene, NH 03431
603-357-8356

Bread and Roses Cultural Project
P.O. Box 1154
Eatontown, NJ 07724
800-666-1728

Churchill Media
6677 N. Northwest Highway
Chicago, IL 60631
800-334-7830

The Cinema Guild
1697 Broadway, Suite 506
New York, NY 10019-5904
800-723-5522
www.cinemaguild.com/cinemaguild

Delinger's Publishers—Ozark Division
1160 S. Maryland
Springfield, MO 65807
417-869-2666

Documentary Photo Aids
P.O. Box 952137
Lake Mary, FL 32795
407-324-1995

Filmakers Library
124 E. 40th Street
New York, NY 10016
212-808-4980
www.filmakers.com

Films for the Humanities and Sciences
P.O. Box 2053
Princeton, NJ 08543-2053
800-257-5126
www.films.com

Great Plains Network
P.O. Box 80669
Lincoln, NE 68501-0669
800-228-4630

Her Own Words
P.O. Box 5264
Madison, WI 53705
608-271-7083

Interact
1825 Gillespie Way #101
El Cajon, CA 92020-1095
800-359-0961
www.interact-simulations.com

Jackdaw Publications
P.O. Box 503
Amawalk, NY 10501
800-789-0022

317

Kaw Valley Films, Inc.
P. O. Box 3541
Shawnee, KS 66203
800-332-5060

Knowledge Unlimited
P.O. Box 52
Madison, WI 53701
800-356-2303

Lucerne Media
37 Ground Pine Road
Morris Plains, NJ 07950
800-341-2293

Media Projects
5215 Homer Street
Dallas, TX 75206
214-826-3863

National Asian American Telecommunications Association
346 Ninth Street, Second Floor
San Francisco, CA 94103
415-552-9550

National Women's History Project
7738 Bell Road
Windsor, CA 95492-8518
707-838-6000
www.nwhp.org

New Day Films
22 Hollywood Avenue, Suite D
Ho Ho Kus, NJ 07423
201-652-6590

The Other Angels Productions
P.O. Box 2083
Boulder, CO 80306-2083
800-984-8845

PBS Video
1320 Braddock Place
Alexandria, VA 22314
800-531-4727

The Phoenix Learning Group, Inc.
2349 Chaffee Drive
St. Louis, MO 63146
800-221-1274

Marjorie Poore Productions
P.O. Box 11471
Des Moines, IA 50336
800-761-4096

Chip Taylor Communications
15 Spollett Drive
Derry, NH 03038
800-876-2447

Thunderhead Productions, Inc.
Box 4454
West Palm Beach, FL 33402
561-471-2933

Women Make Movies, Inc.
462 Broadway, Suite 500 K
New York, NY 10013
212-925-0606
www.wmm.com

Author/Title Index

Subject Index